Should you read this book? If you think it is interesting that on September 11, 2001, Flight 77 reportedly hit the 77 foot tall Pentagon, in Washington D.C. on the 77th Meridian West, after taking off at 8:20 AM and crashing at 9:37 AM, 77 minutes later, then this book is for you. Furthermore, if you can comprehend that there is a code of numbers behind the letters of the English lang~ , B, C is 1, 2, 3, and using this code rh as 'September Eleventh', 'World Tr< os' equate to 77, this book is definite e are all facts, just the same as it is ı began September 11, 1941, just pı

Table oı ....

About the Author & Book, Number Games | 9/11 to Coronavirus

Hi, my name is Zachary Hubbard, and on September 11, 2001, in addition to everything else you know about that date, I made myself a promise. The promise was, "I will find out who is really responsible for 9/11 and I will do something about it." I said that because I knew I was being lied to about the entire story, and at the same time, I felt that I was being mocked. This was mostly due to it being reported that there was a national emergency, like none other, on the date written no different than 9-1-1, the national emergency dialing code for the United States- only to find out shortly after that World Trade Center construction had started in 1968 in New York, the same year 9-1-1 was made the national emergency dialing code. In addition to those details, I'd always had a strong sense for justice, and doing what was right when given two or more choices. I was also thinking about how if I had made a slightly different decision a summer prior, I might be one of the young men being shipped off to fight the coming war, based in an obvious lie, as some of my friends were, including my buddy Oscar, who I had known since second grade. I was only 18 years old then, in my second week of college, living out of state, but I wasn't anybody's fool. Since then, nothing has changed about my sense of justice, or doing what is right, and I never broke my promise to myself either. That's why, as of the start of 2020, after nearly 19 years of extremely time consuming research, I definitely know the answer to the question of who is responsible for September 11, 2001, and I want the world to know as well- and to be able to prove it in the same way I can, in a way that is truly undeniable, and deep, and evidence based. That is what this book is about, a book that has the power to change the world, in terms of exposing and ending tyranny, and thinking about the way we treat each other and this place we call home, earth. I thank you for taking the time to read it, and I promise you that if you do, you'll enjoy it, and you'll learn way more than you expect, plus you'll develop a skill that will benefit you for the rest of your life. If you agree with the phrase knowledge is power, then this book is for you. Cheers truth seeker. And oh yes, one more thing, you'll also learn that the same cabal behind 9/11, is the same cabal behind the "coronavirus outbreak," and that is because they are two related agendas, that are about building a technocratic surveillance grid so that government and big industry can have a watchful eye on all aspects of our lives, at all times, for the continued sake of power & control. And we must stop it.

1 | Introduction to Gematria, the Language of The Cabal

You've likely heard the term "The Cabal" before, meaning a secretive and political organization. The name originates in Kabbalah, an ancient and widely practiced mysticism. A central belief within Kabbalah that we will focus on for the purpose of this book, is God created the world with language, by combining the number with the letter with the word. This is expressed in the foundational text of Kabbalah, the *Sepher Yetzirah*, or in English, *The Book of Formation*. In its opening paragraph, it states, in reference to God creating the world, "He created His Universe by three forms of expression: Numbers, Letters and Words." This belief about creation from *The Book of Formation* is in line with the beginning of the *Holy Bible*, that begins with *Genesis*, where God speaks the world into existence over the course of six numbered days, before resting on the seventh day and making it holy. Ahead, we'll touch more on the number seven and it being holy because it is an important concept to understand. For now, please recognize that both God and *Genesis* begin with 'G', the 7th letter of the English alphabet.

In Kabbalah, the practice of coding numbers into words is known as gematria, meaning geometry in language. Gematria is very popular in Hebrew studies, and in Ancient Greek studies, where it is known as isopsephy. If you are familiar with *Revelation 13:18*, from the concluding book of the *Holy Bible,* it is a Greek isopsephy riddle. In the *NIV Bible*, the verse reads, **"This calls for wisdom. Let the person who has insight calculate the number of the beast, for it is the number of a man. That number is 666."** In this chapter we will uncover that wisdom, and in the chapters ahead we will use it to understand who The Cabal is, for what purpose they are working towards and why they have encoded the number 666 into world changing events, including September 11, 2001 and the coronavirus pandemic of 2020, as well as smaller but related rituals, including the premature death of basketball superstar Kobe Bryant.

To begin to understand the wisdom of gematria and how the English language is encoded with it, we will start with the most straightforward cipher, known as Simple English Gematria, where A is 1, B is 2, C is 3 and so on, counting each letter as a number using the alphabetic order, up to Z the 26th letter is 26. The Simple English Gematria cipher is as follows:

Simple English Gematria (also known as Ordinal Gematria):

A=1, B=2, C=3, D=4, E=5, F=6, G=7, H=8, I=9

J=10, K=11, L=12, M=13, N=14, O=15, P=16, Q=17, R=18

S=19, T=20, U=21, V=22, W=23, X=24, Y=25, Z=26

Using Simple English Gematria, notice each of the words in the cipher name equate to 74.

Simple = 19+9+13+16+12+5 = 74
English = 5+14+7+12+9+19+8 = 74
Gematria = 7+5+13+1+20+18+9+1 = 74

Gematria is about pairing words together that have matching numerical values and logical relationships. For example, notice how 'Jesus', 'Messiah', '*Gospel*' 'parables' and 'cross' each equate to 74 as well, a very special number as we will come to understand. If you are not familiar with the *Gospel*, it is the story of Jesus, and when Jesus speaks within it, he does so in parables.

Jesus = 10+5+19+21+19 = 74
Messiah = 13+5+19+19+9+1+8 = 74
Gospel = 7+15+19+16+5+12 = 74
Parables = 16+1+18+1+2+12+5+19 = 74
Cross = 3+18+15+19+19 = 74

Paying mind to the fact that gematria is a component of Kabbalah, and the purpose of studying Kabbalah is to better understand the nature of God, the relevance of 74 can be understood by observing a Jewish rule about writing the name of God, a name that is best written G-d as a form of respect, unless it is written while studying the *Torah*, or in prayer. You'll notice G is the 7th letter, and D is the 4th, thus G-d is 7-4, and not by chance, the word 'Jewish' equates to 74 using Simple English Gematria too.

Jewish = 10+5+23+9+19+8 = 74

For another 74, the spiritual leader of Islam, 'Muhammad', is a name equating to 74, and sadly, it is no coincidence that Muhammad Ali died at age 74, June 3, 2016, when it is widely believed that the Prophet Muhammad died at age 63. Consider, June 3rd is expressed 6/3, similar to 63, and further, 2016 is the 63rd triangular number, meaning that when 1 through 63 are added together, the total sums to 2016. If you were following me in 2014, I predicted that Muhammad

Ali would die at the age of 74 because of the significance of the number. Sadly, I was right.

Muhammad = 13+21+8+1+13+13+1+4 = 74

Another spiritual leader to some, is 'Lucifer', summing to 74 as well, and referred to as the Morning Star, not unlike Jesus.

Lucifer = 12+21+3+9+6+5+18 = 74

Building on to our understanding of 74 and how it is used ritualistically, we need look no further than the Freemasons, one of many masonic orders that are based in Kabbalah, among other occult teachings. As we decode the 74s in 'masonic' and 'occult', keep in mind you must believe in G-d to become a member of the Freemason brotherhood. Also keep in mind, the deceased Freemason and Confederate Army war general, Albert Pike, made numerous mentions of Lucifer in his text *Morals and Dogma*, that was immortalized in Washington D.C., known as the "Masonic City,", in a statue of Albert Pike holding the book, until it was toppled in the wake of the George Floyd protests, only for Donald Trump to declare it be re-erected.

Masonic = 13+1+19+15+14+9+3 = 74

Occult = 15+3+3+21+12+20 = 74

For the record, Modern Freemasonry began in 'London', England in the year 1717.

London = 12+15+14+4+15+14 = 74

In light of the relevance of 74, it is not reported in history books by accident that the Freemason and first recognized President of the United States of America, George Washington, had 74 generals. It is also not an accident that the Disney film about the Freemasons, *National Treasure*, begins in the year 1974, nor is it an accident that the United States date of independence is July 4th, a date that is written in the U.S. as 7/4. Adding to the relevance of the number, you'll observe that 'holiday' equates to 74.

Holiday = 8+15+12+9+4+1+25 = 74

Holiday means "holy day", and as was mentioned at the beginning of the chapter, the number 7 is associated with being holy. In light of what we have uncovered so far about 74, consider that 7 is the 4th prime number, and the divisors of 4 sum to 7. For a little math reminder, prime numbers are those that can only be divided by 1 and themselves. As for divisors, those are the numbers that divide into a number. For example, the only numbers that divide into 4 are 1, 2 and 4, and when added together, equate to 1+2+4 = 7. And if you're wondering at this point if it is an accident that the 4th book of the *Holy Bible* is titled *Numbers*, the answer is no.

Coming back to the Fourth of July, as you might be aware, the second, third, and fifth Presidents of the United States, John Adams, Thomas Jefferson, and James Monroe, each died on July 4th. Adams and Jefferson both died July 4, 1826, and then 1826-days later, James Monroe died on July 4, 1831. What makes this all the more chilling is that the word 'killing' has Simple English Gematria of 74, and on the subject of killing, I would encourage you to look up the lyrics to the song *Gematria the Killing Name* by the band Slipknot, as well as the song *Murder by Numbers* by the band The Police, where killing is as simple as A, B, C is 1, 2, 3. I would also encourage you to think about how the giving and taking of life is God's work, but as we will discuss in the pages ahead, there is an organization of people using this code to play God, who for now, we will simply call, The Cabal.

Killing = 11+9+12+12+9+14+7 = 74

Adding to the 'killing' riddle, the Gregorian calendar, that we go by now, pays tribute to the fatal 'stabbing' of Caesar on the Ides of March, March 15th, the 74th day of the year.

Stabbing = 19+20+1+2+2+9+14+7 = 74

As you will learn, killing rituals centered on the number 74 are quite common. In later chapters we will discuss the drowning death of Naya Rivera in great detail, but for now, you can know that it was no accident she posted a photo of herself in a Jim Morrison t-shirt on her Instagram page, February 7, 2019, precisely a span of 74 weeks before her July 8, 2020 death. This is because Jim Morrison was found dead in a 'bathtub', equating to 74, the same as the word 'drown'. And please keep in mind that Jim Morrison was found by his girlfriend, Pamela Courson, who would end up dying in 1974, at the same tragic age as Jim Morrison, 27, another number we will learn more about as we progress through the pages of this book.

Bathtub = 2+1+20+8+20+21+2 = 74

Drown = 4+18+15+23+14 = 74

In case you're getting the idea, "maybe a lot of words happen to sum to 74," I'll have you know that out of the fifty states, only one sums to 74 in Simple English Gematria, and that is the thirty-third state, 'Oregon'. This is similar to how it is written in history books that George Washington had 74 generals, and 33 of them were Masons. It also reminds us that 'Jesus' was put on the 'cross' at age 33 according to most teachings about his crucifixion. And yes, we will learn much more about the number 33, in great detail, in the chapters ahead. It's understanding is essential and it is connected to why the actress Naya Rivera died at age 33 by drowning, as well as why Herman Cain, once a U.S. Presidential candidate, died a span of 33 weeks from his 74th birthday, having been born December 13, 1945, and having died July 30, 2020. As you'll learn, the pattern of 33 and 74 coming together is extremely repetitious, and when it is used in 'killing', the cause of death that is typically reported is false, such as Herman Cain's, which was blamed on "coronavirus".

Oregon = 15+18+5+7+15+14 = 74

*OR = 15+18 = 33 (Oregon's state abbreviation)

Coming back to the Fourth of July, there is another important observation that can be made about the date written 7/4 and the number 74 by running the alphabetic order in reverse, a method known as Reverse Simple English Gematria. Using this cipher, the word 'free' sums to 74, and July 4, 1776 is reportedly the date that the United States made itself free from England, the King and the Crown, the latter of which is the banking cartel out of the City of 'London', whose flag is a red 'cross', and being an independent territory that is located in the center of the 33 sections that London is divided into. Now without further ado, the Reverse Simple English Gematria cipher:

Reverse Simple English Gematria (Reverse Ordinal):

Z=1, Y=2, X=3, W=4, V=5, U=6, T=7, S=8, R=9

Q=10, P=11, O=12, N=13, M=14, L=15, K=16, J=17, I=18

H=19, G=20, F=21, E=22, D=23, C=24, B=25, A=26

Let us now decode the word 'free' using this cipher.

Free = 21+9+22+22 = 74

Using this same cipher, the word 'Roman' sums to 74, and as they say, all roads lead to Rome, including the ones that the City of London were built upon, what was once a strategic Roman trading post. As we decode the word, keep in mind, the Gregorian Calendar was given to us by the Roman Catholic Church, the same calendar that pays tribute to the 'killing' of Caesar by 'stabbing' on the 74th day of the year, and a little further ahead, we'll decode the 74 in 'Roman Catholicism'.

Roman = 9+12+14+26+13 = 74

     In light of the Albert Pike statue we referenced earlier, it should be noted that it fell on Juneteenth, June 19, 2020, the 171st day of the leap year, corresponding with the name 'Albert Pike', equating to 171 with Reverse Simple English. Furthermore, consider that Juneteenth is to remember the emancipation of enslaved people at the conclusion of the U.S. Civil War, that has been celebrated since June 19, 1865, and Albert Pike was a Confederate War General. As you'll begin to understand, as we move ahead, this was not an accident, but a symbolic ritual, and what we will come to know as a number game.

Albert = 26+15+25+22+9+7 = 104

Pike = 11+18+16+22 = 67

<u>Albert Pike = 171</u>

     And for further proof of the ritual and who was responsible for the statue coming down, using the exact same cipher, 'Freemasons' equates to 155, and June 19, 2020, when the statue fell, was the 155th anniversary of Juneteenth. Keep in mind the House of the Temple, the Freemason headquarters in Washington D.C., pays tribute to Pythagoras who said, "Everything is number."

Freemasons = 21+9+22+22+14+26+8+12+13+8 = 155

     Coming back to the Fourth of July, we'll now examine how the name 'Independence Day', as it is called in the United States, equates to 74. To calculate this value we'll use what is arguably the most important cipher, known as Pythagorean Gematria, also referred to as Reduction Gematria. It is based on the alphabetic order and incorporates the rules of numerology. You will notice 'A' through 'I' are '1' through '9' in this cipher, the same as Simple English Gematria, and the change begins with 'J', the 10th letter, that in numerology terms becomes 1+0 = 1, followed by K the 11th letter, that becomes 1+1 = 2, followed by L the 12th letter, that becomes 1+2 = 3 and so on, up to Z the 26th letter becoming 2+6 = 8.

<u>Pythagorean Gematria (also known as Reduction Gematria):</u>
A=1, B=2, C=3, D=4, E=5, F=6, G=7, H=8, I=9

J=1, K=2, L=3, M=4, N=5, O=6, P=7, Q=8, R=9

S=1, T=2, U=3, V=4, W=5, X=6, Y=7, Z=8

Let us now decode 'Independence Day' into 74.

Independence = 9+5+4+5+7+5+5+4+5+5+3+5 = 62

Day = 4+1+7 = 12

Independence Day = 62+12 = 74

Using Pythagorean Gematria, 'alphabetic order' and 'numerical language' each equate to 74 as well.

Alphabetic = 1+3+7+8+1+2+5+2+9+3 = 41

Order = 6+9+4+5+9 = 33

Alphabetic Order = 41+33 = 74

Numerical = 5+3+4+5+9+9+3+1+3 = 42

Language = 3+1+5+7+3+1+7+5 = 32

Numerical Language = 42+32 = 74

In this cipher, 'Roman Catholicism' also sums to 74.

Roman = 9+6+4+1+5 = 25

Catholicism = 3+1+2+8+6+3+9+3+9+1+4 = 49

Roman Catholicism = 25+49 = 74

And for a well remembered U.S. President summing to 74 in Pythagorean Gematria, try 'Richard Nixon', who resigned in 1974, on the date August 9, exactly 212 days after his January 9 birthday. I bring up the 212 days, because if you decode the name of the man who replaced him, 'Gerald Rudolph Ford Jr.', you'll notice it sums to 212 using Simple English Gematria.

Richard = 9+9+3+8+1+9+4 = 43

Nixon = 5+9+6+6+5 = 31

Richard Nixon = 43+31 = 74

To build further on your understanding of how 74 and 33 come together, 'Regis Philbin' equates to 74 with Pythagorean Gematria, and his death on July 24, 2020, was a span of 33 days from his August 25th birthday. Beyond that, every article written about his death, at age 88, mentioned that his hit show, *Live with Regis and Kathie Lee*, began in 1988. In other words, the mainstream media's reporting was letting those know with eyes to see, his demise was a number game.

With the use of Simple English and Pythagorean Gematria, you can begin to appreciate why the English language is made up of 26 letters. By no coincidence is it that 'God' and 'letter' equate to 26 using these two ciphers respectively, and on the subject of 26, I would encourage you to read the first chapter of my first book, *Letters & Numbers,* to learn more about all that dazzles when it comes to the number 26, a number that will be discussed extensively in the pages ahead, as we expose those who are truly playing 'God' over humanity by the gematria code, that again, is based in Kabbalah, a spiritual mysticism, in tribute to God.

God = 7+15+4 = 26 (Simple English Gematria)

Letter = 3+5+2+2+5+9 = 26 (Pythagorean Gematria)

Another related word summing to 26, using Pythagorean Gematria, is 'crusade'. This matters because the story goes that during the time of the crusades, the Knights Templar, who are the holy warriors of the Catholic Church and its Pope, secured the knowledge of Kabbalah after successfully sieging Jerusalem in the year 1099, before bringing it back to the Church. Thus it was the crusades that lead to the Roman Catholic Church's understanding of what is considered God's code, and by tracing through history, as we did in my first book, it appears the Church has been operating by this code ever since. Case in point, it's no accident that the most recent crusades of the holy lands began October 7, 2001, 26 days after September 11, 2001. And for the person reading who does not yet understand the connections between the Catholic Church and the United States as well as its military, that is just ahead. We'll also uncover more about the October 7, 2001 invasion in the pages ahead, a clear 'Templar' ritual.

Crusade = 3+9+3+1+1+4+5 = 26

Once again, it is a belief held within Kabbalah that numbers, letters and words are the magic of the world, and the basis of creation, as well as the existence of all things. In light of this belief, consider the meaning of the word 'spell' and its associations with the crafting of words, as well as magic. When you run the alphabetic order in reverse and use the rules of numerology, the word 'spell' also equates to 26.

Spell = 8+2+4+6+6 = 26

This method is known as Reverse Pythagorean Gematria, or Reverse Reduction Gematria, and the cipher is as follows:

<u>Reverse Pythagorean Gematria (also known as Reverse Reduction Gematria):</u>

Z=1, Y=2, X=3, W=4, V=5, U=6, T=7, S=8, R=9

Q=1, P=2, O=3, N=4, M=5, L=6, K=7, J=8, I=9

H=1, G=2, F=3, E=4, D=5, C=6, B=7, A=8

       Using this cipher, names such as 'George Washington' and 'Jesus Christ' equate to 74, pairing perfectly with what we learned earlier about George Washington, the 'masonic' leader, and his 74 generals, as well as 'Jesus', 'Messiah', *'Gospel'*, 'parables', 'cross' and their Simple English Gematria values, each equating to 74.

<u>George</u> = 2+4+3+9+2+4 = 24
<u>Washington</u> = 4+8+8+1+9+4+2+7+3+4 = 50
<u>George Washington = 24+50 = 74</u>
<u>Jesus</u> = 8+4+8+6+8 = 34
<u>Christ</u> = 6+1+9+9+8+7 = 40
<u>Jesus Christ = 34+40 = 74</u>

       Another name summing to 74 with this cipher, is 'William III'. He is the man responsible for making the City of 'London' an independent territory within London and the nation of 'England', a nation summing to 33 using Reverse Pythagorean, with the Tonnage Act, that we will discuss more ahead. As we decode, don't forget that 'London' is divided into 33 areas, or that it sums to 74 using Simple English Gematria. And relating to this pair of numbers, so often found together, please know that ahead we'll discuss Boris Johnson ending up in the 'ICU', an acronym summing to 33 with Simple English, from coronavirus, on April 6, 2020, 74 days before his 56th birthday, June 19th, 2020, and how the media tracked every last detail of his status in the ICU on April 7th, a date that is written 7/4 in the U.K. It will tie in with how it was reported that the Global Vaccine Summit hosted in 'London' on June 3rd and 4th, 2020, raised at least $7.4 billion, and that £330 million of that sum was pledged by the United Kingdom itself. It will also tie in with how Vera Lynn died on June 18, 2020, 74 days after Queen Elizabeth referenced her song, *We'll Meet Again,* in a rare address to the world, April 5, 2020, on the subject of the coronavirus pandemic.

<u>William III</u> = 4+9+6+6+9+8+5+9+9+9 = 74
<u>England</u> = 4+4+2+6+8+4+5 = 33

The ciphers you have now learned make up four parts of what are one system, and we will refer to them as the base ciphers of the English Language. In the chapters ahead we will use these four ciphers to unlock the riddles that have been laid down by The Cabal, over the centuries, connecting world shifting events, with a focus on September 11, 2001, and the coronavirus pandemic of 2020. As we will soon get to, it is no accident that the World Trade Centers collapsed on the 74th Meridian West in Manhattan, New York, after standing for 33-years, just the same as it is no coincidence that a simulation was conducted for a coronavirus outbreak and pandemic on 'October' 18, 2019, the day leaving 74 days left in the year, in the lone month having a gematria value of 33, and both events taking place in 'New York', a state having Reverse Pythagorean Gematria of 33.

New York = 4+4+4+2+3+9+7 = 33 (Reverse Pythagorean)
October = 6+3+2+6+2+5+9 = 33 (Pythagorean)

Regarding the date of the simulation, October 18, 2019, it happened to be the same day the Military World Games began in Wuhan, China, a contest that originated in Rome. Keep in mind this date was prior to any deadly case of coronavirus being reported in Wuhan or the world, something that would occur in the next month, November of 2019. And in light of this book being titled *Number Games*, we will uncover why the coronavirus outbreak simulation was named Event 201 in chapter four, no doubt a tribute to the Jesuit Order who serves the Catholic Church, out of Rome. It is something that can only be understood and proven through having the wisdom and knowledge of gematria.

For now, to further build on the relevance of 74, and to give you a bit of a preview of the fourth chapter, I'll have you know that one of the co-sponsors of Event 201 was the Bill and Melinda Gates Foundation, an organization that has their headquarters directly across the street from the 74-acre Seattle Center, the home of the Space Needle, that is located on the 47th Parallel North. This becomes all the more interesting when you realize that the first case of coronavirus confirmed in the United States, was done so in Bill and Melinda Gates' backyard, Snohomish County, Washington, and between the couple, and the location, we have two more 74s for our list.

Bill = 2+9+3+3 = 17
and = 1+5+4 = 10
Melinda = 4+5+3+9+5+4+1 = 31

Gates = 7+1+2+5+1 = 16
Bill and Melinda Gates = 17+10+31+16 = 74
Snohomish = 1+5+6+8+6+4+9+1+8 = 48
County = 3+6+3+5+2+7 = 26
Snohomish County = 48+26 = 74

  From the decode above, you can gather the name 'Bill Gates' sums to 33, and it is no accident he was the head of Microsoft for precisely 33-years, or that Microsoft became a public company on March 13, 1986, his 137th day of his age (137 is the 33rd prime number). For another March 13th in his history, he stepped down from his board positions at Microsoft and Berkshire Hathaway on March 13, 2020, 137 days after his birthday. From the decode above, you can also gather that 'Melinda Gates' sums to 47, the reflection of 74, reminding us that Seattle is on the 47th Parallel North, and the Microsoft HQ was relocated to Redmond, Washington, also on the 47th Parallel North, on February 16, 1986, the 47th day of the year. Prior to that, it was headquartered in New Mexico, the 47th state, home of the 1947 Roswell incident, something we'll touch on later.

  Now, to bring even greater clarity, and to shed more light on who The Cabal is and how they've encoded the English language, let us connect a few more important dots. We'll begin with the fact that the oldest known record of the English language traces back to the Monk Byrhtferth, of Ramsey Abbey, in England, and the year 1011. His alphabet looked a bit different than the one we're familiar with today. It was as follows: A, B, C, D, E, F, G, H, I, K, L, M, N, O, P, Q, R, S, T, V, X, Y, Z, ⁊, ρ, Þ, Ð, Æ. You'll notice that J, U and W of the modern English alphabet are missing, and we no longer use the glyphs from the end.

  Thus, the letters of Byrhtferth's alphabet were borrowed from Latin, the language of Ancient Rome, and the civilization that the Catholic Church originates from. In light of this fact, consider that the letters of Latin are used for words, as well as numbers, through the practice of Roman Numerals. In other words, English has Roman Catholic origins, and is based in a language that has alphanumeric qualities. With that in mind, consider that English was being standardized with the 26 letter alphabet and agreed to spellings we use today at the end of the 16th century, the same time the Gregorian Calendar was making its debut, in October of 1582, a calendar system

13

that was given to us by the Catholic Church, and more specifically, Pope Gregory XIII.

As we have briefly touched on thus far, and as we will come to better understand with more examples, the English Language and the Gregorian Calendar are perfectly in tune with one another. If you are new to this work, this is something I have been proving daily, no exaggerating, for seven years straight, every single day, and it is something you will be able to prove daily, for the rest of your days, so long as The Cabal remains in power. To build on our understanding of how gematria and dates come together, let's examine the three independent city-states that exist within larger nations, that are the locations from where The Cabal rules. As you might guess, they all have connections to Rome. They are Vatican City in Italy, a spiritual center, established February 11, 1929; Washington D.C., what was formerly a part of the Catholic Colony (thus why it is between Virginia and Maryland... think Virgin Mary) and is now a military center that is named after a masonic war general, where the cornerstone for its development was laid September 18, 1793, before becoming an independent territory on February 21, 1871; and the City of London, within London, the most powerful banking center in the world, originally built within the fortified walls that were erected by the Romans, who once used it as a trading post. It should also be noted that the City of London is where Modern Freemasonry was established, June 24, 1717, not long after becoming an independent territory on July 27, 1694.

Beginning with the 'Vatican', the name sums to 47 with Reverse Pythagorean Gematria, same as 'Francis', the first Jesuit Pope, and similar to how 'Christian' and 'confession' sum to 47 with Pythagorean Gematria. The date the Vatican was established, February 11, can be written 2/11, similar to the number 211, the 47th prime number. Regarding the number 47, if you have the time, watch the film 'The Two Popes', about the process of Pope Francis becoming the 266th Pope. You'll notice in the beginning of the movie, when he loses the cardinals' vote, the first number shown in the election count is 47.

Vatican = 5+8+7+9+6+8+4 = **47**

Christian = 3+8+9+9+1+2+9+1+5 = **47**

Confession = 3+6+5+6+5+1+1+9+6+5 = **47**

***Francis** = 3+9+8+4+6+9+8 = **47 (Reverse Pythagorean)**

14

The date of Vatican City's establishment, February 11th, can also be expressed as 11/2, similar to 112, a number connecting to the gematria of 'Catholicism' using the Simple English cipher. Furthermore, the Jesuits who operate within the Catholic Church, serve 112 countries, and the word 'Jesuit' itself sums to 42 using Reverse Pythagorean Gematria, not unlike how February 11th is the 42nd day of the Gregorian year.

Catholicism = 3+1+20+8+15+12+9+3+9+19+13 = 112
Jesuit = 8+4+8+6+9+7 = 42

Also noteworthy, on the subject of the Jesuits and the date February 11th, it can be expressed as 2/11, similar to 211, corresponding with the Simple English Gematria of the phrase, 'Jesus, savior of men', summing to 211, a Jesuit motto that is often expressed in Latin as, 'Iesus Hominum Salvator', equating to 266 with Reverse Simple English, and connecting to the fact that Pope Francis is the first Jesuit Pope, and he is the 266th Pope in the history of the Church, one of many mind blowing facts to come. You should also know that the number 266 is one that we will discuss often in the pages ahead, regarding a diversity of topics, ranging from Mike Pence being made the coronavirus czar on February 27, 2020, his 266th day of his age, to the death of Lisa Marie Presley's son on his 266th day of his age, in Calabasas, not long after the death of Kobe Bryant, in Calabasas, 266 days after his wife's birthday, while traveling from Catholic mass.

For one last point on the Vatican's February 11th establishment, the 42nd day of the Gregorian year, it is not by chance that when using Simple English Gematria, 'mathematics' sums to 112, and 'math' sums to 42. And at this point it should be very clear to see the hidden math of the English language is the name of the game. As we decode, consider that 1+1=2, similar to 112, and the *New Testament* begins with *Matthew* and the 42 generations to Jesus.

Mathematics = 13+1+20+8+5+13+1+20+9+3+19 = 112
Math = 13+1+20+8 = 42
New = 5+5+5 = 15
Testament = 2+5+1+2+1+4+5+5+2 = 27
New Testament = 15+27 = 42 (Pythagorean Gematria)

On the subject of 42, it is wise to consider that the Catholic Church built its fortune by literally selling the 'savior' with indulgences, a title summing to 42 in Reverse Pythagorean Gematria, as a means for mankind to escape Purgatory and Hell for their committed sins. Not by chance, 'sin' sums to 42 in Simple English Gematria, and that is likely due to an Ancient Egyptian teaching known as the 42 Laws of Ma'at, or sometimes called the 42 Confessions. They begin with, "I have not committed sin."

Sin = 19+9+14= 42
Savior = 8+8+5+9+3+9 = 42

For another gematria nugget, when you write out the word 'forty-two', it sums to 74 with Reverse Simple English Gematria. Let us not forget the connection with 'Jesus', the savior, and 74.

Forty-two = 21+12+9+7+2+7+4+12 = 74

*This value of 74 is only possible because of the lack of 'u' in forty, a rule that is taught in American English, but is inconsistent in the English language overall, given that 'four' is spelled with a 'u', as is 'fourteen' and 'four hundred'. You will notice that 'forty' sums to 84 with Simple English, and 'United States' sums to 40 with Pythagorean, and 'United States of America' to 84 with Pythagorean, tying in with 'U.S.' summing to 40 with Simple English. In chapters ahead, 84 is a number you will learn much about.

Before transitioning to the next city-state, Washington D.C., this is an opportune time to remind us about Andrew Yang, who was a presidential hopeful in the United States, whose slogan was 'MATH', standing for "Make America Think Harder," before dropping out of the race February 11, 2020, the 42nd day of the year, the most "mathematical" day in the entire Gregorian Calendar year. In addition to 'mathematics', his name 'Andrew Yang' also sums to 112 using the Simple English Gematria cipher. As we decode, know that in the pages ahead, we'll expose the U.S. federal government for what it is, a puppet show, organized by a mathematical scheme, where even the candidates in these predetermined selection processes are on strings. For example, it's no accident that Yang is of Chinese ancestry and he campaigned on the radical concept of giving people $1,000 per month so that they can be phased out of employment due to technology and automation, just prior to the "Chinese virus" as Donald Trump called it, that lead to the shutting down of much of the U.S. economy, and the giving away of $1,200 in fiat currency to every working U.S. adult, including those who were determined to be "non-essential". What it was, was a very sick joke, from The Cabal, who does intend to phase us out, with the technology they've been developing systematically not only to replace us, but to control us, and have surveillance over us,

16

more and more, with each passing day. These are things we will prove beyond a shadow of a doubt in the coming chapters, because this agenda is being achieved by the code.

Andrew = 1+14+4+18+5+23 = 65
Yang = 25+1+14+7 = 47
Andrew Yang = 65+47 = 112

Let us now move on to Washington D.C., the city-state named after George Washington, a favored person of the Catholic Church, because he was tolerant of their operations in the time after the Protestant Reformation, and he was a man who laid the cornerstone for the city on the date of September 18, 1793, a date having very relevant numerology, corresponding with the gematria of the name of the city, including 47. Before decoding the relevant gematria, we will take a moment to decode the date numerology using four different methods, all of which are important, just the same as the four ciphers you have learned to decode the English Language with. These methods are as follows, so be sure to study and use these same steps on all dates you decode going forward, just as we will now do with September 18, 1793, the 261st day of the year, leaving 104 days remaining.

9/18/1793 = 9+18+17+93 = 137
9/18/1793 = 9+18+(1+7+9+3) = 47
9/18/1793 = 9+1+8+1+7+9+3 = 38
9/18/93 = 9+18+93 = 120

Connecting to the date numerology, you will notice, 'Washington D.C.' sums to 137 using Simple English Gematria, 'D.C.' sums to 47 using Reverse Simple English, Washington D.C. is located on the 38th Parallel North, plus the word 'Kabbalah' sums to 38 in Simple English (it also sums to 38 using Hebrew Gematria), and the word 'Illuminati' sums to 120 using Simple English, similar to how Inauguration Day for U.S. Presidents is January 20, or 1/20. Regarding the Illuminati, they were established May 1, 1776, as a masonic order, by Adam Weishaupt, who was Jesuit trained. We'll touch more on their establishment date ahead as another proof of how the numerical value of words sync with the dates of the year, as well as their numerology values.

Washington D.C. = 23+1+19+8+9+14+7+20+15+14+4+3 = 137
Illuminati = 9+12+12+21+13+9+14+1+20+9 = 120
Kabbalah = 11+1+2+2+1+12+1+8 = 38
D.C. = 23+24 = 47

Regarding the number 137, there are a few things you should know. For starters, 'government' sums to 137 with Reverse Simple English Gematria, as does 'White House', and 'authority' sums to 137 with Simple English Gematria, as does 'Morals and Dogma', the masonic text authored by Albert Pike that we referenced earlier, that pays tribute to Freemasonry being based in Kabbalah. Furthermore, 137 is the 33rd prime number, and all of the following words have Pythagorean Gematria of 33. As we decode, keep in mind George Washington was a 33rd° Freemason, who now has a 333 foot masonic memorial built in his honor in Alexandria, Virginia, not to mention the House of the Temple, the Scottish Rite HQ in Washington D.C., has 33 columns on the outside, that are each 33 feet tall, and not by accident.

Masonry = 4+1+1+6+5+9+7 = 33
Federal = 6+5+4+5+9+1+3 = 33
Secrecy = 1+5+3+9+5+3+7 = 33
Order = 6+9+4+5+9 = 33

To give you a recent example of how the numbers 33 and 137 come together in ritual, or what I often refer to as number games, consider the story of 33 year old Naya Rivera's dead body being recovered in a lake on July 13, 2020, a date that can be expressed as 13/7, like 137. Furthermore, she was a star of the hit TV show Glee, and 7 years earlier, in the 7th month July, the first member of the hit TV show was found dead, a young man named Cory Monteith, on July 13, 2013. Even further, when Rivera's body was discovered, it made her the third member of the show to tragically die young, factoring in with her age of demise, 33. Also factoring in, she had starred in the 33rd episode of the show *Devious Maids*, that aired July 13, 2015, where she dies in the episode, and she had also starred in the 2014 film *At the Devil's Door*, where she wears a red sweater, with of course, the number 33 on it. In light of the title of the film, it is important to remember that where she drowned, Lake Piru, is a name related to the word devil. That is because in Finnish, Piru is a word for devil.

Next, for a relevant history lesson on the Illuminati, George Washington penned a letter to a man named William Russell, September 28, 1798, expressing his concerns about the Illuminati and their plans to overturn all religion and government through the means of conspiracy. Regarding "conspiracy", the Illuminati was established by Adam Weishaupt on May 1st for this very reason. Notice the value of his name in light of 'conspiracy' and even the stereotypical insult for truth seekers, that is so often 'tinfoil hat', using Pythagorean Gematria for each.

Adam = 1+4+1+4 = 10
Weishaupt = 5+5+9+1+8+1+3+7+2 = 41
<u>Adam Weishaupt = 10+41 = 51</u>
Conspiracy = 3+6+5+1+7+9+9+1+3+7 = 51
Tinfoil Hat = 2+9+5+6+6+9+3+8+1+2 = 51

  As you can gather, they all sum to 51, much like the date May 1st, or 5/1. If you're like me, the number 51 should remind you of the well known location that is often associated with conspiracy, Area 51. And speaking of Area 51, for those who contend Stanley Kubrick filmed the moon landing there, you should know that the word 'moon' sums to 51 with Reverse Simple English. It was for this reason SpaceX reportedly launched the first private rocket to dock at the International Space Station, May 30, 2020, 51 days before the 51st anniversary of the moon landing. Keep in mind, that launch was scheduled for 3:22 EST, and Adam Weishaupt, the founder of the Bavarian Illuminati, died November 18, 1830, the 322nd day of the year, an infamous number we will learn more about later in relation to Skull and Bones, an offshoot of the Bavarian Illuminati. The number 51 also connects to the riddle of 'Naya Rivera', a name equating to 51 with Pythagorean, the same as 'Lake Piru' with Reverse Pythagorean, as well as the words 'just the two of us' with Pythagorean, the latter being the words she left on her final social media post, on Instagram, just before her reported drowning, that we will discuss in even greater detail in the chapters ahead. So no doubt, the next time someone throws the programmed stereotype at you, "tinfoil hat", or mocks you for referencing the "Illuminati", you'll have some gems to drop on them, and don't be surprised if that often regurgitated insult is hurled at you for sharing the incredible knowledge of gematria. Should you experience this treatment from anyone, remember, this language is for people with wisdom, something that most people don't have, and are seemingly incapable of, almost as if they are under a spell, very possibly because of the lifelong programming they've been subjugated to through popular media, most of which is produced by The Cabal. In other words, you are blessed, so know that, truly.

  Back on the subject of the United States capital city, it should be noted that prior to the cornerstone being laid, Washington was first recognized as a territory on July 16, 1790, a date with numerology of

19

130, corresponding perfectly with the Simple English Gematria of 'Washington', also summing to 130.

7/16/1790 = 7+16+17+90 = 130

Washington = 23+1+19+8+9+14+7+20+15+14 = 130

Furthermore, the July 16th date of establishment was 144 days after George Washington's February 22, 1790 birthday. This matters because 'The United States of America' sums to 144 with Reverse Pythagorean Gematria. The name also sums to 261 with Simple English Gematria, and the date the cornerstone was laid, September 18, 1793, was the 261st day of the year. It is also for this reason that the U.S. dollar bill is 2.61 inches tall. Even further, if you use Pythagorean Gematria, the name 'The United States of America' sums to 99, and the United States of America was named as such on September 9, 1776, emphasis on 9/9. To take it further, the nation began with 13 colonies, that are represented in the 13 stripes of the U.S. flag, and if you write out 'thirteen', it has a Simple English value of 99. This connects to the fact that the Bavarian Illuminati was established with 13 families on a date with 99 numerology, May 1, 1776. Furthermore, from their establishment to the naming of 'United States of America', September 9, 1776, was a span of 132 days, not unlike the number of rooms in the White House. The distance of 132 days matters because 'United States of America' sums to 132 with Reverse Pythagorean Gematria when you leave 'the' out. For another 132, 'Catholic Church' equates with Simple English. And for another parallel to the Church, the date the cornerstone was laid, September 18th, leaves 104 days in the year, and 'Roman Catholic Church' equates to 104 with Reverse Pythagorean, similar to how 7/4/1776 has 104 numerology as follows, 7+4+17+76 = 104. Thus it is another reminder, all roads do lead to Rome, and the Church. Now, let us practice decoding.

The = 2+8+5 = 15; United = 3+5+9+2+5+4 = 28

States = 1+2+1+2+5+1 = 12; of = 6+6 = 12

America = 1+4+5+9+9+3+1 = 32   **7+4+1+7+7+6 = 32*

<u>The United States of America = 15+28+12+12+32 = 99</u>

Thirteen = 20+8+9+18+20+5+5+14 = 99

5/1/1776 = 5+1+17+76 = 99

You will notice that if you leave 'the' out, 'United States of America' sums to 84 with Pythagorean Gematria. In light of the naming of the country being well coordinated with the establishment of the Bavarian Illuminati, that was founded by Adam Weishaupt, a trained Jesuit, an operative of the Catholic Church, it should come as no surprise that 'Jesuit' sums to 84 using Simple English, and the title of the Jesuit leader, 'Superior General', sums to 84 using Pythagorean. Furthermore, if you write 'The Catholic Church', it sums to 84 in Pythagorean, and 'The Jesuit Order' sums to 84 using Reverse Pythagorean.

Jesuit = 10+5+19+21+9+20 = 84
Superior = 1+3+7+5+9+9+6+9 = 49
General = 7+5+5+5+9+1+3 = 35
Superior General = 49+35 = 84
The = 2+8+5 = 15
Catholic = 3+1+2+8+6+3+9+3 = 35
Church = 3+8+3+9+3+8 = 34
The Catholic Church = 15+35+34 = 84
The = 7+1+4 = 12
Jesuit = 8+4+8+6+9+7 = 42
Order = 3+9+5+4+9 = 30
The Jesuit Order = 12+42+30 = 84

If you've read George Orwell's *1984*, you might be starting to understand why he chose the year for the title of his novel, and if you've seen the film based on the book, you're very familiar with the red and black color theme. They are colors of the Jesuits, and this same color scheme is used in another important and related film that is based in a 1984 setting, *V for Vendetta*, where the main character wears a Guy Fawkes mask, and Guy Fawkes was a Jesuit. As a heads up, the number 84 is one that will come up repetitively in the chapters ahead regarding the Jesuits, and will surely be one to continue to come up as time goes on. Case in point, as I am finishing this book, it has been reported on May 20, 2020, that the former Jesuit Superior General has died at age 84. To understand why he died on the date he did, look no further than the fact that May 20th leaves 225 days in the year, and his birth name 'Adolfo Nicolas', sums to 225 with Reverse Simple English Gematria. Even more, he died on the 191st day of the current Superior General's age, Arturo Sosa, who was born November 12, 1948, and 'Society of Jesus' sums to 191 using Simple English Gematria. If you're not aware, the official name of the Jesuit Order is the Society of Jesus. As for Sosa being 71 years old at the time of

Nicolas' death, that ties in perfectly with the next point that needs to be made about the history of Washington D.C. and its significant dates.

On February 21, 1871, Washington D.C. became an independent city-state, with the *District of Columbia Organic Act of 1871*. The act merged the town of Washington, and the Jesuit territory of Georgetown, into one self governing territory. This was done as a means to invite international investment, due to the territory becoming impoverished, and some areas being in ruins, as a direct result of the U.S. Civil War that had recently concluded and largely bankrupted the nation. The year '71 matters because 'Catholic' sums to 71 using Simple English Gematria, and the date February 21, or 2/21, matters because 'The Bavarian Illuminati' sums to 221 using the same cipher. At the same time, the Jesuit motto, 'Jesus, savior of men', equates to 221 with Reverse Simple English, and once again, the Illuminati was founded by the Jesuit, Adam Weishaupt. What is even more hidden is the gematria of 'District of Columbia Organic Act of 1871', summing to 201 in Reverse Pythagorean, similar to how 'The Jesuit Order' equates to 201 with Reverse Simple English, another very special number to the organization that we will take apart in chapter four, when we dissect Event 201, the coronavirus outbreak simulation of October 18, 2019, that again, took place on the same day the Military World Games began in Wuhan, China, a festival with origins in Rome, like the Catholic Church, and Jesuits. For now you can know the following about the number in relation to the Jesuits, and that is the Jesuits were reportedly saved by Catherine the Great, who preserved the Jesuit Order, by defying Pope Clement XIV, who ordered the Jesuits to be suppressed on July 21, 1773, and they were, except for the 201 that were protected by Catherine, the leader of Russia at the time. This number becomes all the more fascinating when you recognize that Pope Francis, the first Jesuit Pope, is also the first to live in Suite 201 at the Vatican, a stat pairing perfectly with his birth name, 'Jorge Mario Bergoglio', equating to 201 with Simple English, the same as 'Ignatius of Loyola', the founder of the Jesuits, as well as the name 'Domus Sanctae Marthae', the official name of Suite 201. I should also note that Adam Weishaupt, the Jesuit, eventually changed the name of the Bavarian Illuminati to 'Order of Illuminati', equating to 201 with Simple English, reminding us of Inauguration Day, 20/1.

Another important fact about the date of the District of Columbia Organic Act of 1871, February 21st, is that it is the 52nd day of the year. With regards to 52, the head of the Catholic Church is the 'Pope', and not by chance, the title sums to 52 using Simple English Gematria, same as the phrase 'The Cabal'. Their mission is to rule over 'earth', a name also summing to 52 in Simple English, and a number pairing with the number of weeks in a year, 52, and the number of cards in a deck, 52. For a few more relevant terms equating to 52, 'government' and 'White House' sum to 52 using Pythagorean Gematria, and 'authority' and 'president' equate using the Reverse Pythagorean cipher. Just wait until we get to Donald Trump's role in The Cabal's schemes, the man who attended Fordham University, a Jesuit school, in 1964, 52 years before becoming 'president' elect, and 56 years before the 'coronavirus' outbreak. I bring up the part about 56 years because it is a number you will become very familiar with in chapter four. For now, you can know that 'Washington D.C.', 'Society of Jesus' and 'coronavirus' each equate to 56 in Pythagorean Gematria. You can also know that when we get to Chapter 18, about how 'George Perry Floyd' fits in with The Cabal's agenda, a name summing to 201 with Simple English Gematria, we'll breakdown the changing of Washington D.C.'s 16th Street to 'Black Lives Matter' Plaza on June 5, 2020, in tribute to George Floyd, a date that can be expressed as 5/6, similar to the number 56, and reminding us that the Civil Rights Act of '64 came 56 years earlier, and 'Black Lives Matter' sums to 56 using Pythagorean Gematria.

      Moving on to the third city-state, the City of London, its origins are so old, the date of establishment has been lost to time. Its autonomy came however, with the Tonnage Act, that established the Bank of England and respective territory as an independent entity, July 27, 1694. The Tonnage Act, also known as the Bank of England Act 1694, made the bank and territory an independent 'corporation', thus why the City of London is also commonly referred to as the City of London Corporation. In light of this fact, notice how the numerology of the date of establishment corresponds with the Simple English Gematria of 'corporation', summing to 144.

7/27/1694 = 7+27+16+94 = 144
Corporation = 3+15+18+16+15+18+1+20+9+15+14 = 144

      A moment earlier, we covered how 'The United States of America' has gematria of 144, and that Washington D.C. was established 144-days after George Washington's birthday. This is a number relevant to the 'Jesuit Order' as well, summing to 144 with

Simple English Gematria, and it reminds us that Donald Trump, Jesuit educated, posed with Pope Francis, at the Vatican, May 24, 2017, the 144th day of the year.

Jesuit = 10+5+19+21+9+20 = 84
Order = 15+18+4+5+18 = 60
Jesuit Order = 84+60 = 144

      Adding relevance to the number 144, Ignatius of Loyola, the founder of the Jesuit Order, would often conclude his letters with the phrase, "Go forth and set the world on fire." If you take the time to apply the code, you'll notice that in Pythagorean Gematria, that phrase sums to 144 as well. And in light of the Jesuits operating on behalf of the Catholic Church, it is important to know that the nation of England has been under Catholic control since the Treaty of 1213, when King John pledged England and Ireland to the papacy. This was agreed to on October 3, 1213, a date with 38 and 26 numerology, connecting both parties involved. 'King John' sums to 38 with Reverse Pythagorean, and 'papacy' equates to 26 with Pythagorean. As a reminder, 26 is the number associated with 'God', as well as 'crusade', and this historical event, the Treaty of 1213, wasn't long after the Catholic Church came into possession of the code, after the Knights Templar returned with it from the crusades.

      Going back to the date of July 27th, the date of the Tonnage Act, it is written 27/7 in the United Kingdom, much like 277. The number 277 is the 59th prime number and this matters because 'London, England' sums to 59 in Pythagorean Gematria, whereas 'Freemasonry' sums to 59 with Reverse Pythagorean. Consider, Modern Freemasonry was established in the City of London in the year 1717, and the number 59 is the 17th prime. Furthermore, the United States of America declared its independence from England in 1776, 59 years later, and 'Independence Day' sums to 277 with Reverse Simple English. For another point, the word 'Mason' sums to 17 in Pythagorean Gematria, tying in perfectly with the year 1717, the establishment of Modern Freemasonry. Also relevant to the discussion is the fact that from the Jesuits being recognized by Rome in 1540 to the establishment of Modern Freemasonry in 1717, is 177 years later, and where 'The Jesuit Order' equates to 177 with Simple English, 'New World Order' equates to 177 with Reverse Simple.

      What is essential to understand is Modern Freemasonry claims its roots in the Knights Templar, who serve the Catholic Church, same

as the Jesuits. Even further, there are many Freemasons who are also
Jesuits, as well as being members of other masonic orders. As we will
come to understand, there is a thin line between these secret societies,
that is most clearly seen in Washington D.C. This is because it was
once the Catholic Colony, also known as Rome on the Potomac, and
controlled by the Jesuits, but is now known as the Masonic City,
named after the Freemason, George Washington. Even with the newer
name, Washington, it still has a heavy Jesuit presence due to
Georgetown University, the first Jesuit university established in the
United States, by John Carroll, when he was 54 years of age, on
January 23, 1789. It matters that he was 54, born January 8, 1735,
because 'John Carroll' and 'Jesuit Order' both equate to 54 in
Pythagorean Gematria. Furthermore, the number 54 is symbolic in
terms of time. This is because we're on the Gregorian calendar, a solar
calendar, and the word 'sun' sums to 54 in Simple English Gematria.
If you're not aware of the Jesuit logo, it is the sun, with the letters IHS
inside, as well as the cross and three nails, the latter symbolizing those
used in the crucifixion of God's son, Jesus Christ.

　　And for the record, January 23, 1789 was a date with
numerology of 49 and 130, both connecting to the gematria of
'Washington', as well as a date with 113 numerology, connecting to
the value of 'Scottish', summing to 49 and 113. Consider further, both
'Georgetown' and 'Scottish Rite' sum to 57 using Pythagorean, and
'George' Washington, the Freemason, having a first name equating to
57 with Simple English, would turn 57-years-old, February 22, 1789,
days later, just before becoming the first recognized President of the
United States, April 30, 1789. I'll add that Washington's inauguration
date had numerology of 140, connecting to 'Washington' with Reverse
Simple English, and numerology of 32, connecting the 'Scottish' Rite
and the Jesuits, as well as 'America'. We'll touch on 32 just ahead.
For more relevance to number 57, four of the first six U.S. Presidents
were inaugurated at that age, and in light of the nickname of the capital
city, 'Rome' on the Potomac, it should be noted that 'Rome' sums to
57 with Reverse Simple English. As for the four U.S. Presidents to be
inaugurated at age 57, they were George Washington, Thomas
Jefferson, James Madison and John Quincy Adams. And for a final
point about Georgetown's establishment, and how it pays tribute to the
Jesuits, as well as the Scottish Rite, the date January 23rd can be
written 23/1, similar to 231, the 21st triangular number. This matters

because the word 'Jesuit' sums to 21 with Pythagorean, and 42 with Reverse Pythagorean, just the same as how 'Georgetown' equates to 42 with Reverse Pythagorean, connecting back to the Vatican being established on the 42nd day of the Gregorian year.

To further illustrate the relationship between the Jesuits and Scottish Rite, the 32nd degree of the Scottish Rite shares a motto with the Jesuits, in Latin, "Ad majorem Dei gloriam." In light of it being the 32nd degree, keep in mind there are 32 sun rays in the Jesuit logo, and using Pythagorean Gematria, 'Scottish' sums to 32, as does 'America'', the nation  established on July 4, 1776, a date with numerology of 32. In the same cipher, 'Christ' also sums to 32, reminding us that we're talking about the Society of Jesus. To take it further, the Latin motto, "Ad majorem Dei gloriam," sums to 115 using Reverse Pythagorean, similar to how 'Masonic' and 'France' sum to 115 with Reverse Simple English (*also spelled, *Ad maiorem Dei gloriam). The reason France matters is because the Jesuits were formed in France, and the Scottish Rite came to power there, the same nation where many of the Masonic founders of the United States of America studied. If you're up for a TV show, take the time to watch *Knightfall*, set in France. It is focused on the Knights Templar's fallout with the Catholic Church, at a time when Pope Boniface VIII was focused on making all Kings and Queens of Europe bow the knee to the Roman Catholic Empire. You'll get a kick out of the mention of 65 Knights Templar orders in Europe in episode six, knowing that 'Knights Templar' and 'Christianity' sum to 65 in Pythagorean Gematria, and to be a member of the Knights Templar, you must be Christian.

Coming back to the latin phrase, Ad majorem Dei gloriam, it means, "For the greater glory of God." The translated phrase sums to 351 with Reverse Simple English, the 26th triangular number, bringing us back to the Simple English Gematria of 'God', summing to 26. And on the subject, let us now appreciate how the Council of Nicea, in the year 325, that was held by the Catholic Church to bring about how to worship the offspring of God, factors in. To make a long story short, the Church, who had brought many pagans under its rulership, was having trouble with people worshiping the sun in the sky, instead of worshiping the son of the virgin birth, who died on the cross, for man's sins, and this was a problem they wanted remedied.

Following the trail of the Catholic Church giving birth to the Knights Templar, and the Knights Templar being the roots of Modern Freemasonry, and that you must believe in God, or G-d, to be a Freemason, and Catholicism worshiping the Son of God, established and made clear in the year 325, it makes sense that 'Scottish Rite of Freemasonry' sums to 325 using Simple English Gematria. At the same time, 'City of London Corporation' sums to 325 with Reverse Simple English Gematria, and it too is under Jesuit and Freemason control, meaning ultimately, it is under Catholic control. Ahead, in chapter three, we will uncover what happened on March 25, 2020 or 3/25, while the Bank of England was 325-years-old, the heart of the 'City of London Corporation'. It will connect continents, and many loose ends not yet tied.

To finish our introduction to gematria, the language of The Cabal, let us take a moment to think about the flag of the city-state, Washington D.C. On it are three stars that symbolize the unholy trinity. That is the Vatican, the City of London, and D.C. itself. With that in mind, we'll now decode the word 'trinity' using Reverse Simple English and Reverse Pythagorean. You will notice the word sums to 74, as well as 47.

Trinity = 7+9+18+13+18+7+2 = 74
Trinity = 7+9+9+4+9+7+2 = 47

At this point, we have connected how the numbers 74 and 47 correspond with each of the three city-states, and we have learned the mathematical relationships between the digits 7 and 4. One thing that has not been stated yet is the numerology of 74 and 47 equates to 11 (74 is 7+4=11 and 47 is 4+7=11), what is known as the "master number." This is because the digit 1 is the only number that divides into all numbers, corresponding with the belief that God is in all things, and God is the master of all things. The number 11 is also the first repdigit, meaning a number that is made up of the same repeating number (11, 222, 3333, 44444, etc.), plus, in numerology terms, when you repeat a number, you magnify its power. With that in mind, I want you to pay mind to the plethora of 47s encoded in these key words that pertain to Washington D.C., arguably the most powerful city in the world, that once again, had its cornerstone laid, September 18, 1793, a date with numerology of 38, 47 and 137, all numbers summing to 11 in numerology terms.

D.C. = 23+24 = 47 (Reverse Simple English)

27

Government = 2+3+5+4+9+4+5+4+4+7 = **47** (Reverse Pythagorean)
Authority = 1+3+2+8+6+9+9+2+7 = **47** (Pythagorean)
President = 7+9+5+1+9+4+5+5+2 = **47** (Pythagorean)
Trump = 7+9+6+14+11 = **47** (Reverse Simple English)
*Caesar = 3+1+5+19+1+18 = **47** (Simple English)
White House = 4+1+9+7+4+1+3+6+8+4 = **47** (Reverse Pythagorean)
Republican = 9+5+7+3+2+3+9+3+1+5 = **47** (Pythagorean)
Whig = 23+8+9+7 = **47** (Simple English)
Democrat = 5+4+5+3+6+9+8+7 = **47** (Reverse Pythagorean)

For a few more examples, it's not an accident that Donald Trump was in the 47 story Midtown Hilton Hotel the night of the rigged selection, and it's not an accident Obama became President at age 47, alongside the 47th Vice President, Joe Biden, who was at the center of the 'Ukraine' investigation (pure theater), a nation summing to 47 with Reverse Pythagorean. It's also not an accident that Abraham Lincoln said, "Four score and seven years ago," or that the United States' birthday can be written 4/7. Speaking of which, the masonic compass and square used by the Scottish Rite out of 'France', a nation summing to 47 with Simple English, is set at 47 degrees, in tribute to the 47th Problem of Euclid, otherwise known as the Pythagorean Theorem. It is wise to note, Pythagoras is considered by some to be the first Freemason and the name 'Pythagoras' equates with 'Washington' in all four base ciphers, a perfect match. Try your skills out and see for yourself. Other words having logical relationships and perfect matches are plentiful, try 'witch' and 'broom', or 'judge' and 'gavel'. Speaking of which, the latter two sum to 47 using Simple English, and not by chance, Trump's first picked Supreme Court Justice, Neil Gorsuch, was confirmed on April 7, 2017, emphasis on 4/7. As for the 47th Problem of Euclid, it symbolizes how to establish a perfectly square 'foundation', a word summing to 47 with Pythagorean Gematria. This pairs well with the fact that L'Enfant, the French Freemason, laid out D.C., the land of 47, where the Washington Monument's cornerstone was also laid on July Fourth.

In case you're reading this and seeing the connections and saying things such as, "So what? or, "What is the value of knowing this?" I want to say two things. One, you've been missing out for years, and two, you will. Case in point, Monday Night Football, November 11, 2019, the Seattle Seahawks of Washington State were at the San Francisco 49ers, as big underdogs, on the 130th birthday of

Washington State. Not by chance, the Seahawks coach, Pete Carroll, was going for his 130th regular season win, and his 140th win including the post season, corresponding with the Gematria of 'Washington', summing to 130 and 140, and sure enough he got them, paying those who took the Seahawks to win more than triple their money. I don't mean to promote gambling, but what I do promote is awareness of how the show is being scripted, and who is responsible, and how in the world of sports, you can prove it every single day. Of course, American football is credited to Walter Camp, the Scottish Rite Freemason, and it is no accident the NFL had its first Super Bowl in its 47th season. It was foundational.

To say a few more things about 47, the reflection of 74, the number we started with --- in Hebrew, the word 'Elohim' sums to 47. This is a common name for God of the Old Testament. This factors in with how the name God can be written G-d, the 7th letter and the 4th. As was mentioned earlier, The Cabal is playing God with this knowledge, and not by chance, the title 'The Cabal' sums to 47 with Reverse Pythagorean.

The Cabal = 7+1+4+6+8+7+8+6 = 47

It is for this reason the 33rd President, Harry S. Truman, who became a 33rd degree Scottish Rite Freemason, October 9, 1945, was used to pass the National Security Act of 1947, that went into effect on September 18th, the anniversary of the cornerstone being laid for the city of Washington D.C., a date that has much to do with the 'Roman Catholic Church'. Prior to being enacted, it was introduced in the Senate, a Roman concept, on March 3rd, or 3/3, and it was signed into law by Harry S. Truman, on July 26th, the day leaving 158-days left in the year. Truman's signing date matters because the word 'Freemasonry' sums to 158 with Reverse Simple English, and the date August 15th, or 15/8, is the date the Jesuits were founded in France in 1534, before being officially recognized by Rome, September 27th, 1540. This act created the NSA, and the CIA, things that have been used to both spy on the public, and steer the public, in the interests of The Cabal who control the nation by the code, and no doubt these agencies. Speaking of which, if you've never seen the film *The Truman Show*, you must. It is about a man who has every inch of his life secretly tracked and recorded, for the sake of being broadcast on a reality TV show, without him ever knowing about any of it. Of course, The Cabal also controls 'Hollywood', summing to 33 with Reverse

Pythagorean Gematria. And if you didn't know, Hollywood is a reference to the wood of Holly trees, that have been historically used by druids, to make wands, for magic spells. And again, "spelling" is the word, and the name of the game.

For your learning, I must mention Truman's birthday, May 8, 1884, emphasis on 5/8, as well as the year '84. Using Pythagorean Gematria, 'Freemasonry', 'secret society' and 'Solomon's Temple' each equate to 58. Of course, Freemasonry is a secret society, and most of its secrets are in legends of Solomon's Temple. It is for this reason that Donald Trump announced from his 58 story Trump Tower, that he was running for U.S. President in the 58th U.S. Presidential Election. The significance of the number is also why he hired the 58 year old Steve Ray for inauguration day, and it connects to why Hillary Clinton wrote the book, 'What Happened', summing to 58 with Pythagorean Gematria, about why she lost the election. Regarding Hillary, keep in mind Freemasonry is a fraternity for men. And when you apply Reverse Pythagorean Gematria, you'll notice the word 'fraternal' sums to 58 as well.

One question we have not yet fully answered, is why go through all this trouble of mathematical calculation, and date planning, and name and word coordinating? As covered, this code is associated with God's way of operating, as it is taught in Kabbalah. Furthermore, there is another important set of occult teachings that the secret societies, including The Cabal, are heavily invested in, and that is Hermeticism. It has 7 sacred principles. The third is 'vibration', summing to 47 with Pythagorean Gematria. This principle expresses that everything, including every number, every letter, every word, every color, every smell, every sound, etc., carries a vibration, and these vibrations have consequences that influence the world. Thus, if you can harness these energies and use them strategically, you can influence outcomes, something that The Cabal is heavily interested in. Keep in mind the word 'energy' sums to 74 in Simple English Gematria, same as 'weapon' and 'nuclear'. This pairs well with the 'Trinity' Test, where Trinity sums to 74 and 47, the first 'nuclear' test, taking place in the 47th state, New Mexico. In the next chapter we'll talk about how this event, part of the Manhattan Project, pairs with the World Trade Centers falling on the 74th Meridian West, in Manhattan, and the site of 9/11 being called Ground Zero, a term that is used to describe the point above or below ground where an atomic or nuclear weapon explodes. Another event from recent history, also tying in, was the massive earthquake in Southern California, on July 4, 2019, or 7/4, just days before the 74 year anniversary of the Trinity Test, that took place July 16, 1945. This earthquake's epicenter was located on a military base, and not coincidentally. And much like 9/11, it created a sense of fear, and that is the energy and vibration The Cabal specializes in, pumping it 24/7/365, for the sake of control.

For another 74, the word 'Tarot' sums to 74 using Simple English, as in Tarot cards, and ahead you'll learn much about them, including the 19th card of the Tarot deck, The Sun card, and what the Gregorian Calendar, a solar calendar, has to do with 19 year cycles. It has everything do with why September 11th happened in 2001, blamed on 19 hijackers, and why the Covid-19 pandemic happened in 2020, 19-years later. In Chapter 18 we'll bring together George Floyd, who yelled, 'I can't breathe', summing to 74 with Reverse Pythagorean, and why it was reported an officer kneeled on his neck for 8 minutes and 46 seconds, in the Twin Cities, not unlike how the first plane hit the Twin Towers, at 8:46 AM, on September 11, 2001. George Floyd's killing happened in Gemini as well, the astrological sign known as the Twins. And as we'll get to, it was no accident that they scheduled the pretrial for his murder for September 11, 2020, the 19 year anniversary of the infamous day, especially when the surname 'Floyd' sums to 19 with Reverse Pythagorean.

On the subject of 9/11, you're likely aware that three buildings fell that day, and it was referred to as the New Pearl Harbor. Those buildings were numbered 1, 2 and 7, similar to the date of Pearl Harbor, December 7, or 12/7, much like 127, corresponding with the Reverse Simple English Gematria of 'Ground Zero', summing to 127. The third building to fall, Building 7 was 47 floors tall, and each floor had 47,000 square feet of space. Adding insult to injury, it was known as the 'Salomon Brothers' Building, not too far off from Solomon's Temple, and the name 'Salomon Brothers' sums to 211, the 47th prime. Keep in mind, the demise of the World Trade Center was blamed on 'Osama bin Laden', who was referred to as the 'Cave Dweller' by President George W. Bush. Not by chance, both his name and his nickname sum to 47 using Pythagorean Gematria. And trust me, that's just where the riddles begin, that we will dive much deeper into next chapter. And with regards to these very clear patterns, when you have a moment, I would encourage you to look into the 'BBC', summing to

74 with Reverse Simple English, reporting that Building 7 had fallen, well before it began to collapse. If you have forgotten, Building 7 collapsed several hours after the Twin Towers, and it was not hit by a plane, becoming only the third steel framed building to ever collapse from a fire in history, all three of which collapsed on September 11, 2001, in what is arguably the most obvious lie ever told.

On the subject of 9/11, and introducing this knowledge to you, I would be amiss to skip the Dancing Israelis, who were arrested in 'New Jersey', a state summing to 47 with Reverse Pythagorean, on the day of September 11, 2001, for celebrating the attacks. They were then sent back to Israel, the nation that was recognized as a nation by the United Nations, November 29, 1947, where they went on live television and admitted they were in the U.S. to document the events of 9/11, meaning they had foreknowledge. Keep in mind, 'Brooklyn, New York', a neighbor of Manhattan, sums to 74 with Reverse Pythagorean, and I bring this up because it is the most 'Jewish' neighborhood in the world, outside of Israel, and my first book, *Letters and Numbers*, teaching about the 'Gematria' of the 'English' language, as well as 9/11 and the Dancing Israelis, as those subjects have never been taught before, was banned March 15, 2019, the 74th day of the year, by Etsy, a Jewish owned company out of Brooklyn, without reason, despite having all positive reviews, and hundreds of reviews, and over 10,000 sales. When we get to the chapter on Jesuits, we'll discuss their Jewish origins, like Gematria. We'll also expose Anthony Fauci, Head of NIH since 1984, the Jesuit, from Brooklyn, who said on January 10, 2017, at Georgetown, a pandemic was coming for the Trump administration, in very specific terms.

To close, there is one last thing you must know about the number 47. It is that the word 'time' sums to 47 with Simple English Gematria. Consider, the Tropic of Cancer is at 23.5 degrees North and the Tropic of Capricorn is at 23.5 degrees South, thus separated by 47 degrees, and they are used to measure 'time' and the respective solstices of the northern and southern hemispheres, thus the tropics measure the sun. As you will come to understand, this is what it's all about for The Cabal. Using the code, to control humanity, and control time as we know it. This includes controlling what we know about the past, present and future. To quote George Orwell's *1984*, "Who controls the past controls the future. Who controls the present controls the past."

2 | 1968, the Year of Coronavirus & the 9/11 Master Plan

1968 was a very significant year, full of tragedy and plotting. In terms of tragedy, one of many included a gunshot that ended Martin Luther King Jr.'s life on April 4th, 4/4, the well remembered Civil Rights leader. For your gematria learning, his demise was on a date corresponding with the word 'kill', summing to 44 using Simple English, and 'shooting' summing to 44 with Pythagorean, same as 'execution'. Making matters all the more suspicious, his murder came one year to the day of his speech, *Beyond Vietnam: A Time to Break Silence*, given April 4, 1967, at the Riverside Church in New York, where he said the heart of all that was wrong in the United States, including racism, was the U.S. military agenda that was responsible for bringing so much hatred, death, destruction and darkness into the world. Perhaps it isn't a coincidence then that 'military' sums to 44 with Pythagorean Gematria, or that our history books state the assassination of Caesar took place in 44 B.C., a man who lead one of the greatest militaries of all time. After all, they do say the victors write the history books, and all roads lead to Rome. As for the Jesuit influence in the English language, and its once secret gematria code, do not look past the fact that the word 'infantry' has Pythagorean gematria of 44, or that 'soldier' equates to 44 with Reverse Pythagorean. In the case of the first word, infantry, it has infant in it, showing that The Cabal knows what they're doing, taking advantage of the youth, and exploiting them for the purpose of their militaristic agendas. And with regards to sol-die-r, it has the words sol and die in it. Of course, sol is the Spanish word for sun, and it is the beginning of the word solar, relating to the sun's energy. At the same time, the last letter in the word is 'r', the 18th letter, corresponding with the gematria of 'IHS', as well as 'sun', as well as the age most young people join the military at. Furthermore, the Jesuit logo is the sun with the acronym IHS in the middle of it, and you must keep in mind, the text *Art of War*, by Sun Tzu, emphasis on Sun, was translated in 1772 by a Jesuit, in France. And further, some historians contend there never was a Sun Tzu, a man who is believed to have died at either age 46, or 47, where 'Catholic' and 'Vatican' equate to 46 and 47 respectively, and of course, 'France' also sums to 47, reminding us of L'Enfant, who laid out Washington D.C., the "47 city," and the heart of The Cabal's military empire. And if at this point, you're thinking about the number 44, and MLK, and you're wondering about 'Barack

Obama', a name summing to 68 with Simple English (think 1968), who became President at age 47, and who became the 44th President, elected 44-years after the Civil Rights Act, and who ran his campaign on 'hope', summing to 44 with Simple English, then you're wondering about the right things, and yes, your questions will be answered.

After MLK, another well remembered gunshot came, ending Robert Kennedy's life, June 6th, 6/6, the man who brought the news of MLK's murder to the minds of many with his televised words. Also not by coincidence, 'Robert Kennedy' sums to 66, the same as his assassin, 'Sirhan Sirhan', both with the Pythagorean cipher, complimenting the date of death, 6/6. Patterns such as these bring new meaning to the age old expression, "Your number is up." We'll touch more on both assassinations ahead, and we'll even discuss JFK's and Lincoln's, because they all come together through one number, that points with great intensity at the Jesuit Order. And for those that hate cliffhangers, I'll give you half of the story now. Martin Luther King Jr. was not born with the name. He was born Michael King Jr. The name he assumed, Martin Luther, was the name of the leader of the Protestant Reformation, against the Catholic Church, that transpired after he published the *95 Theses* exposing the Church's wrongdoings. For his efforts, the Jesuit Order was created, with the purpose of killing Martin Luther and his followers. Not by chance, the Jesuits were recognized by Rome on September 27th, the day leaving 95 days left in the year, to counter the *95 Theses* and Martin Luther's campaign. And that brings us to the fact that Martin Luther King Jr. was killed on the 95th day of 1968, a leap year, and also on a date with 95 numerology. 4+4+19+68 = 95. That's the half of it. For your learning, you should also know that 'Jesus, savior of men', a Jesuit motto, equates to 95 with Reverse Pythagorean, and of course, MLK was a follower of Jesus Christ.

Moving on, the infamous year included the 1968 Pandemic, also known as the Hong Kong Flu, that reportedly killed at least one million and as many as four million people. 1968 was the year the term "coronavirus" was coined. 1968 was the year of what is believed to be the first documented HIV case, coming from 'City Hospital', summing to 68 in Reverse Pythagorean. 1968 was the year 9-1-1 was established as the emergency dialing code in the U.S. with the first call made on February 16, 1968, the 47th day of the year. 1968 was the year World Trade Center construction began in New York, on the 74th Meridian West. 1968 was also the year George W. Bush, the President at the time of 9/11, graduated from Yale and Skull and Bones, a man with a July 6, 1946 birthday, meaning September 11th is the 68th day of his age every year. *Seriously, what are the odds of that?*

Answer: About 1 in 365

Let us not forget his father's speech, the 41st President, George H.W. Bush, on September 11, 1990, 11 years to the day, about a "New World Order," and it being "freer of terror". Of course the word 'terror' sums to 68 with Reverse Simple English. As we know, that was W's favorite word. And more than a decade later, I'm still trying to figure out how to correctly write the way he would pronounce it. Ter-eh? Teruh? Terrra? No matter how, W's father H.W. was a member of Skull and Bones, the same as his father, Prescott, and the same as W. himself, and fittingly, 'Skull and Bones' sums to 41 with Pythagorean Gematria, tying in with H.W. being the 41st President, and September 11, 2001 taking place on a date with 41 numerology (9/11/2001 = 9+11+20+01 = 41). Even further, the attack was blamed on 'Al-Qaeda', summing to 41 with Simple English, similar to how 'Saudi Arabia' equates to 41 with Pythagorean, where the majority of hijackers were said to be from. Keep in mind 41, is the 13th prime number, and Skull and Bones is the U.S. offshoot of the Bavarian Illuminati that was established with 13 families on May 1, 1776. Skull and Bones is also a fraternity located at building number 322 on the Yale campus, a number they identify by. Just ask Tim Russert, who prior to his untimely death at age 58, asked both George W. Bush and John Kerry about being in Skull and Bones and the significance of 322, while they were the two respective candidates for U.S. President in the 2004 race- Bush representing the Republicans, and Kerry representing the Democrats. Adding to the relevance of the number, as we covered earlier, the founder of the Bavarian Illuminati, Adam Weishaupt, died November 18, 1830, the 322nd day of the year, leaving 43 days remaining.

As for the son, George W. Bush, being the 43rd President, he and his father attended Yale, as stated. This matters because 'Yale' sums to 43 with Simple English, and you might recall how George W. Bush was announced the 43rd President Elect after Florida called the election in his favor. This was funny at the time because his brother

35

Jeb was the current and 43rd Governor of Florida, and not by chance, 'Florida' sums to 43 with Reverse Pythagorean Gematria, same as 'masonic'. On the masonic tip, the letters D.C. are 4.3. And don't forget that before H.W. was the 41st President, he was the 43rd Vice President. And prior to that, he was the 11th Director of the 'CIA', an alphabet agency with an acronym summing to 68 in Reverse Simple English.

1968 was the beginning of a new age, and not a positive one for humanity, but one that we're feeling the consequences of today. It is probably no accident then that the word 'age' sums to 68 with Reverse Simple English, or that 'Solar System' equates to 68 with Reverse Pythagorean, seeing as how it is the movement of the planets in relation to the sun and stars that dictates the age. As I write this, HBO has announced they're removing 'Gone with the Wind', summing to 68 in Reverse Pythagorean, from their movie platform, a classic title, that opened the 1968 Cannes Film Festival, that was ended prematurely by civil unrest and rioting. The reason for its 2020 removal, in the words of HBO, is that it needs to be culturally "reframed" in the wake of George Floyd's death, and the rioting caused by the video of his death being shown in mainstream media thereafter. Thus, if the times are changing, so is the age, but we must understand these things are being forced, and not coming about naturally, or to anyone's benefit, except The Cabal's.

For one more spark of the mind on the rigged selection of George W. Bush, and for the purpose of exposing how rigged the game is, when Florida was called in his favor, he received the winning 271st Electoral College vote, the 58th prime number, connecting to the Pythagorean Gematria of 'George W. Bush', summing to 58. And yes, that is the same cipher that 'Freemasonry', 'Rosicrucian', 'Secret Society' and 'Solomon's Temple' equate to 58 in. At the same time, 'Bush' sums to 58 with Reverse Simple English, reminding that Tim Russert, who asked Bush and Kerry about Skull and Bones, didn't make it past the age of 58, dying on his 38th day of his age, where the words 'death', 'murder', 'killing' and 'RIP' each have gematria of 38 (Tim Russert, May 7, 1950 – June 13, 2008, the day leaving 201 days left in the year). Next time you see the movie poster for *Murder by Numbers*, you'll be sure to notice two letters are changed to numbers, the 'e' to a '3', and the 'b' to an '8', thus 3 and 8, like 38. And on the subject of 58, never forget, King James, who has the KJV Bible named after him, died at age 58, unexpectedly. He was a Rosicrucian and a Freemason. And for another reminder, 'biblical' sums to 58 with Reverse Pythagorean. *We'll touch more on King James and the biblical riddle when we get to Kobe Bryant's suspicious death, January 26, 2020, a day after being passed by LeBron James in all time points scored, aka King James, in Kobe's hometown, Philadelphia. Never mind the Church of Philadelphia is referenced in *Revelation 3:7*, thus a city name having biblical roots, or that a cartoon named Chamberlain Heights foreshadowed Kobe's death in a helicopter crash in a November 16 episode, written 16/11, like 1611, the year the *King James Version Bible* was published. And while we're at it, never mind that 'Los Angeles Lakers' and 'Kobe Bryant' each equate to 58.

Back on the subject of 1968, it was the year the *Quran Code* was reported to be discovered, showing how the holy book is encoded with the number 19 from cover to cover through simple calculations, such as how the 114 chapters of the text (or 114 Surahs) are divisible by 19. *19x6 = 114. 1968 was also the year Mohamed Atta was born, said to be the ringleader of the 19 hijackers on 9/11, and the oldest of the group, having turned 33 on September 1, 2001, a standout age for self sacrifice. It almost makes you say, "Jesus Christ." For the record, it was reported that his hijacked craft, Flight 11, flew into the 110 story World Trade Center towers, that appeared as a massive number 11 in the skyline of the 11th state, New York, on the 11th day of the month. In light of the Jesus Christ point, consider, September 11, 2001 is New Year's Day on the Christian Coptic Calendar, and it is a date some researches contend is the true birthday of Jesus, coming just three days after September 8th, the date the Catholic Church celebrates as the Virgin Mary's birthday. Furthermore, the name 'Jesus' sums to 11 with Pythagorean Gematria. When you're aware of this, you can understand why '*Revelation*' sums to 121 with Simple English, a number having a square root of 11, and being the concluding book of the *Holy Bible*, dealing with the return of Jesus, and the suffering the world must endure before that time. Keep in mind when you add 1 through 11 together, it sums to 66, and Revelation is the 66th book of the *Bible,* and the final book of the '*New Testament*', summing to 66 with Reverse Pythagorean. For another, 'math' sums to 66 with Reverse Simple English, and of course, the *New Testament* begins with the *Book of Matthew.*

Coming back to the man born in 1968, Atta, who died at 33, on what some would argue is Jesus' birthday, it is noteworthy the word 'crucifixion' sums to 68 using Pythagorean Gematria. Another relevant word equating to 68, in light of the story of Jesus beginning in the book of _Matthew_, is the word 'mathematics' itself, using the Reverse Pythagorean cipher. Related to the value of 'mathematics' summing to 68, the subject 'sacred geometry' equates to 68 with Pythagorean Gematria. If you have read my first book, _Letters and Numbers_, you are well aware of the relationships between the gematria of the English Language, and the sacred numbers of sacred geometry and how those numbers connect to spiritual traditions, including Christianity and Jesus. For example, the most important shape in sacred geometry is the Flower of Life, that is made up of 61 overlapping circles, and those circles represent all of creation. Using Reverse Simple English, Jesus sums to 61, not unlike how 'Church' sums to 61 with Simple English, or 'Christian' sums to 61 with Reverse Pythagorean, same as 'Christmas'. To take it a bit further, there are 13 circles in what is known as the Fruit of Life in sacred geometry, that rests in middle of the Flower of Life, not unlike Jesus and his 12 disciples, or the sun and its 12 constellations, thus 13 and 13. Adding to the riddle with Jesus, who spoke in riddles, the word 'fruit' sums to 74 with Simple English, and 61 with Reverse Simple English, the exact same as 'Jesus', and 'cross'.

Returning to Mohamed Atta, what was reportedly leading him to his great sacrifice, on the 74th Meridian West, at the age of 33, were the "master" orders from 'Osama bin Laden', or 'Cave Dweller', as the 'President' called him. Not by chance, 'Osama bin Laden', 'Cave Dweller' and 'President' each equate to 110 with Simple English Gematria, same as 'Adolf Hitler', the biggest historical villain next to Osama, who was born April 20, 1889, the 110th day of the year. This set of 110 pairs perfectly with the 110 story tall Twin Towers, that were proposed by the 'Rockefeller' family, a surname summing to 110 with Simple English as well. In the 10th chapter of this book we'll discuss the Rockefeller Foundation's 2010 document, _Scenarios for the Future of Technology & International Development_. In the document, it brainstorms the future potential control structures of the world, and there is one referred to as "Lock Step" style government, where there is a massive surveillance grid for the populace, authoritarian rule, and much pushback from the people. I bring this up, because in the time of coronavirus and the writing of this book, massive surveillance grids are being installed by governments worldwide under the guise of tracking carriers of the virus, and we do live in a very authoritarian top down structure style of government whether we realize it or not, and at the moment I am finishing this book, there is massive pushback worldwide, as protests are held across the globe, in remembrance of George Floyd, who was seen being murdered by a police officer on mass-mind-control sets across the world (the TV).

In George Floyd's memory, the name Martin Luther King Jr. is being invoked, who was of course, assassinated in 1968, at the age of 39, not unlike how 'George' or 'Gemini' both sum to 39 in Pythagorean Gematria, and George was killed in one the Twin Cities, Minneapolis, in the time of Gemini, the Twins, on the 93rd Meridian West. The 93 matters because 'Minneapolis, Minnesota' and 'Martin Luther King Jr.' sum to 93 in Pythagorean, similar to how 'Malcolm X' sums to 93 with Simple English, and the two civil rights leaders only met once in history, March 26, 1964, a date with 93 numerology. Like King, Malcolm X was also killed at age 39, on a date with 44 numerology, February 21, 1965, by an assassin, 'Thomas Hagan', whose name sums to 44 with Pythagorean, and who received 44 years in prison, to match MLK's 4/4 expiration, connecting with James Earl Ray, the accused killer of MLK, who died April 23, 1998, 44 days after his 70th birthday on March 10th. For the record, Malcolm X's assassin was a member of the 'Nation of Islam', summing to 58 in Pythagorean, same as 'Audubon Ballroom', where Malcolm X was shot dead. And to connect it back to George Floyd, he was killed by a 44-year-old 'officer', a title summing to 44 in Pythagorean, same as 'overseer', on the 44th Parallel North, in Minneapolis, by a man named 'Derek Chauvin', summing to 58 with Pythagorean as well. Not by chance, the name 'Chauvin' alone sums to 33 in Pythagorean, the same as 'police', and the same as 'race war'. At the same time, 'federal' also sums to 33 with Pythagorean, and this is why Donald Trump first deployed 'federal' 'police' to Oregon, the 33rd state, who were reported to be snatching George Floyd protesters off the street with military tactics and unmarked vans. Keep in mind, the headlines about federal police in Oregon first emerged on July 18, or 18/7, like 187, corresponding with the gematria of the nation's federal government headquarters, 'Washington D.C.', equating to 187 with Reverse Simple

English, the same as 'Society of Jesus'. At the same time, 'Portland' equates to 44 with Reverse Pythagorean, the same as 'Chicago', and this is why Trump announced he was dispersing federal police to Chicago, after having success in Portland. You could say, he was executing the federal 'police state' by the numbers, a term equating to 44 with Pythagorean Gematria. And in case you're not familiar with what a police state is, I'll use Google's definition, only because they're one of the key companies in helping execute it, as we'll get to. There definition is as follows, "Police State. A totalitarian state controlled by a political police force that secretly supervises the citizens' activities." I suppose the only difference being that in 2020, it is no longer a secret, and as we move ahead through this chapter, and this book, you'll understand, more and more, this is exactly what is being built, a police state, in the United States of America, and across the world, something that has been in the works for several decades. Furthermore, it is being implemented based on a series of lies, that in recent history, includes 9/11 and the coronavirus outbreak of 2020.

Speaking of the number 44, later in the chapter, I'll teach you about the greater significance of the World Trade Centers falling to the ground, 44 days after Tisha B'Av, also known as the 'Ninth of Av', summing to 44 with Reverse Pythagorean. It is the Jewish day to remember the destruction of the Two Temples, similar to the two towers, or Twin Towers, that were bombed in '93, and had their bombing blamed on the 'Blind Sheik', a nickname summing to 93 with Simple English. And on the subject of 93, it is a number you must understand the meaning of. It represents time, in two ways. One, we are told through science, that the sun is 93 million miles away, and the sun is the timekeeper of our Gregorian calendar. This becomes all the more interesting when you realize 'God's Son', 'Nazareth' and 'Crucifix' each sum to 93 with with Simple English. Never mind that we measure time with the thought of B.C., or "before Christ", and after. And never mind that in 2012, science claimed they had traced the date of Jesus crucifixion to April 3rd, what is the 93rd day of the Gregorian year, tying in with the crucifixion lasting from 9 AM to 3 PM in the *Bible*. The second time association with the number 93 is the planet 'Saturn', having Simple English Gematria of 93. Saturn is the most distant planet from the sun, to the naked eye, known as the keeper of time to the occult. It is for these reasons Flight 93 was part of the September 11th ritual, and the second plane to hit the Twin

Towers was reported to have crashed into the structure at 9:03 AM. For another related thought, the words 'Atomic Bomb' sum to 93 using Simple English, and the research for its creation was called the Manhattan Project. Of course, the World Trade Centers were in Manhattan, and when they collapsed, the site was called Ground Zero, a name that was only used to describe the point above or below ground where an atomic or nuclear bomb had detonated, prior to September 11, 2001.

With that in mind, ask yourself, what energy was used to turn those buildings to dust as they fell to the ground, falling into nice little neat piles, covering New York in fine layers of the towers' remains? Could it have been a 'weapon', developed by the Manhattan Project? Could it have been an atomic bomb? And why did the U.S. military detonate over 1,000 atomic and nuclear bombs, many of them below ground, for the better part of a century, anyway? Not by chance, underground testing concluded September 23, 1992, shortly before the '93 WTC bombing on February 26th, that presented the authorities with an opportune time to work under the buildings that were attacked below. Could this have been when the charges were set? No matter the answer, in the decades since the collapse of the World Trade Centers, there have been many health related deaths for the people of New York, and many questions unanswered. In my opinion, it is fair to ask if fallout from the possible blasts is the culprit. And for one last point about 93, at least for now, the last surviving pilot to drop the atomic bomb on 'Japan', a nation summing to 93 with Reverse Simple English, died at age 93. He was Theodore Van Kirk.

Adding to the 110 list, and coming back to George Floyd, his death occurred in 'Minnesota', a state summing to 110 with Simple English. And once again, it was reported that a police officer knelt on his neck for 8 minutes and 46 seconds, similar to how Mohamed Atta reportedly crashed into the World Trade Center at 8:46 AM, local. For another, 'Dave Chappelle', the comedian with a name equating to 110 in Simple English, made a bit in tribute to George Floyd, titled 8:46. To take it further, the name 'George Floyd' sums to 119 with Simple English Gematria, not unlike the way the majority of the world writes the date September 11th, or 11/9. And adding further to the riddle, the last time there was as big of a social push with marches and protesting, prior to those in remembrance of George Floyd, were the marches

41

inspired by the Stoneman Douglas High School shooting in Florida, a school named after a woman from Minneapolis, Marjory Stoneman Douglas, where the school shooting happened Valentine's Day, February 14, 2018, a span of 119 weeks from the George Floyd killing video being released, May 26, 2020. The 119 pattern also reminds of the Rodney King riots, that the George Floyd riots have been compared to. Those began April 29, 1992, after the police officers involved in his assault were acquitted, on TV. Of course, April 29 is the 119th day of the Gregorian year, and 'Fraternal Order of Police' sums to 119 with Pythagorean Gematria. If you're not familiar with the F.O.P's logo, it has an 'all seeing eye' on it, summing to 119 with Simple English. And for a couple more 119's, Osama bin Laden was reported dead May 2, 2011, a span of 119 weeks after Barack Obama became President Obama, January 20, 2009. Osama? Obama? Better yet, Osama bin Laden's father reportedly died in a plane crash, September 3, 1967, the day leaving 119 days in the year, and a date that can be expressed as 9/3. For the record, 1967 was the year of the 'Six Day War', won by Israel, and summing to 119 with Reverse Simple English, pairing with how the symbol on Israel's flag, the 'Star of David', sums to 119 in Simple English, just like 'Orthodox'. For another, 'New Jersey' sums to 119 with Reverse Simple English, where the Dancing Israelis were arrested on 9/11, at the 'Doric Apartment Complex', summing to 322, the number of Skull and Bones, with Reverse Simple as well. If you haven't heard President Eisenhower's farewell address, where he warns the U.S. people of the coming 'Military Industrial Complex', summing to 322 in Simple English, you should seek out that speech. He was warning us that something like 9/11 was coming if we didn't stop the growing thirst for conflict that our nation's military strategy was based on. But who could have been behind all this? Look no further than the 'Vatican', summing to 119 with Reverse Simple English, the heart of the same Church that has been waging wars, especially with Islamic regions of the world, for centuries. And for those who doubt this now, make sure you finish the book, because you won't doubt it later.

To connect the dots even further between culture shaping events we've already drawn parallels between, let us examine the number 33. In the case of Rodney King, he was beaten on March 3rd, or 3/3, by the 'LAPD', summing to 33 with Simple English. This is similar to how 'police' sums to 33 with Pythagorean, and how Trayvon

42

Martin was buried on March 3rd, and how the rioting began after Floyd's killing on East 33rd Street in Minneapolis, and that the killing officer 'Chauvin' has a surname summing to 33 with Pythagorean, and that the COPS TV show was dropped by Paramount after its 33rd season because of the George Floyd protests while Detroit was erecting a statue of RoboCop in 2020, 33 years after the 1987 film (during a time of a national discussion about defunding human police). The number 33 is a hallmark of The Cabal, and it has everything to do with why the World Trade Centers lasted for 33 years, 1968 to 2001, and why Jesus was crucified at the youthful age of 33. As we're beginning to understand, these tragic and impactful events of modern and biblical times, are being contrived, in accordance with scripture, to fulfill biblical prophecy. Not by chance, the word '*Bible*' sums to 33 with Reverse Pythagorean, as does 'Sunday', the only day of the week that has a connection to the number, and the day that was made the one to worship on by force, by the Catholic Church, reminding that the Jesuit logo is the sun, connecting to the naming of the day, Sunday. And for the record, 'Sunday' and 'Jesuit' are the exact same in three out of the four base ciphers, summing to 21, 78 and 84. And in light of scripture, and number games, think about how *Genesis 11:9* is where the story of God destroying the Tower of Babel ends, in light of the demise of the Twin Towers on 11/9. And as for the word 'prophecy', it sums to 110 with Reverse Simple English Gematria, bringing clarity to why it is used in the way it has, from 9/11, with the 110 story towers, to George Floyd's killing in 'Minnesota'.

To connect a gematria based relationship with 33 and 119, consider that 'pineal' sums to 33 with Reverse Pythagorean Gematria, as in the pineal gland, or the mind's eye, and the masonic phrase 'all seeing eye', that relates to the pineal gland, sums to 119 with Simple English. Through the TV, or better referred to as the *tell-a-vision*, The Cabal has a window into the mind's eye of the masses, and through the TV, as well as other popular media, they are actively programming the populace, with regularly scheduled programming, as they so often call it. This programming's purpose it to steer the behavior of people in the direction of their ongoing agendas- agendas that boil down to giving The Cabal greater and greater control over humanity, while disarming the people of their God given liberties, under the guise of safety and protection. Their objectives are arrived at through the repetitive strategies of "order out of chaos", while broadcasting fear,

43

before delivering a predetermined solution. The other important point is that they achieve these objectives with greater and greater spiritual wickedness as time passes on.

To take it further, there is an occult belief about spiritual ascension up the 33 bones of the human vertebrae that leads to enlightening the mind's eye, or the 'pineal' gland of a person. It is in this belief where the occult significance of 33 resides, and the likely reason for both 'people' and 'person' equating to 33 with Pythagorean Gematria. The name of the belief is 'Kundalini', summing to 58 with Reverse Pythagorean, complimenting the 58 values of 'Freemasonry' and 'secret society' as we covered prior. For another 58, the four letter name of God, 'Tetragrammaton' sums to 58 with Pythagorean, and Kundalini is about connecting with God. It is because of Kundalini that Freemasonry is fixated on the number 33. And despite Freemasonry being about self improvement, including spiritual, and that being the true purpose of the knowledge they study, including the *Bible*, Kabbalah, Kundalini, Hermeticism and Alchemy --- The Cabal has taken the knowledge and turned it on its head, pushing darkness to prevent the people of this earth from reaching enlightenment. They do this, because people in the dark, without light, are much more easily contained, controlled, and exploited. And by the way, 'they' sums to 58 with Simple English. Now you'll know what to say the next time someone asks the common question, "Who are they?"

What is being done to humanity at this moment in history, is the knowledge of our ancestors is being inverted. And instead of helping people spiritually ascend, The Cabal is using their mass media mind control weapons, to pump non-stop fear, division, and chaos, encoded with occult wisdom, to keep us in a low vibrational state, so that we are less likely to think, and more likely to follow, out of fear, with a cowherd (coward?) mentality. Thus those of us who have the light, and who aren't afraid, are those who will help free our brothers and sisters from darkness, and that is why it is important we never quit in our quest, and we know our self worth no matter how difficult the path of truth becomes. That includes not only helping our friends and families, but also strangers who will listen. In doing so, we can help them escape the matrix of misinformation, that steals their time, does damage to their energy levels, and programs them with the wrong thoughts and behaviors. Helping them escape the matrix includes avoiding false history, politics, bogus religious teachings, news, mass mind control entertainment, and even pro sports, that are rigged to the core, and synced with the agendas.

Case in point, 1968 was the year the New York Jets went on to have their only Super Bowl winning season, starring Broadway Joe, who guaranteed it. New York? Jets? 9/11? Never mind that 'Joe Namath' sums to 33 with Pythagorean, similar to 'New York' equating to 33 with Reverse Pythagorean, and his team's feat would begin a 33 year countdown to the demise of the buildings that were engineered and advertised to withstand impact from a commercial jetliner because of how tall they were, towering over the rest of Gotham City, as it is known in Batman, where in the 33rd episode of the old hit TV show, titled *Fine Finny Fiends*, Skull and Bones is referenced as being part of the Bruce Wayne family legacy. And for your gematria learning, the alumni of Skull and Bones are referred to as 'Bonesmen', summing to 33 with Pythagorean Gematria.

1968 was also the year Boeing, in Seattle, Washington, debuted their jumbo jetliner. The city of Seattle is noteworthy because the construction firm that built the World Trade Centers, Magnusson Klemencic Associates, is headquartered in Seattle, Washington as well, and the name, 'Seattle, Washington', sums to 68 with Pythagorean Gematria. For another dot you might otherwise not connect, the Seattle Seahawks won their only Super Bowl, 48, that was hosted by New York and New Jersey, at the Jets stadium. When the MVP of the game took the podium to speak after its conclusion, a man grabbed his mic and said, "9/11 was an inside job." Keep in mind the common terminology for an inside job, is 'false flag', summing to 48, same as 'Seahawks', both using Reverse Pythagorean. Furthermore, the MVP of Super Bowl 48 was 'Malcolm Smith', summing to 48 with Pythagorean Gematria. Think about it. *What are the odds?* To get even more astronomical, the 'Seattle Seahawks', summing to 43 with Pythagorean, won the game with 43 points. It's a fitting score because 'football' sums to 43 with Reverse Pythagorean, and the sport is credited to Walter Camp, a Skull and Bones member who attended 'Yale' summing to 43, as covered.

This should clear things up the next time you see the *Batman* film, *The Dark Knight Rises*, where a football stadium explodes, only after section 322 is shown. For another kick, the only player on the field who survives the fictional blast in the film, is number 86, reminding of August 6th, the date of Hiroshima, a date that can be expressed as 8/6, or 6/8. Adding to the number riddle, Hines Ward, the retired NFL receiver, who played the part of number 86 in the film, finished his NFL career with 86 touchdowns (85 receiving, 1 rushing), and of course wore 86 for his NFL team, the Steelers, that played at Heinz Field... When you have eyes to see, you realize, pro sports are nothing but number games, and absolutely weaved in as part of the matrix of riddles the cabal has wrapped around the populace. This knowledge will also bring new meaning to that often repeated line by sports commentators, "you couldn't have scripted it any better." It truly is a slap in the face, especially when you see what's going on.

If you're not familiar with what a false flag is, it is when someone uses pirate tactics, flying a flag that is not their own, but of an an enemy, and doing something terrible, so that the terrible act will blamed on the enemy whose flag was used. This was done when the U.S. bombed Pearl Harbor with its own military, but with planes that had the flag of Japan painted on their sides, giving The Cabal leverage to get the people of the United States behind the idea of joining World War II, against Germany and Japan. That historical false flag is not much different than how on 9/11, the "New Pearl Harbor" as it has been called, the U.S. and its allies, Israel and Saudi Arabia, attacked the World Trade Centers, the Pentagon, and the minds of the people of the world, so that the atrocities could be blamed on a region of the world that was ripe for invading. Of course, this region is ripe with resources, including oil, the opium that is now flooding the streets of the U.S. in the form of heroin, and the mountains of Afghanistan that are full of the resources needed to make the computers and phones we use today. On the subject of 'false flag', it should be noted that it sums to 33 with Pythagorean Gematria, the same as 'Hawaii'. Again, the World Trade Centers were attacked after existing for 33 years, and the attack on them was a catalyst for war, the same as the attack on Pearl Harbor, in Hawaii. Furthermore, both 'Pearl Harbor' and 'order out of chaos' equate in gematria terms, and 'Pearl Harbor' also equates with 'World War'. Even further, both 'World War' and 'Pearl Harbor' equate with 'Art of War', the Jesuit translated text, on military tactics. And as I will continuously remind you of in the pages ahead, the U.S. Civil War began April 12, 1861, the 102nd day of the year, the 9/11 attacks were said to have lasted 102 minutes, and both 'World War' and *'Art of War'* equate to 102.

To further illustrate how entertainment ties in with the world of recorded history, there is a 'Hollywood' film titled *Glass* that was released at the beginning of 2019. It is about a terrorist who wants to demolish brand new skyscrapers, reminiscent of the World Trade Centers. In the film, they are having their grand opening on December 7th, Pearl Harbor Day. The name of the fictional buildings are the Osaka Tower, referencing the Japanese city of Osaka. These details in the fictional movie are how the Cabal gets their laughs, taking advantage of a public, that is still largely sound asleep, and not able to connect the obvious dots of history. What isn't as obvious about the riddle, is the title *'Glass'*, summing to 58 with Simple English, and 77 with Reverse Simple English. The number 77 was extremely important in the September 11, 2001 ritual, where Flight 77, hit the 77 foot tall Pentagon, on the 77th Meridian West, exactly 77 minutes after taking off, where according to the *9/11 Commission Report*, the plane took off at 8:20 AM and crashed at 9:37 AM. Adding to the number 77 list, 'September Eleventh' and 'World Trade Center' both sum to 77 using Pythagorean Gematria, as does the phrase 'order from chaos', a tactic of the Jesuits, as well as Masons, that is also sometimes worded ordered out of chaos. At the same time, 'United States' and 'Secret Society' sum to 77 using Reverse Pythagorean. In light of the name of the country summing to 77, keep in mind the 77th Meridian West, that cuts through the nation's capital, is nicknamed the American Meridian. Furthermore, construction on the Pentagon began September 11, 1941, with emphasis on the year '41, since 'U.S.A.' sums to 41 in Simple English, and the 9/11 attack occurred on a 41 date numerology, reminding us that Pearl Harbor was attacked December 7, 1941. Tying the events together even more closely, the Hollywood film Pearl Harbor released May 25, 2001, a span of 110 days from the 110 story World Trade Centers demise on September 11th. This is similar to how the George Floyd murder pretrial begins September 11th, a span of 110 days from his May 25, 2020 killing in 'Minnesota', equating to 110.

For a bit more on entertainment and pro sports being used as part of The Cabal's web of deceit, mockery, and misinformation, think about the New York Jet, Mo Lewis, wrecking the quarterback Drew Bledsoe of the New England Patriots, who wore number 11, right after the September 11, 2001 attacks. This occurred September 23, 2001, 12 days after the attack, giving rise to Tom Brady, who still wears the number 12, all these years later, and the New England Patriots, in the time of the PATRIOT Act. Do I dare mention Tom Brady was born in '77? To appreciate the script, you must recognize that the PATRIOT Act became effective October 26, 2001, 45 days after the attack. This matters because 'Patriot' sums to 45 with Reverse Pythagorean, and 'New England' sums to 45 in the same cipher, and also with regular Pythagorean Gematria. Furthermore, the day Tom Brady took over the team, September 23rd, was the day leaving 99 days left in the year, and both 'New England' and 'PATRIOT' equate to 99 with Simple English. Also, the date the PATRIOT Act was enacted, October 26th, leaves 66 days left in the year, and 'PATRIOT Act' sums to 66 with Reverse Pythagorean. Let us not forget 66 is the 11th triangular number, and football is a game of 11 on 11, and September 11, 2001 was perhaps the greatest 11 ritual of all time. And on the subject of 66, ahead I will teach you about Jewish Gematria, where the acronym 'NFL' sums to 66, and 1966 was the start of the NFL's first Super Bowl season.

In terms of how news and sports are scripted together, it is for this reason that Tom Brady left the New England Patriots in 2020, at the time of coronavirus, while the nation and its patriots were falling. The ritual is undeniable when you know gematria. For example, he made clear he was going to the Tampa Bay Buccaneers on March 16th, a date written 3/16, like 316, and 'Tampa Bay Buccaneers' equates to 316 with Reverse Simple. Furthermore, it was the next day, March 17th, that he officially signed with his new team. That was on a date that can be written 17/3, like 173, and this date matters because 'Knights Templar' sums to 173 with Simple English. Again, they were the order of knights that served the Catholic Church and its Pope, until they were banned by the Church, Friday, October 13, 1307. At that point, many of them fled and went into hiding, becoming pirates, or "buccaneers". Furthermore, Tom Brady moving on to play 'football', in 'Florida', at the age of 43 is no accident, because both words equate to 43. Keep in mind, the pirate symbolism in his new team, the Tampa Bay Buccaneers, also reminds us of the pirate symbolism in the Oakland Raiders, the team that was screwed with the "tuck rule", January 19, 2002, emphasis on 1/19, to launch the New England Patriots very, very scripted dynasty, that lasted nearly two full decades. And if you look carefully, you'll notice the skull and crossed swords symbolism of the Tampa Bay Buccaneers logo is eerily similar to the Skull and Bones symbolism of the powerful 'Yale' fraternity that had Bush in office (thanks to Florida), when 9/11 happened, as well as the emergence of Tom Brady, the New England Patriots, and the PATRIOT Act. *With these topics in mind, I'd encourage you to look into maritime law, the law of the sea, and how it is what U.S. law is based in. These things are not an accident, instead, they are evidence of who created this land we call the United States of America, and as we are learning, they are entities connected to the Catholic Church.

Since we brought up Tom Brady's departure from the New England Patriots, we must also bring up Cam Newton, of the Carolina Panthers, being signed by the Patriots to replace him, June 28, 2020, during the time of the George Floyd protests. In the wake of his signing, CNN ran a front page story, "The New American Patriots", with an image of Colin Kaepernick, the NFL QB who grew his hair out like a Black Panther and said he was paying tribute to 1968 Olympic protesters, as well as Beyonce, who dressed up as a Black Panther for the Super Bowl 50 halftime show, where Cam Newton lost, as well as Lin-Manuel Miranda, the rising star of the Broadway hit, *Hamilton,* a play where black men replace men who were white, historically speaking- sort of like Newton replacing Brady. Of course, Cam Newton is another star quarterback in the NFL, who for all of his career, has played with a black panther on his helmet, as a black man, playing for the Carolina Panthers, a team the Patriots defeated in Super Bowl 38, and where 'Panthers' equates to 38 with Pythagorean. In light of this information, you must keep in mind, the Black Panther Party was founded by Huey P. Newton, having the same surname as Cam Newton. The riddles don't end there however. The name 'Huey P. Newton' equates to 131 with Reverse Simple, and Cam Newton was born May 11, 1989. the 131st day of the year, in the same year Huey P. Newton died, on August 22nd. That date happened to be 83 days after Cam Newton was born, a number corresponding with the gematria of 'football' and 'murder', both equating to 83. Again, 1983 was the year the song '*Murder by Numbers'* released. Beyond that, Newton's NFL career came to an unexpected pause in the previous season when he was benched by his head coach for a rookie, a storyline that has lead to him signing with the New England Patriots, with 131 career games played under his belt. You should know, 131 is the 32nd prime, and both 'America' and 'NFL' equate to 32, the latter being the league with

32 teams. Furthering the parallels between Huey and Cam, in Super Bowl 50, the game Cam Newton and the Panthers lost to the Denver Broncos, Newton became the 58th QB to start in a Super Bowl, corresponding with the gematria of 'Huey P. Newton' in Pythagorean, as well as 'Oakland' in Simple English, both equating to 58, and the latter being where the Black Panther Party was established by Huey P. Newton, in 1966, the first NFL Super Bowl season. I bring this up because Super Bowl 50 was played in the Bay Area, not far from Oakland. *And you should also know I called why that would be the Super Bowl matchup, and why the Broncos would win, and why number 58 Von Miller of the Broncos would be the MVP of the game, in October, four months before all of it happened, causing the USA Today's Big Lead to write a feature article about me, while downplaying the relevance of what I was teaching, gematria, and how the NFL, and world of professional sports were rigged by the code, and in accordance with news and history- something you can prove every single day with this knowledge. If you would like to read the article, it is titled *"Conspiracy Theorist "Proves" Freemasons Rigged AFC and NFC Championship Games"* by Ryan Phillips, Jan 27, 2016. You'll notice he pays tribute to the number 47 in the last paragraph, and not by accident. And for a similar read, you can examine the article *"Wacko YouTuber, uh, 'Proves' World Series Was Rigged"* by Sean Newell of Vice News, also targeting me. If you do read the Vice article, notice he makes fun of my research on the number 52. Then, after reading the article, take the time to decode his name, 'Sean Newell'. As you will find out, his name equals 52, making him the perfect person to write what he did. And I'll add, had an article been written about me every time I called a sports championship seasons and months in advance based off of this knowledge, there'd be many more articles to reference. And I'll also add, to further the point about Cam Newton and the Black Panther Party, his June 28, 2020 signing by the Patriots came a span of 97 days after he was released by the Panthers on March 24, 2020, and it was a span of 74 days after Bill Belichick's birthday, April 16, 2020. In addition to that, June 28, 2020, the date of the signing, had 74 date numerology, and 'Black Panther Party' sums to 74 with Pythagorean, as well as 97 with Reverse Pythagorean. Keep in mind 'Bill Belichick' also sums to 97 with Simple English, and he won the Super Bowl in the 97th NFL season. You might recall that game with the 25 point comeback over

the 'Falcons', equating to 25 with Pythagorean Gematria, on the date February 5th, or 2/5, to conclude the 97th NFL season, where 97 is the 25th prime number, and it was that same season they moved the touchback to 25 yards, from 20. Of course, the date of the Super Bowl could also be expressed 5/2, like 52, and Belichick and Brady became 5 and 2 in Super Bowls together, by the numbers.

Coming back to 1968, one of the most important events of that year was the release of the film *2001: A Space Odyssey*. It is about technology, and more specifically A.I., or artificial intelligence, overtaking humanity. This phenomenon has a name, and it is called the singularity. It is when technology reaches a point that changes humanity forever, and there is no going back, in the sense that technology advances past the capability of humanity, and begins to control humanity. Consider, this is a concept that is much easier to grasp in 2020, than it was in 1968 when the film was made. And speaking of the year 2020, the year of coronavirus, you will notice in gematria terms, the word 'singularity' and 'coronavirus' are the exact same in all four ciphers, both summing to 155 in Simple English, 56 in Pythagorean, 142 in Reverse Simple English, and 70 in Reverse Pythagorean. And rest assured, by the end of the book you will have notes full of how all four of these numbers have been used ritualistically, day after day, to contrive the coronavirus narrative in mainstream headlines. But for now, do not forget that the term coronavirus was coined in 1968, the start of a planned 'age' by The Cabal- an age with a planned outcome to use technology to control humanity, to a much greater extent than it ever had before. Fast forward 52 years later, the number corresponding with 'prophecy' and 'technology' using Pythagorean Gematria, to 2020, **when we should all be seeing clearly**, and this reality has never been more apparent.

For example, two of the world's largest technology companies, Google and Apple, are cooperating with world governments to systematically track the location of every cell phone on the planet that are using their operating systems, for the explained purpose of seeing if people are obeying what is being called the "New Normal", the laws being installed worldwide, in the time of coronavirus. These laws include curfews, only traveling to certain locations, maintaining social distancing, wearing face coverings, and not posting or sharing information that goes against "official" narratives. Keep in mind this level of surveillance is piggybacking off of the PATRIOT Act, installed

51

after 9/11, that gave the U.S. government the right to track and monitor all of its citizens. Furthermore, the PATRIOT Act lead to the collecting of untold bytes of data, that are the phone calls, text messages, emails, library visits, bank records, medical records, etc. of its people. Also keep in mind, this was done in the snap of fingers to those who were told their entire lives they were free, and protected from the government infringing on their privacy. And let us not forget, just prior to September 11th, Google was becoming a household name, and most people were getting small computers in their pockets, that we call cellphones. It is this device specifically that has given big brother a way to peep into the lives and communications of its people. And it is this same device, now in the wake of coronavirus, that is being used to track our every movement. And it is this same device, that is evolving, with built in AI, that automates our tasks for us, and answers our questions, always listening. And I repeat, always listening. Also not by chance, the 'coronavirus' pandemic, summing to 56 in Pythagorean, is taking place at the same time 5G (doesn't 5G look a bit like 56?) technology is rolling out worldwide, that gives big brother the systems of surveillance capability to track as many phones with detail, as they are. Worse yet, U.S. citizens are being asked to snap photos of people violating "mandatory mask" orders and to send those images to government agency phone numbers so that facial recognition technology systems can be tested and improved by them.

Of course, all of these infringements on our liberties are spoon fed to us. They are introduced as caring gestures by the authorities, to keep us safe, that we should welcome, or else fear being called "paranoid", or a "conspiracy theorist" by those around us. God forbid anyone question anything is the collective sentiment. And shouldn't we all feel safe now, with the watchful eye of world governments on us? As we'll get to in later chapters, the U.S. surveillance system in the aftermath of coronavirus, is known as the TRACE Act, and was introduced as H.R. 6666, not far off from 666, the number of the beast from *Revelation*. If you're not familiar with 666 and *Revelation*, there is a prophecy that the people of the world will be made to take the mark of the beast, on either their forehead, or their right hand, and if they do not, then they will not be allowed to buy or sell. In modern times, that could mean not being able to work, or go to school, or use any form of public transit, or shop at most markets. And on the subject of the number 666, it is no accident that Stanley Kubrick, the director of *2001: A Space Odyssey*, died 666 days before January 1, 2001, on March 7, 1999. It should also be noted that March 7 is the 66th day of the year, and 'number of the beast' sums to 66 in Pythagorean Gematria. And again, 666 is referred to in the *Bible*, the text that is 66 books in length, as the 'number of the beast'. It's also not an accident that Microsoft, Bill Gates' old company, filed a patent on March 26, 2020, with the number W02020060606, clearly paying tribute to 666. This patent is for a future cryptocurrency that will monitor your rate of body movement, that will in turn calculate your earnings based on effort. Imagine what that will lead to. Sadly, these things should come as no surprise, because the number 666 has been associated with computers since Apple priced their first consumer computer at $666.66, in 1976. This becomes all the more fascinating when you learn Sumerian and Reverse Sumerian Gematria, because words such as 'computer' and 'internet' equate to 666 using them. With these ciphers, you multiply the Simple English cipher, and the Reverse Simple English cipher by 6. The ciphers are as follows.

Sumerian Gematria:

A=6, B=12, C=18, D=24, E=30, F=36, G=42, H=48, I=54

J=60, K=66, L=72, M=78, N=84, O=90, P=96, Q=102, R=108

S=114, T=120, U=126, V=132, W=138, X=144, Y=150, Z=156

Reverse Sumerian Gematria:

Z=6, Y=12, X=18, W=24, V=30, U=36, T=42, S=48, R=54

Q=60, P=66, O=72, N=78, M=84, L=90, K=96, J=102, I=108

H=114, G=120, F=126, E=132, D=138, C=144, B=150, A=156

It is Sumerian Gematria where 'computer' equates to 666, and it is Reverse Sumerian where 'internet' equates to 666. And while we're at it, another word summing to 666 in Reverse Sumerian, is '*Genesis*', the opening book of the *Bible*, that tells the story of Adam and Eve, and the forbidden fruit, that was not to be eaten from. Now think of Apple's logo, the fruit, with a missing bite. And for the most hardcore of coincidence theorists, who might possibly be reading this page at this very moment, are you seriously going to shrug off the $666.66 price as "coincidence?" Surely this isn't, nor is H.R. 6666.

For a little more learning, there is one more cipher that you must know, and it is the most important outside of the base ciphers that you learned in chapter one. It is known as Jewish Gematria, and it pays tribute to the order of the English letters from when they were part of the Latin alphabet. The cipher also pays tribute to Hebrew Gematria and Greek isopsephy in the way it assigns number values to letters. Before I reveal the cipher, I must inform you that 'isopsephy' sums to 666 with Reverse Sumerian, and remind you that *Revelation 13:18*, about the number of the beast, 666, is a Greek isopsephy riddle.

Jewish Gematria:

A=1, B=2, C=3, D=4, E=5, F=6, G=7, H=8, I=9,

K=10, L=20, M=30, N=40, O=50, P=60, Q=70, R=80, S=90, T=100,

U=200, X=300, Y=400, Z=500, J=600, V=700, W=900

As was mentioned earlier, 'NFL' sums to 66 in this cipher. Another relevant calculation to know based on the contents of this chapter, is that 'Al-Qaeda' sums to 102 with Jewish Gematria, and the 9/11 attacks were said to have lasted 102 minutes, again, connecting back to *'Art of War'*. They even made a film about this fact titled *102 Minutes That Changed America*. Better yet, Tisha B'Av sums to 911 with Jewish Gematria, and it is the day to remember the destruction of the Two Temples, similar to the Twin Towers. To get a little mathematical, 911 is the 156th prime number, and 'false flag' sums to 156 in Jewish Gematria. It only figures then, from the date underground nuclear testing concluded, September 23, 1992, to the date of the '93 WTC bombing, was 156 days later, reminding that 'Robert Kennedy' summing to 156 in Simple English, was shot on June 5th, the 156th day of the year. And oddly enough, there are only two numbers, zero through 100, that when written out as words, sum to 156 with Simple English. They are 'thirty-three' and 'twenty-eight' ('Space Odyssey' also sums to 156 with Simple English and 'Kennedy' sums to 33 with Pythagorean). This matters because the World Trade Centers existed for 33-years, but they were only open for 28, having their grand opening on April 4, 1973. In light of April 4th, recall where we began, with Martin Luther King Jr. being killed on April 4th, in 1968. In a non leap year, April 4th is the 94th day of the year, connecting to the fact that 'World Trade Center' sums to 94 with Reverse Pythagorean and 'terror' sums to 94 with Simple English.

Thus, from the grand opening, their fate was sealed. As we mentioned prior, the Twin Towers fell 44 days after Tisha B'Av, a Jewish holiday that concluded July 29, 2001 in that year. The holiday is also known as the 'Ninth of Av', summing to 44 with Reverse Pythagorean.

This brings us to what I said at the beginning of the chapter, there is a number that ties together the assassinations of Martin Luther King Jr., Robert Kennedy, JFK, and Abraham Lincoln, and that number is 144. When you write out the word 'forty-four', and the date 'April Fourth', they both sum to 144 in Simple English, the same as 'Jesuit Order'. So, MLK was shot on April 4th, Robert Kennedy was reported dead at 1:44 AM on June 6th, JFK, the 44th term president, died at the start of 'Sagittarius', summing to 144 with Simple English, same as 'Kennedy Curse', and Abraham Lincoln was shot on April 14th, or 14/4, in the year 1865. Even more, MLK's assassin not only died 44 days after his birthday, but he also died on a date with 144 numerology, April 23, 1998 (4+23+19+98 = 144). As we covered in chapter one, this number not only connects to the Jesuit Order, but also 'The United States of America'. More importantly, it is a number that represents time. In Jewish Gematria, the word 'time' itself sums to 144, complimenting 'clock', summing to 44 with Simple English. Beyond gematria, consider that each day on earth, there are 1,440 minutes, and the square root of 144 is 12, the number we track the months of our year with, and the number of hours we divide the day with. Like I said at the end of the first chapter, time is EVERYTHING to these people, and The Cabal, lead by the Jesuits, lays down their rituals daily, like clockwork, using the *Bible's* scripture, where 144 is a relevant number, especially to Hebrew Gematria studies, largely because of how the number 144,000 is referenced in *Revelation 7*. For a few last points, JFK and RFK were killed at 'Dealey Plaza' and the 'Ambassador Hotel', respectively, both summing to 54, same as 'Jesuit Order', and reminding us that the thing dictating time, the 'sun' sums to 54 with Simple English. Furthermore, one of Lincoln's assassins, John Surratt, was a Jesuit agent, born 'John Harrison Surratt', equating to 266 with Simple English, and 95 with Pythagorean, both numbers that are extremely specific to the Jesuit Order, and that will come up time and time again as we progress through the pages of this book. Plus, let us not forget MLK, was killed on the 95th day of 1968.

3 | 222 Months Later, From 9/11 to the Coronavirus Pandemic

Measuring from September 11, 2001, the date of the infamous attacks on the World Trade Center, to March 11, 2020, the date the World Health Organization declared a global coronavirus pandemic, was precisely 222 months later. This matters for a number of reasons. We'll begin with the Jesuit and Freemason motto, 'order out of chaos', summing to 222 with Reverse Simple English. The motto ties in with the often heard phrase spoken by politicians, "Never let a good crisis go to waste." It is a simple strategy that involves creating a problem, or a group of related problems, that allows the problem creator to then offer a solution, to a party that does not know the true origins of the problem, so that the problem creator can become the authority figure and expert on the matter before solving the problem they've created. This strategy results in a desirable outcome for the problem creator, and usually not for the party looking for a solution that has been deceived by the conspirator. This is because the unknowing party ends up giving up something valuable, that they would not otherwise have given up, unless it resulted in them believing it was a fair exchange so that they could be protected from the new problem or problems. This concept also ties in perfectly with what we discussed about 'false flag' attacks in the last chapter. For example, knocking down towers, then blaming the attack on a man in a cave, and then offering security from terrorist threats in exchange for giving up the right to privacy from government and big tech intrusion, is how this strategy works. Regarding coronavirus, the same tactics are being used to setup and actively test a surveillance grid, for the entire nation's smartphone carrying population, under the guise of keeping us safe from germs. Only the deceived fall for it, time and time again, because they are made afraid, through mainstream media, that is controlled by The Cabal, that pumps fear, anxiety and confusion, 24/7/365. With that said, hopefully by the time you're done reading this book, you'll be ready to go full Roddy Piper from the film *They Live.* And if you have no idea what I am referencing, you need to seek out the film *They Live* as soon as you finish reading today, because it is important we achieve the outcome that is reached in the film, and preferably with a lot less violence. That outcome is stopping the mainstream media's biggest weapon of all, the TV, from poisoning the world every single day, by shutting it down. And I must say, the movie is a beautiful illustration of how the language of gematria gives a person a new lens, or enhanced perspective, that allows them to see through the matrix of misinformation that they are bombarded with every single day. Not by chance, *They Live*'s motto is 'They live, we sleep', summing to 74 in Pythagorean, similar to how 'gematria', 'English', 'occult' and the rest of our learning from the first chapter sums to 74.

Returning to the subject of "order out of chaos", an important point needs to be made. The word 'chaos' alone sums to 19 with Pythagorean Gematria. This matters because from 2001, the year of the September 11th attacks, to 2020, the year of the coronavirus pandemic, is 19 years later. The number 19 gains its relevance with the Tarot deck, because the 19th card is the sun card, and we are on a solar calendar system, the Gregorian calendar, where the sun dictates time. Before the Gregorian and Julian calendars, the most common way to keep time throughout the world was by the 13 cycles of the moon that are easily observed and counted. What is interesting about the moon in relation to the Gregorian calendar, is that every 19 years, the moon appears in the same place in the sky as it was 19 years prior, also meaning that it will be in the same place 19 years later. This is why on the Hebrew calendar, the oldest ongoing calendar in the world, every 19 years, the Hebrew holy days fall on the exact same date, and are organized by the cycles of the moon. This point about 19 also relates to why the first case of coronavirus confirmed outside of mainland China, in the world, was confirmed in 'Seattle', one of the few large cities in the world equating to 19 with Pythagorean Gematria. Let us not forget, the World Trade Centers in New York were built by the firm from Seattle, or that the World Trade Organization protests in Seattle, that gained much international attention, began precisely 93 weeks before the demise of the World Trade Centers in New York, where 93, is a number representing time, and highly relevant to 9/11, as covered.

The next 222 in the ritual connecting September 11, 2001, coming 222 months prior to the coronavirus pandemic, is 'Wuhan Coronavirus', summing to 222 with Simple English. Of course, this is the culprit being used to spring forth the 'order out of chaos' agenda, yet again. 'New York, New York' also sums to 222 with Simple English, meaning 'New York' alone sums to 111, reminding us that September 11th leaves 111 days left in the Gregorian year. The reason New York, New York matters, is because it was the most impacted city in the world on September 11, 2001, and in terms of coronavirus, it has once again been reported as the hardest hit city in the world in terms of cases and deaths, as of the time of the publishing of this book, July of 2020. Furthermore, Event 201, simulating the coronavirus outbreak, took place in New York, October 18, 2019. And not by chance, if you write out 'Event Two Zero One', those numbers spelled out sum to 222 with Simple English. And then for the clincher, the main sponsor of Event 201, the 'World Economic Forum', has a name equating to 222 with Simple English as well. They're out of Switzerland, same as the World Health Organization, the United Nations, and the Bank of International Monetary Settlements. Of course, Switzerland is the land of Knights Templar bankers, who serve the Catholic Church. This is also why the Swiss Guard protect the Vatican.

Moving ahead, the 222 value of 'World Economic Forum' pairs perfectly with the ritual of Donald Trump speaking at the World Economic Forum on January 21, 2020, his 222nd day of his age, a man born June 14, 1946. His reason for speaking was to gloat about his trade deal with China, that he signed off on January 15, 2020. This becomes all the more curious when you recognize the official story is that an airline traveler from Wuhan, China, infected with the coronavirus, landed in Seattle, Washington, January 15, 2020, and then tested positive for the virus in Seattle on January 21st, the same day Trump was speaking to the World Economic Forum, that once again, was the main sponsor of Event 201, the coronavirus outbreak simulation, that was co-hosted by 'Bill and Melinda Gates', out of Seattle, summing to 115 with Reverse Pythagorean Gematria, not unlike the date January 15th, or 1/15. At the same time, January 15th can be expresses as 15/1, like 151, and 'pandemic' sums to 151 with Reverse Simple English Gematria, and further, January 15, 2020 had numerology of 56, connecting to 'coronavirus' with Pythagorean. Never mind that on January 22, 2020, the day after the first case of coronavirus was confirmed in the United States, Netflix debuted the documentary *Pandemic*, starring Bill Gates. And while we're at it, never mind Netflix's other recent documentary at the time, *Explained: The Next Pandemic*, also starring Bill Gates, that released November 7, 2019, just before the first case was confirmed in the world, where Gates laid out the year that would become 2020, before it happened, almost as if he was a prophet, or, if he had the script. Also, not by chance, November 7th leaves 54 days in the year, connecting to 'Jesuit

Order'. And better than that, *Explained: The Next Pandemic* equates to 251 with Simple English, the 54th prime number.

If you check the notes of Trump's speech to the World Economic Forum, from that same day, you will notice the start time was 11:47 local, master numbers, where once again, 'president', 'White House', 'Trump', 'government' and 'authority' each equate to 47. This detail jives with the fact that the World Health Organization, just down the road from the World Economic Forum, has an establishment date of April 7th, or 4/7, or 7/4, signature numbers of The Cabal. It also syncs with the fact that Seattle, Washington, Bill Gates land, is on the 47th Parallel North. These details serve as a reminder of the repetitive nature of the code, and that Donald Trump is a puppet on strings, a man that became President at 70 years, 7 months and 7 days old. And because I knew the code then, I said then, 'order out of chaos' sums to 777 in Jewish Gematria, and he'll be the order out of chaos president. These days, it is hard to say otherwise.

Coming back to the distance of 222 months from 9/11 to the coronavirus pandemic's declaration, and the phrase 'order out of chaos' equating to 222, it is important we understand what the digit 2 represents in numerology terms. Keep in mind, in numerology, all numbers are dualistic, meaning they have two sides, one positive, one negative. On the positive side, the number 2 symbolizes the ability to come together, to build, to create, and in The Cabal's eyes, they are building their New World Order. It is their one world government, united with one language, and one electronic and easily traceable currency, under one watchful eye, one illicit act at a time, thus why in New York, it went from the Twin Towers, to 'One World Trade Center', a name equating to 93 with Pythagorean, the number related to time, and being a signature of The Cabal. On the subject of 93 and the number 2, remember, 93 represents time in two ways, through the sun, said to be 93 million miles away on average, and 'Saturn', the keeper of time, counting time in darkness, as opposed to the sun, with its light. At the same time, the number 2 represents the possibility of being taken apart, or deconstructed, and that is what we the people of the world are witnessing at this time. The dismantling of the world as we knew it, so that it can be replaced with something that is more beneficial in the eyes of The Cabal. A world where their power and influence is omnipresent, and we have little opportunity to escape their watchful eyes and listening ears, that are the screens, cameras, listening devices and surveillance systems of the world. It will also be a world where more and more of the wealth is controlled by them. Case in point, it was no accident June 4, 2020, when mainstream media reported that tech billionaires had increased their net worth by $565 billion in the time of the pandemic, with 56 year old Jeff Bezos of Amazon being named the biggest beneficiary, 144 days after his January 12th birthday. As we know, those numbers scream Jesuit Order and Society of Jesus. It was for this same reason that on July 2, 2020, it was reported that Jeff Beezos had broken his own personal record, becoming worth $172 billion exactly 172 days after his birthday. Keep in mind, the Jesuit motto 'Ad maiorem Dei gloriam' equates to 172 with Simple English, and where 'Beezos' equates to 72, so does 'Jesuit Order', corresponding with the date July 2nd, or 7/2. Furthermore, with Simple English, 'Amazon', 'Vatican' and 'Francis' each equate to 70 with Simple English, whereas 'coronavirus' equates to 70 with Reverse Pythagorean Gematria, and you have to love that the first Jesuit Pope is Francis, in light of the Jesuits coming from 'France', equating to 47, also like 'Vatican', and reminding us that Amazon is headquartered in Seattle, on the 47th Parallel North, and they are truly taking over the world in the time of 'coronavirus' and the 56th Mayor of Seattle (essentially an employee of Amazon since the company owns Seattle), 'Jenny Durkan', whose name sums to 47 with Pythagorean. And just wait until we get to her big "56 ritual" on her 47th day of her age, July 4, 2020, a date that can be written 4/7, after her 'Summer of Love' comments on CNN, with 'Chris Cuomo'.

Beezos wasn't the only one raking it in though. So were the big bankers, in Switzerland, where Trump gloated on January 21st, and where Bill Gates said on January 22, 2017, also at the World Economic Forum, "I think uh- an epidemic, either naturally caused or intentionally caused, is the most likely thing, to cause, say 10 million excess deaths- uh, and, the, it's pretty surprising how little preparedness there is for it." He then stuttered out, "Now it's tricky because this is a global problem." Regarding those Swiss bankers, reminding us that Bill Gates comes from a family of bankers, they stood to make a killing in profit from interest, after the Senate approved at least $2 trillion, and as much as $6 trillion in stimulus on March 25, 2020. To appreciate that sum of money, realize that 1 trillion seconds is nearly 32,000 years, so if you made $1 per second, you'd have to work for 32,000 years to make your first trillion. As for the date March 25th, or 3/25, it should remind you what you learned about the Bank of England, being 325 years old at the time of the pandemic, and the territory they control, 'City of London Corporation' equating to 325 in gematria. Consider, their flag is the Knights Templar red cross, which is very similar to the flag of Switzerland, and March 25, 2020 was the 85th day of the leap year, corresponding with the Simple English Gematria of 'Templar', summing to 85. Furthermore, in Tarot, the 20th card is the Judgement card, and the card's illustration also bares a red cross.

If you have never heard the phrase, *all wars are bankers wars*, now you have. With that in mind, consider the Knights Templar were once the military might of the Church during the time of the crusades, and the world's first bankers, because they had the ability to protect the assets of others, as well as all that they had pillaged from the Holy Lands while crusading. Furthermore, for centuries, war has been a profitable game for the Catholic Church, and it is for this reason, Washington D.C., under their control, invaded Afghanistan, October 7, 2001, the day leaving 85 days in the year. The difference between 2001 and 2020, is that the war this time is on germs, instead of boogiemen in caves on the other side of the world. And keep in mind, 19 years before 2001, it was October 14, 1982, when the War on Drugs was declared, the day leaving 78 days left in the year. No matter the difference, the same outcome was reached for the bankers, and that was profit through the interest of the loans given to governments to fight their truly needless wars, at the expense of the people of the nations duped by these horrendous lies, who will forever pay the bills with their tax burdens, freedoms, and with the lives of their children.

For one last point on Trump's January 21st appearance at the World Economic Forum, from that date to March 25, 2020, the date of the biggest loan in world history being given the go ahead, was a span of 65 days, connecting to the gematria of 'Knights Templar', 'Switzerland', 'United Kingdom', 'Bank of England', and 'pandemic'. It also connects to the gematria of 'Decade of Vaccines', equating to 65, that Bill Gates launched, January 29, 2010, with ambitions of vaccinating the world's population, exactly one decade before January of 2020, when the first case of coronavirus in the U.S. was confirmed in his own back yard, not to mention, Gates established his vaccine alliance organization, Gavi, in Seattle, July 12, 1999, and now it is headquartered in 'Switzerland'. Those are things we will dissect more in the chapter dedicated to Bill Gates. And for another 65 in Switzerland, CERN, established in Switzerland on September 29, 1954, was 65 years old at the time of the pandemic and massive bank loan given to the United States. They're the scientific organization credited with the creation of the world wide web, or the internet as we know it. CERN is also an organization that gained much attention because of the *Da Vinci Code* series, with the title *Angels & Demons*, something we'll touch more on when we get to Tom Hanks, who starred in the film series, including the title *Inferno*, that released on Bill Gates 61st birthday, October 28, 2016, a date with 74 numerology.

As we'll soon learn, *Inferno* is a film involving a storyline of a billionaire attempting to depopulate the world by means of a virus, a narrative that has a major parallel with the ambitions of Bill Gates himself. In the chapter dedicated to the actor, we'll learn not only about that, but also how Hanks ties in with the larger coronavirus ritual. And in case you have forgotten, he was the first major celebrity to be diagnosed with the virus, along with his wife Rita Wilson, both of whom starred in the film *Sleepless in Seattle*, set in the city where the first case of coronavirus was confirmed in the United States, and of course, the home of Bill Gates and Jeff Beezos. For now, I should note, in light of what we have learned so far about the number 93, the actor's full name, 'Thomas Jeffrey Hanks', as well as 'Wuhan Coronavirus', both equate to 93 with Reverse Pythagorean, matching the year 1993, when *Sleepless in Seattle* released. As another reminder, because it can't be said enough, all of these rituals have everything to do with time. And on the subject, recall that in Tarot, the 20th card is the Judgement card, and in Pythagorean Gematria, 'Tarot', 'time' and 'judge' each equate to 20, corresponding with the year 2020 and the fact that 'Saturn', summing to 93, is connected to not only time, but death and judgement. Furthermore, there is something referred to as the 27 year return of Saturn, and from 1993, to 2020, is 27 years later, a number corresponding with the Pythagorean Gematria of 'ritual', equating to 27. And for the coincidence theorist out there, who might be in doubt, from Tom Hanks' July 9, 2019 birthday, to his coronavirus diagnosis news on March 11, 2020, the same day the pandemic was declared from the World Health Organization in Switzerland, it was his 247th day of his age, corresponding with the gematria of 'Seattle, Washington', equating to 247 with Reverse Simple English. Again, it's all about 'time', and you can prove it every single time, with gematria. And as we'll learn in the next chapter, 2020 is 247 years after the "201 Jesuits" that saved the order, a fact that is not unrelated to the name Event 201, the name of the coronavirus outbreak simulation of October 18, 2019, the same day the Military World Games began in Wuhan, China, games that trace back to the year 1995, emphasis on '95, and Rome, the home of the Jesuits.

On the subject of the number 95, a number we have learned is highly symbolic to the Jesuit Order, and Anthony 'Fauci', the Jesuit, the man having a surname equating to 95, and being born on Christmas Eve, 1940, a date with 95 numerology, I want to conclude this chapter with a powerful example of how rituals are performed in accordance with the calendar and gematria, and I want you to appreciate how special the ritual was of Anthony Fauci's "wild first pitch" to open the shortened MLB season due to coronavirus, on July 23, 2020, when the defending MLB championships, the Washington Nationals, lost to Anthony Fauci's hometown New York Yankees. In that same game, the man considered to be the best pitcher in baseball, who lost to the Nationals in the World Series a season earlier, Gerrit Cole, made his debut with the Yankees, earning his 95th career win in the regular season. Not only that, he had signed with the Yankees on December 11, 2019, his 95th day of his age, having been born September 8, 1990, what is considered the Virgin Mary's birthday. With regards to his date of birth, it is the 251st day of the year, which is the 54th prime number, and in addition to 'baseball' equating to 54, a game of 54 outs, so does 'Jesuit Order'. Furthermore, July 23, 2020, was the day that is celebrated as the 'heliacal rising' of Sirius, the Dog Star. Fittingly, the word 'Sirius' has Simple English Gematria of 95, and 'heliacal rising' equates to 251 with Reverse Simple English, corresponding with Cole's birthday. Beyond that, and adding to our ongoing list of 56, 'Opening Day' and 'First Pitch' equate to 56 with Pythagorean, the same as 'Anthony Fauci', 'Washington D.C.', and 'Society of Jesus'. And with regards to the latter two names, they sum to 187 as well, the same as 'New York Yankees', who Cole was making his debut for. Plus, July 23, 2020, the "coronavirus season" start date, was a date with 70 numerology, and a span of 155 days from Fauci's upcoming birthday, where 'coronavirus' equates to 56, 70, 142 and 155 with the base ciphers, and the NBA season was suspended on its 142nd day, 3/11/20, and NASCAR returned on 5/21/20, the 142nd day of the year, and fittingly the 98 car won on 5/21. *521, 98th prime.

4 | Event 201, The Jesuit Order, Anthony Fauci & The Pope

"There is no question that there will be a challenge to the coming administration in the arena of infectious diseases, both chronic infectious diseases and the sense of already ongoing disease, and we certainly have a large burden of that, but also there will be a surprise outbreak." - Anthony Fauci, Georgetown University, Washington D.C., January 10, 2017, speaking on "Pandemic Preparedness"

It's fitting that Anthony Fauci was speaking at Georgetown University, the oldest Jesuit university in the United States, when he revealed the planned conspiracy to force a pandemic down our throats, in a speech I highly encourage you to listen to. You'll notice, his remarks came 10 days before the Jesuit educated Donald Trump, who attended Fordham University, became the 45th President. Of course, it was Trump's coming administration that Fauci was referencing in the quote above. And Anthony Fauci himself is a Jesuit educated man, having attended Holy Cross. When you pair these details with the fact that the Military World Games, dating back to 1995, and Rome, began in Wuhan, China, October 18, 2019, the same day Event 201 took place (the coronavirus outbreak simulation), and when you understand what the number 201 represents to the Jesuits, who operate on behalf of Rome, the odds of all of this being coincidence are next to impossible, and at the same time, these same facts reveal the responsible party for the conspiracy that is the coronavirus pandemic. They also reveal the theater of the debacle, such as why Donald Trump blamed Anthony Fauci for the poor coronavirus response by the federal government on July 11th, 2020, the 201st day of Anthony Fauci's age, and again on July 19th, the 201st day of 2020.

To better understand the relevance of the number 201 to the Jesuit Order, we must rewind the hands of time to July 21, 1773, when Pope Clement XIV, the leader of the Catholic Church, suppressed the Jesuits. Before we get to the meaning of the number 201, just take a moment to think- the Jesuits were so bad, they were stopped by the institution they operated on behalf of, because simply put, Pope Clement XIV could no longer tolerate the circulating rumors of Jesuit crime, corruption and conspiracy. It couldn't be more telling, could it? As they say, some things never change. Anyhow, after their banning, Catherine the Great of Russia came to their rescue, protecting the 201

Jesuits in her nation that she had acquired through the First Partition of Poland in 1772, so that the activities of the organization could go forward, despite the wishes of the Pope, and they did. And something to ponder is the Pope suppressed them on the 202nd day of the year, after the completion of the 201st day, July 20th. Another thing to ponder is that 'The Jesuit Order' sums to 177 with Simple English, and 201 with Reverse Simple, and Catherine the Great's husband was assassinated a decade earlier, on July 17, 1762, a date that can be expressed as 17/7, not unlike 177, in what is still an unsolved mystery. Relating to this fact is that on July 17, 2020, the 258 year anniversary of his assassination, a distance in time corresponding with the gematria of 'number of the beast', Cardinal Zenon Grocholewski of Poland was found dead. There can be little doubt this was a ritual, because the title 'Cardinal Zenon Grocholewski' equates to 281, and he died on his 281st day of his age, having been born October 11, 1939, the year World War II began when Hitler invaded Poland. Of course, that invasion came on September 1st, and then two days later, on 9/3, or 3/9, in '39, Britain and France declared war on Germany. In light of the date, let us not forget that 'Great War' sums to 39 with Pythagorean, and World War II was a continuation of the Great War, also known as World War I. For another, *'Art of War'*, the Jesuit translated text, sums to 39 with Pythagorean, whereas 'art' alone equates to 39 with Simple English. Let us also not forget the significance of 93. Furthermore, with regards to Grocholewski dying on his 281st day of his age, that is the 60th prime number, and the word 'order' equates to 60 with Simple English, meaning he was a perfect ritual sacrifice for the Jesuit 'Order', and likely paying tribute to their history of being saved by Catherine, and through Poland, where he was a Cardinal.

In addition to 'The Jesuit Order' equating to 201 with Reverse Simple English, let us not forget that the founder of the Jesuits, 'Ignatius of Loyola', had a name equating to 201 with Simple English, and at the same time, the first Jesuit Pope, Francis, was born 'Jorge Mario Bergoglio', also equating to 201 with Simple English. Let us also not forget that he is the first Pope to live in Suite 201 at the Vatican, named the 'Domus Sanctae Marthae', also equating to 201 with Simple English, and even further, 'Catholic Pope' equates to 201 with Reverse Simple English. With the growing list of number 201 connections in mind, don't forget that Adam Weishaupt, who was a

Jesuit, created the Bavarian Illuminati, and later changed the name to 'Order of Illuminati', summing to 201 with Simple English as well. These facts are extremely important, because again, Pope Francis, the leader of the Vatican at the time of the coronavirus pandemic, is the first publicly Jesuit Pope, in the history of the 266 men who have held that title, another number we will learn much about ahead.

In terms of the number 201, the Jesuit Order, and their ongoing agenda, by the numbers, recall what we uncovered in chapter one about the 'District of Columbia Organic Act of 1871', equating to 201 with Reverse Pythagorean. It was the legal move that made Washington D.C. an independent city-state within the United States of America, the same as the City of London within England, and Vatican City within Italy- with all three, or the 'trinity', having Catholic origins, and of course 'Catholic' equating to 71 with Simple English, much the same as the year of the Act, 1871. Furthermore, keep in mind this Act only occurred because the United States was bankrupt due the Civil War, and as was stated earlier, the Act of 1871 opened the door for foreign investment into the nation's capital, and for foreign control. Not by surprise, it was the Catholic Church and Jesuits who had financed the 'Confederate' Army, where 'Confederate' sums to 201 with Reverse Simple English, for the purpose of dividing the nation, so that the planned objective of taking the nation's capital could be reached, and was, with the District of Columbia Organic Act of 1871. As per usual, it was the tactic of "order out of chaos," meaning it was no different then, than it is now. I'll also note, 'Confederate' equates to 51 and 57, the same as 'Rome'.

To build on this point about Washington D.C., the Catholic Church, and the Jesuits, let us not forget that Washington D.C.'s location, prior to its existence, was once known as Rome on the Potomac, thus why it is between Virginia and Maryland, not to be confused with the Virgin Mary, that the Catholic Church worships. Furthermore, the Jesuit territory of Georgetown was merged with Washington in the 1871 Act. And to bring it together even further, let us do a bit more decoding with Pythagorean Gematria. With this cipher, 'Washington D.C.', 'Society of Jesus', 'Anthony Fauci' and 'coronavirus' each sum to 56. So does 'Paris, France', where the Jesuits were created. And so does 'unemployment', that was caused by the outbreak. And if you want to add more to that list, 'toilet paper' and 'mind control' equate in the same way, something that goes without saying unless you weren't living during the "Great T.P. Rush of 2020". In case you weren't alive, the unprecedented rush for toilet paper was caused by the mainstream media reporting coronavirus could cause a toilet paper shortage, that instantly lead to the fluffy butt wiping paper selling out worldwide, and even the non fluffy kind, giving it more street value than cocaine, and almost as much as hand sanitizer.

For another point about 56, in light of coronavirus being a continuation of the "order out of chaos" agenda, that included September 11, 2001- the 'three' planes that hit the World Trade Center and Pentagon buildings were said to be Flights 11, 77 and 175. If you add the three numbers together, they sum to 263, the 56th prime number. Keep in mind the 'Rockefeller' family, a surname summing to 56 in Pythagorean, was behind the World Trade Center construction project, as covered, and has an extensive history in the nation's capital, 'Washington D.C.' Adding to the intrigue of the number, the word 'three' has Simple English Gematria of 56, connecting with the three planes impacting targets on 9/11. And for something additional to consider, the word 'light' has Simple English Gematria of 56 as well. This matters because the third verse of *Genesis* is when God says, "Let there be light." Once again, The Cabal, who is playing God, is using this knowledge to keep us in darkness, by inverting the truth.

Moving down the list of 56 connections, consider President Donald Trump attended the Jesuit school, Fordham University in 1964, 56 years before 2020, the year of the "pandemic". This pairs well with the fact that coronavirus showed up in the United States January 15, 2020, a date with 56 numerology, and Donald Trump declared a national emergency due to the virus, Friday, March 13, 2020, also a date with 56 numerology. Never mind that the World Health Organization told the world to "prepare for pandemic" on February 25, 2020, the 56th day of the year. Furthermore, consider New York's 56th Governor, Andrew Cuomo, who also attended Fordham University, and who became the daily spokesperson used by all news outlets to give us the latest on coronavirus, and who had a younger brother on CNN, 'Chris Cuomo', a name summing to 56 with Reverse Pythagorean, who reportedly caught the virus and spoke about it for weeks on live CNN broadcasts, made solely for the purpose of scaring people into staying home. And as if that isn't enough evidence of the agenda already, Jesuit educated 'Gavin Newsom', equating to 56 and

155, the same as 'coronavirus', who went to Santa Clara University, ordered Californians to stay home on March 19, 2020, telling them at the time of the stay home orders, that in "8 weeks", the same as 56 days, "56%" of the citizens would have "coronavirus". How specific! Right? Not more than 50%, or nearly 60%, but "56%" in 56 days. For a runner up, I'd go with Lori Lightfoot, who as the 56th Mayor of Chicago, requested $56 million in federal funds to track the people of Chicago, under the guise of the virus, and the T.R.A.C.E program. She made this request May 26, 2020, the same day the George Floyd killing video went viral, and 70-days before her August 4th birthday, the same as 'Barack Obama's birthday, 8/4, the man who accepted the presidency in Chicago, winning the 56th U.S. Presidential Election, and who has matching name gematria with 'Lori Lightfoot', equating to 76, the same as 'Floyd the Landlord', George Floyd's porn name, that happens to be the number matching 'slave' and 'negro', and reminding that the Million Man March was on the day leaving 76 days left in the year, in Washington D.C., October 16, 1995.

As for the point about 70 days before Lightfoot's birthday, 'coronavirus' sums to 70 with Reverse Pythagorean, another huge number with the ongoing agenda that we will be buried in examples of by the conclusion of the book, such as the World Health Organization researching 70 potential vaccines for coronavirus, with the lead pharmaceutical company being 'Moderna', summing to 70 with Simple English, or the fact that the first case of coronavirus confirmed in the United States was in 'Snohomish County', summing to 70 in Reverse Pythagorean, or that 'Melinda Gates', also summing to 70 with Reverse Pythagorean, was one of the main hosts of Event 201, or that the name 'Francis', summing to 70 with Simple English, the same as 'Vatican', is the name of the first Jesuit Pope (Pope = 56 Reverse Simple English), or that Trump was 70 years old when he became President, or that Kobe Bryant, who was in a legal battle with a pharmaceutical company when he unexpectedly died while traveling from a Catholic mass in a helicopter crash, ended up being buried in 'Corona del Mar', summing to 56 and 70 in the same ciphers as 'coronavirus'. For another set of words equating to 56 and 70, the same as coronavirus, it is the 'CARES Act', the massive stimulus for the economy that Trump signed into law on March 27, 2020, to supplement the financial setbacks caused by the coronavirus outbreak.

Let us now rewind to the part about the 8/4 birthdays of Lori Lightfoot and Barack Obama, and let us not forget what we learned in chapter one. 'Jesuit', 'The Jesuit Order', and 'The Catholic Church' each sum to 84 in gematria, and so does 'United States of America'. While we're at it, so does 'Abraham Lincoln', the president who "saved the union." That was the president Obama was compared to, only because Obama represented the Land of Lincoln, 'Illinois', a state name summing to 54, the same as 'Jesuit Order'. As we'll learn more about, Lincoln was assassinated in a Jesuit plot involving John Surratt. And if you want to bring Jewish Gematria into it, 'Obama' sums to 84 as well. There is also a mathematical relationship between him being the 44th President, and having the name and birthday connection to the number 84. That relationship is the divisors of 44 sum to 84, and to go further, the divisors of 84 sum to 224, connecting to the fact that 'Anthony Stephen Fauci', the full name of our chief culprit, sums to 224 with Simple English.

Speaking of 84 and Fauci, it brings me to 1984, the year Anthony Fauci became the head of the NIH, standing for the National Institute of Allergy and Infectious Diseases, on the date of November 2, or 11/2. His first day on the job reminds us that the Jesuits operate in 112 countries, and 'Catholicism' sums to 112 with Simple English. At the same time, that same date can be written 2/11, and the Jesuit motto, 'Jesus, savior of men', equates to 211 with Simple English. Of course, 1984 was the year George Orwell warned of, a member of the Fabian Society, established in 1884. In addition to 'Jesuit' summing to 84 with Simple English, it also sums to 78 with 'Reverse Simple English. I bring this up because the coronavirus pandemic was declared March 11, 2020, the 71st day of the year, corresponding with the gematria of 'Catholic', and 78 days after Anthony Fauci's birthday on December 24, 2019. For your learning, jot down 'Wuhan Coronavirus' and 'order out of chaos', because they both sum to 78 as well. And while you're at it, remember that George Floyd's birthday, October 14, leaves 78 days in the year, and further, that on his chest, was tattooed the Scottish Rite symbol, for "order out of chaos." And don't forget, the Jesuits and the Scottish Rite share traditions and ideologies, and gematria as well, because both 'Jesuit' and 'Scottish Rite' equate to 78. As we'll get to later, the motto "order out of chaos" corresponds perfectly with George Floyd's age of death, 46, because the Latin words for "order out of chaos", are "Ordo Ab Chao", summing to 46 with Pythagorean Gematria, and similar to how the word 'chaos' alone sums to 46 with Simple English. These are things we will uncover much further in the eighteenth chapter, but for now you should remember that 'George Perry Floyd' sums to 201 with Simple English, and civil unrest was part of the Event 201 simulation, that no doubt, the George Floyd killing video helped bring about.

Returning to Anthony Fauci, you could also correctly say that March 11th, the date the pandemic was declared, was his 79th day of being 79 years old, being born on Christmas Eve, December 24, 1940, rather than saying the outbreak began 78 days after his birthday. This is important because 'Society of Jesus' sums to 79 with Reverse Pythagorean, corresponding with the true name of Jesus, that is 'Yeshua', summing to 79 with Simple English. And if you're grinning that his birthday is Christmas Eve, I'm right there with you. As they say, Santa and Satan aren't spelled with the same letters by accident.

On the subject of 'Jesuit' summing to 84 and 78, so does 'savior' with the same ciphers, and that is who the Jesuit Order claims to serve. One wonders if this purpose might have been hijacked long ago, or if that ever even was their true purpose. But to rewind the hands of time, the founder of the Jesuits, Ignatius of Loyola, died July 31, 1556, emphasis on the year '56, exactly 84 days before his October 23rd birthday. He was the 'Superior General' of the Jesuits, a title summing to 84 in Pythagorean, as we learned earlier. He was replaced by the man he co-founded the Jesuits with, Diego Laynez, who happened to be Jewish. Thus, it is important to note that despite the Jesuits serving the Catholic Church, not everyone in their ranks, not even in their founding members, are Catholic. Thus, ulterior motives within the order are entirely imaginable, and possible, and likely.

Consider the fact that some in the Jewish faith take all the teachings of the *Talmud* literally, meaning they consider non Jews to be less than human, and a class of people who are to be used as slaves in the Jewish utopia that will begin after their messiah arrives, who they are actively praying for. For a moment, imagine if people with this ideology infiltrated something as powerful as the Catholic Church, that has greater power than any nation on earth, and how that infiltration might be used to help them fulfill the objectives of creating a worldwide class of "goyim" slaves, as some of us are referred to in the '*Talmud*', summing to 71, the same as 'Catholic', with Simple English. And to take the thought a step further, the word 'Catholic' sums to 145 in Reverse Simple English, reminding of the date zionist Israel declared itself a nation, May 14, 1948, a date written 14/5. It was 'David Ben Gurion', summing to 145 with Simple English, who first declared Israel's existence that very day, and ever since, taxpayers of the world, living in nations that have nothing to do with Israel, have been sending their hard earned money to it, whether they support the existence of the nation, or not. And to rewind the clock even further, decades earlier, on November 2, 1917, the *Balfour Declaration* was written, addressed to Lord Rothschild, a Zionist Jew, declaring intentions for a Zionist home in Israel, for the Zionist Jews of the world. The date November 2nd is crucial for four key reasons, two of which you already know. One, the date is expressed as 11/2, similar to 112, the number of nations the Jesuits operate in. Two, 'Catholicism' sums to 112 with Simple English. Three, 'Zionist' sums to 112 with Simple English. And four, 'Judaism' sums to 112 with Reverse Simple English. Thus, these impossible coincidences are the fingerprints of an agenda, being methodically planned and executed, in accordance with time. And for additional numbers that bring together the Jesuits and Zionism, both 'Jesuit' and 'Zionism' equate to 84 and 42. This is similar to how 'Masonry' equates to 84, and 'Freemason' to 42.

As a reminder, at the time of the finalizing of this book, the former Superior General of the Jesuits, Adolfo Nicolas, died at age 84, in 'Japan', a nation summing to 42 with Simple English, on May 20, 2020, the day leaving 225 days left in the year, matching the Reverse Simple English value of his name. Also noteworthy, his name, 'Adolfo Nicolas', sums to 54 with Pythagorean, and 72 with Reverse Pythagorean, the exact same as 'Jesuit Order', and reminding that Catherine the Great saved the order in 1772, emphasis on '72, the same year *Art of War* was translated in France. Let us also not forget, Adolfo Nicolas died on the 191st day of the current Superior General's age, Arturo Sosa, who was 71 at the time, born November 12, 1948, and 'Society of Jesus' sums to 191 with Simple English. For some additional historical perspective, Diego Laynez, who replaced Ignatius of Loyola, died January 19, 1565, a date that can be expressed 19/1, not unlike 191, the 43rd prime, connecting to the gematria of 'Jesus Christ', summing to 43 with Pythagorean. Of course, the date can also be written 1/19, similar to 119, and reminding us of arsenic, abbreviated A.S. on the periodic table, or 1.19. It is the poison Jesuit assassins have used for centuries to kill their targets and it is the 33rd

element on the periodic table, complimenting the fact that 'arsenic' sums to 33 with Pythagorean Gematria. At the same time, it has an atomic mass of 74.9, once again bringing 33 and 74 together. Furthermore, if you look into this history of the 33 day Pope, Pope John Paul I, he went to bed on the Jesuit Order's birthday, September 27, 1978, and he never woke up again. Many contend he was poisoned with arsenic, because he had pledged to rid the Vatican Bank of its mafia ties, connecting to the fact that 'mafia' sums to 33 with Reverse Pythagorean. To make a long story short, he was replaced by Pope John Paul II, who would lead the church for 26 years, before dying on April 2, 2005, emphasis on 4/2, at the age of 84. And again, 'Jesuit' has gematria values of 42 and 84. Also noteworthy, he died 46 days before his upcoming birthday, May 18th, and that matters because 'sacrifice' sums to 46 with Pythagorean, similar to how *Genesis 46* begins with a sacrifice. And second, 'Catholic' sums to 46 with Reverse Pythagorean, matching the number of books in the Catholic *Old Testament*, 46. That's also the age JFK was assassinated at, who was the 35th President, and only Catholic one to date. Not by chance, 'Catholic' sums to 35 with Pythagorean Gematria, same as 'Holy See', that the U.S. has had diplomatic relations with the Holy See since 1984. If you're not hip, the Holy See is Vatican City and the Pope.

As for the point made earlier about 225 in the death of Adolfo Nicolas', it has a connection to Event 201, a simulation that lasted 3 hours and 45 minutes, as advertised. This is the equivalent of 225 minutes, and connects to the fact that the day after the 'George Perry Floyd' killing video, the Catholic Church of Minnesota settled a lawsuit with a payout of $22.5 million. This becomes all the more interesting when you realize George Floyd reportedly died on his 225th day of his age, at 46, being born October 14, 1973, and dying May 25, 2020. So where could they be going with the ritualistic use of this number? The biblical concept, 'The Great Tribulation' sums to 225 with Simple English. It is from *Revelation*, the concluding book of the *Bible*, and it is part of biblical prophesy, forecasting a time of suffering- including war, famine, and disease- subjects that are very relatable in 2020. Speaking of which, the year itself, 2020, reminds us that the 20th card of the Tarot deck is the judgement card, and the word 'judge' sums to 20 with Pythagorean Gematria, same as 'Tarot', 'time' and 'cross'. The latter of which, has been used to symbolize the four seasons of time, since the Pagans. I bring this up because the 20th card of the Tarot deck is illustrated with 'St. George's Cross', summing to 78 in Pythagorean, matching the number of cards in the Tarot deck, 78, as well as the gematria of 'Jesuit' and 'Wuhan Coronavirus'.

This factoid about time and judgement pairs with the historical milestone that was passed on August 20, 2019, when according to U.S. history, it marked 400 years since the first slaves arrived in Virginia, at Point Comfort, on August 20, 1619. If you're not familiar with *Acts 7:6 and 7:7* from the *Bible*, please take a moment to read them. They are as follows:

Acts 7:6-7 (NIV)

6 God spoke to him in this way: 'For four hundred years your descendants will be strangers in a country not their own, and they will be enslaved and mistreated. **7** But I will punish the nation they serve as slaves,' God said, 'and afterward they will come out of that country and worship me in this place.'

As I was telling my community in September of 2018, nearly a year in advance, this milestone was approaching, and knowing how The Cabal uses the scripture in the way a football coach uses a playbook, it didn't look good for the United States. To clarify, that's because *Acts 7:7* is about a nation being punished after the 400 years of slavery milestone, and 'United States' sums to 77 with Reverse Pythagorean, not unlike 7:7, or the fact the very same number was used very ritualistically on September 11, 2001, with Flight 77, as covered. And regarding the prior verse, *Acts 7:6*, recall how 'slave' sums to 76. And for another, consider the fact that *Acts* is the 44th book of the *Bible*. As we covered, 'Floyd the Landlord' sums to 76, and he was killed by a 44 year old officer on the 44th Parallel North.

I bring these facts up, because in the wake of his killing, 'Black Lives Matter' reemerged as a powerful entity, summing to 56 with Pythagorean Gematria, the same as 'Society of Jesus', and reminding us that the BLM movement came to national attention after the killing of 'Michael Brown' in 2014, another person with a name summing to 201, and in his case, using the Reverse Simple English cypher. As we'll discuss again later, Brown was killed in 'Ferguson, Missouri', equating to 84, and where both 'Ferguson' and 'Missouri' equate to 42 alone, numbers of the Jesuits. And as another reminder, in the Event 201 simulation, that you can watch on YouTube at the time of the publishing of this book, the subject of civil unrest is part of the simulation, which was brought about after the televised killing of 'George Perry Floyd', or 201. What was also part of the simulation is governments reopening too soon, a mistake that results in rapidly rising death tolls from coronavirus infections in poor communities. Of course, these are the exact places that George Floyd protests are taking place, worldwide, at the same time governments are reopening too soon, according to authority figures on the matter, such as Anthony Fauci and his business partner Bill Gates, the latter person being one of the main sponsors of Event 201. It only figures then, that his birth name, 'William Henry Gates', sums to 201 with Simple English Gematria, and 84 with Pythagorean.

Adding to the Gates riddle, and to our number 65 list that we began earlier, in the Event 201 simulation, 65 million people die over the course of 18 months, and making this all the more peculiar, is the fact that the simulation was done on Melinda Gates' 65th day of her age, and the word 'pandemic' sums to 65 with Simple English. Keep in mind her birthday is August 15th, matching the date the Jesuits were first formed in Paris, August 15, 1934, a little more than six years before their recognition by Rome, September 27, 1540. Furthermore, Melinda Gates is from a devout Catholic family, with links to the Jesuit Order, and at this moment in history, her and Bill Gates are actively building Jesuit high schools in the United States of America, with a focus on the very Zionist city of Chicago, where Lori Lightfoot is the current mayor, and the 56th. When we get to the Gates family, we will come to understand that this couple, who married 65 days after Bill Gates 38th birthday, numbers corresponding with the Simple English and Pythagorean Gematria of 'pandemic', are pawns on the chessboard, who were born for their arranged marriage and the roles they're currently playing in the mainstream. They're effectively chosen narrators, and made important in the minds eye of the masses, because they're rich, and on TV. As they say, "money talks". For now, I'll leave you with this thought. It is no accident William Henry Gates Sr. is 94 years old at the time of the coronavirus pandemic, and Bill and Melinda were married on January 1, 1994, in light of 'coronavirus pandemic', 'Seattle, Washington' and 'terror' each equating to 94, reminding us that the World Trade Centers, built only to be taken down for an agenda, opened on the 94th day of 1973. Let us not forget, the Gates family has a history in banking, and the City of

London became an independent banking corporation in 1694, emphasis on '94. Furthermore, this number points straight to the 'Roman Catholic Church', equating to 94 with Pythagorean Gematria, and no doubt, that is the entity that is behind the puppet that is Bill Gates, who as we'll get to, launched his Decade of Vaccines, on his 94th day of his age, January 29, 2010, in 'Davos, Switzerland', also equating to 94, something we'll touch more on ahead.

This brings us to the first Jesuit Pope, Francis, born 'Jorge Mario Bergoglio', again, summing to 201 with Simple English. He became the 266th Pope on March 13, 2013, or 3/13/13, where 3 is the 2nd prime, and 13 is the 6th prime. 3/13/13? 2/6/6? The number 266 is extremely important to the Jesuits, because of what the IHS in their sun logo represents. In Latin, IHS stands for 'Iesus Hominum Salvator', summing to 266 with Reverse Simple English. It also sums to 122 with Reverse Pythagorean, and 'Pope Francis' sums to 122 with Simple English. This becomes all the more interesting when you realize that Pope Francis is named after Saint Francis of Assisi, and 'San Francisco', summing to 122 with Simple English, and located on the 122nd Meridian West, is also named after Saint Francis of Assisi. Do I dare mention that the Church of Satan was established in San Francisco in 1966, and 'satanic' sums to 122 with Reverse Simple English? Or how about the fact that the predominantly Catholic and Jewish Supreme Court of the United States made abortion legal on January 22, or 1/22, when 'abortion' sums to 122 with Reverse Simple English? Forgive me father, but it reminds us that Martin Luther, leader of the Protestant Reformation, authored two books speaking out against two groups. They were the Catholic Church, with the *95 Theses*, and *Talmud* practicing Jews, with the title *On the Jews and Their Lies*. It makes me wonder, could it be that those forces joined at the same moment in history, to protect their own interests, and unite against a common enemy, Martin Luther and his followers, who were having serious sway? It is biblical prophesy, from *Revelation*, that in the end, there will be a powerful Cabal of false Jews, who are described as liars, and their name is 'The Synagogue of Satan', summing to 223 with Simple English, similar to how 'Philadelphia' sums to 223 with Reverse Simple English. This matters because the letter written in *Revelation* about The Synagogue of Satan, is written to the Church of Philadelphia. Keep in mind 223 is the 48th prime number, and the nation of Israel, was established in 1948.

Looking back, it's probably not an accident Martin Luther died in 1546, just six years after the Jesuit's recognition by Rome. They were hunting him after all. And he did die on his 101st day of his age, born November 10, 1483, before dying February 18, 1546, and 'Holy See' does sum to 101 in Simple English. For your learning, 101 is the 26th prime number, and as you learned, 'God' sums to 26, who the Jesuits and Church claim to serve. Furthermore, the Jesuit motto shared with the Scottish Rite, 'For the greater glory of God', sums to 351 with Reverse Simple English, the 26th triangular number. It's been said by Jesuit whistleblowers before, their assassins will kill a man, woman and child, and then say, "For the greater glory of God." Chilling, eh? It almost reminds you of the mainstream propaganda used against Muslims, with accused Islamic terrorists screaming, "God is great!" In fact, the hit TV show South Park has a banned episode, titled *201*, and that episode is dedicated to making fun of Islam and the Prophet Muhammad, not to be confused with 'Muhammad Ali', a well known name, equating to 201, as well as 42, the latter like 'Jesuit'.

I should note, the Latin motto for IHS also translates in English to 'Jesus, savior of mankind', which we have touched on. That phrase equates to 83 in Pythagorean, not unlike 'Yeshua', summing to 83 with Reverse Simple English. Keep in mind, Pope Francis was 83 years of age at the time of the pandemic, a number reminding of the Pope who gave us the Gregorian calendar, Pope Gregory XIII, who died at age 83 (born January 7, 1502, dead April 10, 1585), pairing with the fact his name 'Gregory XIII' sums to 83 with Pythagorean, and that the calendar is synced with the life of Jesus, or Yeshua. And with that thought in your mind, recall how the English language is credited to the Church, and so is the calendar, and as I stated prior, the Jesuits perform all their rituals in accordance, using the calendar and gematria, without missing a beat. Case in point, recall when Pope Francis, the 266th Pope, spoke at the White House, beginning at 9:23 AM local, on September 23, 2015, the 266th day of the Gregorian year. It was flawless execution. And don't overlook that he did it with Obama on his arm, the winner of the 56th U.S. Presidential Election, in light of the word 'Pope' summing to 56 with Reverse Simple English, and 'Society of Jesus' summing to 56 using Pythagorean. Not to mention, Obama's birthday is 8/4, and the United States and Holy See, or Vatican City, have had diplomatic relations since 1984, that were established on the date January 10, or 1/10, something like 110. You could say it was a fitting date for partners in contriving 'prophecy'.

On the subject of number 84, another major 84 ritual with Pope Francis and the Gregorian calendar, was the death of his Jesuit friend, and the longtime leader of Cuba, 'Fidel Castro', a name summing to 112 with Simple English. That was because Castro died 433 days after shaking hands with Pope Francis, and 433 is the 84th prime number. The date of their meeting was September 20, 2015, the 263rd day of the year, and as you know, the 56th prime. Furthermore, the date of Castro's death was November 25, 2016, having 52 numerology, connecting to the Simple English Gematria of 'Pope', and having 72 numerology as well, corresponding with the gematria of 'Jesuit Order'. Bringing meaning to the number 72, in Kabbalah, there is a belief that *Exodus 14:19-21*, reveals the 72 names of G-d. This is something I encourage you to research for your own learning. For now, please understand, this is further evidence of how this organization is using this knowledge to truly play God. And if you doubt that, Fidel Castro's son died 433 days after Fidel himself, February 1, 2018, at the age of 68, with his demise blamed on suicide. As for the son dying at age 68, his father's name, 'Fidel Castro', equated to 68 with Reverse Pythagorean. And it is also worth noting that when Fidel died, it was 59 days after the Jesuit Order's birthday, September 27th. This matters because 'Pope Francis' equates to 59 with Pythagorean, and 'kill' equates to 59 with Jewish Gematria.

On the subject of 59, if you know the name 'Roberto Calvi', it sums to 59 with Pythagorean Gematria, and he disappeared 59 days after his birthday, on June 10, 1982, born April 13, 1920. I bring him up because he was known as God's Banker, the man with mob ties who was allowed access to the Vatican Bank. He was found 7 days later, on the 17th, where 59 is the 17th prime, and 17 is the 7th prime, hanging dead, from the 'Blackfriars Bridge', summing to 145 in Simple English, similar to 'Catholic' equating to 145 with Reverse Simple English. In light of him being called God's Banker, keep in mid 'God' sums to 17 with Pythagorean Gematria. He was also found dead 30 days after Pope John Paul II's May 18th birthday, and 'mafia' sums to 30 with Pythagorean Gematria. Furthermore, there was a message with him dying in '82. Pope 'Pius XII', summing to 82 with Reverse Simple English, died at age 82, and was the one responsible for creating the Vatican Bank on the date June 27, 1942. That was an interesting date, because 'Society of Jesus' sums to 187 with Reverse Simple English, and June 27th leaves 187 days in the year. Never mind the year '42, and what you've learned about 42 so far.

Coming back to Pope Francis, and 84, he will turn 84 on December 17, 2020, a date that is the 351st day of the year in non leap years. On that day, should he be blessed to make it, his age will match his birth numerology, born December 17, 1936, a date giving him 84 numerology on his birth chart, fitting for the first 'Jesuit' Pope. And regarding the number, if you go back in time, to September 11, 2013, the mainstream media carried the story of Pope Francis trading in the old 'popemobile', a name summing to 54 in Pythagorean, same as 'Jesuit Order', for a 1984 Renault. With gematria, you can fully understand the joke. And please don't overlook that the news fell on September 11th, the anniversary of the most tragic day in U.S. history. Furthermore, that date can be written 11/9, not unlike 119, connecting to both 'Vatican' and 'Francis' in Reverse Simple English. *It was 119 days after Francis' birthday when Notre Dame burned, April 15, 2019.

Regarding his 1984 Renault, please recall that in the days after Donald Trump became President of the United States, Amazon, the company established in 1995, with clear Vatican ties, began reporting that George Orwell's *1984* had risen to best seller out of the blue. This was reported Wednesday, January 25, 2017, by Amazon, and all of mainstream media. What's funny about the timing of the announcement, the 25th day of the year, is best decoded with Pythagorean Gematria, where 'Amazon', 'Trump' and 'Pope' each equate to 25, and if you use Reverse Pythagorean, the word 'time' also sums to 25. On the subject, I encourage you to take the time to watch the film *In Time*, where the plot is set in the future, in a world where time is literally money, and when you turn 25 years old, a timer begins on your physical body, and if it runs out, you die. Not by chance, both 'death' and 'time' equate to 25 in Reverse Pythagorean, not unlike 'Dayton', summing to 25 with Pythagorean, where the film begins. Also not by chance, the film is about the battle between rich and poor. And with that thought in mind, let us not overlook that the year 2020 is 25 years after the establishment of Amazon in '95, and the year that Jeff Beezos turned 56 years old, having been born on January 12th, 1964. Of course, Amazon is the same company siphoning the wealth of the people of the world right now, who are told to stay home, and essentially, if they need something, to buy it online, meaning buy it from Amazon.

Coming back to *1984*, authored by George Orwell after the World Wars, about a future world, where people are ruled over by screens, and censorship and suppression are the favored tools of those who control with authoritarian measures- it is subject matter reminding a lot of the times we are living in today, and Donald Trump has called for these types of measures numerous times himself, routinely asking for his critics to be shutdown, whether they're *Saturday Night Live*, news outlets, or social media platforms. Of course it is all part of a show, but it is a show with meaning, and it informs us where we are in The Cabal's ongoing agenda, that has been foretold through popular media, including *1984*, as well as films such as *The Matrix* and *Fight Club*, both immensely popular in the period of time leading up to September 11, 2001. If you haven't seen those films, *The Matrix* is about a man who sees through the illusions of his world and joins a team to fight the film's version of The Cabal, and who also is shown carrying a passport with an expiration date of September 11, 2001. As for *Fight Club*, it is about a secret society coming together to fight corporatism, world trade and big banks. The film ends with a city skyline collapsing in free fall, from demolitions, reminiscent of the World Trade Centers demise on September 11, 2001. And keep in mind, the author of *Fight Club*, Chuck Palahniuk, is from the Seattle area, the same city that's home to the firm that built the World Trade Centers. The term for this imagery in popular media, such as the collapsing skyline in *Fight Club*, is called predictive programming, and it is something my first book *Letters and Numbers* explains and exposes with numerous examples. It is also something we will touch more on in the chapters ahead as we expose the predictive programming for 9/11 and coronavirus.

As we near the end of this chapter, I want to teach you one more cipher, for the purpose of further cementing the point that all number games of The Cabal, are time based. Before revealing the cipher, I want to take you back to July 18, 2016, a date that can be written 18/7, much like 187, and a date that came a span of 187 days from Inauguration Day for Donald Trump, January 20, 2017. Of course July 18th was the date his G.O.P. convention began in

Cleveland, Ohio. In Gematria terms, 'Society of Jesus', 'Washington D.C.' and 'Paris, France', the original home of the Jesuits, all sum to 187 with Reverse Simple English. Adding to the list, what is etched on the Scottish Rite headquarters in Washington D.C., 'Ancient & Accepted Scottish Rite of Freemasonry', sums to 187 with Pythagorean Gematria. And for another related name equating to 187, 'George Washington' sums to 187 with Simple English. And in a cipher known as Satanic Gematria, both 'time' and 'Ohio' equate to 187 as well. This cipher is very simple, it begins with A = 36, B = 37, C = 38 and so on, counting up to Z = 61, and where 666 is the 36th triangular number.

Satanic Gematria:

A=36, B=37, C=38, D=39, E=40, F=41, G=42, H=43, I=44

J=45, K=46, L=47, M=48, N=49, O=50, P=51, Q=52, R=53

S=54, T=55, U=56, V=57, W=58, X=59, Y=60, Z=61

Not by chance, when you decode 'Satanic Gematria' using this cipher, it sums to 666. And even further, 61 is the 18th prime number, and 6+6+6 sums to 18. These values sync with the gematria of 'IHS', the Jesuit acronym, equating to 36 with Simple English and 18 with Pythagorean. Furthermore, 'Jesus Christ' sums to 151 with Simple English, the 36th prime number, and 'Jesus' equates to 61 with Reverse Simple, the 18th prime. Thus, think light and dark, and black and white, which is symbolized in Masonic and Vatican checkerboard flooring. Think duality. And think *Revelation 13:18*, which references 666, the number of the beast, but also the number of a man.

Adding to the relevance of the number 187, from Donald Trump's June 14th birthday each year, to Pope Francis' December 17th birthday, is a span of 187 days. Furthermore, Donald Trump was the winner of the 58th U.S. Presidential Election, held in 2016, after announcing he was running from the 58 story Trump Tower, and before hiring the 58 year old Steve Ray for Inauguration Day. This becomes all the more interesting when you realize that 'Pope Francis', 'calendar', 'zodiac', 'Gregorian', and 'solar cycle' each equate to 58 in gematria terms, and once again, the Catholic Church is credited with the Gregorian calendar, based on the solar cycle, as well as the roots of our English language. It should also be noted, 'Trump', 'Francis', 'time' and 'Ohio' each equate to 47, same as 'The Cabal', 'Vatican',

'President', 'White House', 'government' and 'authority'. Thus, these two Jesuit puppets, one the face of the Vatican, the other the face of the United States and Washington D.C., the latter being arguably the most powerful Jesuit city in the world, are not only in sync with each other in terms of the distance of their birthdays, but they are named accordingly, sharing the same gematria, and the same numbers, that again, pay tribute to time, and who is in control of it.

Further adding to the relevance of number 187, is the fact that John F. Kennedy was assassinated November 22, 1963, in the 187th year of the United States' existence, and 'JFK Assassination' sums to 187 with Simple English Gematria. At the same time, with Sumerian Gematria, where you multiple the alphabetic order by six, the phrase 'JFK Assassination' sums to 1122, not unlike the date November 22nd, or 11/22. Keep in mind he was killed in Dealey Plaza, named after George Dealey, a Scottish Rite Freemason, and we just learned about the 187 connection with the Jesuits and the Scottish Rite, a number also associated with homicide through police codes.

With regards to JFK dying in 1963, there is an important point to be made about 19 years cycles, something we covered earlier. Keep in mind 1963 was 19 years before 1982, the year '*TIME*' magazine named the computer as Person of the Year- the only time a non living thing was given the honor by the magazine. Consider further, 1982 was 19 years before 2001, the year the PATRIOT Act transpired, allowing the U.S. government to use computer technology to track its people as it never had before. Then even further, 2020 came another 19 years later, and that was the year the governments of the world made it clear they would be tracking all people at all times through smartphones, that are personal computers, with the government's bolstered internet technology, 5G. Again, every 19 years the moon syncs with the Gregorian calendar, and in Tarot, the 19th card, is the sun card. Also, let us not forget the 'order out of chaos' agenda, where 'chaos' equates to 19 with Pythagorean Gematria. At the same time, it was JFK who warned against secrecy, and those who operate by means of infiltration, which is a key strategy of the Jesuit Order. To revisit his quote from April 27, 1961, these were his exact words. "For we are opposed around the world by a monolithic and ruthless conspiracy that relies primarily on covert means for expanding its sphere of influence- on infiltration instead of invasion, on subversion instead of elections,

81

on intimidation instead of free choice, on guerrillas by night instead of armies by day. It is a system which has conscripted vast human and material resources into the building of a tightly knit, highly efficient machine that combines military, diplomatic, intelligence, economic, scientific and political operations." Of course, he was speaking about the Jesuit Order, reminding us that he died 177 days after his May 29, 1963 birthday, corresponding with the gematria of 'The Jesuit Order', as well as 'New World Order'.

And for one last point on 187 and the Jesuits, let us rewind to 1984. On January 14, 1984, Ray Kroc, "The Founder" of McDonald's, who joined the company in '54, died. Then precisely 187 days after his death, on July 18th, or 18/7, a McDonald's was shot to pieces in 'San Ysidro', California, a town summing to 56, not unlike 'Society of Jesus', and also 119, not unlike 'Vatican'. Furthermore, the shooter's name, 'James Huberty' equates to 177, the same as 'The Jesuit Order', and reminding us that JFK was killed exactly 177 days after his own birthday, in the 187th year of the nation's existence. To go even further, 'San Ysidro, California' sums to 95 with Pythagorean Gematria, a very important number to the Jesuit's establishment as we learned, who were formed to counter the 95 Theses, and recognized by Rome on the day leaving 95 days in the year, September 27th. It reminds us that the surname of the Jesuit 'Fauci', sums to 95 with Reverse Simple English, and he was born December 24, 1940, a date with 95 numerology. It also reminds us of the fact that Event 201 took place on October 18, 2019, the same day the Military World Games began in Wuhan, China, games that trace back to the year 1995, and to Rome, the home of the Vatican. As we'll get to, 1995 was the year Bill Gates was declared the world's richest man, on the most fitting date, the same day that Corona typewriters filed for bankruptcy, and also what would have been his mother's birthday, but she had recently passed, in '94. And on the subject of Corona typewriters, before long, we'll learn why Tom Hanks, Madonna and others were posing with them, and saluting the number 201 at the same time, during the time of the "pandemic," including John Krasinski, of the hit TV show The Office, that ran exactly 201 episodes, and not by accident.

As for the date Bill Gates was declared the richest man, and Corona typewriters folded, it was July 5, 1995, and on the 25 year anniversary of those things happening, on July 5, 2020, it was reported that Nick Cordero, the Broadway actor, who reportedly had a leg amputated before losing a lung to coronavirus, had died from the same disease, on the 187th day of the leap year, corresponding with 'Society of Jesus'. Furthermore, his death came precisely 201 days after Pope Francis' 83rd birthday, Mr. 201, who lives in Suite 201, reminding of the song *'Murder' by Numbers*, and why it released in 1983. On that same date, another top story, Vanessa Guillen's body was identified in 'Killeen, Texas', a town summing to 187, a girl who had been missing since April 22, 2020, 74 days earlier- a number that should remind you of both the Society of 'Jesus' and 'killing'. It was reported that her body was found June 30th, on the 70th day since the disappearance, but because of decomposition, they could not identify her until July 5th. Again, the significance of the 70th day is that both 'Vatican' and 'Francis' sum to 70 with Simple English, a stat that pairs with the fact these stories came 201 days after Pope Francis' birthday, on the 187th day of the year, and they also fell on a date that can be written 7/5, matching the Reverse Pythagorean value of 'Catholic Church', equating to 75. At the same time, 'Catholic Church' sums to 69 with Pythagorean, and her body was found 69 days after she disappeared, or on the 70th day since her disappearance. Keep in mind this happened at Fort Hood, a military base that is no stranger to rituals by the numbers, as I wrote about in my first book. And for even more 'Jesuit' fingerprints, 'Hood' sums to 42, the same as 'Jesuit'. Furthermore, the date of Nick Cordero's and Vanessa Guillen's fateful news, was a date with 52 numerology, corresponding with the gematria of 'Pope', using Simple English, summing to 52, the same as 'devil'. Keep in mind, this was just days before the news of Naya Rivera's drowning, in Lake Piru, or "Lake Devil", that came 187 days before her birthday, and on the 191st day of the year, July 9th, or 7/9, what was a date with 56 numerology, corresponding with the fact that 'Society of Jesus' equates to 56, 79, 187 and 191.

To close with the topic at hand, the number 201, and to better understand and why it is so important to the Jesuits, I want to leave you with a word. It is 'Triclavianism', equating to 201 with Reverse Simple English. It is the simple belief that Jesus was crucified with 'three' nails, an idea that is captured in the Jesuit logo, depicting the three nails and the cross, inside of the sun. As you have learned, 'three' has

gematria of 56, the other very special number to the 'Society of Jesus'. Of course, this fits in with the concept of the trinity and the three independent city states, ruling over the world. Also relevant, 'Triclavianism' sums to 93 with Reverse Pythagorean, corresponding with the 93 gematria values of 'crucifix', 'God's son', 'Nazareth', and the fact that Jesus is crucified in the *Bible* between 9 AM and 3 PM. At the same time, let us not forget that the sun in the sky, is said to be 93 million miles from earth, or that in recent times, modern science supposedly traced the date of Jesus crucifixion to April 3rd, the 93rd day of Gregorian year. Let us also recall that 'Saturn' equates to 93, the keeper of time, connected to death and judgement. And let us also recall that 'Wuhan Coronavirus', equating to 93, is a time based ritual, that carries the threat of death behind it. Besides the numbers, the point to takeaway with the Jesuit fixation on Triclavianism, is that it is related to death and killing, something the Jesuits have used as leverage and as a weapon for centuries, to accomplish their political endeavors. This syncs with the fact that 'capital punishment' also sums to 201 with Simple English. And with the thought of number 'three' on the brain, and knowing that controlling time is the object, consider there are three phases of time- the past, the present, and the future. And that brings us back to George Orwell's quote, "Who controls the past controls the future. Who controls the present controls the past." And as we know, the most effective way to control people is with fear, especially the threat of death.

It is to say, the Jesuits are controlling time and fulfilling prophecy by the code. And on the subject of 'prophecy' you should know it sums to 666 with Jewish Gematria, similar to how 'three nails' equates to 666 with Sumerian Gematria. At the same time, 'IHS' sums to 36 with Simple English, the acronym in the center of the Jesuit logo, just above the 'three nails', and 666 is the 36th triangular number, not to be confused with 'Jesus Christ', summing to 151 with Simple English, the 36th prime number. Ahead, when we discuss the Clade X pandemic simulation, you'll come to understand why it was really carried out May 15, 2018, 666 days before the coronavirus pandemic was declared on March 11, 2020, proving Anthony Fauci correct, the Jesuit, who said at the Jesuit university Georgetown, this would happen, to the Jesuit educated president, Donald Trump, on the date of January 10, 2017, a date that can be written 1/10, similar to how 'prophecy' equates to 110 with Reverse Simple English.

5 | Crimson Contagion Pandemic Drills & the New York Times

   Crimson Contagion was a series of pandemic simulations that were carried out by the U.S. federal government in 2019. The New York Times brought these simulations to light in a March 19, 2020 article, days after the coronavirus pandemic had been declared, by focusing on one of the events that took place August 13th through 16th, in Chicago. The scenario for the simulation the NYT investigated involved airline travelers who were returning from China, to Chicago, Illinois, when they unknowingly started the spread of a virus that became a pandemic. The forecast from the simulation, per the New York Times who reported on it, was that the virus would infect 110 million people in the United States, leading to 7.7 million hospitalizations, and killing 586,000 (5+8+6+0+0+0 = 19). Never mind that this is the plot of the 2011 film *Contagion*, or that The Cabal went with the numbers 110 and 77 again, while encoding 19 in the death toll. Furthermore, the virus used for the simulation was described as a respiratory virus, similar to coronavirus, or Covid-19.

   As for the New York Times choosing to focus on the Chicago simulation, the reasoning becomes clear with our gematria lens. 'Chicago' sums to 37 and 46, similar to how 'virus' sums to 37 and 46. And in light of the "order out of chaos" agenda, don't forget that 'chaos' sums to 46 with Simple English, reminding of the killing of 46 year old George Floyd, on the corner of Chicago Avenue in Minneapolis, the city the hero of the film *Contagion* calls home, not to be confused with Chicago, where his wife cheats on him, after returning from China. For your learning, please also note that 'virus' and 'chaos' share gematria values of 26, 46 and 89 using our four base ciphers. Confirming that the virus as well as chaos encoding of 'Chicago' is why the New York Times focused on Chicago's Crimson Contagion exercise, the name of the virus from the same drill was 'H7N9 Influenza', summing to 183, the same as 'order out of chaos', and even 'Pearl Harbor', another event blamed on asians. Let us not forget 'Wuhan Coronavirus' also equates with 'order out of chaos'.

   What should give you a laugh, in the Crimson Contagion simulation, per the New York Times, the World Health Organization, established April 7, 1948, emphasis on 4/7, declares a pandemic on the 47th day of the outbreak. As we know, the number 47 symbolizes 'time' and 'authority', and if I didn't mention it earlier, the Event 201 simulation that happened not long after, October 18, 2019, was on a date with 47 numerology. The findings from the Crimson Contagion simulation were that the United States was not financially prepared, or well enough organized, to fight a severe pandemic, and that it would cause chaos within federal government ranks, mostly along the lines of what agencies would take on what responsibilities. In the simulation, conflicts occurred between FEMA, HHS and the Department of Homeland Security, the latter being created in the wake of September 11, 2001, the day Building 7 fell, for no good reason, a building standing 47 stories tall.

In terms of the timing of the exercise, it began August 13th, exactly 155 days before the first case of coronavirus reportedly landed in the United States, January 15, 2020. This matters, because in Simple English, 'coronavirus' sums to 155, and by this book's end, we'll have a long list of how the number 155 relates to the "coronavirus pandemic". They'll include things such as the news on June 3, 2020, the 155th day of the year, that George Floyd's autopsy results revealed he had coronavirus at the time of his death, and the former Superior General of the Jesuits died May 20, 2020, 155 days after Pope Francis' birthday, the first Jesuit Pope. They'll also include findings such as the Clade-X pandemic exercise, that took place May 15, or 15/5, exactly 666 days before the coronavirus pandemic was declared on March 11, 2020. We'll get to that exercise next chapter. In addition, we'll eventually cover Hulu releasing a new TV show called *The Great* on May 15, 2020, about Catherine the Great, the Empress of Russia, who once saved the 201 Jesuits, not too far off from Event 201, the coronavirus outbreak simulation. We'll even tie in the diagnosing of Nadia, the tiger, as the first nonhuman to test positive for coronavirus, in a year where International Tiger Day fell on July 29, 2020, the day leaving 155 days in the year. And yes, International Tiger Day is a real thing.

Coming back to the start date of August 13th, it can be expressed as 13/8, similar to 138. This matters because 'federal' sums to 138 with Reverse Simple, and 'Donald Trump' sums to 138 with Simple English. Of course, it was his Department of Health and Human Services that carried out the exercise. Furthermore, the name 'Department of Health and Human Services' sums to 151 with Pythagorean, similar to how 'pandemic' sums to 151 with Reverse

Simple, and once again, the date of the first case of coronavirus in the United States, January 15th, can be expressed as 15/1. When we get to the chapter on big tech, we'll discuss the event named 'The Great Reset', summing to 151 with Simple English, as well as 74 with Reverse Pythagorean. It is scheduled for January of 2021, and is being hosted by the World Economic Forum, the same organization that has been planning how to manage the world's financial interests in the time of a pandemic for decades, just as they did at Event 201, with the coronavirus outbreak simulation. And staying true to the order out of chaos formula, the 2021 event is about how to move forward as a people, in the world reshaped by coronavirus. Never mind that in Tarot, the 21st card is The World card, or that Agenda 21, from the 1990s, focused on changing the world in a drastic way by 2021, as we'll learn about later, and that event has the same ambitions as the upcoming conference, The Great Reset. And adding insult to injury, The Great Reset for 2021 was announced on June 3, 2020 the 155th day of the year. Keep in mind, in light of 'The Great Reset' summing to 151, it is the 36th prime number and June 3rd can be expressed as 3/6, similar to 36. Also, 666 is the 36th triangular number, and in Jewish Gematria, as we have learned, 'prophecy' sums to 666, what The Cabal is fulfilling, using the scripture as the script. As we also know, they are led by the Society of Jesus, and that reminds 'Christianity' sums to 155 with Simple English, and 'Jesus Christ' sums to 151 with the same cipher. And once again, time as we count it, on the Gregorian calendar, is aligned with the life of Jesus Christ, where it is counted in terms of before and after Christ. In that breath, let us not forget that '*Bible*', 'Jesuit' and 'math' all equate to 21, factoring in with the year 2021, emphasis on '21, and it being in the 21st century.

Coming back to the agency responsible for the Crimson Contagion exercise, it is noteworthy that 'Department of Health and Human Services' sums to 182 with Reverse Pythagorean, and 'Year of the Rat' sums to 182 with Reverse Simple. Just wait until we get to the predictive programming chapter and dissect the 2007 film *Pandemic*, where a virus is brought to the United States from Australia, via Flight 182, only to have the CDC scientist board the plane, and announce that his name is Ratner. Adding to the joke, the actor's name for Dr. Ratner is 'French Stewart', a name equating to 191, the same as 'Society of Jesus'. For the record, the Year of the Rat began on January 25, 2020, Dean Koontz's 201st day of being 74 years

87

old, the man born July 9, 1945, and the man who authored *Eyes of Darkness* in 1981, a work of fiction involving details of a secret military operation out of Wuhan, China to spread a virus. Adding insult to injury, the name of the virus is 'Wuhan 400', a name that when written out as words, 'Wuhan Four Hundred', sums to 201 with Simple English. Plus, what did we learn earlier about *Acts 7:6-7*, and 400 years, and how that ties in with the pandemic? The name 'Wuhan Four Hundred' also sums to 84 and 78, the same as 'Jesuit', and 231, the 21st triangular number, corresponding with the 21st century, and the fact that 'Jesuit' sums to 21 with Pythagorean Gematria. In case you're wondering what the Year of the Rat has to do with anything, for one, it is Chinese, and two, rats are known for spreading disease and illness. Regarding the second reason, it's probably no accident that Microsoft's video game platform released a title in 2019, called '*A Plague Tale: Innocence*', equating to 84, the same as 'William Henry Gates', the former CEO of Microsoft, where you fight off disease ridden rats to survive, for the entirety of the game.

Another point that needs to be made about the exercise is that the gematria of the name 'Crimson Contagion' equates to 243 with Reverse Simple English. This is similar to how 'Central Intelligence Agency' sums to 243 with Simple English, and coordinates with the fact the coronavirus pandemic began while the United States of America was 243 years old, having turned 243 on July 4, 2019. As we'll get to in the chapter dedicated to Kobe, his full name 'Kobe Bean Bryant' also sums to 243 with with Reverse Simple, and his death is part of the greater coronavirus ritual, that again, is time based.

In light of the New York Times breaking the news of Crimson Contagion, I want to make a point about the man who was in charge of the paper and its operations at the time of the March 19th article. That was their CEO and President, Mark John Thompson, a Jesuit educated man, having attended Stonyhurst College. Before he was with the New York Times, he was with another media titan, the 'BBC', summing to 74 with Reverse Simple English, the number pairing with 'London' and the rest of the words from the long list we uncovered in chapter one. As we know, the Jesuits work by the code, explaining why the March 19, 2020 article, about the 2019 pandemic exercise, Crimson Contagion, was published just 8 days after Covid-19 was declared a pandemic. Keep in mind 19 is the 8th prime and March 19th

was the day California became the first state to enact stay at home orders, under the leadership of Gavin Newsom, after his "56%" scare. March 19th was also the 79th day of the leap year, corresponding with the Reverse Pythagorean of 'Society of Jesus', that again, Gavin Newsom, the Governor of California is a member of, same with Anthony Fauci, who was on his 79th day of being 79 years old when the pandemic was declared on March 11th.

Delving deeper into the New York Times and its CEO, the name 'Mark John Thompson' sums to 78 with Reverse Pythagorean, the same as the paper, 'The New York Times', that was established on a date with 78 numerology, September 18, 1851, the same day the cornerstone was laid for Washington D.C., in 1793. As you'll recall, that day leaves 104 days left in the year, corresponding with the gematria of 'Roman Catholic Church'. As for the 78 connections to the New York Times, they remind us that the words 'Jesuit' and 'New York' equate to 78 with Reverse Simple English. Furthermore, if you leave 'the' out, and just decode 'New York Times', you will notice it sums to 177, not unlike 'The Jesuit Order', or 'New World Order'- or 'propaganda'. And keep in mind the New York Times is sold worldwide, and is a propaganda publication that actively uses the term "conspiracy theorist" to describe people who question government and mainstream narratives, including the coronavirus pandemic, 9/11, the moon landing, and the JFK assassination. Regarding the moon landing, it happened on July 20, 1969, the 201st day of the year, in the time of Cancer, the astrology sign that appears as a 69, and reminding that in astrology, the sign of Cancer is ruled by the moon. And regarding JFK, he was a man who was reportedly killed 177 days after his own birthday, in the middle of a location named after a newspaper mogul, George Dealey, who was also a member of a secret society, the Scottish Rite of Freemasonry. Adding to the list, 'Kennedy' sums to 78, similar to how 'Jesuit' and 'Scottish Rite' equate to 78, along with the two fraternities favorite tactic, 'order out of chaos'. And with regards to Gavin Newsom and "order out of chaos", he lit the fire of fear under California, and across the nation with his March 18th speech about the coming rapid spread of the deadly virus, on the 78th day of 2020. That was when he announced the stay at home orders for his state for the following day. And do you know who didn't mind those orders? Jeff Bezos of Amazon and all the big box retailer chief executive officers that were allowed to stay open, while mom and pop stores were told to close and stay home… and go out of business. If not they were warned, they might die otherwise, and if not that, then be fined and jailed and have their business licenses taken from them for not following the new health safety protocols. Thus part of the order that was installed through the new rules of government, due to the chaotic coronavirus, was more business traffic through corporate giants, and almost none through small business. In this breath, it should be noted, when CNN wrote about how billionaires had taken $565 billion more of the pie of America's wealth on June 4, 2020, during the time of the pandemic, they began their measurement date on March 18th, the 78th day of the year, and the article was written precisely 78 days later. Effectively, CNN was publishing the words of the gloating Cabal, richer by the second, who once again, successfully had directed the world's people into its trap, with its media weapons.

Coming back to the New York Times and JFK, the 78 connections also remind us that John F. Kennedy addressed the American Newspaper Publishers Association, April 27, 1961, in New York, speaking about the impact of secret societies on the press as well as the nation (the same quote we examined last chapter), only to end up dying in a plaza named after a newspaper publisher, who was in a secret society. And then further, having a movie made about it, the *Zapruder Film*, by 'Abraham Zapruder', a name equating to 153 and 72, the same as 'Jesuit order'. Zapruder was also a Scottish Rite Freemason of the 33rd degree. Keep in mind many Jesuits are Freemasons, and not by chance, 'Freemason' sums to 42 with Pythagorean Gematria, whereas 'Jesuit' sums to 42 with Reverse Pythagorean. At the same time, if you use the Sumerian cipher, where you multiply the alphabetic order by six, G, the 7th letter, becomes 42, and that is the letter in the middle of the Freemason logo, surrounded by the compass and square, instruments of measurement, reminding of how well measured everything is in these rituals we are exposing are. And let us not forget 'math' sums to 42 with Simple English, or Andrew Yang's ritual on the 42nd day of 2020, February 11th.

Coming back to JFK. Another important point about his same speech where he touched on secrecy, is that he spoke extensively about Fidel Castro, Cuba's Jesuit dictator, from the nation located off the shores of the Southeastern United States. Think about that in light of The Cabal's "order out of chaos" mantra, because Castro was a man who was used on nightly news broadcasts as an excuse to pump fear into the hearts of Americans for decades, due to the threat of nuclear warfare and annihilation. The media coined this threat at one point as the 'Cuban Missile Crisis', summing to 78 with Pythagorean. The results of this headline driven skirmish were financial excuses to pump untold amounts of dollars into military activities that we'll likely never know the extent of, and wage wars against communism, as we did in 'Vietnam', summing to 84 and 42, the same as 'Jesuit', and elsewhere, as we did more quietly, with guerrilla tactics. And for the record, the Cuban Missile Crisis began October 16, 1962, the day leaving 76 days left in the year, corresponding with the gematria of 'Castro', equating to 76 with Simple English. It serves as a reminder, all Jesuit rituals are executed by the code, and when you recognize the code, it brings new meaning to popular phrases, such as the "the theater of war."

As you can now understand, with the knowledge of gematria, you can identify who are the puppets, people such as Castro and JFK, and who are the puppeteers, the Jesuits and other powerful secret societies that fall under their umbrella, including the Scottish Rite and Knights Templar, as well as the Knights of Malta, all of whom serve the Catholic Church. You can also better appreciate the saying, "The world is a stage," while knowing who directs the performance. And for anyone who might be upset by me calling John F. Kennedy a puppet, don't let the drama take you. All good theater needs heroes and villains, and through the story of the Kennedy brothers, their outspoken words, and their untimely assassinations, both in perfect numerical rituals, that only could have transpired with the properly named actors, an entire generation learned to tuck their heads like turtles, and steer clear of going against authority. It's all part of how we've arrived at where we are in 2020, with people handing over their rights, obeying the commands of big brother, and strapping a mask across their face, a sign of the silenced, with very little evidence there is any threat of a killer virus, other than one that threatens the elderly, specifically those with preexisting health problems- something that is also true of the seasonal flu and pneumonia.

For another point on John F. Kennedy, that will connect with what we're living out today, his most odd speech was at the site of the Berlin Wall, on June 26, 1963, or 26/6, not unlike 266, the cherished number by the Jesuits, that you just learned about regarding Pope

Francis, the 266th Pope, the first Jesuit. It was titled *Ich bin ein Berliner*, and was about the recently built Berlin Wall being a symbol of division. Of course, that wall would eventually fall on November 9, 1989, another 11/9 or 9/11 date. Not by accident, 56 years after the Inauguration of JFK, on January 20, 2017, or 20/1, like 201, Donald Trump, "Mr. Wall," was compared to JFK. This was because Donald's wife Melania was the first to wear baby blue for a presidential inauguration since Jacqueline Kennedy in 1961. Keep in mind, shortly before the inauguration, Donald Trump had become the 45th President Elect on the anniversary of the fall of the 'Berlin Wall', November 9, 2016, after the election was called in his favor in the early hours of the day. And understand, it was not an accident that the election was called after November 8th, the voting date, it was a ritual, and it was because 'Berlin Wall' sums to 45 with Pythagorean, and 63 with Reverse Pythagorean. Regarding the latter number, 2016 is the 63rd triangular number, and it connects us back to the year of JFK's demise.

Consider the duality, as well as the mockery, since Donald Trump ran on building walls, going against what JFK was preaching in the 1960's, and what Pope Francis, the 266th Pope, the first Jesuit, is speaking today. Again, JFK's speech at the wall was 26/6, June 26, 1963, 149 days before his assassination, the 35th prime number, bringing an end to the 35th president, who had a May 29th birthday, the 149th day of the year, and who defeated Richard Nixon in the 1960 election, on Richard Nixon's 305th day of his age. Should I add *'Zapruder Film'* sums to 149 with Simple English, the title of the footage that recorded his death? Once again, 'Catholic' sums to 35 with Pythagorean, and JFK is the only Catholic President of the United States to date. This is likely due to the fact that if Presidents were Catholic, as often as they are Supreme Court Justices and politicians, people might catch on to the scheme.

For more vital information regarding the November 9, 2016 announcement, the name 'Donald' in Jewish Gematria sums to 119, similar to how the date is expressed as 11/9. And better than that, if you look into Donald Trump's television commercial history, you'll find that he did an ad for Serta mattresses, years before he ran for president, about counting sheep (what they do on voting day). Not by chance, 'Serta' sums to 63 with Simple English, and again, 2016 is the 63rd triangular number. In that commercial he talks to two digital sheep in the hallway of a hotel he owns, and each of the sheep are standing on pillars, with numbers on their side. In the rear, you can see the sheep is numbered 11, and the other, in the front, is numbered 9. Part of the ad's dialogue is being born for something you were supposed to do. Could they have been referencing the predetermined presidency of Donald Trump? If you doubt it, consider Donald Trump's last words for the ad are, "Looking good number 9, looking good!" and the number 45 is the 9th triangular number and 2016 was a 9 year (2+0+1+6=9). As for the name Trump, it is the newer surname of the family that was named Drumpf just generations ago. What's funny about the newer name 'Trump', is that it relates to Tarot cards, where the terminology originates, "Trump card." With this in mind, please note that 'Tarot cards' equate to 119 with Simple English. And better yet, at the time Donald Trump was elected, there was a hit TV show about the White House and presidency titled *House of Cards*. In that show, the President was played by Kevin Spacey, who was accused of sexual assault, at the same time Donald Trump was accused of the same misconduct, and his character was named President Francis Underwood, and he won election in the year 2016 as well. With gematria this becomes more fascinating because 'Francis' sums to 119 with Reverse Simple English, the name of the Pope, and 'Underwood' sums to 119 with Simple English. If you want to test your skills, the show is full of gematria, and you'll understand why there is an assassination attempt on the president in Season 4, Episode 4, along with many other related things. In that breath, it is worth remembering, that despite Donald Trump being the 45th President in number, he is only the 44th person to be president because of Grover Cleveland, who had a split term, messing up the count ever since. If that's news to you, look it up. Grover Cleveland is counted as the 22nd and 24th U.S. President. And for one last point, the name 'Francis Underwood' sums to 243 with Reverse Simple English, similar to 'Central Intelligence Agency', and reminding us that at the time of the pandemic, a few years after Anthony Fauci said Donald Trump would face a surprise outbreak in his pandemic preparedness remarks, the United States of America was 243 years old. Of course, that also corresponds with the gematria of 'Crimson Contagion', the simulation that was in sync with coronavirus showing up in Seattle, Washington, in the United States of America.

Because we discussed the number 78 extensively in it, I want to educate about the 78th verse of the opening book of the *Bible*, *Genesis 3:22*, a number that should remind you of Yale's Skull and Bones, a secret society that identifies by the number 322. Using Simple English Gematria, '*Genesis*' sums to 78, and there is something extremely fascinating about this verse, the one about "knowing good and evil." It is the fact that the number 322 is encoded into *Genesis 3:22* using Reverse Pythagorean for both the *King James Version* (KJV) and the *New International Version* (NIV), despite different wording being used for each. Please read the encoded sections of *Genesis 3:22*, where the first word "And," through the last word "evil," equate to 322 for both.

Genesis 3:22 (NIV)

22 And the Lord God said, "The man has now become like one of us, knowing good and evil.

Genesis 3:22 (KJV)

22 And the Lord God said, Behold, the man is become as one of us, to know good and evil:

The number 322 gains greater significance when you decode 'Abrahamic Religions', summing to 322 with Reverse Simple English. If you are not familiar with the Abrahamic Religions, they are Judaism, Christianity and Islam, and all three religions are based out of the *Torah*, that begins with *Genesis*, the first book of the *Bible*. Keep in mind 'Abrahamic' alone sums to 187 with Reverse Simple, the same as 'Society of Jesus'. This becomes all the more interesting when you realize that the *Torah* is 187 chapters long. Furthermore, 'Ancient Mystery Religions' also sums to 322 with Reverse Simple, and those are the ancient spiritual knowledges that include Hermeticism, Kundalini, Alchemy and of course Kabbalah, that gematria is related to. And with that in mind, let us read the entirety of *Genesis 3:22*.

Genesis 3:22 (NIV)

22 And the Lord God said, "The man has now become like one of us, knowing good and evil. He must not be allowed to reach out his hand and take also from the tree of life and eat, and live forever."

After reading the verse, please notice the mention of the "tree of life". It is important to know that the physical model for Kabbalah is called the Tree of Life as well. This part of the *Bible* comes just after the serpent tricks Adam and Eve into eating from the tree that they were forbidden to eat from by the Lord God. It also comes the verse before being kicked out of the Garden of Eden by Lord God. With regards Kabbalah, there are two sides to the Tree of Life. One is about light and spiritual ascension, thus it is good, and the other is about understanding darkness, or what is evil. It is the evil side of the Tree of Life that The Cabal uses for their sorcery, and it is known as the Qliphoth. And if you can believe it, the word 'Qliphoth' has Reverse Sumerian Gematria of 666, the same as '*Genesis*', a number we still have much to learn about.

For another familiar number, the name 'Tree of Life' sums to 56 with Pythagorean, and the phrase from *Genesis 3:22*, 'Knowing good and evil', sums to 201 with Simple English. As we have learned, these are numbers corresponding with the 'Society of Jesus', summing to 56 in Pythagorean, and 'The Jesuit Order', summing to 201 in Reverse Simple English, who were founded by 'Ignatius of Loyola', summing to 201 with Simple English, the same as 'Jorge Mario Bergoglio', the birth name of Pope Francis, the first Jesuit Pope, and the first to live in Suite 201. Adding to the list, 'The Holy Bible' sums to 201 with Reverse Simple English and it is because of this one verse, in the 1,189 chapters of the *Bible*, that these numbers have been chosen. This is because it is the verse that explains what it is all about, knowing good and evil. Ultimately, that is the groundwork for all spiritual teachings, knowing what is good and what isn't, and how to behave accordingly. Unfortunately for us, The Cabal is going to make us choose between good and evil, to take the mark of the beast, 666, or not, as we'll get to in the chapter on the big tech takeover.

And as mad as it is, this is how the numbers are chosen and used in the gematria based rituals that become the foundational encoding of the propaganda that is broadcast in the mainstream, to program the masses. Case in point, the United States people began to be locked down by the governors of the nation in clumps on March 22, 2020, emphasis on 3/22, with New York leading the way. I'll remind you, that in the hit TV series *Batman*, in the 33rd episode, it is revealed that Batman's family legacy includes the creation of Skull and Bones, and New York is the city *Batman* is set in, only it is known as 'Gotham City', summing to 149, just like 'Skull and Bones'. While we're at it,

95

in the film *Enemy of the State,* also set in New York, when Will Smith's character checks his watch at 1 hour and 49 minutes into the film, it shows the time on the screen as none other than 3:22. If you haven't seen *Enemy of the State,* it's about the government's surveillance state that is used to keep tabs on the populace. It released just before 9/11, and was predictive programming for the PATRIOT Act, plus more. I highly suggest you watch it, for the sake of becoming aware of how we are teased with the truth in the world of Hollywood and mainstream media.

For another example of how the numbers encoded in the *Bible* become the numbers encoded in the fabric of the details that make up mainstream propaganda we are bombarded with, think of the coronavirus image you keep seeing being shown in the mainstream media, with the red triangles all over it. It was illustrated by two people, having name gematria values of 201 and 56. One was the lead illustrator, 'Alissa Eckert,' having a name summing to 201 and 84 in the same ciphers as 'The Jesuit Order', and the other was Dan Higgins, summing to 56 in Pythagorean, same as 'coronavirus' and 'Society of Jesus'. And to tie in the 78 piece, for the 78th verse of '*Genesis*', let us not forget Event 201, the coronavirus outbreak simulation, was hosted in 'New York', a state having gematria values of 78 and 666, the same as '*Genesis*'. Then for another, the virus was named 'Wuhan Coronavirus', summing to 78 with Pythagorean.

On the subject of 78, let us not forget the 78 cards of a Tarot deck, or that 22 of those cards are Trump cards, because at this moment, we are being trumped, as well as trounced, by The Cabal, in the time of their puppet Donald Trump. And strangely enough, the 22nd card in a Tarot Deck is The Fool, and all of these men turned 22 years old in 1968, the infamous year we dissected in chapter two. They were Bill Clinton, George W. Bush and Donald Trump, the latter of which is playing the "the fool" during the time of 'Wuhan' Coronavirus, where coronavirus was coined in 1968, and 'Wuhan' sums to 22 with Pythagorean Gematria, and 2020, the year of the outbreak, incorporates the same key digits. And on the subject of 22, please also recall, it is named the Master Builder number, and in Pythagorean Gematria, 'master' equates to 22, the same as 'Wuhan'. Furthermore, if you pair the Master Builder concept with the year '68, when Donald Trump was 22, and the fact that 'mathematics' has gematria of 68, as does 'Donald John Trump', you can begin to understand the riddle of his legacy, from the buildings in his name, TRUMP, to the virus he is said to be dropping the ball on, causing the United States to lead the world in supposed coronavirus deaths. And please keep in mind, Donald Trump is indebted to the international cabal, due to the numerous bailouts he has received in his business career, that have been given to him by this same group. And for all the "Q'Anon" types out there, please know that 'Q'Anon' sums to 201 with Jewish Gematria, and 74 with Reverse Simple, hallmarks of the Jesuits. Beyond that, it equates to 25 with Pythagorean, the same as 'Trump' and 'Vatican'. Furthermore, the Anon part of Q'Anon is short for Anonymous, an organization that takes its symbolism from Guy Fawkes, the Jesuit, who was part of the same society that was eventually saved with the 201 Jesuits who were protected by Catherine the Great. Thus if you have been taken by Q, you have been taken by "controlled opposition," and more specifically, the enemy, so I sincerely hope this book is opening your eyes to the truth of the matter.

For one last point on Crimson Contagion, and the Jesuit backed New York Times calling attention to the Chicago simulation, let us not forget that it took place in the time of the 56th Mayor of Chicago, 'Lori Lightfoot', a name equating to 68, the same as 'Barack Obama', the latter being the man who won the 56th U.S. Presidential election, in Chicago, and who like Lightfoot, has an August 4th birthday, emphasis on 8/4. *And never mind that Obama defeated John McCain in that election, the U.S. Senator from 'Arizona', the state equating to 84 and 42 in the same ciphers as 'Jesuit'. Furthermore, from the day Lori Lightfoot took office as Mayor of Chicago, May 20, 2019, to the day Crimson Contagion concluded, August 16, 2019, was her 89th day in office, corresponding with the gematria of both 'virus' and 'chaos'. Again, as we have covered earlier, Lightfoot requested $56 million to "contract trace" the people of her city, the same day 'chaos' was breaking out, in her city and elsewhere, due to the viral video showing the killing of George Floyd, on the corner of Chicago Avenue. That was May 26, 2020, a date with 71 numerology, corresponding with the gematria of 'Catholic', and a span of 71 days from her upcoming 58th birthday, or otherwise said, 70 days before her birthday, the latter number corresponding with 'Vatican' and 'Francis', as well as 'coronavirus', which again, sums to 56 and 70.

6 | Clade X Pandemic Exercise & the Pandemic 666 Days Later

The Clade X pandemic exercise being scheduled for May 15, 2018, precisely 666 days before the coronavirus pandemic was declared on March 11, 2020, was no accident. This was apparent even before H.R. 6666 was introduced on May 1, 2020, the anniversary of the establishment of the Bavarian Illuminati. As a reminder, H.R. 6666 was legislation designed to let us know that the U.S. Government was using coronavirus as an excuse to track all of us through our personal cellphone computers, something that should remind us of the fact that 'computer' and 'internet' equate to 666, and the U.S. federal government partnered with Google and Apple for the data collection operations, where the latter company sold their first personal computer to the U.S. market at the price of $666.66, and the other company, Google, is led by their CEO, 'Sundar Pichai', a name equating to 201 with Reverse Simple English. In light of what we learned last chapter, about *Genesis 3:22*, Kabbalah, the Tree of Life, the Qliphoth, 666 and 201, I want you to read what is posted below. It is from the start of the Clade X presentation, and it was the first slide shown to the attending audience. As you read it, please know that this simulation was put on by the same people who did Event 201, including 'The Johns Hopkins University', as alumni refer to the school, equating to 322 with Reverse Simple English, and also being a university founded by the Skull and Bones member, 'Daniel Coit Gilman', a man having a name equating to 95, reminding us that the Jesuits are fixated on 95, and the Bavarian Illuminati was founded by the Jesuit, Adam Weishaupt, who died November 18, 1830, the 322nd day of the year, and that Skull and Bones, the fraternity that identifies by the number 322, was established as an offshoot of the Bavarian Illuminati, also known as the 'Order of Illuminati', equating to 201.

Clade: klād/

A clade (from Ancient Greek: klādos, meaning "branch") is a group of organism that consists of a common ancestor and all its lineal descendants, representing a single "branch" on the tree of life.

There is much symbolism in that definition. You can begin with the mention of lineal descendants, not unlike The Cabal, that is based in bloodlines. This is something the mainstream media often reminds us of when they show how the ancestry of U.S. Presidents connect to each other, and to European royalty as well. For your gematria learning, and because the definition also brings up the tree of life, consider 'blood', 'tree' and 'evil' all share gematria of 48 using Simple English. At the same time, 'Illuminati' sums to 48 with Pythagorean, and 'Freemason' sums to 48 with Reverse Pythagorean. Perhaps you have heard of the book, *The 48 Laws of Power?* And it isn't to say that all blood, or all trees, or all Freemasons are evil, but it is to say that there is a bloodline that has determined to do evil for the sake of the good it brings them, as shortsighted as it is, turning the point of *Genesis 3:22* on its head. And it is for this reason that they must be exposed, for the betterment of humanity. After all, 'they' are the ones that made the word 'live' and 'evil' out of the same letters, showing the intentions they had for us. And with the thought of their intentions for humanity in mind, and remembering that the Gregorian calendar was coming into existence at the end of the 16th century, the same time English was being standardized with the letters and spellings we use today, perhaps then it is not a coincidence that the 16th card of the Tarot deck, is The Tower card? If you have not seen it before, it is illustrated with a lightening bolt setting the tower afire, and causing people to jump from its windows, reminiscent of September 11, 2001, and reminding that the story of the destruction of the Tower of Babel ends with *Genesis 11:9,* and that 'Tarot cards' sums to 119 with Simple English. Of course it was the destruction of the Twin Towers in New York, that catapulted the propaganda as George W. Bush once put it, that lead to the PATRIOT Act, the was the predecessor of the TRACE Act (H.R. 6666), the latter being the legal instrument granting the U.S. federal government the right to have surveillance over all of its people, at all times.

For the record, the oldest surviving set of Tarot Cards, known as the Visconti-Sforza deck, was created for the Duke of Milan's family, in Italy, around the year 1440. And isn't it funny the oldest remaining Tarot cards date back to Italy of all places, like the Catholic Church? In light of the estimated year of 1440, consider what they call the recording of time- history. This is similar to "his story," and the Jesuit logo has the letters IHS in it, a reshuffling of HIS. And in light of history being a recording of time, let us not forget that 'time' sums to 144 in Jewish Gematria and there are 1,440 minutes in a day, similar to how 'Jesuit Order' sums to 144 with Simple English. Let us also not forget that the calendar we keep track of time with was given to us by the Catholic Church, and it is synced with the life of Jesus, the son of God, not to be confused with the sun of God, despite the fact that the Catholic Church makes its followers worship on Sunday.

In light of Jesus, let us not overlook that in the definition of the word clade, given to the Clade X audience, it points out that the word has Greek origins, reminding us of the civilization that wrote the *New Testament* and the story of Jesus, including *Revelation 13:18*, about 666, the number of a man, the number of the beast. They were also the powerful empire that came before Rome, that practiced isopsephy, the Greek word for gematria. They were also the civilization that calculated the distance of the sun as 93 million miles, the number corresponding with the gematria of 'God's Son', 'Nazareth' and 'crucifix', each equating to 93 with Simple. This calculation was made during the 'Hellenistic Period', summing to 93 with Pythagorean. It was the period of time when Greece was falling, and Rome was coming into being. And keep in mind, Rome brought with it the practice of 'triclavianism', the crucifying of its criminals, with three nails, and a word having gematria of 93 and 201, reminding us that 'Roman' equates to 201 with Jewish Gematria.

Moving on, as mentioned, Clade X was hosted by 'The Johns Hopkins University', and Johns Hopkins was founded by Daniel Coit Gilman, a member of Yale's Skull and Bones, the 322 gang. With regards to Daniel Coit Gilman, his birthday is recorded as July 6, 1831, the same day of the year as George W. Bush, another member of Skull and Bones, who was born July 6, 1946. What makes July 6th significant, is that it is the 187th day of the year, connecting to 'Society of Jesus'. Even further, his name 'Daniel Coit Gilman' equates to 76, the same as 'Skull and Bones', a detail that reminds us of how prophecy is being contrived, and *Acts 7:6* is very much a part of the ritual. At the same time, it reminds us of how the calendar and language are connected, and that Skull and Bones is under the Jesuit umbrella, meaning that it serves the Church. To bring Skull and Bones even closer to the Catholic Church, their symbolism, the skull and crossbones, comes from how the Knights Templar, who served the Church, would bury their dead, in an ossuary. And to connect the name 'The Johns Hopkins University' to the Church, it sums to 353 with Simple English, the 71st prime, and 'Catholic' equates to 71 with Simple English. It reminds us that the CDC, who Johns Hopkins works closely with, has a July 1, 1946 date of establishment, or 7/1, and 'CDC' sums to 71 with Reverse Simple English. Never mind that 'Catholic' also sums to 46, corresponding with the year of establishment. Even more, the CDC is headquartered on the 84th Meridian West in Atlanta... Better yet, the director of the CDC, at the time of the "pandemic", is Robert Redfield, an alumni of Georgetown, the nation's oldest Jesuit University. And further still, the date he took the reigns, was March 26, 2018, the 65 year anniversary of the introduction of the polio vaccine, and a date that can be expressed as 26/3, like 263, the 56th prime number, corresponding with 'Society of Jesus'. And for the overkill, 'Robert', as well as 'Robert Redfield', both equate to 78 and 84, the same as 'Jesuit'.

Coming back to the date of the Clade X exercise, May 15th, as covered, it can be expressed as 15/5, similar to 155, connecting to the Simple English value of 'coronavirus'. May 15th is also the 135th day of the year in non leap years, connecting to the Reverse Pythagorean Gematria of 'Central Intelligence Agency', summing to 135, not unlike the Simple English value of 'Gina Cheri Haspel'. I bring up Gina Cheri Haspel, because she was being confirmed as the head of the CIA at the time of Clade X, and she was sworn in two days later, May 17, 2018, the 137th day of the year, the number connecting to 'Washington D.C.', 'government', and 'authority'. She was also born October 1, 1956, emphasis on '56, meaning the simulation came 32 weeks and 2 days after her birthday. Let us not forget the 11th director of the CIA, the Skull and Bones member, 322, George H.W. Bush.

If you take the time to watch the 26 minute highlight reel of Clade X, you'll be astonished by what the simulation projects. To give you a quick synopsis, a terrorist organization that operates in the U.K. and Switzerland, that goes by the name 'ABD', summing to 74 with Reverse Simple English, unleashes a virus on the world for the sake of depopulation, with a goal of reducing the earth's human population to what it was in the preindustrial age, something like the plot of the movie *Inferno*. If you haven't seen the film, it is about a billionaire who wants to depopulate the world with a virus, and it happened to release on Bill Gates 61st birthday, October 28, 2016, a date with 74 numerology, as well as 54. The film even runs 2 hours and 1 minute in length, thus appearing as 2:01 in length on any DVD or Blu-Ray player, corresponding with the Simple English Gematria of 'William Henry Gates', summing to 201 in Simple English. Again, his

101

organization was one of the main sponsors of Event 201, that took place October 18, 2019, the day leaving 74 days left in the year. Of course, Bill Gates is also the billionaire who at his 2010 TED Talk, stated we needed to reduce the world's population by 15%, and stated further, the goal can be achieved if we do a "good job with vaccines". I bring this up, because in the Clade X simulation, as many as 900 million people die worldwide, what is said to be 12% of the world's population.

If you compare this loss of life to what is projected on the Georgia Guidestones, it's minimal. Those massive stone monuments call for reducing the world's population to 500 million, what the earth's population was prior to the industrial age. And to put it in perspective, more than 13 out of 14 living people would have to die for the mark to be achieved based on the statistic that more than 7 billion people are currently living on earth. If you're not familiar with the Georgia Guidestones, I encourage you to research them. You'll find that they were placed where they are in Elberton, Georgia, March 22, 1980. That date can be expressed as 3/22, not unlike 322, or 22/3, not unlike 223. For your learning, 'masonic' sums to 223 with Jewish Gematria, and at the same time, 'novel coronavirus' sums to 223 with Simple English. Let us not forget, March 22nd was the date when Gotham City (New York) and much of the United States was told to stay at home by their government and mainstream media. March 22nd is also a date of killing in the film and television series *The Purge*, that we'll discuss in the chapter on predictive programming.

Regarding the masonic connection, in the simulation, the terrorist organization 'ABD', summing to 74, like 'masonic', is named A Brighter Dawn. This isn't too far off from the Hermetic Order of the Golden Dawn, founded in the 19th century by British Freemasons William Robert Woodman, William Wynn Westcott, and Samuel Liddell Mathers (just wait until we get to Marshall Mathers). For another parallel, the name 'A Brighter Dawn' has gematria of 221, the same as 'The Bavarian Illuminati'. The name 'A Brighter Dawn' also sums to 67, the 19th prime, the number of 'chaos', and the number concluding the name Covid-19. At the same time, 'Wuhan' sums to 67 with Simple English and the Event 201 simulation took place on a date with 67 numerology. And for one more, the name of the organization sums to 77, in the same cipher as 'secret society'. This corresponds with 'Zurich', also equating to 77, and in the simulation, the organization's lab is raided in 'Zurich, Switzerland', summing to 223 with Reverse Simple English, syncing with 'novel coronavirus'.

In the Clade X simulation, the virus causes world markets to crumble, with the DowJones falling 90%. This leads to protests, along with rioting, largely due to the imposed mandatory two week quarantine of all people by world governments. In turn, these acts of civil disobedience are met with "violent police crackdowns" in the language of the simulation, that tire out as the population is devastated by the virus. In addition to massive deaths, especially in poor communities, there is massive unemployment and hunger, leading to, as the simulation puts it, a "mass exodus" of people from major cities. This is biblical language. These events lead to vaccines without any clinical trials being rushed to the market. They fail. In the U.S., the President is no longer in command, and neither is the Vice President. Instead, it is the Speaker of the House, who oversees the government body that has lost a third of its members to death, similar to how the Supreme Court is operating with 7 justices instead of 9 due to fatal infections. Per the simulation, the world as we knew it is no longer, with essential services collapsing, including the medical industry, meaning insurance and hospitals. And in the end, the nation's healthcare is nationalized, but the world will never recover to where it was prior to the outbreak. And with regards to the end, what is finally developed in the simulation, after two years of effort, is the Omega Vaccine. Of course, Omega is the final letter of the Greek alphabet, thus fitting for bringing an end to the virus, and especially in a simulation titled Clade X, where clade is a Greek word. Likely not by chance, 'Omega' has gematria of 22 and 23, same as 'Wuhan'. And further, the word 'Omega' sums to 94, not unlike 'coronavirus pandemic', or 'Roman Catholic Church', and reminding yet again, that Bill Gates launched his decade of vaccines on his 94th day of his age, January 29, 2020, in 'Davos, Switzerland', equating to 94, the same as his hometown, 'Seattle, Washington', where the virus entered the U.S.

For another thought about Omega, it is the 24th letter of the Greek alphabet. And in light of the Georgia Guidestones calling for the world's population to be reduced to preindustrial levels, the same call made by the terrorists in the Clade X exercise, there is something important about the year 2024, emphasis on '24. It is that the Georgia

Guidestones will turn 44 years old on March 22nd of that year. The state 'Georgia', as well as the word 'genocide' equate to 44 with Pythagorean Gematria. At the same time, 'kill' and 'clock' sum to 44 with Simple English. Adding to the riddle, the stone monuments stand 19'3" tall, not unlike 193, the 44th prime number. And then there is *Acts*, the 44th book of the *Bible*. To go further, Georgia is the 4th state in order of statehood, and the number four is associated with death. This belief comes from Mandarin Chinese and Japanese, where the word for four is pronounced the same as the word for death.

If you take the time to watch both the Clade X and Event 201 simulations, you'll see that the same woman is used as the main narrator, playing the part of a nightly news anchor, for a fictional network, GNN. What's odd about this, is GNN is the fictional news network in the *Left Behind Series*, about the apocalypse and rapture. Also odd, is that the chosen name for her character is Jeanne Meserve. The name 'Jeanne Meserve' sums to 55 with Pythagorean Gematria, similar to how 'satan' sums to 55 with Simple English, and the first rule of satanism, is to worship yourself, or serve yourself. Meserve? Rest assured, this detail in the simulation coming 666 days before the planned pandemic was a tribute to The Cabal's master. For the coincidence theorist who might be doubting that this is the case, the name 'Jeanne Meserve' also sums to 136, not unlike 'baphomet', the latter being a symbol of the Church of Satan, and a symbol the Knights Templar were accused of worshipping. Of course, the Knights Templar once fled to Switzerland, where the terrorist organization 'ABD' is raided in the Clade X simulation. And as a reminder, Switzerland is also the home of the United Nations, World Economic Forum, World Health Organization, and CERN, the latter of which carefully encodes 666 in their logo. In their case, it is only fitting, because they gave us the internet as we know it, and 'internet' sums to 666, the same as 'computer'.

Regarding the gematria of 'Clade X', there is much that stands out. With Simple English Gematria, it sums to 49, a number corresponding with 'Washington', where the first case was confirmed outside of mainland China, and also *Revelation*, the book of the *Bible* that made the number 666 infamous. With Pythagorean Gematria, 'Clade X' sums to 22, the same as 'Wuhan', the master builder number, reminding that there are 22 chapters in *Revelation*.

The name 'Clade X' also sums to 113 with Reverse Simple English, and this is paramount because the pandemic was declared by the World Health Organization on March 11, 2020, a date that can be expressed as 11/3. Keep in mind the main sponsor of the event, 'Johns Hopkins University', has a name equating to 113 with Pythagorean Gematria. At the same time, 'apocalypse' sums to 113 with Simple English, and that is an alternate word for *Revelation*. For another thought, 'Scottish' sums to 113 with Simple English, and Washington D.C., where Clade X was hosted, is home of the Scottish Rite Freemasons, who have a headquarters their, the House of the Temple. And for the most important 113 of all, 'coronavirus pandemic' sums to 113 with Reverse Pythagorean. Also noteworthy, 'Clade X' sums to 32, not unlike 'America', or 'Scottish', and reminding us of the 32 sun rays on the Jesuit logo, an organization that shares a motto with the 32nd degree of the Scottish Rite, as we have learned.

To close, it is important to point out that in the Clade X simulation the virus begins in Caracas, Venezuela. This matters because in the Event 201 simulation, the virus begins in South America as well, but Brazil instead. These details are paying tribute to the fact that the Agenda 21 conference took place in Brazil, on April 23, 1992, where April 23 is the 113th day of the year in non leap years. Furthermore, later that same year, on June 3, 1992, the 155th day of the year, the United Nations conference began where the goals of Agenda 21 were agreed to. As we'll learn, the goals of that conference coincide with what is being achieved by the world elite in the time of the coronavirus pandemic, and those goals were set to be achieved by the start of the year 2021. Also ahead, we'll learn more about the World Economic Forum's planned event for January of 2021, 'The Great Reset', announced June 3, 2020, having gematria of 151, just like 'pandemic', and just like 'Sustainable Development Goals', from Agenda 21. And let us not forget that 'Jesuit' sums to 21 with Pythagorean Gematria, or 'Saturn', the keeper of time, also equating to 93, the same as 'Wuhan Coronavirus'. Let us also not forget that the World Economic Forum was the main sponsor of Event 201. And finally, I would be amiss to not let you know that 'Brazil' sums to 68 with Simple English, reminding us of all the planning and plotting that took place in 1968, the infamous year we covered in chapter two. It ties together perfectly with the fact that 'Wuhan' sums to 68 with Reverse Simple English, and coronavirus was coined in '68.

7 | Operation Dark Winter & the "Darkest Winter" Warning

Operation Dark Winter was another simulation carried out by Johns Hopkins. It took place on the dates of June 22-23, 2001. The concluding date was fitting, written 23/6, because 'Operation Dark Winter' sums to 236 with Simple English Gematria. Strangely enough, the concluding date was also the six year anniversary of the death of Jonas Salk, who we will learn more about in the eleventh chapter. The purpose of the simulation was to prepare for how to deal with a bio-terrorist attack, where the terrorist organization's weapon of choice was anthrax. As you might recall, that is precisely what happened later in 2001, when numerous media outlets, as well as U.S. Senators Tom Daschle and Patrick Leahy, reported receiving letters containing anthrax poison, where the postmarks for the first letters containing anthrax were dated September 18, 2001, the date in history that the cornerstone for Washington D.C. was laid, and the date the New York Times was founded, who also happened to be one of the media networks that reportedly received a letter. This date is curious, because September 18th was precisely 87 days after the Operation Dark Winter simulation had ended, and 'anthrax poisoning' sums to 87 with Pythagorean Gematria. The second set of letters were mailed October 9th, or 10/9, 109 days after the first day of the simulation, or a span of 109 days from the second. This is also curious because 'military' sums to 109 with Reverse Simple English, and in the end, the federal government said that the anthrax was military grade, and had likely been obtained from a U.S. military facility. The prime suspect, per the feds, was Bruce Edwards Ivins, who eventually committed suicide on July 29, 2008, a date with 44 and 64 numerology, and also being the day leaving 155 days in the year. For your learning, please know 'kill' sums to 44 with Simple English, and 64 with Reverse Simple English. And please know, when these 44 and 64 dates roll around, suspicious deaths happen, something I have educated about in my first book, and something we will talk about later with the deaths of C.T. Vivian and John Lewis, both on July 17, 2020, a date with 44 and 64 numerology.

As for the gematria of the name 'Bruce Edwards Ivins', it equates to 263, the 56th prime, as well as 79. As a reminder, 'Society of Jesus' equates to 56 and 79. Also important, since the anthrax attacks followed the events of September 11, 2001, let us not forget that the three planes that impacted structures on that date, Flights 11, 77 and 175, when added together, equate to 263. While we're at it, the

106

name 'Bruce Edwards Ivins' also sums to 110, reminding us of how tall the WTCs were in New York, and the connection the number has to 'prophecy', or should I say contrived prophecy? And for one more point, 'anthrax poisoning' sums to 84 in the same cipher as 'The Jesuit Order'. It is fitting, because the Jesuits are known for poisoning their enemies throughout history.

In light of The Johns Hopkins University being founded by a Skull and Bones member, the same university that was responsible for the anthrax attack simulation, it is worth pointing out that the first letters were mailed from 'Trenton, New Jersey', summing to 202 with Reverse Simple English. In the same cipher, 'Skull and Bones' equates to 202. And keep in mind the 202nd minute of each day is expressed as 3:22. similar to 322. Furthermore, in 2020, Connecticut basketball star 'Stanley Robinson', equating to 202, was found dead on the 202nd day of the year, July 21st, and Skull and Bones is from Connecticut, located at Yale. And in light of the attack coming one week after September 11, 2001, where the number 77 was very well encoded into the ritual of Flight 77, hitting the 77 foot tall Pentagon, on the 77th Meridian West, 77 minutes after taking off- 'Trenton, New Jersey' also sums to 77 with Pythagorean Gematria, the same as 'September Eleventh' and 'World Trade Center'.

Because of these anthrax mailings, it was reported that 5 people were killed and 17 more were injured, impacting 22 people in total, the master builder number. In addition to that, the attacks coming on the back of September 11th had most of the United States, and much of the world, in a state of complete fear. If you were watching the nightly news at that time, they had you believing nowhere was safe. We were told by the same media to be on the lookout for terrorists, possibly packing suitcase bombs, and to use extreme caution when opening our mail. That said, even then, people weren't barricading themselves in their homes, as many have done in the time of the coronavirus scare.

That brings us to the testimony of Rick Arthur Bright, on May 14, 2020, Israel's 72nd birthday, who told the people of the United States to prepare for the "darkest winter in modern history" because of the coronavirus pandemic, and if significant action wasn't taken to curb the spread of the virus before then, there would be unprecedented deaths. Bright? Dark? Symbolism? It is wise to consider that the term "corona" relates to the faint edge of light shown around the sun in the time of a solar eclipse. It is also wise to note that the Jesuit logo pays tribute to the sun's corona. And with the Society of Jesus in mind, the phrase 'darkest winter in modern history', that was emphasized in nearly all mainstream news headlines after Bright's testimony, sums to 373 with Simple English, the 74th prime number. As you know, 'Jesus' sums to 74 with Simple English, along with 'cross', 'Messiah', *'Gospel'* and 'parables', and Jesus' birthday is celebrated in winter, at the end of the Gregorian Calendar year. Adding to the ritual and identifying who is responsible is that the full name of the speaker, 'Rick Arthur Bright', equates to 191 with Simple English, the exact same as 'Society of Jesus' and 'Winter Solstice'.

As for the timing of his remarks, they were actually brought to mainstream attention on May 13, 2020, when the nightly news announced that Rick Bright, the ousted director of BARDA, or the Biomedical Advanced Research Development and Authority, an office charged with developing medical countermeasures, would testify before the U.S. Congress and explain why the United States of America could expect the "darkest winter". The news hype came precisely 222 days before the Winter Solstice, December 21, 2020, corresponding with the 222 value of 'Wuhan Coronavirus'. You could also say it came a span of 223 days from the solstice, corresponding with the gematria of 'novel coronavirus', where both names are routinely used by the mainstream media. That means his testimony was 221 days before the solstice, or a span of 222 days, the latter being code for 'order out of chaos', and the former being code for 'The Bavarian Illuminati'.

To close, an important point that Rick Bright made, is the United States of America needs a federal coordinated effort to help decrease the spread of the virus across the entire nation, and if that is not done, then there will be dire consequences. In other words, it is a push for greater federalization, a concept that brings we the people closer to the idea of one government, that will bring us one step away from the New World Order, a one world order, being achieved. This subject matter is what the U.S. Civil War was much about, and we the people are being driven down a similar road at this moment in history, something that is plain as day to see, and something that is a topic we will explore further when we get to the chapter on the killing of 'George Perry Floyd', a man having a name equating to 102 with Pythagorean Gematria, reminding us that the Civil War began April 12, 1861, the 102nd day of the Gregorian year.

8 | Donald Trump's Vaccine Plan, Operation Warp Speed

Before we get to Donald Trump's vaccine plan, Operation Warp Speed, let's refresh our memories of the ritual he participated in on the date of January 21, 2020, at the World Economic Forum, in Switzerland. On that date, he gloated at the headquarters of the main sponsor of Event 201, about his recent trade deal with China, while at the same time, on the same date, the first case of coronavirus was being confirmed in the United States, from Wuhan, China. And as a reminder, it was being confirmed in Seattle, Washington, the home of the Bill and Melinda Gates Foundation, one of the major sponsors of Event 201. And as discussed, the odds of Trump's ritual being a coincidence dramatically decrease when you realize the Donald was at the 'World Economic Forum' on his 222nd day of his age, and 'World Economic Forum' sums to 222, the same as 'Wuhan Coronavirus' and 'order out of chaos', reminding us that the coronavirus pandemic was declared exactly 222 months after September 11, 2001, in 'New York, New York', summing to 222, where Event 201 was hosted, and further, when you write out 'Event Two Zero One' it also sums to 222.

Thus, having well established that The Cabal and those it puppeteers, including Donald Trump, are practitioners of the code, it will be in this lens that we examine his proposed plan for administering vaccines via the U.S. military. We'll begin with the date of his Operation Warp Speed proposal, May 15th, written 15/5, like 155, connecting to 'coronavirus', as well as it being the two year anniversary of Clade X. In light of the connection to 666 and Clade X, I should note that 'vaccination' equates to 666 with Sumerian Gematria. I should also mention, the plural, 'Freemasons', sums to both 155 and 56, the same as 'coronavirus', and the U.S. capital is named after a Freemason. Of course, it is named 'Washington D.C.', summing to 56, the same as 'Society of Jesus' and 'Anthony Fauci', linking with the fact that Donald Trump attended the Jesuit school, Fordham, in New York, in 1964, 56 years before 2020. I bring all this up now because Donald Trump became very popular with television audiences before becoming President during the time of the game show he starred in, 'The Apprentice'. Of course, The Apprentice is the name of the first degree earned after joining Freemasonry, and modern Freemasonry falls under the umbrella of the Jesuits. And in that breath, please remember that 'Freemasonry' equates to 58 with Pythagorean Gematria, and Donald Trump announced he was running for the 58th U.S. Presidential Election from his 58 story Trump Tower, before hiring the 58-year-old Steve Ray for Inauguration Day- causing Hillary Clinton to write the book 'What Happened' about why she lost to Donald Trump, a title also summing to 58 in Pythagorean Gematria.

As we have learned, both the Jesuits and the Freemasons celebrate the motto "order out of chaos". And with the Jesuits in mind, the name 'Operation Warp Speed' sums to 266 with Reverse Simple, the same as how the Society of Jesus motto, "Iesus Hominum Salvator" sums to 266, and similar to how Donald Trump made Mike Pence the coronavirus czar on February 27, 2020, the 58th day of the year, and Mike Pence's 266th day of his age, being a man with a June 7, 1959 birthday. On the subject of Mike Pence, I should note that his full name, 'Michael Richard Pence' sums to 155 with Simple English, the same as 'coronavirus', and similar to the date May 15th, or 15/5. As for the Jesuit motto, 'Iesus Hominum Salvator', please recall that is also sums to 122, connecting perfectly with 'Pope Francis', a name summing to 122, and him being the 266th Pope, the first to be a member of the Society of Jesus. Furthermore, connecting the name to the Jesuits even more clearly, 'Operation Warp Speed' sums to 95 with Reverse Pythagorean. As we have learned, the Jesuits were formed September 27th, the day leaving 95 days in the year, to counter the 95 *Theses* authored by Martin Luther, reminding of MLK's demise on the 95th day of 1968. And even more related to the subject at hand, let us not forget the Jesuit, Anthony 'Fauci', having a surname summing to 95, and being a man born December 24, 1940, a date with 95 numerology. Of course he was standing over Trump's shoulder on the day of the May 15th announcement, emphasis on 15/5, as he so often has been during the time of the "pandemic".

To go even further, and to show that each of the base ciphers are relevant to this name, 'Operation Warp Speed' and 'Coronavirus pandemic' both equate to 220 and 94 using Simple English and Pythagorean, where the number 94 connects to 'Roman Catholic Church'. As for the name 'Warp Speed' alone, it equates with 'military' in the same two ciphers, summing to 107 and 44. This only makes perfect sense, because as Donald Trump explained, this would be a military operation, with the nation's forces being used to administer the vaccine to the populace as quickly as possible, once it was ready, and even warned that the vaccine could come from China. To bring more relevance to the military and 44, at the time of finishing this book, the official narrative for the first confirmed case of coronavirus in the world, traces to the date November 17, 2019, in Wuhan, China, the day leaving 44 days left in the year (and a date having 67 numerology). When you consider Clade X and Event 201 were categorized as war game simulations with a virus, and you don't neglect that the Military World Games, that originated in Rome in '95, were beginning the date of Event 201- the role of military becomes all the more clear in these agendas that are taking hold. Let us not forget, on September 11, 2001, part of the Pentagon's excuse for why the military did not respond more quickly to stop the terrorists from flying planes into their targets, was because of the war game simulations that were taking place at the same time, causing much confusion and providing the perfect window for the attack that we now collectively remember as 9/11, a swell date for a national emergency. You might also recall that September 11, 2001 was 44 days after the 'Ninth of Av', summing to 44, the Jewish annual holiday to remember the destruction of the Two Temples, the second of which was destroyed in 70 CE, by the Romans, reminding us that 'Vatican' equates to 70.

Another pertinent point is that Donald Trump's Operation Warp Speed was announced May 15, 2020, 30 days before his 74th birthday on June 14th. This distance of 30 days matters because 'vaccine' sums to 30 with Pythagorean Gematria, the same as 'corona', and Trump's big statement from the speech was that he believed science could have a vaccine for coronavirus by the end of 2020. This pairs well with the fact that the pandemic was declared March 11th, much like 11/3, and similar to 113, the 30th prime number. Let us not forget that 'coronavirus pandemic' also sums to 113, same as 'Clade X', and in that simulation, as well as Event 201, the top objective was to develop a vaccine, and administer it to the populace, by whatever means necessary, even by cutting corners such as no trial vaccines, something that is considered very dangerous by the medical world.

Not by chance, 19 days after Trump's May 15th remarks, the 'Global Vaccine Summit', summing to 201 with Simple English, was hosted in London, England. It was reported that the event raised "at least $7.4 billion, corresponding with the Simple English Gematria of 'London', and reminding that Event 201 was October 18, 2019, the day leaving 74 days in the year. Furthermore, the Global Vaccine Summit began June 3rd, the 155th day of 2020, corresponding with the Simple English value of 'coronavirus', 155, and pairing with the date of Trump's big vaccine goals, May 15th, or 15/5. Even further, it ended on June 4th, a date that can be written as 4/6, not unlike 46, representing 'ordo ab chao', as well as 'chaos' and 'virus'.

One thing I am currently wondering about, that seems unrelated at first, is if it is a coincidence that on June 14, 2020, Donald Trump's 74th birthday, it also happened to be the concluding day of the PGA's 74th Charles Schwab Challenge, that was won by a 'Jewish' golfer, Daniel Berger, born April 7th, or 7/4 (the same date Trump's tower burned in 2018). Consider, this was the first PGA event after the break in their season caused by coronavirus, and Charles Schwab is an investment firm for the financial markets. This matters because Daniel Berger won the tournament 68 days after his birthday, and 'market' as well as 'golf' equate to 68, same with 'Donald John Trump', 'The Apprentice', and 'Mar-a-Lago', the latter being Trump's favorite golf resort. Adding insult to injury, it was reported that Trump returned to playing golf on May 23, 2020, a date with 68 numerology, after being advised to stop on March 8th, the 68th day of the year, of course, due to coronavirus, coined in 1968 (In light of the date 5/23, 'Donald Trump' equates to 523 using Satanic Gematria). As you'll learn in due time, the world of scripted sports and the world of scripted news go hand in hand, including the scripted events of world leaders, and perhaps through this story, The Cabal was hinting at who might have a big hand, in a big ritual, that involved international markets, where The Cabal was literally stealing the wealth of the people of the world, for the benefit of the very top earners, such as the Jeff Bezos types. Case in point, on July 22, 2020 it was reported that Beezos had made more than $13 billion in the last 24 hours due to surging Amazon stock prices, and his wealth had climbed past Nike, McDonald's, and Costco, to nearly worth as much as 50% of the DowJones. Never mind that was his 193rd day of his age, 56, and 'Roman Catholic Church' equates to 193 with Simple English, and 193 is the 44th prime number, corresponding with the gematria of 'Seattle', equating to 44, the city sitting on what could be the Cabal's favorite parallel, the 47th, corresponding with the gematria of the 'Vatican', equating to 47, that was established on 2/11, like 211, the 47th prime number.

If that wasn't enough, on that same date, Trump's 74th birthday, June 14, 2020, Israel, a 'Jewish' nation, named a section of the Golan Heights 'Trump Heights', equating to 74, after Donald Trump. As we know, Donald Trump likes golf, and more importantly than that, he likes Israel, having visited their on Jerusalem Day, before dashing off directly to the Vatican, to pose with Pope Francis on May 24, 2017, the 144th day of the year. What is concerning about this is mainstream Israeli publications such as Haaretz, Times of Israel, and Jewish Standard are discussing Donald Trump as the possible Jewish 'Messiah', where both 'Jewish' and 'Messiah' equate to 74. This becomes all the more disturbing when you realize that there is a shekel being sold in Israel with Donald Trump's head on one side, and the Third Temple on the other. Furthermore, the proceeds of this coin are going to be used to build the Third Temple, that will be built at the time of the Jewish Messiah, per prophecy. And what adds to the concern, is the fact that Israeli and U.S. media brought attention to the coming Trump Heights territory on September 16, 2019, the day leaving 106 days left in the year, the number corresponding with the Simple English value of 'prophecy', equating to 106. That was precisely a span of 39 weeks from the funding being approved for the development on Trump's birthday, and there are 39 books in the *Old Testament*, the Jewish section of the *Bible*. It was also a date with 44 and 64 numerology, connecting to the gematria of 'Israel' and 'Zion', both equating to 44 and 64, and reminding that there were 44 kings of ancient Israel, and Donald Trump is the 44th person to be President of the United States, despite being number 45.

With regards to number 45, *'Holy Bible'* sums to 45 with Pythagorean and Reverse Pythagorean Gematria, and in the holy text, the warnings of *Revelation* are through the sounds of trumpets, not too far off from the Trump-Pence presidency. If you'd care to add to your 45 list, 'Mike Pence' sums to 45 with both Pythagorean and Reverse Pythagorean as well, the same as *'Gutenberg'*, the name of the first published *Bible* in the world. And going beyond gematria, the year the King James Bible was published, 1611, King James turned 45 years old, having been born June 19, 1566. Thus, there can be no doubt that the riddles we are facing in the time of the Donald Trump presidency, are absolutely biblical, and relating to *Revelation*. This is something we will take apart further ahead when we dissect the meaning of the first case of coronavirus being confirmed outside of China, in the United States, January 21st, or 1/21, like 121, while Trump was gloating about financial wealth at the World Economic Forum, instead of human decency. As you'll learn, there is a great significance to *'Revelation'* and 'coronavirus outbreak' equating to 121, the same as the big players at Event 201, the 'Bill and Melinda Gates Foundation', 'Johns Hopkins University' and 'World Health Organization', each equating to 121 as well, in light of what the agenda is ultimately about. You'll also realize it was no accident SiriusXM made channel 121 the coronavirus pandemic channel on March 6, 2020, the 66th day of the year, reminding us *Revelation* is the 66th book of the text, and even more, March 6, 2020 was a date with 49 numerology, corresponding with the Pythagorean Gematria of '*Revelation*', as well as 'Washington' and 'America'. And even further, that the date can be expressed as 3/6, similar to 36, where 666 is the 36th triangular number, and 666 is the number of the beast, that will either have to be taken or denied by the person who chooses in *Revelation,* in the time of the Great Tribulation. As a reminder, that choice is- do they want to be able to buy or sell? Of course, per the *Bible,* 666 is taken on the forehead or the right hand, and many people are having their foreheads scanned at this very moment to see if they're healthy enough to enter stores and clinics, so that they can buy or sell. If you ask me, it is clear symbolism.

On the subject of the Trump-Pence presidency and trumpets, please recall what transpired when an earthquake struck Salt Lake City, Utah, March 18, 2020, knocking the trumpet out of the Angel Moroni's hands at the town's iconic Mormon temple. What made this event extremely fascinating, is that where 'Moroni' sums to 78 with Reverse Simple, 'Salt Lake City' sums to 78 with Reverse Pythagorean, and March 18th was the 78th day of the leap year. As you know, this numbers connects to the gematria of 'Jesuit' and 'Scottish Rite', each equating to 78, and the founder of the Mormon faith was Joseph Smith, a Scottish Rite Freemason, who was killed on June 27, 1844, emphasis on '44, and on the day leaving 187 days left in the year- and a date with 95 numerology. At the same time, the March 18th earthquake was 88 days before Donald Trump's 74th birthday, and where 'Mormon' sums to 88 and 74, 'Trump' sums to 88 and 47. Furthermore, the Mormon's quietly opened a temple next to the Vatican on January 15, 2019, 61 weeks and 1 day before this earthquake, which also fell on a date with 61 numerology, corresponding with the gematria of 'Jesus', 'church', and 'Christian', as well as 'God' with Jewish Gematria. *Ahead, we'll talk about military technology and earthquakes. And if that topic frightens you, help me do something before they're administering our vaccines too…

9 | H.R. 6666, Contact Tracing, ID2020 & the Big Tech Takeover

In light of the TRACE Act being H.R. 6666, it should be noted that the word 'TRACE' has gematria overlap with 'beast' in three out of the four base ciphers, equating to 34, 47 and 88. At the same time, 'TRACE' equates to 20 with Pythagorean, and it is going into effect in 2020. Of course, 666 is the number of the beast, as written about in *Revelation 13:18*. Adding to the riddle, the TRACE Act stands for 'Testing, Reaching And Contacting Everyone Act'. The full name sums to 183 with Pythagorean, and 222 with Reverse Pythagorean, similar to how 'order out of chaos' sums to 183 with Simple English, and 222 with Reverse Simple English. Furthermore, the acronym 'TRACE' sums to 222 with Satanic Gematria, the cipher you learned about at the end of chapter four, where if you write out the cipher name, 'Satanic Gematria', it sums to 666 using the method.

Cementing the fact that this legislation is evidence of the order out of chaos agenda, and paying tribute to the significance of 666, is that it was introduced on May 1, 2020, a date with 46 numerology, corresponding with the gematria of 'chaos', 'ordo ab chao' 'virus', and 'Chicago', the latter being the hometown of the man who introduced H.R. 6666, a man who was also born in 1946, who we will discuss ahead, and who was perfect for introducing the bill having four sixes in the title. Keep in mind, 'Illinois' equates to 54, the same as 'Mark of the Beast', and 'Jesuit Order'. If you want to go even further, 'May' is one of two months equating to 42, the other being 'February', and the 'beast' rules for 42 months in *Revelation*, reminding that 'Washington' state, where the first case of coronavirus was confirmed in the U.S., is the 42nd state in order of statehood, and 'Washington' has gematria overlap with '*Revelation*' and 'America', as well as 'Scottish', as in the Jesuit's Freemason buddies. And most important of all, May 1st is the 121st day of the Gregorian year, corresponding with the Simple English Gematria of '*Revelation*', and reminding that coronavirus was confirmed in the United States on January 21st, or 1/21, like 121.

The goal of the TRACE program, not surprisingly, is to trace everyone through their cellphones for the purpose of contacting everyone who might cross paths with the infected, as an extra precaution to help stop the spread of the virus. The new medical term for this is "contact tracing." And as you know, it is only made possible because of the 'computer' and the 'internet', both words having gematria values of 666, as well as 42. And as you can imagine, it will only be a matter of time before big brother is telling us the added benefits of the TRACE Act, and why it should be here to stay, even after the time of coronavirus. All they will have to say is, "it could stop the next pandemic." And sadly, very few will ask the necessary question, "But what about my privacy?" Of course, the average person in 2020 thinks along the lines of, "Well, if I stay out of trouble, I won't have to worry about any problems with the government." And more and more are thinking in terms of, "I hope some government creep isn't checking out my nudes." But what they're not thinking is, "How am I ever going to be able to help my people organize to take a stand against tyranny, if the watchful eyes and listening ears of the tyrants are always on me, for the exact purpose of sniffing out the type of dissent I intend?" Those not considering the latter question need to ask themselves where society is being directed, and is it good? Better yet, should there be a stand? While they're at it, they need to go back and read George Orwell's *1984* for some perspective.

As for the man who introduced H.R. 6666, his name was written 'Bobby L. Rush' on the bill, summing to 56 in Reverse Pythagorean, similar to the 56 value of 'coronavirus' and 'Washington D.C.'. Furthermore, from his 73rd birthday, November 23, 2019, to the day he introduced the bill, May 1, 2020, was 5 months and 8 days later, similar to the Pythagorean Gematria value of 'contact tracing', summing to 58, and reminding us that the U.S. military's technology branch is DARPA, established in 1958, the same year as NASA, in part because 'science' sums to 58 with Simple English. Also, don't overlook that Bobby L. Rush was in his 74th year of his life when this happened, or that he first ran for office in 1974, because it ties in with how he once founded the 'Black Panther Party' branch in Illinois, an organization summing to 74 with Pythagorean Gematria- and a party that was created by 'Huey P. Newton', a name summing to 58 with Pythagorean as well. Recall what we learned about Cam Newton, of the Carolina "Black" Panthers, signing on Bill Belichick's 74th day of his age, June 28, 2020. And if any coincidence theorists are still reading, you must not have been following four months before Super Bowl 50 was played, when I explained why the Denver Broncos would beat the Carolina Panthers in the Bay Area in Super Bowl 50, where the Black Panthers were founded, the latter team being one with a black panther on their helmet, making Cam Newton, emphasis on

116

Newton, the QB of the Carolina "Black" Panthers at the time, the 58th quarterback to start in a Super Bowl. Sure as the sun, it happened, and Beyonce even dressed up as a Black Panther for the halftime show. And not to gloat too much, but I also spelled out why number 58, Von Miller of the Denver Broncos would be the MVP of the game, drafted one pick after Cam Newton in 2011, and sure as the sun, he was. For one more, Super Bowl 50 was the "golden" anniversary of the NFL's signature game, hosted by the 49ers, named after the 1849 California Gold Rush, and it was held on February 7, 2016, the 38th day of the year, corresponding with the Simple English value of 'gold', equating to 38, not unlike Gerald Ford, the 38th President of the United States, who allowed Americans to once again purchase and own gold, overturning FDR's 1933 orders that took the right to purchase gold away. Ford's orders went into effect on December 31, 1974, the same year 'Richard Nixon', summing to 74 in Pythagorean, resigned. And keep in mind Denver is from the 38th state in order of statehood, and 'Colorado' sums to 38 with Pythagorean, same as 'Panthers', the latter team who lost in Super Bowl 38 to the New England Patriots, thus a fateful number for them. Another way the fatefulness of this number is evident, is with the death of Tupac Shakur, the son of a Black Panther leader, his mother, Afeni Shakur. That's because Tupac died on September 13, 1996, a date with 38 numerology, a number corresponding with 'death', 'murder', 'killing', 'rapper', 'nigga' and even 'Africa', as well as 'R.I.P'. In case you're wondering, Notorious B.I.G. also died on a date with 38 numerology, like how 'Pop Smoke' summing to 38, died at the beginning of 2020 while renting the house of the 38-year-old daughter of John Mellencamp. If you've read my first book, you know these riddles of 38 and death are endless, and as of recently, George Floyd has joined the club. With ease, I could write another book on those that have transpired since the release of my first book, in March of 2018, just over two years ago. To make a long story short, the world of celebrity and reality TV, is deadly business.

On the subject of Pop Smoke's death at age 20, on February 19, 2020, where 'death' equates to 20, I should note his death was very much related to the Jesuit Cabal. This was made clear in a few ways. First, he was on born July 20th, the 201st day of the year. Second, after his death, the rapper Jadakiss announced that out of respect for Pop Smoke's passing, he was pushing back the release of his new album, to March 6, 2020, an album in tribute to Ignatius Jackson, not to be confused with Ignatius of Loyola, the former being a friend of Jadakiss', from the hip hop industry, and who went by the name 'Icepick', equating to 38 with Pythagorean. As for Jadakiss, he was born 'Jason Phillips', equating to 191, the same as 'Society of Jesus'. And further, 'Jason Phillips' and 'Jadakiss' each equate to 61 and 74, the same as 'Jesus'. Also, don't overlook that March 6th can be written 3/6, similar to how 'IHS' equates to 36. At the same time, Ignatius Jackson died at age 44, on June 6, 2017, a date written 6/6, and the album in tribute to him was released on the 66th day of 2020. Furthermore, his age of death connects to the gematria of his surname, 'Jackson', equating to 44, as well as the fact that the album released while Jadakiss was 44 years old. And on the subject of the name Jackson, Pop Smoke was born 'Bashar Jackson', and in light of him being killed on the 50th day of the year, it reminds of the then 44 year old rapper 50 Cent, born Curtis Jackson, who looks a lot like Pop Smoke, and who immediately came out and said he would help get Pop Smoke's posthumous album finished, which he did, on a 50 date numerology, July 3, 2020. As for the number 44, and what we learned earlier, 'shooting' equates to 44, and that is what reportedly took Pop Smoke's life, similar to how MLK and Malcolm X were killed in "44 rituals" and in shootings. In the case of Ignatius 'Jackson', it was 'cancer', equating to 44 with Simple English, the same as 'chemo' and 'kill'. As for the other big Jesuit clue in his death, it came on July 9, 2020, when it was reported that '5' people had been arrested in his murder, the news coming on the 191st day of the year, and a date written 7/9, as well as having 56 date numerology, connecting to the base cipher gematria values of 'Society of Jesus', equating to 56, 79, 187 and 191. As for the 187 connection, 50 Cent's birthday is July 6th, the 187th day of the year. And on the subject of the July 9th arrests, don't overlook that 'murder' equates to 79, or that July 9th is O.J. Simpson's birthday, a man born 'Orenthal James Simpson', equating to 84, and being a person that is another story for another time.

Getting back on track, a point worth making about the 'Black Panther Party', that Bobby L. Rush, who gave us H.R. 6666 was a foundational member of, is that the name sums to 191 with Simple English, identical to the 'Society of Jesus'. This reminds us that 'Black Lives Matter' sums to 56 in Pythagorean, the same as 'Society of Jesus', and it also reminds us 2020 is 56 years after the U.S. Civil Rights Act, and 54 years after the establishment of the BPP in 1966.

And it does make sense that it would be the 'Jesuit Order' behind each entity, the BPP and BLM, because a Jesuit motto is divide and conquer, and these political parties have historically been about division. And it isn't to say that there isn't merit for the existence of both organizations, the BPP and BLM, it is only to point out that they have ultimately fueled the divide between races in the nations they have operated in, as they were intended to, by the Jesuits. Case in point, on June 23, 2020, Shaun King, the leader of Black Lives Matter, was receiving mainstream attention for tweeting the night prior that he believed white Jesus was a symbol of white supremacy, and all statues depicting white Jesus should be torn down. Not by accident, the date of this news was on the day leaving 191 days left in the year, corresponding with both 'Society of Jesus' and 'Black Panther Party'. And I'll add, while he is correct to an extent, it does not mean the people who believe in white Jesus are white supremacists, and it is through instances such as this one, through his not so careful, but very intentional words, that the greater divide is created- because a divided people, are more easily controlled. And it is in instances such as these, where you are reminded that communication is 95% nonverbal.

As for 'Bobby L. Rush' summing to 56, recall the word 'singularity' sums to 56, a word that is identical to 'coronavirus' using all four base ciphers. It is the word that explains the moment in history where technology advances to a point that creates an irreversible change in humanity. In other words, it is the moment we are at now. Case in point, days after the introduction of H.R. 6666, 'Boston Dynamics' out of Massachusetts, a company name summing to 56 in Pythagorean, unleashed 'Spot', summing to 70 with Simple English. This is similar to how 'coronavirus' and 'singularity' sum to 56 and 70, as well as having overlap with all four base ciphers. The purpose of Spot, the robotic dog, that was first deployed in Singapore, was to identify people who were not practicing "social distancing" during the time of coronavirus, and then present them with a friendly voice recording, through the mouth-speaker of Spot, telling them to increase their distance in relation to the people around them. It was also reported that future generations of Spot could be equipped with cameras and sensors designed to read the body temperatures of people so as to "spot" who might be infected with the virus. Just imagine a future version of the robotic dog, where he is equipped with facial recognition technology, and is commanding you by your name, to stand back 6 feet, or to seek medical attention, or to surrender yourself to authorities. In a not so distant future, all of this could become a reality because all of your personal information could be uploaded to a database, or a cloud, that Spot has access to, including your face. And at the rate we're going, it's very likely.

To paint the picture more clearly about the riddles being laid down before our eyes, that are coming straight from biblical scripture, I'll go with an example many can relate to. You've likely already had the experience of your forehead being scanned by a computerized wand for a temperature reading as a means to determine if you might be one of the infected before entering a building, such as a business, or a doctor's office. I personally had it happen to me at the dentist office in May of 2020. The next time someone reads your forehead, remember, that is the place that the mark of the beast is taken in *Revelation*, during the time of 'the great tribulation', having gematria of 225, a period we will learn more about when we discuss the killing of George Floyd on his 225th day of his age, in Minnesota, and the Catholic Church of Minnesota settling with the families of sexually abused children, for $22.5 million days after, and just a week after the death of the Jesuit leader, 'Adolfo Nicolas', having name gematria of 225, and dying on the day leaving 225 days in the year, May 20, 2020.

For another glimpse into the future, just prior to Spot being unleashed on the streets, on March 26th, or 26/3, sort of like 263, the 56th prime, Microsoft published patent W02020060606. You'll notice the 666 at the end of the patent name, separated by zeros. What this patent was for was described as, "A cryptocurrency system using body activity data." In other words, it is computer technology, monitoring the workload of the body, as a means to determine the level of pay in electronic currency, or cryptocurrency. It isn't hard to imagine technology such as this being implemented at an Amazon warehouse near you in the not too distant future. This way Jeff Bezos, just down the street from Microsoft, will have no problem at all detecting who his most productive workers are, at any given minute, at any given location, or who might have taken one extra minute, going over the limit on their 15 minute break period, and who needs to be punished, while having access to the data of potentially millions of people at once. Of course, governments, who Amazon, as well as other tech giants build the technology for, will have the same capability.

While considering technological capability such as this, you have to keep in mind the mainstream media talking points that are being used in the time of coronavirus to prep the minds of the masses for the New World Order, including the elimination of paper money because of its ability to carry and spread germs. The killing of George Floyd over a counterfeit $20 bill even became part of this discussion, because electronic currency would eliminate the possibility of counterfeit money. These details factor in with how days before the reported George Floyd killing, Steve Mnuchin announced the Federal Reserve would not be debuting the new $20 bill with 'Harriet Tubman' on it as planned, a name summing to 201, the same as 'George Perry Floyd'. The encoded details reveal that both stories, regarding Harriet Tubman and George Floyd, were part of the planned mainstream narrative, that was foretold at Event 201, as well as Clade X, where pandemics were forecasted that involved predictions of immense changes to life as we know it, as well as resistance and rioting. In total, from the mainstream media programming, to the war games simulations with viruses, it is all done so that The Cabal can normalize us to the process of these coming transitions, thus why it has been named the "new normal", having gematria of 43, like 'pandemic', 47, like 'foundation', and 115, reminding of January 15th, when the first case of coronavirus was reportedly discovered outside of mainland China. At the same time, 'masonic' and 'Freemasons', the plural, both sum to 43 and 115, and we know how many degrees the Scottish Rite of 'France', the nation summing to 47 and 115, sets their compass at, 47°. Let us not forget, 'Paris, France', equating to 56, is the home of the Jesuits, or how 115 connects the Jesuits and the Scottish Rite.

On the subject of digital currency, something that is an objective of The Cabal, simply because it will ensure that they can track every last penny of the masses, preventing any possibility of tax fraud, such as not paying taxes on your tips, as many people in the service industry tend not to do, we must look at Visa's published patent, May 14, 2020, the day that was Israel's 72nd birthday. For your gematria learning, both 'money' and Bitcoin' sum to 72 with Simple English, similar to how 'Jesuit Order' equates to 72, and we know who the money managers often are. Look no further than Skull and Bones member Steve Mnuchin, the Treasury Secretary. Furthermore, on May 14, 2020, Visa published their patent for 'Digital Fiat Currency', summing to 119 with Reverse Pythagorean, similar to 'all seeing eye', summing to 119 with Simple English, the latter being the object that is shown on the U.S. $1 bill, atop the unfinished pyramid, made of 13 layers of bricks. On that same dollar bill design, there is a 'Star of David', summing to 119 with Simple English, hidden in the grouping of stars above the head of the bird, that is debated as being an eagle or a 'phoenix', the latter being a symbol for order out of chaos, and having gematria of 46, the same as 'ordo ab chao'. As for the 'Star of David', also known as the Seal of Solomon, it is the symbol on the flag of Israel. And in light of the 13 layers of bricks, it is important to know that the House of the Temple, the Scottish Rite headquarters in Washington D.C., modeled after Solomon's Temple in Jerusalem, has an unfinished pyramid on the top, also made out of 13 layers of bricks. Keep in mind Solomon means sun and moon, and the moon is on a 13 month cycle, whereas the sun is moving about the 12 constellations, thus 12 sets of stars and one nearer star, that we call the sun, thus 13. This parallel to the Freemasons becomes all the more important when you look at the drawing submitted with Visa's published patent for how the digital currency will work. If you take the time to examine the provided illustration in the patent, there is a rectangle drawn in the top right corner, with the word 'Architect' written inside of it. Directly above the word 'Architect' is the Freemason compass and square. For your learning, the G in the middle of the Freemason logo, surrounded by the compass and square, stands for 'Grand Architect'. One of the central masonic beliefs is that God is a master mathematician, and God built the world in his image, using geometry, or what is also referred to as sacred geometry. It is why this knowledge of gematria, meaning geometry in language, is used by The Cabal, in repetitive fashion, along with the routine use of other important symbols to them, such as the circle, the triangle, the pyramid and the all seeing eyes. Again, they are playing the part of God, in what is believed to be God's language- letters, numbers, and words, as well as geometric shapes.

Speaking of God, on the U.S. dollar bill, it is written 'In God We Trust', as well as 'Annuit Coeptis'. Both phrases sum to 58 with Pythagorean Gematria, the same as 'Freemasonry' and 'secret society', as well as 'Solomon's Temple'. The latter belonging to the Freemason king, who per *1 Kings 10:14*, received 666 talents of gold each year in weight. I bring this up because Visa's patent for the digital fiat currency was filed on November 8, 2019, a date with 58 numerology. This date was precisely 188 days before the May 14th publishing date, a number that also matters because 'Bavarian Illuminati' sums to 188 with Simple English, and the U.S. fiat currency dollar bill denominations sum to 188. They are the 1, 2, 5, 10, 20, 50 and 100 dollar bills. It all makes sense when you consider these same bills are full of Illuminati symbolism. And in undressing these rituals, it becomes clear who is behind Visa, the card that is accepted worldwide. Let us not forget the Bavarian Illuminati was founded by Adam Weishaupt, the Jesuit and Freemason, with 13 families. And on the subject of 13, I would encourage you to look up The Economist cover from January 9, 1988, that depicts a phoenix rising out of the ashes, and the title of the cover is 'Get ready for a world currency'. Keep in mind, that date can be written 9/1, like 91, the 13th triangular number, and 'phoenix' sums to 91 with Simple English. At the same time, the date can be written 1/9, like 19, and 'chaos' equates to 19 as well as 26. With regards to 26, 'Phoenix' also equates to 26, the same as 'dollar' and 'bank'. And let us not forget the phoenix symbolizes the strategy of order out of chaos. Furthermore, the title of the cover equates to 137, the 33rd prime number, and September 1, 2021, will mark 33 years since it was published.

Another point that should be made clear is both 'God' and 'dollar' have gematria of 26, as does the word 'bank'. Adding to that list is the word 'virus', and while we're at it, so does the name 'China', the blamed party for coronavirus, the perfect problem for The Cabal, that allows them a convenient excuse to push their agenda forward, including a surveillance state, as well as an entirely trackable currency, meaning your neighborhood drug dealer doesn't have much time left. Just wait until 'Spot' the robotic dog is dragging him down the street. And speaking of Spot, the letters for the word 'dog' are a reshuffling of the letters in 'God', meaning it also sums to 26.

Coming back to the point about May 14th, I want to remind you who was born on that date, in 1984, the infamous year. It was Mark Zuckerberg, the face of 'Facebook', summing to 58 with Simple English, reminding that DARPA was established in 1958. If you're not aware already, DARPA's LifeLog experiment, meaning a U.S. military experiment, the equivalent of Facebook, concluded February 4, 2004, the exact same day Facebook launched. Notice that date can be written 4/2, similar to 42, connecting to the gematria of 'computer' and 'internet', as well as 'Freemason', 'Zionism' and 'Jesuit'. Furthermore, February 4, 2004 was 266 days after Mark Zuckerberg's

19th birthday, the Jesuit tribute number, as we have learned, pairing well with the fact that 'Mark Zuckerberg' was not only born in '84, but his name sums to 84 with Reverse Pythagorean, the same as 'The Jesuit Order', and similar to how 'Jesuit' sums to 84 with Simple English. Beyond the gematria, Jesuit and Israel comparisons, and ignoring the fact that Mark Zuckerberg was known for traveling around wearing a hoodie with the Star of David hidden on the inside of it early in his Facebook days, it is important to point out what Facebook and the rest of social media platforms were up to during the time of coronavirus. Of course, they were busy censoring people such as myself, labeling us as "fake news" and the like, despite posting very well researched and credible information that is backed in years of evidence, data analysis and correct predictions. At the same time, they are likely helping big brother build a database of "rabble rousers", or otherwise said, those questioning mainstream and "official" narratives. What can be confirmed at this time, is world governments are announcing they have facial recognition technology for at least 3 billion of the world's people, and this has been achieved by collecting data and images from the world wide web, and connecting names and government identification numbers to the faces they belong to. Of course, most of this is possible because of Facebook.

And if you're wondering, the same types of rituals have been taking place with Jack Dorsey, and still are. On May 28, 2020, Donald Trump targeted Dorsey's brand, 'Twitter', having gematria of 74 and 47, with an executive order. This was 191 days after Jack Dorsey's 43rd birthday, where 191 is the 43rd prime, and both numbers connect to the 'Society of Jesus'. Trump's beef was that two days earlier, on May 26th, Twitter had labeled his tweets as potentially inappropriate. This issue on the 26th of May, sparked headlines stating "the 26 words that created the internet" could be finished. It was a number game in plain sight, not unlike September 11th, that lead to the invasion of Afghanistan 26 days later. If you are not familiar with the 26 words, they are *47 U.S.C. § 230*, a Provision of the Communication Decency Act, that state, "No provider or user of an interactive computer service shall be treated as the publisher or speaker of any information provided by another information content provider." It is this same provision that prevents social media companies from being sued for content posted on their platforms, meaning Donald Trump was aiming to open up the door for lawsuits, potentially going both ways, something that could be a real threat to any content creator on any social media platform, who does not have anywhere near the bankroll big tech does. I bring this up, because as we know, in the U.S. courtroom, "justice" is usually about who can afford the best lawyers.

Back on the subject of the surveillance state, in addition to things tracking us on the outside, such as phones, websites, cameras and robotic dogs, they will soon be tracking us from within, under our skin, and very likely with practically invisible computers that are flowing through our bloodstreams. This is becoming all the more clear because of announcements such as what MIT out of Massachusetts shared on December 18, 2019. On that day, they announced, that with the funding provided by the Bill and Melinda Gates Foundation, they had developed a computerized dye, that can be injected into the blood stream of a person, along with a vaccine, for the purpose of permanently containing all of the person's medical records within their own body, so that it can never be lost, and quickly accessed in an emergency. Thus it isn't a stretch to imagine a future dye that not only holds our medical records, but all of our records, including those relating to education status, job history, financial, marital, criminal, etc. No doubt this is something that will be pushed for by politicians and even nightly news anchors, because it will be explained that with such tracking, we can not only help stop the spread of viruses, but we can quickly identify who the threats are in our society, plus better than that, we can improve the flow of society, from decreased wait times at the DMV, to the doctor's office, to the grocery story, and better still, we can make sure children are no longer kidnapped, because we'll always know where they are. To envision how this technology might be utilized by the authorities, imagine going through the scanner at the airport, that currently invades your privacy by seeing if there are any physical weapons or contraband on your person. In the future however, it will be more invasive, because it will read the computerized data that is flowing through your veins. This reading will then allow TSA to quickly detect if you are in compliance with the orders of big brother, including having all of your latest vaccines.

This very idea, internal computerized tracking, has been in development by organizations such as Microsoft and the Rockefeller Foundation for several years. In fact, a technology in this area that the two have partnered in developing is named ID2020. Think how fitting it is that in the days before the start of the year 2020, MIT announced their computerized dye, ready for human bloodstreams, that was funded by Bill Gates' own foundation, the former head of Microsoft. If you are not familiar with ID2020, it is a biometric scan of your body that reveals your personal data, much like a driver's license, or passport, or medical card. It is being marketed by the Rockefeller Foundation as "Private, Portable, Persistent and Personal." I must say, it is very Orwellian. And let us not forget that the name 'Rockefeller' sums to 56 with Pythagorean Gematria, the family who financed the World Trade Centers, and who has strong ties to the nation's capital, a city having a name also equating to 56 with Pythagorean, the same as 'coronavirus'. In this regard, it is likely no coincidence that on May 11, 2020, a date with 56 numerology, it was reported the White House had begun contact tracing its staff to prevent the spread of the virus.

What many people don't know about the Rockefeller family, often associated with oil and investment, is that they have a long history of working with vaccines as well. Going back 95 years, to 1925, was when the Rockefeller Institute in New York attempted to research a vaccine for the 'Yellow Fever'. After that, they began actively researching vaccines for other common disease and illness, such as smallpox. And more recently, in 1984 of all years, they began a global effort to vaccinate all children worldwide. Talk about big business. When you realize that petroleum products are essential in the medicine business, you begin to understand how the Rockefeller's became involved with medicine and vaccines in the first place.

The point to take away from this chapter, is we as a people are being moved, by very wealth and powerful interest, in a direction, where we will have no privacy, and where every last detail about us will likely be accessible, down to our current heart rate, by government types, operating at a distance, through computers, peering into our lives. The hope is that you will help raise awareness of this agenda so that we as a people, who are not yet totally shackled and under the watchful eye, can stop what is taking place, and collectively say we do not consent to this agenda. The alternative is being bullied and spied on by big brother, while being mocked at the same time, with events such as Global Citizen's, 'One World Together At Home', summing to 266 with Simple English. If you missed this event, put on by The Cabal, for the benefit of the New World Order, April 18, 2020, 38 days after the 'pandemic' was declared, it was to raise money for first responders helping with the COVID-19 crisis. As you learned earlier, 'pandemic' sums to 38 with Pythagorean Gematria, and the ritual couldn't have been placed or named any better. I should note that 'One World Together At Home' also sums to 113, similar to 'coronavirus pandemic', reminding us that the pandemic began on March 11th, or 11/3. Furthermore, it reminds us of Agenda 21, that took place on the 113th day of the year, because Global Citizen was born out of Agenda 2030, Agenda 21's predecessor.

For one last point on the subject of the big tech takeover during the time of coronavirus by the numbers, and the Jesuits being behind it all, it was no accident that on July 29, 2020, the day leaving 155 days left in the year, and a date with 56 numerology, the U.S. Congress made Mark Zuckerberg of Facebook, Jeff Beezos of Amazon, Tim Cook of Apple, and Sundar Pichai of Google, testify before congress, about whether their companies were purposefully attempting to achieve monopolies in their respective industries. Of course, they all denied it, knowing congress wasn't going to do anything beyond ask "tough questions" during the hearing, or better said, political theater. And let us not forget this same federal government, and Google and Apple, in a joint effort, were actively spying on the U.S. populace through their smartphones at this same time. And you'll recall, the numbers 155 and 56 connect to not only the gematria of 'coronavirus', but also 'singularity', where both words overlap with all four base ciphers. And in case you need a reminder, the singularity relates to a point where technology overtakes humanity, and these four CEOs were the faces of the companies that were helping achieve this exact thing at this moment in history. Also, let us not forget that 'The Great Reset', to begin in 2021, which has very much to do with using technology to reshape the world, especially in terms of keeping people at home so that they do not commute and burn fossil fuels, was announced on June 3, 2020, the 155th day of the year. As for more Jesuit fingerprints, you'll recall that Mark Zuckerberg established Facebook February 4, 2004, 266 days after his May 14, 2003 birthday, Jeff Beezos was 56 years old at the time of the outbreak (and everything else we've discussed about him), 'Sundar Pichai' equates to 201, and Tim Cook replaced Steve Jobs, who died at age 56, on October 5, 2011, 223 days after his February 24th birthday, having been born in 1955. And with regards to the date Jobs died, it was the day leaving 87 days left in the year, connecting to the gematria of 'number of the beast', reminding us that Apple priced their first consumer computer at $666.66.

10 | The Rockefeller Foundations's 2010 Coronavirus Clue

Before we get to the Rockefeller Foundation's writings from 2010, that gave away the very well planned and thought out "coronavirus pandemic," the same one we are currently living out, I want to revisit something. In concluding the ninth chapter, we discussed the encoding of 113, a number corresponding with the gematria of 'coronavirus pandemic', as well as the date the pandemic was declared, March 11, 2020, a date often written 11/3, not unlike 113. To add to our list, 'Rockefeller Foundation' also sums to 113 with Reverse Pythagorean. It reminds us of how the One World Trade Center opened on November 3, 2014, a little more than 13 years after the Twin Towers demise, a date that can be written 11/3 as well. As you know, the One World Trade Center replaced the World Trade Centers (two became one), a project proposed and initially financed by the Rockefeller family, that ended with tragedy when it crumbled down on September 11, 2001. Regarding November 3rd, in early 2020, Donald Trump was asked if he might move the presidential election from November 3, 2020 because of the threat of coronavirus, to which he responded by saying "no," and adding that, "It's a good number," referencing the date. Imagine what he could have meant by that, being of 'Scottish' ancestry. In case you have forgotten, 'Scottish' sums to 113 with Simple English. For another thought, on March 11, 2002, a date that can also be written 11/3, the Tribute In Light began, filling the New York skyline with two massive beams of light, that were to remember the fallen towers from six months earlier. I bring these things up to begin the chapter because the Rockefeller Foundation was launched in 1913, four years after the Walter Reed Army Medical Center was opened in Washington D.C., the land of the 'Scottish' Rite, on a campus that was 113 acres in size. In addition to the Rockefeller's having much history and influence in the nation's capital, the greater parallel is that the hospital, Walter Reed, is named after a Yellow Fever researcher, and the Rockefeller Foundation got their feet wet in the vaccine business attempting to solve the same illness. Let us not forget that 113 is the 30th prime, and 'vaccine' sums to 30 with Pythagorean Gematria. And for another reminder, the 'Clade X' simulation, also equating to 113, was centered on the primary goal of developing a vaccine and distributing it to the world's entire populace. It was put on by 'Johns Hopkins University', located just outside of Washington D.C., also equating to 113. Let us not forget this simulation took place 666 days before the pandemic was declared, connecting to the fact that 'vaccination' sums to 666 in Sumerian Gematria, same with 'mandatory'. At the same time, 'New York', summing to 666 in Sumerian Gematria, hosted Event 201, the simulation that was a continuation of Clade X, and that was also focused on developing and distributing a vaccine to solve the pandemic for the people of the world.

In light of the coronavirus pandemic, and the influence of the Rockefeller family and their foundation, it is interesting to look back to May of 2010. In that month, the Rockefeller Foundation released a document titled 'Scenarios for the Future of Technology and International Development'. The title summed to 907 with Reverse Simple English, the 155th prime number, the latter number corresponding with 'coronavirus' as well as 'singularity'. It also summed to 313 with Reverse Pythagorean, the 65th prime number, the latter number corresponding with 'pandemic'- reminding of the 65 million killed in the Event 201 simulation, and the 'CARES Act' being passed by the U.S. Senate for the world's big bankers, 65 days from Donald Trump gloating about world trade to the World Economic Forum. As a reminder, 'CARES Act' equates to 56 and 70, same as 'coronavirus'. And speaking of number 56, the 'Rockefeller' Foundation document we are about to dissect was prepared with the help of the 'Global Business Network', summing to 263 with Simple English, the 56th prime, making them a perfect partner for the foundation. And on the subject of 263, as another reminder, the three planes that impacted buildings on September 11, 2001, Flights 11, 77 and 175, add up to 263- and the Rockefellers were behind the WTCs.

On the subject of 263, if you want to understand how the world elite have truly mocked us in the time of coronavirus, look up the March 26, 2020 cover of The Economist, that says "Everything's under control". You'll see that it depicts the hand of God holding a leash that is around the neck of a masked person who is walking their own leashed dog, that also has a mask over its snout. In addition to the date being written 26/3, like 263, the 56th prime, 'The Economist' equates to 56 with Pythagorean Gematria. At the same time, the title of the cover, 'Everything's under control', equates to 311, much like the date the pandemic was declared, March 11th. Furthermore, the title equates to 121, similar to January 21st, when coronavirus was confirmed outside of mainland China, and reminding us that

'*Revelation*' equates to 121, and accepting the mark of the beast, part of the story of *Revelation*, is very much part of the planned and coming agenda that we are being made to live out as a people.

Moving on, and getting to the topic at hand, within the document, '*Scenarios for the Future of Technology and International Development*', it laid out four potential scenarios for the future of global development in a technology based world. Those four scenarios were titled and captioned as follows. 1. "Lock Step. A world of tighter top-down government control and more authoritarian leadership, with limited innovation and growing citizen pushback." 2. "Hack Attack. An economically unstable and shock-prone world in which governments weaken, criminals thrive, and dangerous innovations emerge." 3. "Clever Together. A world in which highly coordinated and successful strategies emerge for addressing both urgent and entrenched worldwide issues." 4. "Smart Scramble. An economically depressed world in which individuals and communities develop localized, makeshift solutions to a growing set of problems."

As you can gather, the Lock Step and Hack Attack scenarios are currently playing out at the time of writing this book, with authoritarian top-down orders being given by world governments, requiring citizens to do things such as stay at home, wear masks and obey curfew, while at the same time dangerous innovations are emerging, pushed by organized crime, that is big government, including the surveillance and body tracking technology systems discussed in the last chapter. Unfortunately, the scenarios of Clever Together and Smart Scramble aren't taking place at the extent they should, and that is because as a people, we have been raised to compete with one another, rather than cooperate with one another. It is to say we don't know how to get along as well as we should be able to, and it is something we must work on. Many of us have also been made dependent on others, rather than self reliant and able. These problems are largely due to the education (more like socialization) many of us have received, and the culture we have been raised in, both being insufficient and lacking in terms of teaching good values and common decency. That said, if the government fell, I imagine in time, those who survived the chaos, would learn to unite and work together, because it would be the only way forward. The human way forward. At least I would hope.

Coming back to the document, this is what is written, word for word, in the larger Lock Step scenario section, that was published in May of 2010. "In 2012, the pandemic that the world had been anticipating for years finally hit. Unlike 2009's H1N1, this new influenza strain—originating from wild geese—was extremely virulent and deadly. Even the most pandemic-prepared nations were quickly overwhelmed when the virus streaked around the world, infecting nearly 20 percent of the global population and killing 8 million in just seven months, the majority of them healthy young adults. The pandemic also had a deadly effect on economies: international mobility of both people and goods screeched to a halt, debilitating industries like tourism and breaking global supply chains. Even locally, normally bustling shops and office buildings sat empty for months, devoid of both employees and customers." From the same section, it also reads, "However, a few countries did fare better—China in particular. The Chinese government's quick imposition and enforcement of mandatory quarantine for all citizens, as well as its instant and near-hermetic sealing off of all borders, saved millions of lives, stopping the spread of the virus far earlier than in other countries and enabling a swifter post-pandemic recovery." As of May 2020, China is being complimented for its quick and mandatory lockdown of its citizens, and in the U.S., we're being told China's rate of new cases for the virus is far below that of the United States, that was slower to lockdown, and more lenient. In other words, this simulation was pretty spot on, including this part, "During the pandemic, national leaders around the world flexed their authority and imposed airtight rules and restrictions, from the mandatory wearing of face masks to body-temperature checks at the entries to communal spaces like train stations and supermarkets. Even after the pandemic faded, this more authoritarian control and oversight of citizens and their activities stuck and even intensified. In order to protect themselves from the spread of increasingly global problems—from pandemics and transnational terrorism to environmental crises and rising poverty—leaders around the world took a firmer grip on power." And no doubt, we can rest assured that is exactly what will happen, unless we do something about it. The document then goes on, "At first, the notion of a more controlled world gained wide acceptance and approval. Citizens willingly gave up some of their sovereignty—and their privacy—to more paternalistic states in exchange for greater safety and stability.

Citizens were more tolerant, and even eager, for top-down direction and oversight, and national leaders had more latitude to impose order in the ways they saw fit. In developed countries, this heightened oversight took many forms: biometric IDs for all citizens, for example, and tighter regulation of key industries whose stability was deemed vital to national interests."

The details of the scenario are astonishing to look at in the midst of what we're living out, even mentioning ID2020 through the language of "biometric IDs," something that went into development by the Rockefeller Foundation shortly after the proposed scenario, and partnering with Microsoft in its development, the company once headed by the man who has a foundation of his own, the Bill and Melinda Gates Foundation, that like the Rockefeller Foundation, claims to be about humanitarianism, but really appears to be about wealth and power creation, off the projects he supports and convinces world governments to get behind and spend for. Aside from the year 2012 used in the scenario, as opposed to 2020, and a higher death toll caused by birds, instead of bats, this simulation describes to a tee what is taking place in the world right now, the same world where it was reported on June 4, 2020, that Rockefeller types, led by Jeff Bezos, had gained $565 billion more in wealth as a result of the pandemic, that was only just beginning. That is because this scenario, no doubt, was the chosen path forward by the world elite, that includes the Rockefeller Foundation and the Bill and Melinda Gates Foundation, as well as the names you don't know, because they lurk in the shadows, something we'll touch more on ahead, in the chapter where we discuss Bill Gates and his "Decade of Vaccines" plan, as well as other things.

As you consider this level of planning and detail, keep in mind this same philanthropic group, the Rockefeller Foundation, is derived from the same family that forced the World Trade Centers on New York City, decades before September 11, 2001, for the sole purpose of knocking them down, only as a symbol, to push forward their New World Order agenda, as they did. On the subject, please research Aaron Russo's film, *America; Freedom to Fascism*, where he discusses how he witnessed firsthand a member of the Rockefeller family speaking about the events of 9/11, years before they transpired. If you don't know the history of how the construction of the World Trade Centers came about, they were proposed by the Rockefeller family at a time when office space was vacant in New York, and landlords were already struggling to get the desired amount of rent from their tenants due to the many vacancies and bargains in the city. Thus, the last thing they wanted were new buildings, bigger than any before in the city, full of office space- exactly what the WTCs were.

On the subject of bats, the differing detail from the Lock Step scenario, and the Rockefeller's, a big money family, like that of Bruce Wayne, in Batman, it is worth pointing out that on February 3, 2020, the U.S. mint released a new quarter. For the first time ever, the design was a fruit bat. Not by chance, 'fruit bat' equates to 56 with Reverse Pythagorean Gematria, similar to how 'coronavirus' sums to 56 with Pythagorean, the same as 'Rockefeller', and this news was prominent at the same time experts were explaining how the coronavirus likely came from bats, just as the killer pandemic does in the film *Contagion*. For the record, 'fruit bat' also sums to 34 with Pythagorean Gematria, and it released on the 34th day of the year, February 3, 2020. Adding insult to injury, the designer of the new quarter was 'Richard Masters', summing to 222 with Reverse Simple English, corresponding with the long list of 222 rituals you learned about in the third chapter, including 'Wuhan Coronavirus' summing to 222, and the coronavirus pandemic being declared 222 weeks after September 11, 2001, an event that also had a lot to do with money, as I wrote about in my first book. In other words, the new quarter was not a coincidence, but instead, was what I call "coincidence programming"- a tactic of the mainstream media's regularly scheduled programming. If you pay attention, the mainstream media is often presenting stories that seem related, but are described by the mainstream as being "only coincidental", such as the quarter and the virus. And do I dare add that the news about the quarter was first broken by outlets such as USA Today on January 10, 2020? That date can be written 1/10, not unlike 110, the number connecting to the surname 'Rockefeller', equating to 110, the same as 'prophecy', and reminding us how the World Trade Centers were 110 stories tall, and how a span of 110 days from their demise, the movie Pearl Harbor released, only for the attacks of 9/11 to be referred to as the New Pearl Harbor. It reminds us that if you look into the history of cinema, there has always been big money behind it, especially that of industries who are interested in using cinema to help sell products, as well as culture, the latter being so that their products become more enticing. And when you think industry, you think Rockefeller. And when you think cinema and themes, you might acknowledge that for the last twenty years, there have been many post apocalyptic titles, preparing us for the type of draconian world that is being built around us.

To finish, I should mention the deaths of John D. Rockefeller, the man who made the family name what it is, and David Rockefeller, who spearheaded the building of the World Trade Centers in New York. There is a clear parallel, through a very familiar number. John D. Rockefeller died May 23, 1937, a date with 84 numerology, and David Rockefeller died March 20, 2017, 84 days before his June 12th birthday. In light of Ignatius of Loyola dying in 1556, emphasis on '56, and the 'Rockefeller' connection to 56, let us not forget Ignatius of Loyola died 84 days before his birthday as well. In the case of John D. Rockefeller, he died on the 143rd day of the year, corresponding with the Reverse Pythagorean Gematria of 'Scottish Rite of Freemasonry', and David Rockefeller died on March 20th, or 3/20, the Spring 'equinox', having a Reverse Simple value of 84. Furthermore, that date appears similar to the number 320, and 'Roman Catholic Church' equates to 320 with Reverse Simple English. If you're a sport buff, you might also recall how the "Big 3" on the Cleveland Cavaliers, LeBron James, Kyrie Irving, and Kevin Love, became the first teammates to combine for 101 points in a game, the night before the death of David Rockefeller, at age 101, a stat that matters, because the Rockefeller family came to power in Cleveland.

For one last nugget on the Rockefeller family, look up the cover of 'Newsweek', from April 3, 1967, the 93rd day of the year, and a date with 93 numerology as well. 'David Rockefeller', summing to 93 with Reverse Pythagorean is on the cover, reminding us of the '93 WTC bombing. In that article he discussed the future of banking, and the World Trade Centers, that of course would be bombed in 1993, and were reportedly struck by the second flight, on September 11, 2001, at 9:03 AM, but not hit by Flight 93, that crashed in Shanksville. And for another reminder of the relevance of 93, the structure that now stands where the World Trade Centers once did, is 'One World Trade Center', equating to 93 with Pythagorean Gematria. And let us not forget, the number 93 is also encoded in 'Wuhan Coronavirus', because it is a number symbolizing the keepers of time, 'Saturn' and the sun- and as you know, all of these rituals are 'time' based. Plus, the magazine cover is from the year '67, the 19th prime, and as you know, 'chaos' equates to 19, and 'Wuhan' equates to 67. *Newsweek=666 (R. Sum.)

11 | Bill Gates First Birthday on Jonas Salk's 42nd... & Elvis

October 28, 1956, was one for the vaccination history books. This is because on the same date, 'The King', a nickname summing to 74 with Simple English, Elvis Presley, received his polio vaccination on live TV. More specifically, it was on the *'Ed Sullivan'* show, a name summing to 119 with Simple English, the same as 'all seeing eye'. Keep in mind 'all seeing eye' sums to 56 in Pythagorean and '56 was the year Elvis was elevated to international fame, mostly because of the television. In addition to the television coverage, the photo of him receiving his polio shot was published in newspapers across the world. Speaking of which, the Guardian, a paper out of the U.K., wrote a lengthy and detailed article about this same vaccination event from history's past on April 23, 2016, the 113th day of the year. As for why it was written on this date, recall, the number 113 is the 30th prime, and 'vaccine' sums to 30 with Pythagorean Gematria. For one more, the date of Elvis Presley's televised vaccination had 113 numerology (10+28+19+56=113), and together, it should remind us that the coronavirus pandemic was declared March 11, 2020, emphasis on 11/3, and of the simulation 'Clade X'. I highly suggest you read the Guardian article, and I'm telling you, once you learn the code, you'll laugh at the way stories are contrived every single day, in all of mainstream media. *And it won't end, until we end it.

Back on the subject of Elvis Presley's polio vaccine, what made this ritual special, was the timing. It came precisely 42 weeks after Elvis' 21st birthday, a young man at the time, born January 8, 1935, and it came on the date of Jonas Salk's 42nd birthday, the doctor credited with developing the polio vaccine, who was born October 28, 1914. Adding to the ritual, it was Bill Gates' 1st birthday, having been born October 28, 1955, a good year and month for little 'satan', who is now the face of vaccinations across the world- despite the fact that he comes from a family of bankers and lawyers and has personal experience in computer programming and contract negotiating. Sadly, in the present, the world listens to this man as if they don't know the difference between computer viruses and human viruses. Adding to the 42 list, is the word 'birthday', having Pythagorean Gematria of 42, and that Elvis would go on to die at 42. It reminds us that Aretha Franklin would die years after Elvis, after recording 42 albums of her own, as the Queen of Soul, only to die on the same day in history as Elvis, The King of Rock and Roll, August 16, 2018, a date with 42 numerology, and 41 years after Elvis, who passed in 1977, where 'King' sums to 41 with Simple English. On the subject of 42, and how the beast in *Revelation* rules for 42 months, do I dare mention that 'rockstar' has Reverse Sumerian Gematria of 666? This becomes all the more fascinating when you recognize that 'vaccine' sums to 42 with Reverse Pythagorean Gematria, and Bill Gates currently operates his personal foundation out of Seattle, Washington, located in the 42nd state in order of statehood. As we also learned, 'vaccination' equates to 666 with Sumerian Gematria, so consider how perfect it was to do such a thing to one of the world's first "rockstars," on the 'TV', the latter being the acronym for the mass mind control instrument that sums to 42 with Simple English (T is 20 and V is 22), that was broadcasting to nearly the entire world in 1956. For one last point on the number 42, on 'May' 1, 2020, one of two months having gematria of 42, it was reported that Stéphane Bancel, CEO of Moderna, became the first person and pharmaceutical company working on a coronavirus vaccine to send a trial vaccine to Anthony Fauci, the 'Jesuit', at NIH, after just 42 days. Let us not forget that Fauci has been the head of NIH since 1984, or that 'Jesuit' sums to 42 and 84. Personally, this detail reminds me that in the Clade X simulation, vaccines are rushed to the consumer, and are ineffective. For your own sake, imagine rushed vaccines causing even more problems in terms of health consequences and loss of life due to coronavirus, or in the next contrived pandemic. It's fair to imagine, because it has happened before and it appears to be happening now.

Coming back to Elvis Presley's October 28, 1956 vaccine infomercial on Ed Sullivan's show, the result of the ritual was very impactful on the U.S. populace, especially for teenagers, who prior to Elvis Presley's televised needle jab, had been resistant to being vaccinated for polio. In large part, this was because of the reported problems with vaccines, including accidental deaths, that had halted polio vaccinations temporarily in 1955. Another part is people don't like needles. However, after Elvis lent his arm, perceptions changed rapidly, especially due to the fact that a number of other celebrities followed behind Elvis, championing the cause of a healthier world through preventative medicine such as vaccinations. For another point to consider, the polio vaccine had become available to the public on the date of March 26, 1953, more than three years earlier, and up until that point, had mostly only been utilized by parents of infants, with babies being the group most at risk of being infected with polio. Let us not overlook the date, March 26th, or 26/3, like 263, the 56th prime. If you're asking if it was Jesuits then, the likely answer is yes. Consider that the first encyclical Pope Francis wrote, was written with the subject, 'On care for our common home', summing to 263 with Simple English, connecting to the fact that both 'Society of Jesus' and 'pope' equate to 56. That encyclical was dated May 24, 2014, the 144th day of the year, connecting to 'Jesuit Order' and 'time'. In the next chapter we'll talk about how Tom Hanks ended his coronavirus quarantine 263 days after his July 9th birthday, a man also born in '56, along with his wife. It is to say that these numbers and trademarks are rituals of the Jesuits. And as we know, 'Jesuit' also sums to 42, and their logo, the sun, reminds a bit of where Elvis Presley, who departed at 42, laid down his tracks, at 'Sun Record Company', summing to 78 and 84, the same as 'Jesuit'. Keep in mind Elvis was 21 years old at the time of the vaccine ritual, and 'Jesuit' sums to 21 with Pythagorean, similar how the number written out as a word, 'twenty one', sums to 42 with Pythagorean Gematria.

In addition to the date of October 28, 1956, and the number 42 linking the lives of Elvis Presley, Jonas Salk, and Bill Gates together, there is one other common quality, and that is religion. Each of the 'three' men came from Jewish families. In the case of Elvis' family, his mother was buried with the Star of David on her casket, and it is the symbol of 'Zionism', a word equating to 42 with Pythagorean Gematria. Of course, it is Jewish people who predominately practice gematria, and as we learned, it was the Jew Diego Laynez, who co-founded the Jesuits, one of seven founders, reminding us of the 7 continents and the 7 days of the week, a number that connects colors and sound, and a number that 42 is divisible by.

For one last point on the Society of Jesus, reminding us of the 42 generations to Jesus, the same society that is the Jesuit Order, that operates by the code, and kills by the code- Elvis Presley as well as Aretha Franklin died on August 16th, the 228th day of the year. This matters because the word 'death' sums to 228 with Sumerian Gematria. Furthermore, the name 'Sun Record Studios', with its Jesuit matching gematria, where Elvis recorded, sums to 228 with Reverse Simple English. This pairs with 'Martin Luther King Jr.', summing to 228 with Simple English, who died in Memphis, the same as Elvis, in what was also a Jesuit ritual. Let us not overlook that Memphis is a

137

name that is in tribute to Memphis of ancient Egypt, not far from where the pyramids still stand, symbols of mathematics and geometry. As we know, 'math' equates to 42. And if you check the stats, there are 201 remaining layers of bricks, that are intact, on the Great Pyramid at Giza, as of the time these events are happening. That fact even blows my mind. If you want to take it further, the date of Elvis' death, August 16th, can be expressed as 16/8, not unlike 168, and the name 'Gladys Presley' sums to 168 with Simple English, the name of his mother. Of course, she died at age 46, like JFK, connecting to the gematria of 'sacrifice', 'execution', 'Catholic' and the word 'religion' itself. It almost reminds us of Martin Luther, who died in 1546, emphasis on '46, six years after the Jesuit Order was formed, who lead the Protestant Reformation against the Church. His date of death was February 18th, or 2/18, not unlike 218. This is a number of 'death' in what is known as English Extended Gematria, a cipher that pays tribute to Hebrew Gematria and Greek isopsephy. I bring it up because Elvis Presley's mother died August 14, 1958, 218 days after her son's birthday. And the cipher is as follows:

English Extend Gematria:
A=1, B=2, C=3, D=4, E=5, F=6, G=7, H=8, I=9
J=10, K=20, L=30, M=40, N=50, O=60, P=70, Q=80, R=90
S=100, T=200, U=300, V=400, W= 500, X=600, Y=700, Z=800

For practice, let us decode death into the value of 218 using English Extended. Death = 4+5+1+200+8=218. And as we learned earlier, 'death' sums to 38 with Simple English Gematria, corresponding with the fact that Elvis died in 'Graceland', summing to 38 with Pythagorean, the same as 'Memphis', where again, he, The King, and Martin Luther King Jr., both died. And for a related ritual, 'Prince' summing to 38, died in 'Chanhassen', also summing to 38, the same as 'Minnesota', and each word equating to 38 with Pythagorean Gematria, on Queen Elizabeth's birthday. As we learned, his song 'I Would Die 4 U' revealed his fate, dying on 4/21, where U is the 21st letter- and on the date he died, they lit up Niagara Falls purple in tribute to Queen Elizabeth, while never acknowledging that Prince's girlfriend from the time of *Purple Rain* was Vanity, who was from Niagara Falls, and was the person who died February 15, 2016, the 46th day of the year, on the 14 year anniversary of the death of Prince's mother, on what was the day of the 58th Grammy's, a little more than two months before Prince's passing. This becomes all the more chilling when you recognize that both 'Purple Rain' and 'Queen of England' sum to 58, and that Prince died 33 years after recording I Would Die 4 U in 1983, only to die at the age of 57, a difference of 33 years from 90, the age Queen Elizabeth turned the day of his passing. Thus, the riddle tied in with how 'England' equates to 33 and 57. And now both homes, of Elvis and Prince, where both men reportedly died, are considered museums, and are used for financial gain, by the same management firm. There's much more to say on the matter, but we'll save it for later, when we learn about the Boule and 38, in relation to George Floyd's death on 38th Street in 'Minnesota', as well as Kobe Bryant's and Martin Luther King Jr.'s, and the rest of King's family.

In light of all the chatter about 38, keep in mind the words 'Jew' and 'Kabbalah' both have Simple English Gematria of 38. Again, this is how old Bill Gates was when he married Melinda Gates, January 1, 1994, 65 days after his 38th birthday, numbers corresponding with the Simple English and Pythagorean Gematria values of 'pandemic'. Those same numbers also correspond with how 'George Floyd', equating to 65 in Pythagorean, was killed on 38th Street, in 'Minnesota', and then on June 5th, or 6/5, in Washington D.C., on the 38th Parallel North, 'Black Lives Matter' was painted on the streets of Washington D.C. Furthermore, this took place on 16th Street, reminding of the 16th Street Baptist Church bombing, and of the 16th card in 'Tarot cards', having Simple English Gematria of 119, the same as 'George Floyd', and similar to the date of September 11th, or 11/9, because once again, there was the whole "846" thing, connecting to George Floyd and 9/11. And as a reminder, the 16th card is the Tower card. At the same time, let us not forget the Event 201 simulation, that killed 65 million, was conducted on Melinda Gates 65th day of her age, a woman born on August 15th, the date the Jesuits were formed in Paris, France, in 1534, or that 'George Perry Floyd' sums to 201, the same as 'The Jesuit Order', or that Adama Traore was killed in Paris, France, July 19, 2016, the home of the Jesuits, on the 201st day of the year, precisely a span of 201 weeks from the killing of George Floyd on May 25, 2020, and the two men's names were protested in remembrance of on the same date, June 1, 2020, in Paris, a date having 47 numerology, and in 'France', having 47 gematria- a number that connects 'time', 'authority', and 'government', as well as the 'Vatican', the history of London, and 'D.C.', the lands of the respective 'trinity', or three city states that we learned about in the first

139

chapter, plus 'France', in the time of Pope 'Francis', a name equating to 47 as well. And in case you have amnesia, Pope Francis is the first Jesuit Pope, who lives in Suite 201, at the Vatican, and who was born 'Jorge Mario Bergoglio', equating to 201, plus everything else, that if you have amnesia, you probably won't remember anyway, including 'Ignatius of Loyola' summing to 201, the creator of the Jesuits, and the name of Pope Francis' living quarters, Suite 201, named the 'Domus Sanctae Marthae', also equating to 201, and each of the 201 values mentioned equating with Simple English. As for those with good memories, please know there are a mountain of 201 rituals we haven't even touched yet- from Florida's stay at home orders going into effect on April Fools Day, Governor Ron DeSantis' 201st day of his, having been born September 14, 1978- to the Governor of Oklahoma, Kevin Stitt, testing positive for coronavirus, July 15, 2020, his 201st day of being 47 years old, having been born December 28, 1972.

*John Kevin Stitt = 196 (Simple English) *July 15th, 196th d.o.y.

In light of the massive worldwide protests sparked by George Floyd's televised killing, and just so you understand this is bigger than Bill Gates, I should remind about Google, headed by 'Sundar Pichai', a man having a name equating to 201 as well, the same as 'William Henry Gates'. Equally as important, his name 'Sundar Pichai' sums to 123 with Simple English, and he took over as CEO of both Google, and it's parent company Alphabet, on December 3, 2019, at the same time the pandemic was beginning. That date can be written 12/3, not unlike 123, equating with 'conspiracy' in Simple English. And in light of Alphabet Company, think ABC, 123, similar to the date 12/3. The reason Sundar Pichai is important to consider is because Pichai, a name ending with A.I., as in 'artificial intelligence', summing to 113 with Pythagorean Gematria, similar to 'coronavirus pandemic'- he oversees the company that is responsible for much of the world's contact tracing, that no doubt is tracking every last person carrying a smartphone, including those participating in these protests and riots, for the purpose of creating databases of people and their behaviors, especially at this moment in history. Keep in mind these databases are overseen and managed largely by A.I. technology, owned by Google, a company that celebrates its birthday on September 27th, the day the Jesuits were recognized by Rome. Furthermore, this level of tracking is being done to find out who are the order followers, and who are not. And it is not that these numbers are intersecting by accident, but that they are part of a written code, that are encoded into the key details of one interconnected story, written by the Jesuits, that has been created for the purpose of transforming the world and its people. Something that is the next chapter for humanity, if you will, where the least of our problems we'll be the health consequences of the virus.

On the subject of Bill Gates, it is interesting to go back in history, to the date of January 29, 2010. This was the date Bill Gates announced his "Decade of Vaccines." As we have covered, it was his 94th day of his age, corresponding with 'Davos, Switzerland', equating to 94, where he made the announcement, as well as 'coronavirus pandemic', equating to 94. As you know, Switzerland is the nation that is home to the United Nations, World Health Organization (WHO), World Economic Forum, CERN and many of the most powerful banks, including the Bank of International Settlements. In the case of the WHO, it was 'they' that declared the coronavirus pandemic. And let us not forget 'Switzerland' has gematria of 65, same as 'Knights Templar', reminding us that Bill Gates was married to Melinda 65 days after his birthday, on the first day of 1994, and best of all, 'Decade of Vaccines' equates to 65 with Pythagorean, pairing with the fact that at the end of the decade, Event 201, on October 18, 2019, simulated a pandemic that called for a global vaccine after the deaths of 65 million, and again, that simulation was on Melinda Gates 65th day of her age. Adding further to the riddle, his father, Bill Gates Sr., was 94 years old at the time of the start of the pandemic, having been born, November 30, 1925, and reminding that his wife died in 1994, shortly after the wedding of her son. Adding to the 94 list, recall that both 'Seattle, Washington' and 'coronavirus pandemic' equate to 94, and Seattle is the city where the first case was confirmed outside of Wuhan, China, the home of Bill and Melinda Gates. For one more, 'Brazil' equates to 94 in Reverse Simple, where the coronavirus outbreak begins in Event 201, that was co-sponsored by the Bill and Melinda Gates Foundation. It reminds us that Agenda 21 took place in Brazil, a predominantly Catholic nation, and 'Roman Catholic Church' equates to 94 with Pythagorean Gematria. This pairs with the fact that October 28, 1956, the date of Elvis' polio shot was one with 94 numerology (10/28/56=10+28+56=94). Ultimately, 94 breaks down to 13 and 4 in numerology terms, and the number 4 is associated with death, the same as a virus. The number also pays tribute to in the *Bible*, where the fourth book is titled *Numbers*. *4/4, 94th d.o.y.

For another thought on 94, the Kanye West and Jay-Z music video for the song *No Church in the Wild*, from 2011, shows a violent confrontation between masked protesters, and police, where the one number that is front and center in the altercation, is shown on the back of the police officer's helmet who is in the center of the screen, and it is P94. Consider P is the 16th letter of the English alphabet, and the year 1694 is when the Tonnage Act made the City of London an independent city-state, controlled by the 'Bank of England', having gematria of 65, the same as 'United Kingdom', and reminding us that the bank was 325 years old on March 25th, or 3/25, 65 days from Donald Trump gloating at the World Economic Forum, and March 25th being a date when many world governments passed legislation for massive bailout loans that were needed because of the pandemic (order out of chaos), including the United States of America, making the Swiss bankers all the richer off the interest that will be paid to them for generations to come, ensuring their power and influence for the foreseeable future- unless somehow this system is overthrown. Also, in light of the 325 part, recall that 'City of London Corporation' equates to 325, and it was 325 years old at the time, having been established July 27, 1694. It reminds us that 'Scottish Rite of Freemasonry' equates to 325, and of the Council of Nicea in 325 AD, that takes us back to the Catholic Church. Speaking of the Church, the Kanye West and Jay-Z song was on the album *Watch the Throne*, that released August 8, 2011, the day leaving 145 days in the year. As you know, 'Catholic' equates to 145 with Reverse Simple English.

Should you think any of this is coincidental, realize that my YouTube followers and I did a call-in-show as part of a live stream broadcast about this exact scene, from the same music video, in April of 2020, asking how long until this fictional event would become a part of the nightly news, in light of the way 94 had been coded into the ritual we were living out. We had to wait a little more than a month to see it after the people of the world were provoked into confrontation and physical violence with police, because of the viral video of the killing of George Floyd. It is to say, by understanding the code, and how predictive programming is laid down in popular culture, we knew it was only a matter of when and not if, in the same way we have been prepared for this moment we are living out now, the "pandemic," because we knew it was coming as well, and we had the correct timeframe beforehand, understanding the 19 year cycles. It is in these things that is the value of this knowledge. And knowledge is power. And each one teach one. And so on.

Back on the topic of Bill Gates, what else was encoded in his 'Decade of Vaccines', was the number 313, the 65th prime, a number that points most strongly to the 'Knights Templar' and their history of banking and finance, in the respective nations of the 'United Kingdom' and 'Switzerland'. And on the subject of 65, don't forget how in the sixth episode of *Knightfall*, a series about the Knights Templar, that more recently released its second season on March 25, 2019, one year to the big pay day, they pay tribute to 65 by saying there are 65 Templar orders in 'Europe', a continent having Pythagorean Gematria of 35, the same as 'Catholic'- and making too much sense as to why when you think about it. After all, the legend goes, the Kabbalah knowledge came back to the Church with the Knights Templar after the crusades, and from there it spread to European royalty, forming the early roots of The Cabal. Don't forget JFK was killed 149 days after his speech in 'Europe', and 149 is the 35th prime, and he was the 35th President, the only Catholic one to date. For another value encoded into 'Decade of Vaccines', it was 119, using Simple English, the number corresponding with 'all seeing eye', what the world elite attempt to program in all people, the mind's eye, with each ritual they put on, including the one with Elvis, on '*Ed Sullivan*', on Billy's first birthday. At the same time, let us not forget 'Vatican' equates to 119 as well, same as 'Francis', and the Vatican has a giant statue of a pinecone at their fortress, a symbol of the mind's eye, or the pineal gland. And that leaves us with one remaining value from the base ciphers not discussed, where the name of the event, 'Decade of Vaccines', sums to 88 with Reverse Pythagorean. With regards to the number 88, words such as 'program' and 'poison' equate to 88, and in light of what Bill Gates said at his 2010 TED Talk, days after announcing his 'Decade of Vaccines', about the possibility of reducing the earth's human population by 15%, in a strategy leading with vaccines, that is something very much worth thinking about. For people in Africa, and poorer regions of the world, this is especially true, because at the beginning of the same 2010 presentation, Bill Gates shows a picture of African children, who are likely being targeted. At the same time, poor people are hit the hardest in Clade X and Event 201, the latter of which Bill Gates was a main sponsor. In light of what you learned about 'death' and 38, and it being the age

Bill married Melinda at, in what was seemingly part of the ritual that was building up to this pandemic agenda we're currently living out, 'Africa' also sums to 38 with Simple English, a continent that has been used for medical experimentation for longer than Bill or Melinda Gates have been around, and 'pandemic' sums to 38 with Pythagorean.

For some historical perspective, Dr. David Ho told us decades ago, in February of 1998, that HIV traced back to 1959 in the 'Belgian Congo', having Pythagorean Gematria of 59. Adding to the list, the words 'Rasta', 'blues', 'slave' and 'negro' each equate to 59 with Simple English. Beyond that, there's the fact that Motown records came out in 1959 and Black History Month ends on the 59th day of the Gregorian year. And in light of what Bill Gates said, and has been simulated in Clade X and Event 201, this matters because the word 'kill' sums to 59 with Jewish Gematria. Keep in mind, this number has been connected to many sinister rituals that are part of what is known as "black history" over the years, as I explain in my first book. And as we'll soon get to, it's no accident the news of George Floyd's death, came 59 days before the Minneapolis Mayor's birthday, who was 38 years old at the time. And do not misinterpret what I meant by writing "black history". It is to say, that the history of African people is tremendous, and it can't be reduced to a month.

As for Bill's eugenics centered presentation, keep in mind, TED Conferences LLC, that operates TED Talks was formed on the date of February 23, 1984, a date that can be written 2/23, and a date that is the 54th day of the Gregorian year. They're familiar numbers, that should remind you of the Masons and Jesuits, as well as the Rockefeller Foundation, who partners with Bill Gates' foundation, and has had their mission to vaccinate all children since 1984. Adding to the list, the number is even encoded into 'Innovating to Zero', the name of Gates 2010 TED Talk, that sums to 224 with Simple English, where the divisors of 84 sum to 224, and reminding us that 'William Henry Gates' sums to 84 with Pythagorean. On the subject of 84, I should note that 'Mark Zuckerberg', equating to 84 as well, joined Bill Gates and Jeff Bezos as the only men worth $100 billion dollars on August 6, 2020, 84 days after his own birthday. As for Gates' TED presentation, the most concerning remark he makes is where he explains, "First we've got population, now the world today has 6.8 billion people, that's heading up to about 9 billion, now if we do a really great job on new vaccines, healthcare, reproductive health services, we can lower that by perhaps 10 or 15%." His quote brings to light that his father, 84 years old at the time of the 2010 remarks, and 94 years old at the time of the 2020 pandemic, was a co-founder of Planned Parenthood, because they are focused on reproductive health services, another way of saying eugenics, or population control. Ultimately, the point of his speech is that if we don't do something to reduce carbon emissions, we will commit self suicide as a planet due to rapidly changing environments that will destroy the possibility of growing enough food to sustain the world's populace. Strangely enough, or perhaps not so, he claims that the world is way over the limit on carbon emissions, emitting 26 billion tons annually. As you have learned, 26 is the 'God' number, thus why the 'virus', from 'China', both words equating to 26, is being used for the excuse- and in this case, 'carbon' has Pythagorean Gematria of 26 as well, the particle existing in all things, like 'God', and having 6 protons, 6 neutrons, and 6 electrons. That number. Of man. Of beast. It reminds us that 'William Henry Gates' sums to 258 with Reverse Simple English, the same as 'number of the beast'. It is fitting for a 'computer' man, wouldn't you say? Don't forget when Microsoft once bailed out Apple, the $666.66 pricing gang culprits. And for another 258 pertaining to Bill Gates, Gavi was established July 12, 1999, on Bill Gates 258th day of his age, in his 44th year of his life, meaning he was still 43 years old at the time, the latter number corresponding with 'pandemic', as well as 'Lucifer', both equating with Reverse Pythagorean. In light of Gavi being Bill Gates' vaccine business, let us not forget that 'vaccination' equates to 666 through Sumerian Gematria, or that Seattle is on the 47th Parallel North, corresponding with the Simple English Gematria of 'beast'.

As a reminder that these same types of patterns go beyond Bill Gates, I'll bring up the tragic news of the passing of Malik B., the founder of the hip hop group The Roots. He was born 'Malik Abdul Basit', and he died very recently, at age 47, on July 29, 2020, 258 days after his November 14th birthday, having been born in '72, on the day leaving 47 days in the year. On top of that, his full name, 'Malik Abdul Basit' equates to 47 with Pythagorean Gematria, and he died on the day leaving 155 days in the year. With regards to 155 and 47, 'Christianity' equates to 155, and 'Christian' equates to 47, and Christianity teaches about the number of the beast, and Malik B. was a Muslim, reminding us of the crusades, and the 'Vatican', equating to

145

47. For another thought, 'Black Thought', equating to 47 with Pythagorean, is a star from The Roots, and Malik B. died 66 days before Black Thought's 49th birthday, having been born October 3rd, in 1971 (*Revelation = 49, Pythagorean). And as you know, 'number of the beast' equates to 66 with Pythagorean, whereas '*New Testament*' equates to 66 with Reverse Pythagorean, and 666 is taught about in the 66th book of non-Catholic Bibles, where the number corresponds with the gematria of 'math' and 'mankind', and how God regrets making mankind in *Genesis 6:6*. In that breath, it reminds us of how 'Lakers' equates to 66, same with 'Lower Merion', where Kobe went to high school, same with 'LeBron', and 'LeBron James', and how Kobe Bryant scored his career high 81 points in his 666th game career game, on January 22, 2006, scoring 81 out of the teams 122 points, meaning he scored 66% of the team's total. We'll learn more about that subject later in the chapter on Kobe Bryant when we discuss how 'Kobe Bean Bryant', his full name, and 'mark of the beast', both equate to 54 and 81 in the same ciphers- just understand for now, it wasn't an accident the NBA scheduled to play LeBron James and the Lakers against the Toronto Raptors, the same team Kobe scored 81 against, on August 1st, or 8/1, right after the return of the NBA from its 'coronavirus' suspension, in the year of Kobe's death. As you'll recall, the word ritual sums to 81 with both Simple ciphers, forwards and backwards, and these truly are 'satanic' rituals, where 'satanic' sums to 122, explaining why the Lakers scored 122 points, on January 22nd, or 1/22, the same night Kobe scored 81 of the team's points. Also, let us not forget the 'satanic' church was established in 'San Francisco', equating to 122 with Simple English, on the 122nd Meridian West, in the year '66. And with regards to satanic rituals, the day before Kobe died, LeBron James, known as "King James," passed Kobe Bryant in points scored, scoring the 54th points of the game, making it Lakers 54, Philadelphia 76ers 74, in the 74th NBA season, and in Philadelphia, Kobe Bryant's hometown, and on a court with a chopped up black snake, similar to how Kobe Bryant was known as the 'Black Mamba'. At the same time, Philadelphia is the same hometown of 'Malik B.', a rap name equating to 42, reminding us of the way it is encoded in black history, from 'Jackie' to 'Tuskegee', to 'February', as we discussed heavily in my first book, and also how the beast rules for 42 months in *Revelation*, the 66th book of the *Holy Bible*. Let us not forget Bill Gates operates from the 42nd state, Washington. And for

one last point on Kobe, remember that 'helicopter' equates to 666 with Sumerian Gematria, and that Philadelphia is named in *Revelation*, the same as 666. And for a couple last points on Malik B., he was from Philadelphia, the land of the 76ers, a name coming from the year 1776 and the **56 signers** on the Declaration of Independence, and he died on a date with 56 and 76 numerology, that happened to be International Tiger Day, where 'Tiger' equates to 76, and it is a word that has been used in a popular nursery rhyme to replace the 'n-word'. Furthermore, it ties in with the prophecy of *Acts 7:6* that we have been discussing, a number and verse we will continue to build meaningful examples around as we progress towards the conclusion of this book.

Going back to the date of January 29, 2010, the date of Bill Gates 'Decade of Vaccines' announcement, it was a much more numerical ritual than we've already uncovered. Take for example, the fact that Bill Gates pledged $10 billion of his own money to the cause, on the 29th day of 2010, where 29 is the 10th prime number, and 'Davos' sums to 29 with Reverse Pythagorean, the city where he pledged the money for a 10 year project. And please keep in mind Gates was born in '55, the 10th Triangular number and the 10th Fibonacci number, and that he would go on to turn 55 years old later in 2010, meaning he was 54 years old at the time, the 'Jesuit Order' number. Furthermore, the date January 29th can be expressed as 1/29, not unlike 129. This matters because 'Gavi, the Vaccine Alliance' sums to 129 with Reverse Pythagorean, the official name of Bill Gates' personal organization dedicated to creating and distributing vaccines worldwide, an organization that has helped him gain much more wealth than he had from his years as a computer man, in a much shorter time. The date of January 29th also reminds us that Bill Gates mother died shortly after his marriage to Melinda, June 10, 1994, a date with 129 numerology (6+10+19+94=129). She died on the 193rd day of her husband's age, the 44th prime number, corresponding with the values of 'Seattle', 'kill', and 'execution', as well as 'medicine'. At the same time, 'Roman Catholic Church' equates to 193 and 94. Gavi is now headquartered in Switzerland and Washington D.C., and was officially established in 'Seattle, Washington', the 94 city, on a date with 137 numerology (7+12+19+99=137), the 33rd prime number, reminding us of 'Bill Gates' connection to the number, and the fact that his former company, Microsoft, that he was the head of for 33 years, went public 137 days from his birthday, on March 13, 1986.

For a bit more, Seattle was once called 'Alki', summing to 33 with Simple English. And it is now named after 'Chief Seattle', summing to 113 with Simple English, who is remembered for giving his most famous speech, about all things being connected, on the date of March 11, 1854- a standout year, coming 166 years before the pandemic date, March 11, 2020. Never mind they say Chief Seattle was 68 years old when he gave that speech, or that it was a date with 68 numerology (3/11/54=3+11+54=68), reminding us that Seattle's Autonomous Zone was established on June 8th, 6/8, corresponding with the Pythagorean Gematria of 'Seattle, Washington', and also 'Davos, Switzerland', two locations that are the exact same in three out of four ciphers. As for the Autonomous Zone, that's a subject we'll get to later. For now however, please ask yourself- how much of our history might be entirely contrived?

For a bit more on the gematria of Gavi, the full name 'Gavi, the Alliance Network' equates to 96, the same as 'William Henry Gates', 'Gavi Alliance', 'Freemason' and 'corona'. Keep in mind the divisors of 42 sum to 96, and 42 is related to vaccines. It also factors in with Washington state being the 42nd state in order of statehood as we covered at the start of the chapter. For another 42, it is 'New Mexico', equating to 42 with Reverse Pythagorean, where Bill Gates co-founded Microsoft with Paul Allen, the latter man being the one who died by the code, at age 65, in a ritual synced with the Seattle Seahawks, as well as the coronavirus outbreak.

The day prior to Paul Allen's death, the coach of his football team, Pete Carroll, not to be confused with John Carroll, the Jesuit, earned a franchise record with the Seattle Seahawks by achieving his 82nd regular season home win in defeating the Oakland Raiders, corresponding with the Simple English value of 'Seattle', summing to 82. Then Paul Allen died from 'non-Hodgkins Lymphoma' summing to 82 with Reverse Pythagorean one day after. Keep in mind these were computer men, and TIME magazine named 1982's person of the year as, **The Computer**. Adding even more relevance, the shape of the football is known as the 'Vesica Piscis' in sacred geometry, summing to 82 with Reverse Pythagorean, similar to how 'game' sums to 82 with Reverse Simple English. If you run it the other way around, 'Vesica Piscis' sums to 53 with Pythagorean, and this was the 53rd game between the Raiders and Seahawks, who used to be rivals in the AFC West. For another 53, with Pythagorean, you can add 'Pete

Carroll', and it should be noted that it was Pete Carroll's 134th game with the Seahawks, because 'Vesica Piscis' sums to 134 with Simple English. For yet another, you can add 'Microsoft', summing to 53 with Reverse Pythagorean, and again, Bill Gates and Paul Allen cofounded the company Microsoft together. It should be noted the "home" game as it was scheduled for the Seattle Seahawks, was played at 'Wembley Stadium' in London, England, in the NFL's ongoing program with the United Kingdom. This becomes very interesting when you recognize that 'Wembley Stadium' sums to 206 with Reverse Simple English, Seattle is the (206) area code, and the Seahawks had last played the Raiders exactly 206 weeks earlier, reminding that Russell Wilson had 206 passing yards in Super Bowl 48, and Robinson Cano, while with the Seattle Mariners, was suspended 206 days from his birthday, and the first person killed in Seattle's Autonomous Zone, was killed on June 20, 2020, or 20/6. Also curious, Paul Allen's birthday was January 21, 1953, what would eventually become the date for the first case of coronavirus confirmed outside of mainland China, in his home city, Seattle, Washington, January 21, 2020, what would have been his 67th birthday, the 19th prime (Wuhan = 67, Simple English; Seattle = 19, Pythagorean). Don't forget he died at 65 either, because in addition to 'pandemic' summing to 65, so does 'United Kingdom', where the Seahawks coach, Pete Carroll, picked up the milestone, in a game of measurements. And never mind that Pete Carroll used to coach the 'New England Patriots' football team, prior to the Seattle Seahawks, a team summing to 82, the same as 'Seattle'. He also coached the New York Jets, for one season, prior to taking over the Patriots. And of all years, he began with the Jets in 1994, emphasis on '94. Recall, the World Trade Centers, built by the first from Seattle, opened April 4, 1973, the 94th day of the year, and 'World Trade Center' as well as 'terror' equate to 94. Again, it is a web of rituals, on top of rituals, on top of more rituals, that are part of an ongoing storyline, we're living out, that connects sports, entertainment, and news.

As for New Mexico, the original home of Microsoft, the 47th state, and home of the '47 Roswell Incident, not to be confused with Seattle, on the 47th Parallel North, Bill Gates had an incident from there in his early days with Microsoft that exposes what a puppet he is, playing his part as the billionaire money genius, and now philanthropist, telling the world via TV screens why it is good for them to give up privacy, their liberties and to bend over and accept his hyper rushed and big money backed vaccines as a necessity of life. The incident in New Mexico transpired on December 13, 1977, when a mugshot of 22 year old Bill Gates was taken at the Albuquerque, New Mexico police station, for reasons that are said to be lost to time. Look it up. The big goofy smile he uses in the mugshot tells the story and exposes the ritual. It is a smile that reminds us of the many awkward laughs and grins he had during his March 26, 2020 CNN interview about the pandemic, when he spoke for 33 minutes and some seconds with propaganda agents Anderson Cooper and Sanjay Gupta, broadcasting from the 33rd Parallel North in Atlanta and 84th Meridian West. The date of the 1977 mugshot was 46 days after Gates birthday, corresponding with the Pythagorean Gematria of 'Microsoft', as well as the value 'virus'. You could also say it was his 47th day of his age. Furthermore, it was a date with 121 numerology, corresponding with the Pythagorean Gematria of 'Bill and Melinda Gates Foundation', and similar to Paul Allen's birthday, January 21st, or 1/21, the date coronavirus was confirmed in the U.S., in Seattle. Also, it is important to recognize that 'Albuquerque' sums to 58, same as 'fraternal', and in that breath, think 'Fraternal Order of Police', a masonic organization, who has a logo with an 'all seeing eye' on it. Look it up. Only fitting then, 'Fraternal Order of Police' sums to 119, similar to 'all seeing eye'. Never mind that it is the reflection of 911, what you dial for police in the United States. Even further, 'secret society' sums to 58 and 77, and this happened in '77.

For another related ritual, it was Bill Gates getting a pie in the face, on February 4, 1998, when he was 42 years old. Consider the date February 4th can be written 4/2, not unlike 42, and was the date Facebook launched six years later, February 4, 2004. As you know, 'computer' and 'internet' equate to 42, same with 'vaccine'. This was blamed on 'pranksters', summing to 42 with Pythagorean, in 'Belgium', summing to 33 with Pythagorean, the same as 'Bill Gates', Microsoft's CEO for precisely 33 years.

And for a few last rituals, we'll begin with the declaration of Bill Gates as the world's richest man, the year of the release of Microsoft's Windows 95, on the date of July 5, 1995, what would have been his mother's 66th birthday, born July 5, 1929. Keep in mind, the phrase 'number of the beast' sums go 66 with Pythagorean Gematria, and it is taught about in the 66th book of the *Bible,* the concluding book of the 'New Testament', summing to 66. And again, the beast is unleashed for 42 months in *Revelation*. Anyhow, it was declared on that date Bill Gates was worth $12.9 billion, similar to how his mother died on a date with 129 numerology, and with what we learned about Gavi's multiple connections to 129, as well as it being established on Bill Gates 258th day of his age, corresponding with the 258 gematria values for 'William Henry Gates' and 'number of the beast', the ritual seems quite clear. These details bring together what *Revelation* warns of, the 'Synagogue' of Satan'. That's because 'synagogue' sums to 42 with Pythagorean, and 129 with Reverse Simple English. Let us not forget 'sin' alone equates to 42 with Simple English.

Also fascinating, the day Bill Gates was declared the richest man in the world, is the same day Corona typewriters went out of business after 113 years, a tribute to technology, and its advancement, with the computer replacing the typewriter, while also foretelling of what was to come in 2020. It was a fitting date, because both 'Bill Gates' and 'typewriter' equate to 57, similar to how July 5th can be written 5/7, or even 7/5, the latter corresponding with the gematria of 'Catholic Church' and 'New World Order', both equating to 75. At the same time 'vaccine' equates to 57, and as we know, Bill Gates has become the face of vaccines, especially in the time of coronavirus, where the pandemic was declared on March 11th, or 11/3. It was for this reason we predicted in April that on May 7, 2020, we would see big vaccine news in the world. Sure enough, on that day Bill Gates' backed Moderna became the first pharmaceutical company to have their coronavirus vaccine be approved for phase two testing by the Food and Drug Administration of the United States. Let us not forget that 'Moderna' sums to 70, the same as 'coronavirus' and 'Melinda Gates', the latter being the partner of Bill, or that the first case of coronavirus was confirmed in 'Snohomish County' equating to 70 as well, just miles from their foundation. In that same breath, let us also recall that on April 13, 2020, a date with 57 numerology, it was reported the World Health Organization was developing 70 vaccines for coronavirus by TIME and other mainstream publications.

To further prove how coordinated the rituals are, on March 16, 2020, Moderna's trial vaccine began in Seattle, the 56th day since confirmation of the virus on January 21st. As you know, 'coronavirus' sums to 56 with Pythagorean, and March 16th was three days after Trump declared a national emergency, on March 13, 2020, a date with

56 numerology. As for the trial vaccine, it was reported on March 16th that Moderna was aiming to set a record and develop the vaccine in 65 days, which has since passed, but the headlines still exist. The patient's name, was 'Jennifer Haller', equating to 74 in Pythagorean, the same as 'Snohomish County' and 'Bill and Melinda Gates', reminding that Event 201, about getting a vaccine to stop a pandemic, that kills 65 million, took place October 18, 2019, the day leaving 74 days left in the year. At the same time, let us not forget that the Bill and Melinda Gates Foundation is located directly across the street from the 74 acre Seattle Center, where the world's biggest needle is, the Space Needle, a symbol that ties right in with vaccines. As for Jennifer Haller, her name also equates to 137 with Simple English, the 33rd prime, reminding us that Trump's national emergency was declared on March 13th, 137 days from Bill Gates' birthday, on October 28, 2019, that began his 65th year of life. And we know how they love to pair 33 and 74 together, and that 'Bill Gates' equates to 33…

For one last detail, it was 'Kaiser Permanente', summing to 174 with Simple English, and 258 with Reverse Simple English, the exact same as 'number of the beast', who was overseeing the trial 'vaccine', in the 42nd state. At the same time, 'Kaiser Permanente' and 'William Henry Gates' both equate to 96 and 258, the latter being the man who founded his vaccine alliance on his 258th day of his age. And with the number of the beast encoding exposed, let us not forget that 'vaccination' sums to 666 with Sumerian Gematria, or the March 26, 2020 Microsoft patent we learned about, ending with the number 60606, or H.R. 6666, the TRACE Act. Let us also not forget the mathematical relationship between 42 and 96, or how the beast relates to 42. And in the next chapter we'll tie in how Tom Hanks fits into all of this, being the man who starred in *Inferno,* about the billionaire who wants to depopulate the world with a virus, that released on Bill Gates 61st birthday, a number associated with 'God'. Hanks was also in Apollo 13, about the 13th mission in the series of moon missions that resulted in the moon landing, on July 20, 1969, the 201st day of the year- in part explaining why he posted on Instagram, on March 17, 2020, that he was losing to his wife by 201 points in Gin Rummy, while they were recovering from coronavirus. Go figure 'Gin Rummy' equates to 96 and 42 as well. And better yet, go figure he posted this remark next to a picture of a Corona typewriter.

12 | Tom Hanks & the Use of Celebrity to Sell the Pandemic

On March 11, 2020, the same day the World Health Organization declared a 'coronavirus pandemic', it was reported that Tom Hanks and his wife, Rita Wilson, who both starred in *Sleepless in Seattle*, the one set in the "19 city", had contracted Covid-19 while filming a movie about Elvis Presley, of all people, in Australia. On the subject of 19, I'd say it is a coincidence *The Elvis Channel* is number 19 on SiriusXM if not for the fact that 'Elvis' sums to 67 with Simple English, and 'Elvis Presley' sums to 67 with Reverse Pythagorean, the latter equating to 67 in the same way as 'Rita Wilson'. Again, 67 is the 19th prime number, and 'Wuhan' also equates to 67 with Simple English. Making matters all the more interesting, the polio vaccine that Elvis eventually received, first debuted in March of 1953, 67 years prior to March of 2020, the coronavirus pandemic's start. This same numerical ritual factored into the April 24, 2020 story of Tom Hanks donating his corona typewriter to an 8 year old named 'Corona DeVries', in Australia, who had reportedly been bullied because of his first name during the time of the pandemic, a name summing to 67 with Pythagorean Gematria. At the same time, the boy's name equated to 77 with Reverse Pythagorean, and the news came a span of 77 days from Tom Hanks upcoming July 9th birthday, reminding us of the year Elvis died, 1977. And on the subject of SiriusXM, let us not forget that they made channel 121 the coronavirus channel on March 6, 2020, corresponding with the date of the first coronavirus confirmation in the U.S., January 21, 2020, or 1/21, as well as the gematria of 'coronavirus outbreak', 'Bill and Melinda Gates Foundation', 'World Health Organization' and 'Johns Hopkins University', the latter summing to 121 and 113, similar to March 11th, or 11/3, the "pandemic" date.

As for the 'Australia' detail, it is noteworthy, because it sums to 102 in 'Simple English', the same as 'Wuhan, China'. Consider, on March 11, 1918, 102 years earlier, Spanish Flu had been confirmed at Fort Riley, in 'Kansas', a state summing to 65 with Simple English, the same as 'pandemic', at the start of the Spanish Flu pandemic- not to be confused with coronavirus, where *corona* is a Spanish word. It was reported that Spanish Flu originated out of World War I, and 'world war' is a name equating to 102 with Reverse Simple. It is a number that reminds us of 'Art of War', summing to 102 with Simple English, the military strategy book by Sun Tzu, that was translated by a Jesuit in France in 1772. And again, think about his name. Sun Tzu?

The sun? The Jesuits? Keep in mind World War I began in 1914, 142 years later, and 'Jesuit', 'World War' and 'War' all equate to 42, where as 'forty-two' equates to 142. It also reminds us that the American Civil War began April 12, 1861, the 102nd day of the year, and that the 9/11 attack lasted 102 minutes, and on the day of the attack, Donald Trump referenced his insurance firm on the 102nd story of the World Trade Center. Keep in mind, 9/11 was a giant ritual, centered on the number 33, and the word 'magic' equates to 33 with Simple English, as well as 102 with Reverse Simple. And don't get me started on how 'George Perry Floyd' sums to 102 with Pythagorean, whose death ignited a movement that brought down Civil War statues in the U.S. and related historical statues and monuments across the nation, and even the world, after being sparked by rioting on East 33rd Street in Minneapolis. The 102 in his name mattered in this case because the history of 'slavery' is what undermined the destruction, a word summing to 102 and 42. Adding to the list, the term 'social distancing' sums to 102 with Reverse Pythagorean, and Tom Hanks and Rita Wilson became spokespeople for the term, reminding their social media followers numerous times to obey 'social distancing' guidelines, and to stand 6 feet apart, for the sake of our health- as if being driven apart is healthy. For a moment, imagine if a series of people were standing in a line, six feet, six feet, and six feet apart, with the legacy of H.R. 6666 contact tracing them, so as to observe if social distancing guidelines are being followed. While you ponder that, please know that Australia was the first nation to erect a shrine to Elvis Presley, the 'rockstar', even though he never traveled there, on the date of November 26, 1977, exactly 102 days after his August 16th death. And for one last 102, Tom Hanks hosted Saturday Night Live, April 11, 2020, from his own home, in a special coronavirus broadcast, on the 102nd day of the year. And further adding to the list of Jesuit fingerprints, 'Fort Riley', a theorized outbreak point of Spanish Flu, is a name summing to 54 and 153, the same as 'Jesuit Order'.

In light of Hanks and his wife being born in 1956, the year of Elvis Presley's vaccination on television, it is interesting to note that Tom Hanks once starred in *Forrest Gump*, where as a young boy with polio, hampered by consequential leg braces, he taught Elvis his knee shaking dance moves. If you can believe it, the actor chosen to play the brief role of Elvis in the film, was 'Peter Dobson', having a name summing to 56 with Reverse Pythagorean, similar to how 'coronavirus' equates to 56. In light of 'Robert Zemeckis', summing to 70, also like 'coronavirus', being the director of *Forrest Gump*, a man known for encoding numerical riddles in his films, often full of predictive programming, I doubt this fact about the gematria of 'Peter Dobson' is coincidence, especially since '56 was Elvis Presley's breakout year. If you're not familiar with the work of Zemeckis, he did the *Back to the Future* series, that shed light on coming events ranging from September 11, 2001 to the Chicago Cubs 2016 World Series, when they ended the 108 year drought, not unlike the 108 double stitches on a baseball, or the fact that 'Major League' sums to 108 with Simple English, or that the tallest building in Chicago, the Sears Tower, is 108 stories tall. And for the record, we had it nailed in Spring Training, why the Chicago Cubs would end the 108 year drought, in Game 7, of the 112th World Series, on November 2, 2016, emphasis on 11/2, not unlike 112. It was because using Simple English, 'mathematics' equates to 112, and 'geometry' equates to 108, not unlike 'Major League', also summing to 108. And when you think about how tall the tallest building is in Chicago, 108 stories, think builders, think measurement, and think Masons, ancestors of Jesuits. And further, think about how from the Jesuits being recognized by Rome in 1540, to the establishment of Modern Freemasonry in London, England, in 1717, was 177 years later. As you know, 'The Jesuit Order' equates to 177, and so does 'New World Order'. With that in mind, think of the very political Hollywood family, the Kennedy's, where JFK was killed 177 days after his birthday.

And on the subject of 'Major League Baseball', to go on another brief tangent, you should know that it equates to 162 with Simple English, similar to how 'baseball' sums to 162 with Reverse Simple, matching the 162 game season in a "non coronavirus year". It is a fun stat to share with enthusiasts of the sport. And as for Hollywood, think about the film series *Major League* focused on the Cleveland Indians, made by Hollywood, a Jesuit enterprise, because that is what we did, months in advance, calling why the Cubs would beat the Cleveland Indians, in game Game 7, in a *Major League* tribute. Of course, Cleveland is the (216) area code, and the 108 double stitches on a baseball, are also 216 individual stitches.

Moving on, in the same way I don't think Peter Dobson was chosen for the part of Elvis by accident, I also assume it is intentional that the film *Forrest Gump*, that Tom Hanks stars in, is 2 hours and 22 minutes in length, similar to 'Wuhan Coronavirus' equating to 222. Furthermore, 2 hours and 22 minutes is the same as 142 minutes, corresponding with 'coronavirus' summing to 142. Adding on to the riddle, *Forrest Gump* released July 6th, the 187th day of the year, a big number with the 'Society of Jesus', and in 1994, emphasis on '94, a relevant number because 'coronavirus pandemic' sums to 94 in Pythagorean, a number we learned a great deal about while discussing Bill Gates, his marriage, his father, and the loss of his mother in 1994, years before his 'Decade of Vaccines', that began on his 94th day of being 54 years old.

Another film Zemeckis and Hanks collaborated on, was *Cast Away*, and it also factored into the details surrounding Tom Hanks after his coronavirus diagnosis. This is because on March 18, 2020, one week after the pandemic was declared, which was the same day Tom Hanks had been named as the first sick celebrity with the virus, LeBron James went viral for sharing a video of himself in isolation due to coronavirus, captioning it by saying he looked like Tom Hanks in the film *Cast Away*- a film about a man, trapped on an island, who grows very long hair, and a very long beard to match, similar to the beard and hair that comes about with Tom Hanks' character in *Forrest Gump,* when "shit happens" --- such as now, 26 years after the film's '94 release, the big year for Bill and Melinda, with now being 2020, the time the 'virus' has struck, from 'China', at least so we're told, that is being used to change life as we know it, in record time. And for one more reminder, both 'virus' and 'China' sum to 26. I should also note, LeBron James' social media post on the subject was on the 78th day of the year, and as we learned, 'Wuhan Coronavirus' sums to 78 with Pythagorean Gematria, the same as 'Thomas Jeffrey Hanks', the full name of the actor, Tom Hanks. For another, 'Cleveland' sums to 78 with Simple, considered LeBron's hometown. If you haven't seen the film *Cast Away,* it is partly set in Memphis, the home of Elvis, as well as FedEx, the latter being the company Hanks' character works for in the film. It is also scored with Elvis Presley's music. The next time you watch it, you'll likely snicker when you hear Hanks' character complain in the opening dialogue that it took too long for his package to get from Memphis to Russia, taking "87 hours." The reason this is laughable, is because 'Russia' sums to 87 with Simple English. Another thing to consider is that 'number of the beast' sums to 87 with Reverse Pythagorean, and 'beast' and 'time' equate with Simple

English. At the same time, 'The Catholic Church' equates to 87 with Reverse Pythagorean, and we will learn much about this number when we further analyze Naya Rivera's July 8th death, a date that can be written 8/7, and of a woman born in 1987. And on the subject of 87, consider, when Donald Trump signed off on the trillions in international banker loans, with his big devilish grin on his face, on March 27, 2020, it was the 87th day of the year- and of course, 'Trump' and 'beast' equate to 47, meaning he is part of the beast system, not thee beast himself. Also noteworthy, is that 'Cast Away' sums to 93 with Simple English Gematria. As you have learned, this is a number related to time, connecting the sun and 'Saturn' and if you watch the film, you won't miss the joke, because everything in the film is about time, a point that is made abundantly clear through dialogue, and especially since the object that motivates him to stay alive while he is alone on an island for many years, is a watch, to keep the time, given to him by his fiancé. For another 93, you must decode the full name of the actor with Reverse Pythagorean, 'Thomas Jeffrey Hanks', because it also sums to 93 in the same way as 'Wuhan Coronavirus', reminding us of the '93 WTC Bombing, and the eventual demise of the towers that came exactly 93 weeks after the World Trade Organization protests began in Seattle, Washington on November 30, 1999, a date that can be written 11/30, similar to the Simple English Gematria of 'protest', equating to 113.

It was in that year, 1993, that Tom Hanks starred with Rita Wilson in *Sleepless in Seattle*, a movie that concludes in New York, not far from the World Trade Centers, bringing Seattle and New York together yet again. And to think, the NFL's Jamal Adams wasn't even born then, having been born October 17, 1995, and in 2020, on July 26th, the date New York joined the United States in 1788, the New York Jets traded Jamal Adams, number 33, to the Seattle Seahawks, a serious "inside joke." And not to spoil the sequel to *Sleepless in Seattle*, titled *You've Got Mail*, but when Tom Hanks and the love interest meet, you won't miss the 201 behind them, a number that is clearly placed in the shot. As for the first film, if you haven't seen *Sleepless in Seattle*, it begins in Chicago, with the funeral of the wife of Tom Hanks' character, who has died from an unspecified illness. From there, he departs to Seattle for a change of scenery. What is interesting about this, is per the official narrative, the first case of coronavirus in the United States was confirmed in Seattle, and the second was in Chicago, the latter city being the one the New York Times focused on regarding the Crimson Contagion simulation. Keep in mind, both of those cities have their 56th Mayor at the time of the outbreak, Jenny Durkan in Seattle, and Lori Lightfoot in Chicago. And as a reminder, 'Seattle' equates with 'Covid'-19, and 'Chicago' equates with 'virus'. Also interesting, in the opening minutes of the film, you are introduced to the love interest of Tom Hanks, who is located in Baltimore, the home of Johns Hopkins University, and not by chance, the university is referenced almost as soon as the film begins. Of course, it is Johns Hopkins that conducted and participated in the Clade X and Event 201 simulations, and is now the same university keeping track of the coronavirus cases and deaths worldwide, and it is their statistics that are being reported in the mainstream media as facts, when in truth, they are merely number games with great consequences for many people, that need exposing.

As for Hanks' love interest in the film, it is played by the actress Meg Ryan. And on March 11th, the date the pandemic was declared, and the date Tom Hanks and his wife Rita Wilson were reported to have been diagnosed, it was precisely 113 days after Meg Ryan's 58th birthday, celebrated on November 19, 2019. As a reminder 'coronavirus pandemic' equates to 113. Beyond that, her birthday can be written 19/11, like 1911, and you might recall when the DowJones fell 1,911 points on February 24th and 25th of 2020, concluding on the 56th day of the year. For your learning, the number 1911 corresponds with the Jewish Gematria of 'Ancient and Accepted Scottish Rite of Freemasonry', where 'Scottish' alone sums to 113 with Simple English. Equally as important, in 1910 & 1911, a pandemic reportedly occurred in 'Manchuria', equating to 56 and 155, the same as 'coronavirus' and 'Freemasons', that led to the start of the formation of the World Health Organization. Keep in mind, Manchuria is modern day China. Furthermore, 'Manchuria' equates to 43, the same as 'pandemic' and 'Freemasons'. And adding to the riddle, 'The Great Manchurian Plague', as the virus was called in 1911, equals 113 with Pythagorean Gematria, reminding us of what we learned about the 'Rockefeller Foundation', 113, and their history in vaccines, along with Walter Reed, and its retired 113 acre campus.

As for Tom Hanks, March 11th was 8 months and 2 days after his 63rd birthday on July 9, 2019, and 'Seattle', 'Hanks', and 'Covid'-19 each equate to 82. You could also say it was Tom Hanks' 247th day of his age, and 'Seattle, Washington' equates to 247 with Reverse Simple English. Keep in mind 2020 is the year that marked the 247 year anniversary of the banning of the Jesuits by Pope Clement XIV on the date of July 21, 1773, an order that was preserved with 201 Jesuits, only thanks to Catherine the Great, as you know, who now has a hit show about her, that released on May 15th, or 15/5, during the time of the 'coronavirus' pandemic. And back on the subject of March 11th, it was a span of 121 days from Tom Hanks upcoming 64th birthday, something that is interesting for two reasons. One, 'coronavirus outbreak' equates to 121, plus the first case was confirmed on January 21st, or 1/21, in Seattle, Washington. And two, '*Sleepless in Seattle*' equates to 64 with Pythagorean Gematria, and the date of Tom Hanks diagnosis, March 11th, can be expressed as 3/11, similar to 311, the 64th prime number number.

Adding to the intrigue of the ritual, in the most recent film Tom Hanks had starred in prior to the pandemic beginning, he played the part of 'Mr. Rogers', summing to 113 with Simple English. What makes this all the more significant, is that the name 'Fred Rogers' equates to 56 and 155, the same as 'coronavirus'. And for another, the title of the film about Mr. Rogers, '*A Beautiful Day In the Neighborhood*', equates to 155 with Reverse Pythagorean. It also sums to 151 with Pythagorean, similar to 'pandemic'. Even the name '*Mister Rogers' Neighborhood*' sums to 142 with with Pythagorean, similar to how 'coronavirus' sums to 142 with Reverse Simple English. Looking back, the fact that his series *Mister Rogers' Neighborhood* debuted February 19, 1968, the 50th day of the infamous year, where 'America' sums to 50 with Simple English, the land of 50 states and countless territories, and the same year "coronavirus" was coined- it must not have been an accident. It reminds us of the symbolism being used, as The Cabal transitions us from one 'age' to the next, and the significance of 1968 in this ongoing agenda.

For another film that Tom Hanks stars in that appears to have been a clue for the coronavirus pandemic we're now living out, consider the title *Larry Crowne*, that released on July 1, 2011, the CDC's 65th birthday, a number corresponding with the gematria of 'pandemic'. In the film, Tom Hanks plays the part of Larry Crowne, who is given the nickname "Lance Corona". Of course, the word corona is Spanish for crown, reminding us that coronavirus was confirmed in Seattle, Washington, in King County, after being discovered just north of Seattle, in Snohomish County- because the king wears the crown. At the same time, the title 'Larry Crowne' equates to 145 with Reverse Simple, the same as 'Catholic'. And the surname 'Crowne' alone has gematria of 84, not unlike Jesuit, or the fact that the CDC is headquartered in Atlanta on the 84th Meridian West. With these thoughts in mind, recall what we learned earlier about the *Watch the Throne* album, released on August 8, 2011, the day leaving 145 days left in the year. Once again, the symbolism is clear- the throne, the king, the crown, or the "corona."

Years before *Larry Crowne*, in 1993, the same year *Sleepless in Seattle* released, Tom Hanks also starred in the film *Philadelphia*, where he battled the HIV virus. Recall, the first case of HIV in the United States is believed to have been confirmed in 1968, the same year "coronavirus" was coined. What is interesting about the name of the film is *'Philadelphia'* sums to 223 with Reverse Simple, similar to how 'novel coronavirus' equates to 223 with Simple English. As we'll get to in the chapter on predictive programming, the film *12 Monkeys*, where 'monkeys' sums to 102 with Simple English, is about a deadly virus being unleashed on the world for the purpose of depopulation, and it is set in Philadelphia. Let us not forget that Philadelphia is named in *'Revelation'*, summing to 121, and reminding us of the date January 21st, or 1/21. And to tie in the 223 value with *Forrest Gump*, at the end of that film, Gump's love interest dies on the date of March 22nd from an "unknown virus", that is HIV, a date that can be expressed as 22/3, or of course 3/22, like 322. She also dies in the year 1982, emphasis on '82, bringing us back to the 'Covid'-19 and 'Seattle' riddle. Do I dare mention Gump's love interest is named 'Jenny', summing to 68 with Simple English? What makes this last stat all the more interesting is that Robert Zemeicks, the director of *Forrest Gump* as well as *Castaway*, turned 68 years old on May 14, 2020, during the time of the pandemic, and on Israel's 72nd birthday.

Now to get to the gold mine, out of all the films Tom Hanks has starred in to date, the one that stands out at the top of the pack, in terms of coronavirus predictive programming, is from the *'The Da Vinci Code'* series, about the Illuminati, a series equating to 68 with Pythagorean, and that title is *Inferno*. As we mentioned earlier, it was released on Bill Gates' 61st birthday, October 28, 2016, and is 2 hours and 1 minute in length, the same as 121 minutes, or as shown on a DVD or Blu-Ray player, 2:01. As you have learned, the number 61 is associated with 'God', and in this case, the first offering in *The Da Vinci Code* series is *'Angels & Demons'*, summing to 61. Think about that title for a moment. Also, keep in mind 'Year of the Rat' equates to 61, and that is when the "pandemic" was declared. For another reminder, *Inferno* is about a billionaire who wants to depopulate the earth with a virus, not too far off from what Bill Gates said at his TED Talk in 2010, a little more than six years before the release of this film. Keep in mind 61 is the 18th prime number, and the Event 201 simulation took place October 18th, and the simulation projected an 18 month timeline where 65 million would die, and it compared the coronavirus outbreak to the Spanish Flu that began in 1918. As we know, 'IHS', equates to 18. And for the record, *Inferno's* date of release, October 28, 2016, was 111 days after Tom Hank's birthday, corresponding with the Simple English Gematria of 'vaccination'. You could also say it was his 112th day of his age, the number corresponding with the Catholic Church, and the number of countries the Jesuits operate in, 112, and the date of February 11th, or 11/2, the establishment of the Vatican, in the year 1929.

If you have not seen *The Da Vinci Code* series, the entire story centers around the 'Vatican', and its secrets, a location name summing to 70 with Simple English Gematria- a number that connects to the gematria of 'coronavirus', 'CARES Act', 'Melinda Gates', 'Francis', 'Snohomish County', and a long list of details in the ongoing coronavirus story, including the gematria of 'Queensland, Australia', where the boy Corona DeVries lived, the boy that Tom Hanks donated his corona typewriter to, and the same city the pandemic begins in in the 2007 film *Pandemic,* only after a surfer named 'Ames', summing to 70 with Reverse Simple, flies from Australia to Los Angeles. And for a reminder, it is extremely possible that 70 gains its relevance from the year 70 CE, when the Roman's destroyed the second temple, Herod's Temple, that is remembered on Tisha B'Av. The greater event that destruction was a part of is recorded in history as the Siege of Jerusalem, lasting from March to September of that calendar year, 70 CE, almost reminding us of 9/11 in September, and the Tribute in Light on March 11th, as well as the coronavirus pandemic being declared on March 11, 2020. For me personally, it is a fair thought, because right now, as I finish this book, with the hope it reaches your hands- society as we knew it is crumbling around us, like the temple, and like the towers. It is happening in the snap of fingers in a historical context. Or otherwise said, in "new normal" terms, in a flash of light… that might now be scanning your head to make sure you're virus free.

Coming back to *The Da Vinci Code* series, the name of Tom Hanks character in it is 'Robert Langdon', summing to 206 with Reverse Simple English, reminding us of Seattle's area code, the (206), and his starring role in *Sleepless in Seattle.* To add more significance to the number, there are 206 bones in the adult human body, and this becomes all the more interesting when you consider the phrase, "the body is the temple.". With this phrase in mind, 'masonic temple' sums to 206 with Reverse Simple English, and of course, the 'temple', summing to 26, is a place to worship 'God', summing to 26, an entity that is different depending on the spirituality one worships. In the case of The Cabal, it is something more like the 'beast', corresponding with Seattle being on the 47th Parallel North, and as was stated at the beginning of this book, they're using this code to play 'God', or if not that, summon the 'beast', and at this moment in history, their key weapon is the threat of the 'virus', equating to 26, in an ongoing story that has much to do with Seattle, Washington. Speaking of, did I make clear that Seattle based 'Amazon' sums to 70, as well as 25, and was established in 1995, 25 years prior to 2020, the year Bill Gates, of Seattle, was declared the world's richest man, only to be outdone by Jeff Bezos, of Amazon, also out of Seattle? What a small world, right? What a coincidence? Let us not forget Seattle is on the 122nd Meridian West, and 'satanic' sums to 122 with Reverse Simple English. And don't get me started on all the dead rockstars from this city in relation to those numbers, when 'rock' sums to 47 with Simple English, the same as 'beast', and Seattle was the center of the rock world through much of the 1990s. Those deaths include many, and names such as Kurt Cobain, Layne Staley and most recently Shawn Smith, who all died on April 5th, or 5/4, not unlike 54, the number that connects the 'Jesuit Order' and the 'sun', the latter being the object that dictates time, that is the Jesuit logo. I should mention, in Jewish Gematria, 'sacrifice' sums to 206, and that is why on June 20th, or 20/6, in Seattle's Autonomous Zone, it was reported a 19 year was shot and killed, on a date and in a ritual we saw coming a mile away, in the "19 city". Let us not forget that the Autonomous Zone was established next to Seattle University, one of the nation's limited Jesuit universities, on June 8, 2020, a 6/8 date, with 54 numerology.

For more familiar numbers, pointing straight to the Jesuits, the largest building overseeing the Autonomous Zone area was the Odd Fellows Temple, part of an organization that dates back to April 26, 1819, making it 201 years old at the time of the occupation. And as for the building itself, it was established in 1908, making it 112 years old, reminding us of the 112 countries the Jesuits operate in. And two days after the reported killing, on June 22, 2020, the Seattle police announced their intentions to return to their precinct that they had abandoned on June 8, creating the Autonomous Zone. It was not by chance because June 22, 2020 was a date with 68 numerology, in 'Seattle, Washington', the city equating to 68, that we learned about earlier. *For your learning, that date can be expressed as 22/6, like 226, and 'planet' sums to 226 with Jewish Gematria, and 68 with Simple English. This information should shed new light on the '93 WTC bombing, on February 26th, a date that can be written 2/26. Of course, we know what planet is represented by the number 93, 'Saturn', the keeper of time.

On the subject of 206 and *The Da Vinci Code*', Tom Hanks son, Chet Hanks, made his 206th post on Instagram a memorable one. It was a video about his father's and mother's coronavirus sickness, ultimately saying they were going to be okay. Keeping in mind *The Da Vinci Code* is about the Vatican and the Illuminati, it is interesting to note that his March 12, 2020 post, was 221 days after Chet's August 4th birthday, or also put, on his 222nd day of his age. As you'll recall, 'The Bavarian Illuminati' sums to 221, and it was later changed to 'Order of Illuminati', equating to 201, and reminding of Tom Hanks' March 17, 2020 Instagram upload, with the image of his coronavirus typewriter, that has since been donated to little Corona, was about losing to his wife in Gin Rummy by 201 points. Furthering the point about the Illuminati, in Chet's March 12th Instagram video, he decided to talk about his parents illness with his shirt off, showing that in the center of his bare chest, he had the tattoo of the pyramid with the all seeing eye, a symbol associated with the Illuminati, and in part, through *The Da Vinci Code*. In light of the symbolism, keep in mind 'Gin Rummy' equates to 'Illuminati' with Simple English and Pythagorean. And better than that, *The Da Vinci Code*, starring Tom Hanks, released May 19, 2006, the 139th day of the year, corresponding with the Reverse Pythagorean Gematria of 'The Bavarian Illuminati', and also the values of 'Freemasonry' and 'America'. It should remind you how in my first book, we talk about the deaths of Sopranos' stars, James Gandolfini and Frank Vincent, exactly 221 weeks apart, and with Frank Vincent dying second, on September 13, or 13/9, reminding us of the death of 'Tupac Shakur', also on September 13th, and having a name with a Simple English value of 139. Keep in mind, James Gandolfini, died in 'Rome', summing to 51 with Simple English, at age 51, similar to how 'The Sopranos' sums to 51 with Pythagorean Gematria, the same as 'Adam Weishaupt', who founded the Bavarian Illuminati on May 1st, or 5/1, 1776. And in the case of Frank Vincent, he died at 78, corresponding with the Pythagorean Gematria of his full name, 'Frank Vincent Gattuso', as well as the word 'Jesuit'. Also, because Chet Hanks' post was on March 12th, or 3/12, and we're talking about riddles with the Vatican through his father's film series, you should know that 'Jorge Mario Bergoglio' and the name of Suite 201, the 'Domus Sanctae Marthae', both equate to 312, as well as 201.

This leads us to the point about Chet Hanks second Instagram post about his parents sickness on March 20, 2020, the 80th day of the year, corresponding with the Pythagorean Gematria of 'Bavarian Illuminati', equating to 80, as well as the 'Roman Catholic Church', equating to 320. On that day, he uploaded a response video to people accusing his family of being connected to the Illuminati, a viral rumor that circulated after his shirtless March 12th offering- with the all seeing eye in the triangle, front and center, on his exposed chest, being the basis of the claim. In a dry tone, possibly meant to be perceived as sarcastic, Chet Hanks said his family was part of the Illuminati, and before long, all their critics and all conspiracy theorists would be rounded up and put in FEMA Camps, amongst other remarks on the same level, before saying he needed to hurry off to participate in a human sacrifice ritual, where later that night he would be eating a person's pineal gland. What makes all of this so perfect, is that Chet Hank's birthday is August 4, 1990, a date emphasized as 8/4, corresponding with the 'Jesuit' encoding. It's also a date with numerology of 102 and 121, numbers you've become very familiar with. And further, August 4, 1990, was the 216th day of the year, the product of 6x6x6, also leaving 149 days left in the year, the 35th prime, connecting back to the gematria of 'Catholic', as well as 'satan' and 'baphomet', each equating to 35. And in light of *The Da Vinci Code* series being centered on the Catholic Church and the Vatican, we should be reminded that the pandemic was declared and Tom Hanks was announced as being sick on March 11th, the 71st day of the year, connecting to 'Catholic', and his son responded to the diagnosis on March 12th, the 72nd day of the year, connecting to 'Jesuit Order'.

With regards to 'Illuminati' and 'Gin Rummy' summing to 120 and what Chet Hanks was hopefully joking about, the human sacrifice meal, it should be noted that Tom Hanks co-star in *Inferno*, Irrfan Khan, died at age 53, on April 29, 2020, the 120th day of the leap year. Regarding his age of passing, both 'Hanks' and 'Covid'-19 equate to 53 with Simple English. Furthermore, 53 is the 16th prime number, and *Inferno* had released in 2016, emphasis on '16. For more familiar patterns, Khan reportedly died in 'Mumbai, India', equating to 201 with Reverse Simple, and also 113 days after his January 7th birthday. This 113 stands out all the more because his character name in *Inferno*, running 2:01 in length, is 'Harry Sims', summing to 113 with Simple English. Further connecting the 'Catholic' part of *The Da Vinci Code* series, he died 71 days before Tom Hanks' July 9th birthday, and 71 is the 20th prime number, corresponding with the Pythagorean Gematria of 'death', equating to 20. *If you have been following my online work for the year 2020, you know how familiar the 71 and 20 pattern has been in celebrity death.

On a lighter note, a ritual with Tom Hanks I didn't see coming, but had to laugh about when it did, was the announcement of Tom Hanks' and Rita Wilson's antibodies being used to help create the coronavirus vaccine. Keep in mind 'Hanks' and 'Covid'-19 equate in three out of the four base ciphers. And in light of these rituals being about time, the story of their antibodies being used by science was a top headline on April 25, 2020, a date with 49 numerology. In headlines, Tom Hanks referred to it as the 'Hank-ccine', equating to 49 with Reverse Pythagorean, similar to '*Revelation*', as well as 'Washington', 'Scottish' and 'America'. Even further, the news came 75 days before Tom Hanks July 9th birthday, corresponding with 'Catholic Church'. At the same time, it came 182 days after Rita Wilson's October 26, 2019 birthday, corresponding with what we learned about in the 2007 film *Pandemic*, where a viral outbreak is brought to the United States via Flight 182. As a reminder, 'Year of the Rat' equates to 182, as well as 142, the latter like 'coronavirus'. Adding to the ritual, April 25th is the 115th day of the year in non leap years, and 'Tom Hanks' sums to 115 with Reverse Simple English, similar to how 'Bill and Melinda Gates' sums to 115 with Reverse

Pythagorean, a number that should remind us of the first confirmed case of coronavirus in the United States, arriving at Seattle's airport, January 15th, or 1/15. And for the sake of time, we're going to skip Tom Hanks movie *Terminal*, about being stuck in an airport, as many people have found themselves with changing flight laws between states and nations due to coronavirus. And with the 115 list in mind, let us not forget that it is the number, from the Jesuit and Scottish Rite motto, 'Ad majorem Dei gloriam', equating to 115, that brings the two fraternities together, a number that also connects 'France', a nation the *Da Vinci Code* series is also set in.

As a reminder, that motto means "For the Greater Glory of God," and what is odd, is 'Lucifer' sums to 115 with Reverse Simple, the same as 'masonic', but Jesus does not have this connection, despite 'Jesus' and 'Lucifer', both equating to 74 with Simple English Gematria. Or perhaps, it isn't odd, in light of all the sinister agendas we're uncovering, or that *The Da Vinci Code* series is about these exact topics. For further proof of the relevance of the encoding of 115 in 'Tom Hanks' and 'Lucifer', using the same cipher, the next time you watch *Forrest Gump*, pay attention to the scene where he gives his Purple Heart medal from 'Vietnam', summing to 84 with Simple English, to Jenny. You will notice that after he gives away the 5 pointed star, reminding of the nation's 5 sided war department, the Pentagon, he does the baphomet pose, often shown in front of a 5 pointed pentagram, with two fingers pointed up, and two pointed down- in tribute to the phrase 'as above, so below', equating to 222, a number that is similar to how long the film *Forrest Gump* is, 2 hours and 22 minutes. Another detail to catch in that scene, is that the bus Jenny rides away in, is heading from Washington D.C., to Berkeley, in the Bay Area, where the Church of Satan was established in 1966, around the same time period as the film. The next time you watch *Forrest Gump*, also pay attention when Gump is describing the rain in Vietnam- he describes it as if a person was in control of it. This is curious because the U.S. military admitted in the time of Vietnam, to Operation Popeye, a mission that used the latest science of the time to increase rainfall on Vietnamese troops, as a means to flood out their underground tunnel networks. For whatever reason, Zemeckis decided to leave out the part about Operation Popeye in his film *Forrest Gump*, but he did drop a clue as to what was really going on with the weather in the very clever dialogue.

On the subject of Lucifer, there is an important point that needs to be made that connects to the Jesuits. In astrology, the planet Venus, known as the "morning star", is symbolic of Lucifer, the light bringer. And the transit of the planet Venus is said to have been first documented by the Jesuit Priest, Hell Miksa. *What a name right?* For the record, 'hell' and 'Catholic' both share gematria of 71, the 20th prime number, shedding perhaps even more light on why 2020 is the year that it has been. And not by surprise, 'Hell Miksa' and 'Venus' both equate to 54 with the base ciphers, the same as 'Jesuit Order'. And as you learned earlier, 'Jesuit Order' also sums to 144, and I bring this up, because Hell Miksa eventually died on April 14, 1792, a date that can be written 14/4. And also noteworthy, he died a span of 32 days from his 72nd birthday, having been born May 15, 1720. As you know, there are 32 sun rays on the Jesuit logo, and 'Jesuit Order' equates to 72 as well. Also, be sure to keep an eye on this date annually, because there is typically foul play on it. Case in point, on April 14, 2020, it was reported 'Henry George Steinbrenner III' of the Yankees, a name equating to 144, had died unexpectedly on it, 12 days after his April 2nd birthday, where 144 is the 12th Fibonacci number, and 144 has a square root of 12. Furthermore, as you learned earlier, the 'Society of Jesus' and the 'New York Yankees' have quite the relationship. And since I'm bringing up baseball, I should note that Tom Hanks played the part of 'Jimmy Dugan' in *A League of Their Own*. In addition to that title likely having new meaning to you now, his character name equates to 54 and 153, the same as 'Jesuit Order'.

As for science and the tracking of celestial bodies, Tom Hanks also starred in '*Lost Moon: The Perilous Voyage of Apollo Thirteen*', a title summing to 201 with Reverse Pythagorean. At the same time, the word 'Apollo' sums to 201 alone using Jewish Gematria, reminding us that those missions involved the moon landing, July 20, 1969, the 201st day of the Gregorian year. I bring this up, because John Kransinski of *The Office*, also posed with a Corona typewriter during the time of the pandemic, similar to Hanks, who posted an image of his Corona, with the message about Gin Rummy and losing by "201 points". In light of the number 201, consider, the hit show Krasinski starred in, *The Office*, lasted 201 episodes, and clearly not by accident. That is because there is a Jesuit school in town, 'Scranton Preparatory School', summing to 329, and similar to the date March 29th, or 3/29, the date John Krasinski posed with the typewriter, while launching his new news program, *Some Good News* (SGN). And to bring it back to the Apollo missions, Glynn Lunney, a NASA astronaut, was one of the original employees of NASA and was one of the first scientists to work on the Apollo missions, and he was a graduate of Scranton Preparatory School. And do I dare mention that 'Scranton' sums to 112, reminding of the number of countries the Jesuits operate in?

The other celebrity who was caught redhanded with a Corona typewriter, was Madonna. In her case, the typewriter was part of her album artwork for *Madame X*, that released June 14, 2019, on Donald Trump's 73rd birthday and the U.S. Flag's 242nd birthday. Keep in mind, the release date was a span of 222 days from January 21, 2020, when the first case of the virus was confirmed in the United States, and as you know, 'Wuhan Coronavirus' equates to 222. Adding to the ritual, on March 9th, or 9/3, similar to 93, also connecting to 'Wuhan Coronavirus', Madonna cancelled her March 10th and 11th performance in Paris, France, the original home of the Jesuits. Notice, the second show was to fall on the "pandemic" date declaration, and fittingly, '*Madame X*' equates to 38, same as 'pandemic'. Then on May 1, 2020, the anniversary of the establishment of the Bavarian Illuminati, on a date with 46 numerology, Madonna announced she had the antibodies to counteract the 'virus'. In light of 'The Bavarian Illuminati' equating to 221, I should note that from the release of her album, to the confirmation of the virus in the U.S., was also 221 days later, as opposed to a span of 222.

Perhaps the most important ritual Madonna participated in however, in the lead up to the coronavirus pandemic, was her performance at the 64th Eurovision, in Israel, that began on May 14, 2019, on Israel's birthday. Keep in mind 'Israel' sums to 64 with Hebrew and English gematria, and 'Zion' sums to 64 just the same. Never mind that on the exact same day, May 14th, the NBA had the 'Zion' Williamson sweepstakes, where 'Zion Williamson' sums to 74 with Pythagorean, and it was the first major event for the upcoming 74th NBA season. As for the predictive programming in the Eurovision performance, Madonna's backup dancers were wearing gas masks, and collapsing throughout the performance, almost as if they had died. In one section, Madonna hovers over a fallen dancer, and says, "it's not out there, it's in all of us." In light of the way millions have tested positive for coronavirus, despite being asymptomatic, it makes one wonder. I highly suggest you take the time to watch the performance. You will notice she is wearing the same costume, with the patch over the left eye, that she is clothed in for the *Madame X* album. And with that said, let us not overlook the Illuminati's well known one eye symbolism, or that Madonna has a song titled '*Illuminati*'. When you get a moment, be sure to look up the lyrics.

Regarding Madonna, let us not forget that in recent history, Aretha Franklin had died on her birthday, August 16, 2018. This matters because 'Queen' sums to 62 with Simple English, same as 'Madonna', and Aretha was considered the Queen of Soul. Adding to the ritual, four days after Aretha's death, Madonna was chosen to speak at the MTV Video Music Awards about the death of Aretha. In her speech, she told the story of how her personal music career began with $35 in her pocket, no doubt a tribute to 'satan'. Consider, Elvis Presley, who died on the same day as Aretha Franklin, years earlier, was born in 1935, and when he passed, Aretha was 35 years old at the time. It it to say, that these people are owned and operated by The Cabal, and the rituals they participate in are exact- and dark.

Speaking of dark, Idris Elba became the first black celebrity to be diagnosed with the virus, and one day after his diagnosis, asked the black people of the world not to spread conspiracy theories about the coronavirus. Not by chance, the news of his diagnosis was March 16, 2020, a date with 59 numerology, and the 76th day of the leap year. This matters because each of the following words sums to 59 with Simple English, and 76 with Reverse Simple. They include, 'Idris', 'slave', 'negro', 'Rasta' and 'blues'. Let us not forget *Acts 7:6* and the 400 year prophecy that landed on August 20, 2019, or that the Million Man March took place October 16, 1995, the day leaving 76 days in the year, or that Black History Month ends on the 59th day of the year, or that Motown Records was established in 1959. Let us also not overlook that Idris Elba was 47 years old at the time of this ritual, the number that defines 'time'.

All in all, there were several celebrities from the world of entertainment, media, and politics who came down with the virus by the numbers, even jailed movie producer Harvey Weinstein. The news of his illness came on the infamous date of March 22, 2020, the 82nd day of the year, corresponding with the gematria of 'Covid'-19, as well as 'Harvey Weinstein', both equating to 82. Adding to the riddle, he was 68 years old at the time, corresponding with the gematria of 'Wuhan', 'rape' and 'guilty'. The date of March 22nd, or 3/22, also reminds us a bit of another Jewish pervert, 'Jeffrey Edward Epstein', summing to 322 with Reverse Simple English. Furthermore, his name 'Jeffrey Epstein' sums to 163, the 38th prime, and he reportedly died in jail, on Tisha B'Av, August 10, 2019, 163 days prior to his upcoming January 20, 2019 birthday (a date that can be written 20/1). And if you think I'm reaching, look up the news story from July 19, 2020, the 201st day of the leap year, of a restaurant owner burning the table where Epstein and Weinstein used to eat together. The name of the restaurant that received the attention was Main 75. Of course, the number 75 reminds of the New York Times headline from October 6, 1940, a date with 75 numerology, reading "New World Order Pledged to Jews". As you know, 'New World Order' and 'Catholic Church' equate to 75. The latter entity being the one doing the pledging in the headline. And at the same time, 'Jeffrey' equates to 75, so you don't need to ask who backed either of these high profile perverts.

Also on the date of March 22nd, Rand Paul became the first U.S. Senator to test positive for the virus. This was a fitting date for him, because it can be expressed 22/3, similar to 223, the 48th prime, and the name 'Rand Paul' equates to 48 with Reverse Pythagorean. And let us not forget that 'novel coronavirus' sums to 223 with Simple English. At the same time, 'Senator Paul' equates to 142 and 155, the same as 'coronavirus', making him perfect for the ritual. Furthermore, his title, 'Senator Paul', also sums to 43 and 65, the same as 'pandemic'. This fits in with the fact that he represents 'Kentucky', a state summing to 43 as well.

For another 82 riddle with the virus, Sean Payton, the coach of the 'Saints', equating to 82 with Simple English, as well as 19 with Pythagorean, became the first member of the NFL to be diagnosed with 'Covid'-19. That was on March 19, 2020, his 82nd day of being 56 years old. Of course, 'coronavirus' sums to 56. Not long after, Tom Dempsey, who wore number 19 for the Saints, would reportedly died from the virus, on April 4th, or 4/4. This was 83 days after Dempsey's January 12, 2020 birthday, and both 'football' and 'murder' equate to 83. While we're at it, please look up the lyrics to the song *Murder by Numbers*, recorded in 1983, by the band The Police. Again, it is about how killing is the sport of the elite, and it is as simple as ABC, 123. As you have learned, Dempsey's date of death, 4/4, corresponds with the 44 gematria values of 'kill' and 'execution'. And in this case, 'Saints' also sums to 44 with Reverse Pythagorean. If you want to take it further, you could say he died on his 84th day of his age, and the divisors of 44 sum to 84, the latter being a favorite number of the Jesuits. And with regards to the J.O., 'New Orleans' sums to 54, the same as 'Jesuit Order'. Beyond that, his full name 'Thomas John Dempsey', equates to 'Wuhan Coronavirus', both summing to 78 and 210. Taking it another step further, the name 'Dempsey' alone sums to 102, a number that we have learned much about in this chapter.

Personally, one of my favorite coronavirus diagnosis rituals, was when the 56th Governor of New York, Jesuit educated Andrew Cuomo, announced that the head of New York's Port Authority, Rick Cotton, had come down with the coronavirus. This was funny for multiple reasons, including the fact that 'coronavirus' and 'Rick Cotton' sum to 142 with Reverse Simple English, and in Cuomo's same announcement, on March 9, 2020, he said New York had reached 142 total confirmed cases. Keep in mind March 9th can be expressed as 3/9, similar to 39. I've always referred to New York as the "39 state" because all of the following words and acronyms sum to 39 using the base ciphers. They are 'New York', 'empire', 'New York, NY', 'NY' and 'NYC'. Adding to the list, New York joined the United States of America on July 26, 1788, a date with 39 numerology, and the first governor was George Clinton, born July 26, 1739, a man having a first and last name equating to 39, 'George' and 'Clinton'. Beyond that, New York is home to the 39 story United Nations building, and it is the state that hosted the 1939's World Fair. From this day forward, you'll notice how significant the number is to the state, in ritual after ritual. For example, it wasn't an accident in 2018, when ESPN started a 39 day countdown for moving their show *First Take* to New York. The countdown began on July 26, 2018, the anniversary of New York joining the Union, counting down to the date of the first show in the Big Apple, September 3rd, a date that can be expressed as 3/9, not unlike 39. Trust me, when it comes to New York, these rituals are a dime a dozen, and you won't miss them going forward. If you'd like to do some investigating of your own, to put your skills to the test, look into the five NFL Super Bowls won by the state, four by Giants, and one by Jets. You will notice every single one paid tribute to the number 39. And it is for this same reason the Vegas line is currently set at 39.5 points for the upcoming Week 1 matchup between the Buffalo Bills and the New York Jets, September 13, 2020- two teams from New York. Even better, as I send this book off to the press, the New York Yankees and New York Mets have just faced each other in the MLB preseason July 18, 2020, after a 128 day coronavirus break, and the Mets have lost to the Yankees 3-9. Better yet, the Yankees have improve to 12-8 in the preseason, and they outhit the Mets 12-8 in the game. And putting the cherry on top, 'New York Yankees' equate to 187 and 191, the same as 'Society of Jesus', and the 187 corresponds perfectly with the date of the game, July 18th or 18/7, like 187.

The rituals weren't just taking place with the "Yankees" in the United States however. Across the Atlantic, similar things were transpiring. For example, take the case of Boris Johnson, the Prime Minister of the United Kingdom, or who I prefer to call "Bad Barbershop Brother #2", as opposed to Donald Trump, who is #1. All jokes aside, Johnson was reported to have been sent to the ICU on April 6, 2020, to receive treatment for the virus. Not by chance, this was his 293rd day of his age, born June 19th, and the term 'coronavirus pandemic' sums to 293 with Reverse Simple English. Furthermore, the date of April 6th was 74 days prior to his upcoming 56th birthday, on June 19, 2020, and we know how they like to bring 74 and 33 together, such as 'London' and 'England'. In this case, 'ICU' sums to 33 with Simple English. Let us not forget that Boris Johnson became the Prime Minister of the United Kingdom on July 24, 2019, exactly 158-weeks after Theresa May took office on July 13, 2016, and both 'Boris Johnson' as well as 'Freemasonry' equate to 158 with Reverse Simple English, reminding us that the Jesuits were fist formed in Paris on August 15th, or 15/8, in the year 1534. To go further, let us not forget that 'Brexit' sums to 78, like 'Jesuit', and it was the 'order out of chaos' event that triggered the Prime Minister terms for both Theresa May and Boris Johnson.

With politicians on the brain, and to come back to the man we began with, Tom Hanks, it is reported that he is an ancestor of Abraham Lincoln. This was brought attention to in September of 2012 by mainstream press, while Hanks was 56 years old. Of course, Barack Obama was the recent U.S. President who represented the Land of Lincoln, and who won the 56th U.S. Presidential Election, and one wonders if it is an accident that Barack Obama hosted both Tom Hanks and Bill Gates on the same night, to honor them with the 'Medal of Freedom', summing to 68 in Pythagorean, that infamous number, that connects 'Barack Obama' and 'Seattle, Washington', the latter being the city that brings Tom Hanks and Bill Gates together. This was done on November 22, 2016, the 53 year anniversary of the assassination of JFK, tying in 'Hanks' equating to 53, and 'Covid'-19, and the former company of Gates, 'Microsoft', each equating with the base ciphers. It was also a date that came precisely 165 weeks before coronavirus was confirmed in the United States of America. As you'll recall, JFK was killed in Dealey Plaza, named after a Scottish Rite Freemason, and 'Scottish Rite' equates to 165. 'Scottish Rite' also equates to 78, like 'Thomas Jeffrey Hanks', and 57, like 'Bill Gates'. Let us not forget the medal ceremony was in 'Washington D.C.', summing to 137 with Simple English, on Tom Hanks' 137th day of his age- the same city that has the North American headquarters for the Scottish Rite of Freemasonry. The exactness reminds that when Tom Hanks and Rita Wilson returned to the United States, from their coronavirus quarantine, on March 28th, it was 263 days after Tom Hanks' birthday, the 56th prime, and 155 days after Rita Wilson's, having been born October 26, 1956. As you know, 'coronavirus' equates to 56 and 155, and so does 'Freemasons'. In total, it should make you wonder, were these two married for this planned ritual on April 30, 1988, with this eventual planned outcome, 32 years later, reminding of the number of sun rays on the Jesuit logo? Let us not forget that 'America' and 'Scottish' also sum to 32 with Pythagorean. After all, the wedding was 70 days before Tom Hanks' birthday, and 'coronavirus' equates to 70, the same as 'Vatican', the entity overseeing the outbreak. If you ask me, this detail of their wedding parallels the fact that Bill and Melinda were married on the first day of 1994, and as we know, 'Roman Catholic Church' equates to 94.

As we conclude this chapter, please know that across the world, and throughout mainstream headlines, there were hundreds of other celebrity coronavirus diagnosis and death rituals, by the same repetitive patterns we have already identified. If you want to apply what you have learned, and investigate the other related stories, it will be a great way for you to practice and develop your decoding skills, and I promise, you will not be disappointed by what you find, but you might be disgusted. Just keep in mind, we're exposing disgusting people, and when enough people are helping, there will be justice. So thank you truth seeker, for being part of this cause, and being willing to take on this darkness, because it means everything.

13 | Nadia Tiger, Tiger King & the Year of the Tiger, 2022

On April 5, 2020, headlines read, 'Nadia the Tiger' tests positive for coronavirus. As you might imagine, or even recall, it was a story about a tiger, at the Bronx Zoo, becoming the first animal in the nation to test positive for the "deadly virus". To begin with why this matters, 'tiger' sums to 201 with Jewish Gematria. And keep in mind the Bronx isn't too far from the (201) area code in New Jersey, that houses the majority of the pharmaceutical giants of the world, that stand to benefit a great deal from a coronavirus vaccine, especially if it becomes something that is required, and annually. Of course those requirements would be based on how bad the pandemic is, or at least, believed to be. Furthermore, regarding the April 5th date of the news, it can be written 5/4, similar to 54, as in 'Jesuit Order', or as 4/5, similar to 45, in the time of the 45th President, and connecting to 'Holy Bible', as well as 'Gutenberg' equating to 45, as in the first printed Bible, the Gutenberg Bible, and reminding us of how the King James Version was published in 1611, the year King James turned 45 years old. This part about the Holy Bible is crucial, because 'Nadia the Tiger' sums to 121 with Simple English, the same as 'Revelation', the concluding text of the Bible, where the story of the mark of the beast is to be taken, 666, if you want to buy or sell. And because of our gained wisdom, we know how 'vaccination' equates to 666. Adding to this 'Revelation' riddle is the fact that 'Revelation' sums to 49 with Pythagorean Gematria, and the story broke on a date with 49 numerology (4/5/2020 = 4+5+20+20 = 49). Adding further, is that Nadia is considered a beast, and her news story was a riddle, not unlike Revelation 13:18, a Greek isopsephy riddle, about the mark of the beast, that requires wisdom to calculate it. And to that, cheers.

In light of Revelation being part of the Christian section of the Bible, it is important to remind ourselves that both 'Christianity' and 'coronavirus' equate to 155 with Simple English. Let us not forget the Clade X simulation, on May 15th, or 15/5, 666 days before the pandemic was declared. And regarding the number 155, it is symbolic in this story for numerous reasons. For one, the facility Nadia was housed at, the 'Wildlife Conservation Society', equates to 155 with Reverse Pythagorean. At the same time, it sums to 331 with Simple English, the 67th prime number, corresponding with 'Nadia the Tiger', equating to 67 with Pythagorean, and 'Wuhan' summing to 67 with

Simple English. Let us not forget 67 is the 19th prime, and 19 is the number of 'chaos', as in order out of chaos. I should also note the 67th Bilderberg Conference took place in Switzerland, not long before the pandemic began, that was declared from Switzerland. If you're not familiar with the Bilderberg Conference, it began in 1954, emphasis on '54, and it is where world banking, industry and media elite gather annually, to plot against humanity. As for the next big 155, it is the fact that International Tiger Day, a real thing, falls on July 29th every single year, the day leaving 155 days in the Gregorian year. Making this all the more interesting, in 2020, July 29th was the first day of Tisha B'Av, just as it was in 2001, 19 years earlier.

For one last detail on Nadia, she was described as a 'Malayan Tiger', equating to 54 and 72 with the Pythagorean methods, the same as 'Jesuit Order', and similar to how 'sun' equates to 54 with Simple English, and also similar to the date of the news, April 5th, or 5/4. It is a reminder, all of these rituals are time based, and in tribute to our past, as well as where we are going, or better yet, where we are being taken. As we move ahead with this chapter, I will get to the point about how The Cabal are signaling the coming year 2022, the Chinese Year of the Tiger, that ends at the start of 2023, thus 2022-23, corresponding with how 'Wuhan' has Pythagorean values of both 22 and 23, and how they are signaling this through rituals such as 'Nadia', summing to 20 with Pythagorean, a story coming in 2020.

Shortly after the story of Nadia, Pink, the singer, born 'Alicia Moore', equating to 56 and 70, in the exact same way as 'coronavirus', told the story of how her and her 'three' year old son had been battling the illness. As you'll recall, 'three' equates to 56 with Simple English, the same as 'zoo', where Nadia was diagnosed. The image the majority of mainstream media chose to show when the news broke, was Pink holding her child, who was dressed in a toddler's jacket, with a tiger emblem clearly on the front of it. In the details of the story, it was reported how her son carried a 102 degree temperature for two straight weeks, a reminder for all people listening to practice 'social distancing', summing to 102, the same as 'Wuhan, China'.

Days after that, ESPN reported on April 7, 2020, how Tiger Woods was enjoying his annual Masters dinner, 'quarantine style', with emphasis on the phrase, as the media so often does, when there are key numbers behind it. Case in point, 'quarantine style' sums to

201 with Simple English, similar to how 'Tiger' sums to 201 with Jewish Gematria. And yes, for the record, I helped people win a fortune with the 2019 Masters, that Tiger won, by showing how it was in the bag for Tiger Woods to win, nearly a year in advance. How? For starters, the name 'Tiger Woods' sums to 54 with both Pythagorean methods, similar to how Jesuit Order sums to 54 and 144, combing perfectly with the 2019 Masters end date, won by Tiger Woods on Sunday, April 14th, or 14/4, an infamous date in history for the Jesuits, who are credited with the assassination of Lincoln April 14, 1865. And for those familiar with the golf superstar, consider how Tiger always wears red and black on Sundays, the colors of the Jesuits, and in many regards, the Catholic Church itself. The bigger giveaway that the tournament was in the bag for Tiger, was that the 2019 Masters tournament was 22 years after Tiger won his first Masters in '97, and 11 years after he won his last major, where the master numbers are 11, and 22. Plus 'golf' sums to 22 in Pythagorean, the same as 'master', and the same as 'Woods'. To take it to the next level, April 14th was 105 days after Tiger's birthday, the 14th triangular number, and 'golf' equates to 14 with Reverse Pythagorean, similar to 'slave' with Pythagorean. I bring up the word slave because the tournament began April 11, 2019, 102 days after Tiger's birthday, corresponding with the gematria of 'slavery', equating to 102, and the fact that the American Civil War began April 12, 1861, the 102nd day of the year- and beyond that, 'civil war' equates to 43, what is the 14th prime number, and Tiger Woods was 43 years old at the time of the 2019 Masters win. The final piece was that April 14th could also be expressed as Tiger Woods 106th day of his age, corresponding with the gematria of both 'black' and 'prophecy', and while we're at it, 'Black Lives Matter'. This mattered in 2019 because on August 20th of that year, months after the Masters golf tournament concluded, the 400 year prophecy from *Acts 7:6* was fulfilled. And keep in mind both the names 'Tiger' and 'Woods', as well as the words 'slave' and 'master', equate to 76. It was for this reason we were also able to call the Virginia Cavaliers winning the college basketball championship at the start of February in 2019, during Black History Month, when we connected the dot that the first slaves to arrive in America, arrived at Point Comfort, Virginia, on the James River, explaining why so many politicians in the state were being accused of wearing "black face." And not to be a broken record, but I promise you, you'll never look at sports and news the same way

again, because from this day forward, you have the knowledge to see through the scripted rituals, that are intertwined, that are the workings of The Cabal. And better yet, you can see them before they come.

Continuing with the number 76, on April 7, 2020, the date of the news of Tiger Woods 'quarantine style' dinner, Wuhan, China ended their lockdown after 76 days. Again, another tribute to 'Tiger', summing to 76, as in the Chinese Year of the Tiger. And keep in mind Tiger Woods is of African and Asian descent. Also consider that the lockdown in 'Wuhan' had begun on the 23rd of January, a fitting date, since 'Wuhan' sums to 23 with Reverse Pythagorean. At the same time, 'outbreak' sums to 123 and 51 in gematria, and 'Wuhan, China' also sums to 51, meaning that between the date, January 23rd, or 1/23, and the location summing to 51, both outbreak numbers were covered. Adding to the list of words with the same number association, 'conspiracy' equates to 123 and 51, and that is what this was.

The details about 51 and 123 remind us that on March 10, 2020, the 25 year anniversary of the release of the film *Outbreak*, having a plot involving a viral outbreak in the U.S., and the military being deployed to a small suburban town to contain the spread of the virus, Andrew Cuomo, the 56th Governor of New York, deployed the 'National Guard', equating to 56 in Pythagorean, the same as 'coronavirus', on the town of 'New Rochelle', summing to 51 in Reverse Pythagorean, the same as 'Outbreak'. Furthermore, he said the troops would arrive there March 12th, or 12/3, not unlike 123. Keep in mind, March 10, 2020, the date of his announcement, was the 70th day of leap year, and 'coronavirus' sums to 70 with Reverse Pythagorean. As we know, 56 connects to 'Society of Jesus' and 70 connects to 'Vatican'. Consider then that 'New Rochelle' also sums to 177 like 'The Jesuit Order', and March 12th was the 72nd day of the year, corresponding with 'Jesuit Order'. Making those responsible for the ritual all the more clear, Governor Cuomo, born December 6, 1957, was on his 96th day of his age, and 'New Rochelle, New York' equates to 96 with Pythagorean, similar to how 'Corona' sums to 96 with Reverse Simple. As you have learned, the divisors of 42 sum to 96, and the word 'Jesuit' sums to 42, whereas 'Freemason' sums to 42 and 96. You could also say the incident was 95 days after his birthday, reminding us of 1995, the year *Outbreak* released, and the year of the first Military World Games in Rome, as well as the fact that the Jesuits were formed to counter the *95 Theses*. On the subject of 95, and for a related tangent, for all the New York Yankees fans out there, please know MLB star Gerrit Cole picked up his 95th career regular season win, in his Yankees debut, in the first game of the coronavirus shortened season, July 23, 2020, by defeating the Washington Nationals, in 'Washington D.C.', equating to 187, the same as 'New York Yankees' and 'Society of Jesus'. And keep in mind, the Washington Nationals just won the 115th World Series by the numbers to conclude last season, and as we know, D.C. is a Jesuit stronghold, to say the least. And making the ritual all the more perfect, Cole's birthday is September 8th, the one the Catholic Church celebrates as the Virgin Mary's birthday. That is also the 251st day of the year, the 54th prime number, connecting to the gematria of 'baseball', as well as 'Jesuit Order'. Furthermore, the game was on his 320th day of his age, corresponding with 'Roman Catholic Church'. And for one more fastball, right down the pipe, before we get back on topic, you can now understand why Roger Maris hit 61 home runs in 1961, where 61 is the 18th prime number, and both 'baseball' and 'IHS' equate to 18 with Pythagorean. Of course he was playing for the 'Yankees', a name equating to 26, like 'game' and 'God', where the latter word sums to 61 with Jewish Gematria, and should remind of you of the 61 circles that make up the Flower of Life in sacred geometry. Of course, a circle in its three dimensional form, is a ball. As for the year 1995, and getting back on topic, when *Outbreak* came out, as a reminder, it was the year Bill Gates was declared the world's richest man, and 'Amazon' came into existence, the company that is on its way to what Kurt Vonnegut predicted over 50 years ago, the one company to own all things. As we know, 95 matters to the Jesuits, recognized by Rome, on the day leaving 95 days left in the year, to counteract the *95 Theses*. And for one last thought on Cuomo's New Rochelle ritual, both Morgan Freeman, and Dustin Hoffman, the stars of *Outbreak*, were 82 years old at the time, corresponding with the gematria of 'Covid'-19, equating to 82, and the fact that the Jesuit educated Cuomo would go on to issue stay at home orders for New York, beginning March 22, 2020, the 82nd day of the year. I should also note, for his efforts, his name began trending on Twitter with '#PresidentCuomo', a hashtag having gematria of 69, 177 and 201, in the same ciphers as 'The Jesuit Order'. Thus, it was fitting for the Jesuit educated politician. And sadly, it showed that if you manipulate your own people, as Cuomo did, in this Orwellian society we're living in, you can still be loved.

It was shortly after this same time, March 31st, that Samuel L. Jackson was a guest on Jimmy Kimmel's nightly entertainment program, that typically broadcasts from the Masonic Temple of Hollywood. On there he read the book 'Stay the Fuck At Home', with a tiger drawn on the cover, and a title summing to 201 in Simple English. The title also has gematria of 66, 87 and 258, the exact same as 'number of the beast'. Keep in mind 'Corona' sums to 66 with Simple English, and 'Samuel L. Jackson' sums to 87. Showing further why he was chosen for this ritual, the actor's name also equates to 222 (similar to 2022, the Year of the Tiger), the same as 'Wuhan, Coronavirus', and reminding us of the massive ritual with the pandemic being declared on March 11, 2020, 222 months after September 11, 2001. On the subject of 9/11, if you watch the clip of Samuel L. Jackson reading the nicely titled book, you'll see the actor has '*The Long Kiss Goodnight*' movie poster above his shoulder, that he once starred in. If you have never seen this movie before, I won't ruin it for you, but I promise you your jaw will hit the floor, in light of the dialogue, that came before September 11, 2001. Trust me, you won't miss what I intend for you to see and hear if you watch. That same film released October 11, 1996, nearly five years earlier, a date with 136 numerology, the 16th Triangular Number, reminding us of the 16th Tarot card, The Tower. Trust me, after you watch the film, and you hear the dialogue that is SO SPECIFIC to what took place on September 11, 2001, you won't believe it even after you watch it. And then to see how they use Samuel L. Jackson, in this ritual, it is so twisted! Then again, he is the villain in '*Glass*', the film we discussed earlier, where he intends to destroy the Osaka Tower, in a terrorist attack, on the anniversary of Pearl Harbor. And for one last stat on the book Samuel L. Jackson was reading, and to build on our 155 'coronavirus' pattern, the author of '*Stay the Fuck At Home*', Adam 'Mansbach', has a surname summing to 155 with Reverse Simple English. As a reminder, the number 155 is where we started the chapter, with the story of Nadia, the tiger, living at the 155 location, something that relates to this book's cover, which is illustrated with a picture of a tiger. *And for the record, the Detroit Tigers defeated the Kansas City Royals, 5-4, on International Tiger Day, July 29, 2020.

Moving on, around the time of Samuel L. Jackson's late night bedtime story being read on Jimmy Kimmel's show, with the tiger on the cover, *Tiger King* became the number one trending series on Netflix, after debuting on March 20, 2020. Keep in mind, the date March 20th can be expressed as 3/20, like 320, corresponding with the gematria of 'Roman Catholic Church', reminding us who the boss is. Adding to the riddle, the star of the show, Joe Exotic, was born March 5, or 3/5, not unlike 35, the number representing 'Catholic' in Pythagorean Gematria. Adding further to the ritual, it was announced on May 4th, that Nicolas Cage, born January 7th, or 7/1, corresponding with the 71 value of 'Catholic', would play the part of Joe Exotic in an upcoming *Tiger King* series, to air on CBS, the network that uses the all seeing eye for its logo. Adding insult to injury, Nicolas cage was 56 years old at the time of the announcement, that came on the 119th day of his age. As you know, 'all seeing eye' equates to 56 and 119, and at the same time, 'Society of Jesus' sums to 56, whereas 'Vatican' equates to 119. You could also say the announcement came 118 days after Cage's birthday, corresponding with the Reverse Pythagorean gematria of 'Joseph Allen Schreibvogel', equating to 118. That is the birth name of Joe Exotic. In Variety's story on the Nicholas Cage role, they emphasized 'American Vandal' in their May 4th headline, the team behind the upcoming show. Using simple English, their name also equates to 118, reminding us how perfectly these rituals are executed, day after day. And for a more familiar number, the name 'Joe Schreibvogel' equates to 155 with Simple English, the same as 'coronavirus', bringing us back to the ritual with Nadia, at the 155 location, and to International Tiger Day, leaving 155 days left in the year. For a couple more familiar numbers, the name 'Joe Exotic' sums to 47, whereas 'Joe Schreibvogel' equates to 74 with Pythagorean, similar to how his zoo is located in 'Wynnewood, Oklahoma', also equating to 74. It was for this reason, 'Carole Baskin', equating to 47 with Pythagorean, a character from *Tiger King,* was given control of the Zoo on June 1, 2020, a date with 47 numerology. Never mind that 'Oklahoma' alone equates to 76, the same as 'tiger'.

And speaking of Carole Baskin, the Hollywood actress, Tara Reid, born November 8, 1975, a date written 11/8, was named to play the part of Carole Baskin on May 16, 2020, in an upcoming film about *Tiger King.* This was done on the 191st day of Tara Reid's age, corresponding with 'Society of Jesus'. Factoring in, 191 is the 43rd

prime, and the surname 'Baskin' equates to 43 with Reverse Pythagorean, whereas 'Joe Exotic' sums to 43 with Pythagorean. What makes this all the more ritualistic, is that at the same time in the news, another woman, with a very similar name, Tara Reade, was accusing a different Joe, Joe Biden, the presidential hopeful, of sexual assault. As I had pointed out on April 9, 2020, when Tara Reade filed a police report, it was the 153rd day of the Hollywood actress's age, and this was curious because the accuser's full name, 'Alexandra Tara Reade', equates to 153 with Simple English, whereas 'Jesuit Order' equates to 153 with Reverse Simple. In light of the date, April 9th, it can be written 9/4, like 94, reminding that Joe Biden is of the 'Roman Catholic Church', equating to 94. To take it even further, Tara Reade's accusal was on March 25th, or 3/25, and the full name of Joe Biden, 'Joseph Robinette Biden', equates to 325 with Revers Simple English.

For another story that relates, on April 22, 2020, a date with 46 numerology, corresponding with 'virus', it was reported that two separate cats, in two differing parts of New York, had tested positive for coronavirus. Personally, this reminded me of the November 21, 2010 episode of *The Simpsons*, titled *The Fool Monty*. In that episode, part of the plot involves something referred to as "Apocalypse Meow", an epidemic impacting felines. What makes this all the more interesting, is that *The Simpsons* episode released on the 325th day of the year, reminding of the massive 325 ritual that took place during the time of the pandemic, with the 'City of London Corporation' becoming all the richer on March 25th, or 3/25, while having existed for 325 years. Adding to the relevance of *The Simpsons*, in terms of coronavirus predictive programming, on May 6, 1993, or 5/6, they released the episode *Marge in Chains*, about a viral outbreak of Osaka Flu, that is spread by mailed packages. As we decode, keep in mind the writer of *The Simpsons*, Matthew Groening, studied at Evergreen College, just south of Seattle, where the first case of coronavirus was confirmed on January 21st, or 1/21. I bring this up because '*Marge in Chains*' sums to 121 with Simple English, and beyond that, the name reminds us of Alice in Chains, the Seattle based band. Furthermore, don't overlook the release date of the episode, May 6th, that can be written 5/6, similar to 56, the big 'coronavirus' number, or the year of release, '93, reminding of 'Wuhan Coronavirus', equating to 93. I'll also note, 1993 was when *Sleepless in Seattle* released, and in 2007, *The Simpsons Movie* released, where Tom Hanks makes a cameo, and he puts himself in isolation, reminding us of his ritual after his March 11th coronavirus diagnosis. Coming back to the '93 episode, the contents of the mailed package that begins the Osaka Flu outbreak, is a 'Juice Loosener', equating to 151, the same as 'pandemic', and reminding us that the first case of coronavirus to arrive in Seattle, was on the date January 15th, or 15/1, before being confirmed on January 21st. Aside from the numbers, key details to keep track of are that the flu is given an "asian" name, and that it begins with mailed packages, reminding us of Amazon, the package mailing giant, based out of Seattle. And for the record, the writer's full name, 'Matthew Abraham Groening', has gematria of 223, in the same cipher as 'novel coronavirus'. His full name also equates to 119, and so does 'Springfield', the town his show is set in. Let us not forget the many relevances of that number, including the gematria of 'Ancient Mystery Religions', which includes what we're discussing in this book.

For one last point, the term 'cats', bringing household pets and tigers together, has Reverse Simple English Gematria of 65. This is similar to how 'pandemic' equates to 65 with Simple English, and how *The Simpsons* episode about the Osaka Flu released on May 6th, a date that can be expressed as 6/5, not unlike 65. Thus, it made the creatures perfect for the encoded pandemic rituals that they became a part of, in the monstrous lies that were told in popular media, by villains such as Anthony Fauci, Andrew Cuomo, Chris Cuomo, Gavin Newsom, Donald Trump, Deborah Birx, Bill Gates, and so on. And keep in mind, these are the same lies that will benefit Bill Gates and others when the vaccines come around, the man who participated in the many 65 rituals we've uncovered, in the decades leading up to the coronavirus pandemic, including his 'Decade of Vaccines', summing to 65. And to add to your 65 list, the detail from *The Simpsons'* episode mentioned earlier, 'Apocalypse Meow', equates to 65 with Reverse Pythagorean, the same as 'Year of the Rat', that began January 25, 2020, just days after the first confirmed case in the U.S. As we'll get to in the next chapter, the Chinese New Year was Dean Koontz's 201st day of being 74 years old, a ritual we'll learn about next chapter, that was even more prophetic than anything we have discussed yet. And when I say prophetic, please realize I'm saying it with the understanding that this is all being contrived by The Cabal, thus contrived prophecy.

14 | Coronavirus Predictive Programming in Popular Media

The oldest piece of predictive programming I am aware of when it comes to the coronavirus is the *Holy Bible*. The next oldest is Dean Koontz's 1981 novel, *The Eyes of Darkness*. The latter is a novel that includes a plot with details of a military conspiracy, to spread a virus, that is named "Wuhan 400." In light of what you have learned thus far about the number 201, a biblical number, I want you to appreciate the significance of Dean Koontz, who was born July 9, 1945, at the end of the second World War, being on his 201st day of his age, age 74, the day of the Chinese New Year, January 25, 2020, the start of the Year of the Rat. Let us not forget, Event 201 took place October 18, 2019, the day leaving 74 days in the year, or what the meaning of 74 is. Adding to the riddle, using the base ciphers, 'Dean Ray Koontz', the author's full name, and 'Year of the Rat', are identical in three out of four, each summing to 61 with Pythagorean, 65 with Reverse Pythagorean, and 182 with Reverse Simple English. At this point, you should be familiar with 61 and 65 and their meaning, you should even know how they both relate to Bill Gates, Agent 201, and in a moment, we'll discuss more about number 182, in the context of another piece of predictive programming, titled *Pandemic*. Of course what makes the Dean Koontz alignment much more impressive, is the fact that in his 1981 book, part of the plot involves a military conspiracy that uses a virus named 'Wuhan 400', out of a city in China that has a name you can guess. With that in mind, think about what we have learned regarding August 20, 2019, being the 400 year anniversary of slavery, especially since Wuhan Coronavirus came shortly after. Furthermore, consider how the verses in *Acts 7:6-7* correspond with this moment in history, and in the 'United States', equating to 77, specifically, the land of the not so free or brave in the days of the mask, the same land Dean Koontz calls home. With that in mind, know that 'Wuhan Four Hundred', written out as words, sums to 201 with Simple English, so once again, we know who is behind it. Using the rest of the base ciphers, the name 'Wuhan Four Hundred' sums to 78, 84 and 231, the latter being the 21st triangular number, and reminding us that 'Jesuit' equates to 21, 42, 78 and 84, and that 'Georgetown', summing to 42, Washington D.C.'s Jesuit University, was founded 23/1, January 23rd. Altogether, it reminds us of Event 201, taking place on the same day the Military World Games began, in

Wuhan, China, an event that has origins in Rome, from the year 1995. It is to say, familiar patterns.

In terms of the coronavirus outbreak, a crucial detail in the Wuhan 400 virus from Koontz's novel is that it is part of *Project Pandora*, another "fictional" element. The name 'Project Pandora' equates to 222 and 78, the same as 'Wuhan Coronavirus', 'order out of chaos', and 'Event Two Zero One', as well as 'New York, New York', where Event 201 was hosted. Let us not forget that 'Jesuit' sums to 78, the same as 'Scottish Rite', or the 78 cards of the Tarot deck. And of course, there are many other details we can add to the list, such as 'Samuel L. Jackson', summing to 222 and 87, reading the not so nicely titled book, that had a value equating to 201 (last chapter). Or the 'Washington Huskies', summing to 222 and 78, out of Seattle, being one of the first major universities to tell their students to stay home, setting a national trend with all schools because of the virus. And in light of Washington Huskies summing to 222, consider that George Washington was born February 22nd, or 2/22.

To contrast the information you're learning here with how information such as this is presented in the mainstream, I offer this example. The topic of Dean Koontz's same novel using the "Wuhan 400" terminology decades prior to Wuhan Coronavirus was simply called a coincidence by Fox News, and brushed aside, with little explanation for how they could be so sure, on February 14, 2020. Imagine it truth seeker, what a lost potential. Fox News' headline was written one day after the South China Morning Post wrote about the curiosities of Dean Koontz 1981 thriller, in the context of coronavirus, asking- how is it that some works of fiction turn out to be prophecy? What they should have answered with was, look no further than the Jesuits. Case in point, take the book *'The Wreck of the Titan'*, equating to 95. It was about a boat named the TITAN, the largest boat ever built, sinking on its first sail, after hitting an iceberg- while traveling from Europe to America. And yes, that is the exact same story as the TITANIC, that was a sinister plot, and insurance fraud. That book was published in 1898, long before April 14, 1912, the date of the wreck of the Titanic. By the way, April 14th can be expressed as 14/4, not unlike 144, the number syncing with 'Jesuit Order', as well as 'time'. And on the subject of 'time', equating to 47 with Simple English and 144 with Jewish Gematria, the Titanic's demise was 47 years after Lincoln's assassination, where he was shot late April 14th, and died early April 15, 1865, kind of like how the Titanic began to sink late April 14th, and fully submerged April 15, 1912. Adding to the ritual, April 14, 1912 was a date with 49 numerology, and 'iceberg' equates to 49, as does 'America', the destination. If you research the book, you will find the same story is known by a shorter name, '*Futility*', also equating to 49. And further, if you'll recall that the word 'Scottish' sums to 49 and 113, as in the Scottish Rite of Freemasonry, please know that 'Titanic' also sums to 113, a number of deception from the *Talmud*. What makes this all the more fascinating, is that from the date the Titanic fully submerged, April 15, 1912, to the date the Federal Reserve was established, December 23, 1913, was 617 days later, the 113th prime number. If you research the history of the sinking of the Titanic, you'll also learn that a number of very wealthy and powerful men perished with the boat's demise, men who were opposed to the establishment of a central bank, which is what the Federal Reserve is, and what was warned about at the beginning of this nation's existence, especially by Thomas Jefferson, who died, by the numbers, July 4, 1826, as covered. As for the wealthy and powerful men on the boat, they were John Jacob Astor IV, Isidor Straus, and Benjamin Guggenheim. It truly is worth investigating, because many other notable people from society died due to their attendance in what was considered a very special event, the launching of this unprecedented structure in terms of its size, something like the World Trade Centers when they were built. On the subject, as you learned, 'World Trade Center' sums to 94, and they opened on the 94th day of 1973, and in this case, '*Futility*' also sums to 94, similar to 'terror'. To put the loss of life on the Titanic in today's terms, imagine if a headline read something similar to, *Elon Musk, Jeff Bezos, Bill Gates, Mark Zuckerberg, Kim Kardashian & Kanye West die in SpaceX catastrophe!* That would be an eye popper. And on the subject of SpaceX, let's take a brief moment to remember their historic mission launch time of 3:22 EST, on May 30, 2020, what reportedly became the first private space launch to result in a successful docking at the International Space Station. What made this ritual amusing if you were in the know, is that it came 51 days before the 51 year anniversary of the supposed moon landing, that took place on the 201st day of 1969, on July 20th. The reason we can be sure the 51st anniversary is more important to The Cabal than the 50th, is because 'moon' and 'conspiracy' both equate to 51. Keep in mind, some researchers contend that the moon landing was filmed at Area 51, and filmed by 'Stanley Kubrick', a name summing to 54 in Pythagorean, the same as 'Jesuit Order', and 207 with Reverse Simple, not unlike the date 20/7, or July 20, 1969. And please don't get me started on how 'SpaceX' sums to 68, or the story of the 1968 Apollo astronauts reading *Genesis*, for a Christmas Eve broadcast, from space. As a reminder, *Genesis* is the opening book of the *Holy Bible,* that should remind you of *Genesis 3:22,* and how from that verse, 'knowing good and evil', equates to 201. And for your learning, where '*Genesis'* equates to 666 with Reverse Sumerian, NASA, standing for 'National Aeronautics and Space Administration', equates to 666 with Reverse Sumerian. It's almost as if all this time, they have been testing our spiritual impulses with their propaganda, seeing if we do know good and evil- and more importantly, what we'll do about it. Sadly, I think most people have not recognized the evil, and that these stories have ultimately contributed to dividing us as a people, while helping us forget essential concepts and essential values that traditionally have kept people in harmony with each other and the world, such as spirituality and loving our neighbor. Perhaps part of the reason why is because we have been mesmerized at the accomplishments of science and technology, especially those that have been televised, including the moon landing, causing us to forget the basics of life and the necessary traditions of our ancestors.

Coming back to the South China Morning Post's article on the Dean Koontz novel (the same one that made the story go viral), and how it discussed the book within the context of prophecy, it is important to note that it was published on February 13th, the 44th day of the year. This is because using Pythagorean Gematria, 'Dean Koontz' sums to 44, and so does 'prophet'. Using that same cipher, you can add 'military' to your 44 list, because his book involved a military conspiracy. And as a reminder, and as of this moment, the official narrative still reports the first confirmed coronavirus case in the world was recorded on November 17, 2019, the day leaving 44 days in the year, and also a date with 47 and 67 numerology, the latter number corresponding with 'Wuhan', and being the 19th prime, reminding us that 'Seattle' sums to 19 and 44, where the virus would go after Wuhan. Another point about the February 13th article date is it can be written 13/2, like 132, connecting the gematria of 'United States of America', as well as 'Catholic Church', and reminding us that the

White House, built on top of what was once known as Rome on the Potomac, has 132 rooms in it. And possibly coincidental, or not, Donald Trump, the man residing in the White House at the time of the outbreak, turned 35 years old in 1981, the year the book was published, having been born in 1946, where 'Catholic' equates to 35 and 46. While we're at it, 'Dean Koontz' equates to 46 and 145, in the same ciphers as 'Catholic'.

To make another point about the date November 17, 2019, it was the one year anniversary of the Yellow Vest movement beginning in Paris, France, the home of the Jesuits, on November 17, 2018. Keep in mind both 'Society of Jesus' and 'Paris, France' equate to 187 with Reverse Simple, and the date written 11/17, is much like 1117, the 187th prime number. Furthermore, 11 and 17 are prime factors of 187. And beyond that, 'Yellow Vest' equates to 112, the same as 'Catholicism', and reminding us that the Jesuits operate in 112 countries. At the same time, 'Yellow Vest' sums to 158, reminding us that the Jesuits were formed in Paris, France, on August 15th, or 15/8, in the year 1534. *For more number learning, we know that 'France' and 'masonic' equate to 115, but what we have not mentioned is how 11, the master number, is also the 5th prime number, thus 115 contains two numbers that have a mathematical relationship, 11 and 5.

To make a few last points on the Koontz novel, when it was first released, it had a different author's name, an alias Dean Koontz reportedly used. That name was 'Leigh Nichols'. In Simple English, the alternate name equates to 121, the same as 'Revelation', and using Pythagorean, it sums to 67, similar to 'Wuhan'. As for the title itself, 'The Eyes of Darkness' sums to 89 and 199, the latter number being the 46th prime. This matters because both 'virus' and 'chaos' equate to 46 and 89 *and since initially writing this chapter, I am now updating it, because mainstream media has come out and clarified that in his 1981 book, the name Wuhan 400 was not used, instead, it was changed for the later edition, published in 1989. What is worth considering about the 1989 update, is 89 is the 11th Fibonacci number, and 1989 was 31 years before 2020, where 31 is the 11th prime number. 1989 was also the year Hulk Hogan and Randy Savage, as the "Mega Powers" of professional wrestling, made their infamous speech about tearing down the "Twin Towers." Look it up, you won't regret it, and as sad as it is, it might even make you laugh at the same time. At least, that's how it is for me. And once again, 11 is the master number and 9/11 as well as coronavirus were masterplans, centered on it. And for one last point on the Dean Koontz novel, the title *'The Eyes of Darkness'* also sums to 260, not far off from 26, the number corresponding with 'virus' and 'China', as well as 'Covid'-19. Keep in mind the surname 'Koontz' sums to 101, the 26th prime number, and Event 201 took place precisely 101 days after his 74th birthday, on the day leaving 74 days left in the year. And last, the other value of the title is 73, reminding us that in Catholic Bible's there are 73 books, and 73 is the 21st prime number, corresponding with the gematria of *'Bible'*, 'Jesuit' and 'math'.

The next piece of predictive programming worth mentioning is the 2007 film *Pandemic*. It begins with a surfer named 'Ames', which is perfect for the film *Pandemic* because his name sums to 38, the same as 'pandemic'. Better yet, 'Ames' also sums to 70, matching 'coronavirus'. Adding to the list of 70s is that he contracts his pandemic starting illness in 'Queensland, Australia', summing to 70, and then catches an international flight in 'Sydney', equating to 70 as well, setting up the storyline. For another parallel, he is traveling from 'Australia', summing to 102, the same as 'Wuhan, China', to the United States of America, who on April 11, 2020, the 102nd day of the leap year, was reported to have become the nation to have the most recorded deaths in the world from the virus. That was the same day Tom Hanks hosted SNL, who donated his Corona typewriter to the boy in Queensland, Corona DeVries. In the film, Ames is traveling from Australia to 'L.A.', two letters summing to 13 with Simple English, and connecting to how the film came out 13 years before 2020. Even more, the film is 169 minutes in length, having a square root of 13.

On the subject of 38, I should bring up the fact that it was reported on January 25, 2020, in all mainstream media, that the world documented its 38th case of coronavirus outside of mainland China. Keep in mind, just days earlier, on January 21st, the first case was recorded in Seattle, Washington, a city located on the west coast of the U.S., like Los Angeles, the scene of *Pandemic*. For another 38, around this same time, the man referred to as the Chinese doctor who blew the whistle on coronavirus, before being censored by Chinese police on January 3, 2020, reportedly died from the virus. His name was Li Wenliang, and he was said to have passed on February 7, 2020, the 38th day of the year. It was also 118 days after his October 12ᵗʰ birthday, having turned 33, and been born October 12, 1986. As you have learned, 'death' sums to 38 with Simple English, and 118 with 'Jewish'. If you're trying to wake people up to this knowledge, pointing out this pattern of 118 along with the TV show *Numb3rs*, about solving homicides, that lasted 118 episodes, is a good one. Another strong example is the movie poster for *Murder by Numbers*, where it is written *Murd3r 8y Numb8rs*. As a reminder, the words 'death', 'murder', 'killing' and 'R.I.P.' all equate to 38. For one last important point on the good doctor, his name, 'Li Wenliang', equates to 56, the same as 'coronavirus'. Surprised? Me neither.

Back on the subject of the film *Pandemic*, Ames is flying from Australia to Los Angeles on Flight 182, a flight number the movie is sure to make you remember due to how many times it is repeated. As you learned earlier, both 'Year of the Rat' and 'Dean Ray Koontz' equate to 182, a number that breaks down to 11 in numerology terms, the master number. Eliminating the possibility of this being a coincidence, is the fact that when the plane lands in the film, a CDC scientist boards the plane and announces that his name is Dr. Ratner, emphasis on the beginning of the surname, "Rat", as in 'Year of the Rat', having gematria of 142 as well, the same as 'coronavirus'- and 'gematria', the latter being the thing that all of this predictive programming is encoded with. For the record, the reason Dr. Ratner comes aboard is because while the flight was traveling to Los Angeles, the very rapidly deteriorating condition of Ames was reported by the flight crew, thus bringing the experts to the scene. From there, Dr. Ratner leads the patients to a quarantine, where later in the film it is reported "38 patients" broke out, thus starting the 'pandemic'. Around this time a graphic is put up, showing that 65 hours have passed since patient zero was identified, and that there are 11 confirmed cases, corresponding with the numerology of 65 and 38, both breaking down to 11, and both being gematria values of 'pandemic'.

Not to spoil the film, that it is full of riddles, but one part of the plot you should know is 'martial law' is declared, a term equating to 38 in Pythagorean, the same as 'pandemic', and 70 in Reverse Pythagorean, the same as 'coronavirus'- similar to the encoding of 'Ames'. In the martial law section of the film, there is a scene showing "gun loving patriot types" attempting to drive through a military checkpoint, only to be shot to death. What's sick, is when the ambulance comes to take care of the victims, it is number 56, corresponding with not only 'coronavirus', but 'National Guard', who would be deployed if martial law were to occur in 2020, having been made part of the U.S. military in the time after 9/11. And worse yet, at the beginning of the film, when they take the corpse of 'Ames' from the plane, they show a baggage vehicle transporting it, with the word TIGER, in caps, clearly on the side. The vehicle is even numbered 1776, like the year the United States of America was established with the "56 signers". Don't forget 'Tiger' sums to 76, and 1776 was a '76 year, of course. And for one last kick to our metaphorical balls from the makers of this made for TV movie, the outbreak is blamed on the 'Riptide Virus', equating to 82, just like 'Covid'-19, and reminding us of the greater meanings we have uncovered regarding the number 82, connecting the world of computers and technology, to the city of 'Seattle', arguably one of the most crucial cities in the world, in terms of the pandemic scam, and the benefiting parties. If you're like me, you'll feel like you're getting your teeth knocked out when at the end of the film, they arrest a man who is behind the drastic spread of the virus, and they call him of all things, the "rat".

Moving on, more recently, a piece of predictive programming was uploaded to Netflix on November 7, 2019, the day leaving 54 days left in the year. This title was, *'Explained: The Next Pandemic'*, summing to 251 with Simple English, the 54th prime, the number near and dear to the 'Jesuit Order'. The star of this film, Bill Gates, laid out just in time, 10 days before the first confirmed case of coronavirus on November 17th, the coming pandemic, and explained the consequences of this coming pandemic, in a way that now matches what we are seeing in the real world. Keep in mind, this program released at the conclusion of his "Decade of Vaccines", that was sparked with the massive 10 ritual, as covered. Furthermore, November 7, 2019 was a date with 57 numerology, matching the gematria of 'Bill Gates' and 'vaccine'. Even more, it was the 311th day of the year, not far off from how the majority of the U.S. writes the date March 11th, or 3/11, the date the World Health Organization, out of Switzerland, declared the coronavirus pandemic. As we learned earlier, Switzerland is where Bill Gates had described a coming epidemic could be intentional in January of 2017. For that one, I have to thank him.

Also in November of 2019, on the 27th of the month, it was announced that a remake was underway for Stephen King's *The Stand,* about a plague ending humanity as we know it. This was curious for several reasons. For starters, 'Stephen King' sums to 56 in Pythagorean, the same as 'coronavirus'. Also, his novel released in 1978, emphasis on '78, because 'Wuhan Coronavirus' sums to 78 with Pythagorean Gematria. And further, because 'The Stand' has gematria of 44, corresponding with the November 17th date, and the fact that the virus arrived in the U.S. in 'Seattle', once again, summing to 44. Adding to the list, the novel was released October 3rd of 1978, the day leaving 89 days left in the year, corresponding with the gematria of 'virus'. And finally, the first film made about the novel released in 1994, emphasis on '94, corresponding with 'coronavirus pandemic'. It was aired on ABC on the nights of May 8th, through May 12th, concluding on the 132nd day of the year. Please note that 1994 was 26 years before 2020, and 'plague', 'virus', 'China' and 'Covid'-19 each equate to 26 with Pythagorean Gematria.

Speaking of plague, that is the name of the July 13, 2003 episode of *The Dead Zone,* an episode about a deadly plague that can be stopped with 'chloroquine', per the storyline, reminding us of Donald Trump's favorite coronavirus treatment. In light of the release date of the episode, July 13th, a date that can expressed as 13/7, it is important to note that 'chloroquine' sums to 137 with Simple English, the same as 'Anthony Fauci' and 'Washington D.C.', the 33rd prime number. At the same time, 'chloroquine' equates to 65 with Pythagorean, the latter number connecting to 'pandemic'. Keep in mind 'pandemic' equates to 43 as well, and the episode released on a date with 43 numerology. If you want a laugh, look up the April 3, 2020 headline about Anthony Fauci calling chloroquine a 'knockout drug', a phrase equating to 65 with Reverse Pythagorean. Because 2020 was a leap year, the remark was made on the 94th day of the year. And for one last point about the show, its name, '*The Dead Zone*', equates to 53, the same as 'Covid'-19. And on the subject of 53, and *The Dead Zone,* let me say goodbye to the dead, and R.I.P. to the 53 year old Irrfan Khan, of *Inferno,* a film we have said enough about.

On the subject of 2016, the year *Inferno* was released, where 53 is the 16th prime, that is also the year the show *Containment* concluded, on the date of July 19th, the 201st day of the leap year. The show is set in Atlanta, Georgia, the home of the CDC, an agency that turned 74 years old on July 1, 2020. The storyline involves a virus that is part of a top secret conspiracy, that is unleashed in Atlanta, possibly by accident, that the CDC is actively covering up. This is so, until the conspiracy is partially admitted by the agency in the 11th episode. This outbreak leads to quarantine, martial law and eventually civil unrest and rioting. It reminds us that on June 13, 2020, the day leaving 201 days left in the year, the Wendy's burned in Atlanta, after the June 12th killing of Rayshard Brooks by police in the same Wendy's parking lot, a date written 6/12. Keep in mind his killing came after the killing of George Floyd by police in Minneapolis, the (612) area code. The 612 pattern matters because 'police' sums to 612 with Reverse Sumerian cipher, and in the show *Contagion, a* pair of police officers are the main characters. If you have not read my first book, we discuss the pattern of 612 and (612) in relation to the June 12, 2016 Pulse Night Club shooting in Florida, and how 612 days later, on February 14, 2018, Marjory Stoneman Douglas High School was attacked with gun violence, also located in Florida, but named after a woman from Minneapolis. And regarding Stoneman Douglas, the shooting was on Valentine's Day, and 'Valentine' sums to 612 with Sumerian Gematria. If you want to get even more technical, the school was named the Eagles, and had a logo to match the Philadelphia Eagles, who had just won the Super Bowl on February 4, 2018 in Minneapolis, 10 days earlier, corresponding with 'Minneapolis' summing to 55, and 55 being the 10th triangular number. For another, both shootings, June 12, 2016 and February 14, 2018, were on 54 date numerology, a number that points straight to the Jesuits, the same as 112. I bring up the latter number because of the Sandy Hook Elementary School shooting on December 14, 2012, reportedly carried out by 112 pound Adam Lanza, a stat every mainstream news outlet was sure to report, as if it was important. It was not by accident. It was because 'Sandy Hook' sums to 112 with Simple English, and adding onto the list, it was reported that Adam Lanza was born April 22, the 112th day of the year, and had the initials A.L., or 1.12. Not by chance, the Sandy Hook incident was compared to the Dunblane Massacre of March 13, 1996, a date with 112 numerology, that resulted in gun rights being taken away in the U.K. Keep in mind, using Jewish Gematria, 'Dunblane Massacre' sums to 612, same as the phrase 'Orlando Strong', a saying in the mainstream that was used after the 6/12 Pulse Nightclub shooting.

What makes this all the more curious, is the Dunblane shooting came exactly 6,120 days before the Sandy Hook shooting, and both incidents targeted 'First Graders', summing to 144 with Simple English, the exact same as 'Jesuit Order'. You should know I discovered gematria by researching the Sandy Hook shooting, and why the media was constantly mentioning Adam Lanza's weight of 112 pounds. Had it not been for that, all of this might have never been. And for one last point on these shootings, so that you can understand how the same numbers are used ritualistically, whether it is coronavirus, or something else, both 'Sandy Hook Elementary School' and 'Stoneman Douglas High School', equate to 113 with Pythagorean, and 121 with Reverse Pythagorean. As you have learned, '*Revelation*' sums to 121 with Simple English, and 'apocalypse' sums to 113 with the same cipher. It is a reminder, once again, these riddles, that are part of agendas, that are meant to destroy us, are absolutely biblical, such as coronavirus being confirmed in the U.S. on January 21st, and the pandemic being declared on March 11th, shortly after the fulfillment of *Acts 7:6*. And speaking of the number 612 and the *Holy Bible*, *Ephesians 6:12* from the *NIV* reads, "For our struggle is not against flesh and blood, but against the rulers, against the authorities, against the powers of this dark world and against the spiritual forces of evil in the heavenly realms."

To make one more relevant and timely point about the number 112 in regards to Sandy Hook- on May 24, 2020, it was reported a manhunt had begun for Peter Manfredonia, for murders he had been named the suspect in, and he was the nephew of Chris Manfredonia, the latter being the man who was arrested the day of the Sandy Hook shooting, and who was shown in the nightly news as a suspect, because police were unsure about what he was doing behind the school the day of the reportedly tragic incident. In addition to May 24th, the day of the news, being what is typically the 144th day of the year, corresponding with 'Jesuit Order', and in a leap year the 145th, corresponding with 'Catholic', it was 112 days after the reported birthday of Peter Manfredonia, born February 2nd, the 33rd day of the year, the latter number corresponding with the Pythagorean Gematria of 'Newtown', where Sandy Hook Elementary School is. I bring this up because it serves as a reminder of how repetitive the rituals are, and how over the years, the same patterns manifest again and again.

Getting back on the subject of the show *Containment,* and with spirituality in mind, in the eighth episode, part of the story involves people who are trapped in Atlanta's quarantine zone trying to escape. The idea they come up with is to find an old hidden passageway, located in a church, that was used in the days of slavery, and the underground railroad. They are successful in finding this passageway, and as the camera shows them entering the tunnel, it is sure to show the church wall, that has the number 322 on it, in plain sight, a number that should remind you about "knowing good and evil." I'll remind you, in addition to *Genesis 3:22,* and the Skull and Bones association with the number, 'The Johns Hopkins University' sums to 322 with Reverse Simple, and it was founded by a member of Skull and Bones, Daniel Coit Gilman, at Yale, not far from Newtown, Connecticut. At the same time, 'The Johns Hopkins University' sums to 353 with Simple English, the 71st prime, and 'CDC' sums to 71 with Reverse Simple, the agency established on 7/1, or July 1st. It goes to show, that from the top down, it is all clearly part of The Cabal, controlled by the 'Catholic' Church. And since I just brought up Sandy Hook, let us not overlook that 'Connecticut' equates to 46, the same as 'Catholic'.

Let us now rewind to 2011, and to July 19th, what is the 201st day in a leap year, when *Captain America: The First Avenger* released. In the very end of the film, you see Captain America pose in the middle of Times Square and over one shoulder is an ad for a Corona beer, and over the other shoulder is an illustration that looks nearly identical to the coronavirus. For the record, the name *'The First Avenger'* equates to 78 and 84, the same as 'Jesuit', and 177, matching 'The Jesuit Order'. 2011 was also the year *Contagion* released, on the date September 9th, the day leaving 113 days in the year. As you know, 'coronavirus pandemic' equates to 113, and it was declared on March 11th, or 11/3, 666 days after 'Clade X', equating to 113, was put on by 'Johns Hopkins University', equating to 113. And on the subject, have I mentioned the January 13, 2020 article by the U.K,'s Express, emphasis on 1/13, about Pope Francis and the 'apocalypse' a word summing to 113 with Simple English? I recommend you look it up.

As for *Contagion,* if you have not seen the film, it is about a deadly virus driven pandemic, that begins when a bat defecates in a pig sty, contaminating a pig, that is then sold in an open air Chinese market, that leads to a world shifting pandemic, thus it is essentially the same story as coronavirus. In the film, the contaminated pig ends up in a Chinese restaurant, that infects a woman who is traveling home to Minneapolis, Minnesota, the location of the George Floyd killing, that leads to a lot of people dying in a very short period of time. I will add, the movie states the population of Minneapolis as being 3.3 million people and the George Floyd rioting began on East 33rd Street. More importantly, the film involves plot elements including a CDC coverup, a mass outbreak that kills many worldwide, CNN news anchors such as Sanjay Gupta talking about "social distancing" and a rampant debate about what is real information when it comes to choosing between the television and the internet.

Even more chilling than the predictive programming from *Contagion*, is that from the film and TV series *The Purge*, that released in 2013, but begins in the futuristic year 2022, the Year of the Tiger. If you are not familiar with the widely acclaimed titles, they are about a "New Founding Fathers" who take control of the United States of America in 2017 (the same year Donald Trump became President of the United States), and declare a new holiday in their honor, titled *The Purge*. It begins at 7 PM on March 21st and concludes on March 22nd at 7 AM. In that time, crime is legal, including murder, except for murdering people of the ruling class, who are off limits per the new laws of the land. It should remind us of how all these supposed Adam Lanza types who are mad at the world target nonsensical things with their mass shootings, such as schools, malls and theaters- the same places police conduct active shooter drills- as opposed to targeting those who are actually responsible for the oppression they feel, such as governments and major industry, the same people protected in the film on "purge night". On the subject of government, the third film in the series is titled *Election Year*, and it released on July 1, 2016, an election year, the same as 2020. 2016 was also the year Trump was running for President, and the tagline from the film was "Keep America Great." Of course, that is Trump's 2020 reelection campaign slogan, and as we learned earlier, it sums to 138, the same as 'Donald Trump' and 'federal'. It's so blatant, not even those in Q'Anon can call it a "coincidence." *Q'Anon = 201 (Jewish Gematria)

Looking at the release dates of the films in *The Purge* series is very interesting, starting with the first, June 7, 2013, a date that can be written 7/6, similar to 76, as in 'tiger', and the 'Year of the Tiger', in which it begins, 2022, not far off from the 222 gematria of 'Wuhan Coronavirus'. The date can also be written 6/7, and 'purge' sums to 67 with Simple English, the same as 'Wuhan'. In fact, the words 'purge' and 'Wuhan' are the exact same in three out of four ciphers, summing to 23, 67 and 68. Let us not forget, the Year of the Tiger will end at the start of 2023. The date June 7th is also the 158th day of the year, and the Jesuits were formed in France on August 15th, or 15/8. Furthermore, June 7, 2013 was a date with 46 numerology, and 'virus', 'chaos' and 'Ordo Ab Chao' each equate to 46. If you watch the film, the idea of *The Purge* is an order out of chaos concept. The belief by some government leaders in the film is that by allowing the people to "unleash the beast" for 12 hours every year, it prevents them from participating in crime and violence for the remainder of the year, thus resulting in a net gain for society. And in light of the concluding date of March 22nd, 3/22, think about being confronted with this situation, and what would you do per *Genesis 3:22*, "knowing good and evil."

As for the second film in *The Purge* series, it released July 18, 2014, a date associated with homicide thanks to the San Ysidro Massacre. As you know, it can be written 18/7, like 187, the police homicide code, and a number associated with the 'Society of Jesus', as well as 'Paris, France' and 'Washington D.C.', which are Jesuit strongholds. In 2020, July 18th was the date pro skater Ekaterina 'Alexandrovskaya' reportedly committed suicide, having a surname equating to 56, like 'Society of Jesus'. The number 187 can also be associated with 'George Washington' and 'Ancient & Accepted Scottish Rite of Freemasonry'. To go further, 'December Fourteenth' and 'arsenic poisoning' equate to 187 and when George Washington died on December 14th, he did so with a Jesuit doctor by his side. With the Freemasons in mind, the name 'New Founding Fathers', the name of the U.S. leadership in *The Purge*, sums to 277, the 59th prime number, and this film released on July 18, 2014, a date with 59 numerology, a number corresponding with 'kill' in Jewish Gematria. As you learned earlier, 'Freemasonry' sums to 59, and from the establishment of Modern Freemasonry in 1717, to the establishment of the United States of America in 1776, was 59 years later. Plus, 59 is the 17th prime. Plus, 'Independence Day', also sums to 277. Plus, the 59th U.S. Presidential Election is taking place in 2020, where Donald Trump is the incumbent President. Plus Obama is turning 59 years old right before it, August 4th, and his secret service code name,

'Renegade', equates to 59, the same as 'negro' and 'slave'. For one last point on the second film, it was titled 'Anarchy', having gematria of 70 and 119, in the same ciphers as 'Vatican', and gematria of 38 as well, corresponding with 'pandemic' and 'death'.

Moving on to the third film in the series, *Election Year*, it released July 1, 2016, the CDC's 70th birthday, reminding us that Donald Trump became President at age 70, and 'Vatican' as well as 'coronavirus' equates to 70. Furthermore, Trump is the 44th person to be President of the United States, something like the 44 kings of ancient Israel, and this third film in the series released on a date with 44 numerology, a number corresponding with the Simple English Gematria of 'kill'- corresponding with what the film is about. As mentioned, the slogan for the film is 'Keep America Great', the same as Trump's 2020 reelection slogan. Even more, 'Election Year' equates to 60, the same as 'Donald Trump'. And 'Election Year' also sums to 132, reminding us of the connection between the 'Catholic Church', 'United States of America', and the number of rooms in the White House. The fingerprints, in total, are incriminating.

As for the fourth film in the series, it released July 4, 2018, 'Independence Day', summing to 74 as well as 277 (59th prime number), and being a right day for 'killing', as we learned about in the first chapter. This film is focused on the very first purge, set in 2017 (59, 17th prime number). And in light of the 59 connections, it is noteworthy that the second, third and fourth films focus on predominantly poor, and black communities, that the 'New Founding Fathers' see as undesirable, thus why these communities are targeted by mercenary killers, paid for by the 'New Founding Fathers', every annual purge, a very central part of the storyline. As another reminder, the words 'slave', 'negro', 'Rasta' and 'blues' each equate to 59 with Simple English, and if you want to go further, so does 'Tobacco', the product that was related to the killings of Eric Garner, Michael Brown, and George Floyd, a product that has been big business since the time of slavery, and something we'll discuss further ahead.

As for the name of the fourth film in the series, '*The First Purge*', it equates to 71, the same as 'African American', and '*Birth of a Nation*', the latter being a film that was said to disappoint at the box office, when it only brought in $7.1 million its opening weekend, after debuting October 7, 2016, emphasis on 7/10. Never mind that the film was about Nat Turner, the slave who lead an uprising, and who was executed on November 11, 1831, a date with 71 numerology, or that the George Floyd killing video went viral on May 26, 2020, a date with 71 numerology as well. As we know, 'Catholic' also sums to 71, and it is the 20th prime number, reminding us that in 2020, races were provoked, worldwide, in ways they hadn't been for decades, in the election year of Donald Trump, the 'agent provocateur', a term having gematria of 201. To go further, the name 'The First Purge' sums to 172 with Simple English, the same as 'Ad maiorem Dei gloriam', the Jesuit motto, meaning "for the greater glory of God."

Regarding the number 172, it is another favorite number of the Jesuits, reminding us that Jeff Bezos set a new record in personal wealth, becoming valued at $172 billion, 172 days after his 56th birthday, on July 2, 2020. In the same story, it said his 'Amazon' stocks were up 56% for the year. And for another layer, you could also say it was his 173rd day of his age, and 'Roman Catholicism' sums to 173 with Simple English. For another example of the relevance of 172, let us revisit Nick Cordero's death ritual, the Broadway star, that we covered earlier, who passed on July 5, 2020, 201 days after Pope Francis' birthday. What I did not mention prior is that it was also Lin-Manuel Miranda's 172nd day of his age, having been born January 16, 1980. If you are not familiar with Lin-Manuel Miranda, he is the star of *Hamilton*, on Broadway, and he was receiving much recognition in the mainstream for his work with *Hamilton* at the same time Cordero died. For another star with a 172 connection, look no further than Michael Jordan, who was born February 17, 1963, emphasis on 17/2. As we will get to, it's no accident his father died at age 56, or that Kobe Bryant died while Jordan himself was at the tail end of being 56 years old. And on the subject of 56 and 172, let us not forget that '*V for Vendetta*' equates to 172, the film that pays tribute to the Jesuit, Guy Fawkes, who led the Gunpowder Plot on November 5, 1605, the day leaving 56 days in the year.

For some concluding remarks on *The Purge*, cementing who is behind these films, the fifth movie was supposed to release on July 10, 2020, but has been delayed because of the events transpiring in the world, especially the Black Lives Matter protests. It is named '*The Forever Purge*', summing to 72 with Reverse Pythagorean, the same as 'Society of Jesus', pairing with the fact that July 10 is the 191st day of the year, and 'Society of Jesus' sums to 191 with Simple English. Let us not forget, 'Black Lives Matter' and 'Society of Jesus' both equate to 56 with Pythagorean. Furthermore, a television series was spawned on the date of September 4, 2018, emphasis on 9/4, corresponding with 'Roman Catholic Church'. That is also the date leaving 118 days in the year, matching the Jewish Gematria of 'death' and 'homicide'. As of the time of writing this book, the last episode was December 17, 2019, the date of Pope Francis' 83rd birthday, reminding us that 'murder' equates to 83 and the song *Murder by Numbers* released in '83. Even more, 83 is the 23rd prime number, and both 'purge' and 'Wuhan' equate to 23. All in all, these are not good signs for humanity, and The Cabal, through their twisted Hollywood platform, are communicating very negative planned intentions for us as a people, no matter if we are poor and black, or not. Keep in mind, humanity is a chain, and when one part suffers, all will eventually endure suffering. And for one last thought on the television series, in the early episodes, there are multiple important conversations, including one man describing, just before his murder, or "purge", how the government tricked him into his death, by paying him to stay in his house. Think of that line in light of stimulus checks during the time of the "pandemic". There is also separate dialogue in another scene about how the purge is something that came to the United States from 'Europe'. Thanks to gematria, we can be a lot more specific about what they're referring to, that is also backed up by history, because the Catholic Church's favorite word for purge is "crusade."

For another show with the Jesuit fingerprints all over it, predicting a viral outbreak, look no further than *'Between'*, a title summing to 74 with Simple English, just like 'Wiley', the name of the main character of the show, a pregnant teenage girl. From the first episode on, a building commonly shown is the Central District Medical Center, building number 201, and a detail that reminds us Event 201 took place on the day leaving 74 days left in the year. Even more, the show is set in the fictional town of 'Pretty Lake', equating to 56, the same as 'coronavirus'. The name of the town also sums to 133 and 137, like 'government', and 43, like 'pandemic'. The first episode of season one is titled *"School's Out"*, a curious name in light of what happened to our schools, worldwide, due to coronavirus. And with regards to the youth, this is who the show is centered on. The plot involves a conspiracy where a virus is unleashed by authorities, for experimentation purposes, that targets people who are over 21 years of age, meaning 22 and older. Keep in mind 'Wuhan' sums to 22 with Pythagorean, not too far off from the year (2020), and 'Jesuit' equates to 21 with the same cipher. If you take the time to watch the show, you'll laugh in the early minutes of the first episode, when it tells you it is day 4, and the 'death toll', having gematria of 47, is at a count of 47. As a reminder, the number 4 is associated with death. And as a second reminder, Event 201 took place on a date with 47 numerology. And for one last point on the show, it released May 21, 2015. What is interesting about this date is that in a leap year, such as 2020, it is the 142nd day of the year, corresponding with 'coronavirus'. And to prove the relevance, on May 21, 2020, NASCAR returned from its 'coronavirus' hiatus, and true to form, on 5/21, where 521 is the 98th prime, the number 98 car won, driven by 'Chase David Wayne Briscoe', equating to 98 with Pythagorean, at the track 'Darlington Raceway', also equating to 98. The story was that he had just lost his son in a tragedy days before, a suspicious detail. And for another important detail, from Briscoe's 25th birthday on December 15th, to the race, was his 159th day of his age. This matters because 'Ford Mustang', 'Donald Trump' and 'Scottish Rite' each equate to 159, and Donald Trump was critiqued the same day for not wearing a mask while touring the Ford plant, and Briscoe drove a Ford Mustang for the win. Again, it reminds us how sports and news are scripted together. And for one more detail, 'Ford' and 'Trump' equate to 25 with Pythagorean Gematria, and Briscoe was age 25 at the time.

Moving on, let us rewind to the 1990s, the time of VHS tapes, and video rental stores, for a couple more illustrations of how well planned this moment we're living out is. On February 26, 1993, the date of the World Trade Center bombings, the movie *Falling Down* released. The next time you watch the film, having a very curious name in light of what eventually happened to the World Trade Centers on September 11, 2001, pay attention to the surroundings when Michael Douglas' character destroys the convenience store in a fit of rage. You'll see in the same scene, a street sign is shown, and it is none other than Corona St. I'd call it a coincidence if I didn't know better, but I do. And for the record, *'Falling Down'* equates to 54 with both Pythagorean methods, the very important number to the 'Jesuit Order', where their logo, the 'sun', emphasizes its corona. Again, that film came out in '93, reminding us that the 'sun' is 93 million miles away from earth on average. At least, so we're told.

For another film that released that same year, it was 'Demolition Man', equating to 72 and 144 in the same ciphers as 'Jesuit Order', on October 8, 1993, the day leaving 84 days left in the year, reminding of the gematria of 'Jesuit' and George Orwell's *1984*, a book that the film pays tribute to. This is because it is about a world changed by technology, where people are watched and listened to at all times by the government, and should they do so much as swear, they are instantly given a fine. Anyone who watches the film in the post coronavirus era, and who has read *1984*, will get the jokes, including the end of 'toilet paper', summing to 56 like 'coronavirus', and also 'San Angeles', the future merger of San Diego and Los Angeles, that *Demolition Man* is set in. For a couple more familiar numbers, you should get a kick out of how Sylvester Stallone's character receives a compliment for looking good at age 74, and Dennis Leary's character mentions he doesn't want to be a 47 year old virgin. Another detail you won't overlook is the leader of this Orwellian city of San Angeles, who dresses like he is the Catholic Pope, and that is 'Dr. Raymond Cocteau', equating to 72, like 'Demolition Man' and 'Jesuit Order'. As for his name 'Raymond Cocteau' alone, it equates to 158, reminding of the Jesuit formation date, August 15th, and that at the time of coronavirus, the world has its first Jesuit Pope, Pope Francis.

On the subject of the Pope and predictive programming, I should mention what is known as the *Prophecy of Saint-Archbishop Malachy*. It was recorded in the year 1139, in Rome, that the Archbishop of Armagh went their, and prophesied his vision that 112 popes from then, "there will reign Peter the Roman, who will feed his flock, amid many tribulations, after which the seven-hilled city *[Rome]* will be destroyed and the dreadful Judge will judge the people." To clarify things, Pope Francis is 112 popes from then, and while his name isn't 'Peter the Roman', summing to 158 with Simple English, he is the first Jesuit, and the 266th Pope, corresponding with 'Iesus Hominum Salvator', equating to 266, and the phrase for what the letters of IHS stand for in the Jesuit logo. Furthermore, with the emphasis on 'judge', a word summing to 20 with Pythagorean, we are looking at this in context of 2020, and the 20th Tarot card being the 'Judgement' card. What makes this all the more strange, is the name of the prophecy, the 'Prophecy of Saint-Archbishop Malachy', sums to 352 with Simple English, and in 2020, a leap year, Pope Francis' December 17th birthday will fall on the 352nd day of the year. Of course, he is turning 84 years old that day, a man with 84 birth numerology. And for a reminder, 'United States of America', 'The Catholic Church', 'The Jesuit Order' and 'Jesuit' each equate to 84. I should also mention, the 'Prophecy of Saint-Archbishop Malachy' equates to 163 as well, the 38th prime, the number connected to 'pandemic', as well as 'death'. In this case, the event that could wipe out Rome, is an 'earthquake', also equating to 163. *Case in point, on July 21, 2020, the day leaving 163 days in the year, it was reported that there was a massive 7.8 earthquake in the Gulf of Alaska (Jesuit = 78), not far from the HAARP facility, the U.S. military technology base that has the power to quake the ground. Furthermore, it was reported the closest town to the epicenter was 'Perryville', equating to 56, or 'Perryville, Alaska', equating to 187, both numbers connecting to the 'Society of Jesus'. And what you will learn with this knowledge, is how there are even riddles carried out with weather warfare, including earthquakes. For example, the July 4, 2019 earthquake of Southern California came exactly 1,776 days after the South Napa earthquake of August 24, 2014, the largest in the region prior to the July 4, 2019 earthquake. And in terms of the military being responsible, that is something I cover in depth in my first book, and the evidence in the July 4, 2019 example, is that the epicenter was on a military base.

With earthquakes on your mind, I'll remind you that many mainstream outlets published headlines reading 'Half the town is gone', in relation to the August 24, 2016 central Italy earthquake that rocked the nation. And on my first website, I have CNN's story archived, using the same phrasing and emphasis, 'Half the town is gone', and that's because in Pythagorean Gematria, it equates to 84. As I documented on my August 24, 2016 post, the incident came 35 days before the anniversary of the Jesuits being recognized by Rome, September 27th. To make a point about this, I want you to think of the scientist Nikola Tesla, who said he had the technology to shake the earth. He was born July 10, the 191st day, in the year 1856. As you know, 'Society of Jesus' sums to 56 and 191. Furthermore, the name 'Nikola Tesla' sums to 119 with Simple English, whereas 'Vatican' sums to 119 with Reverse Simple. For another Catholic connection, he would die on January 7th, a date that can be written 7/1, similar to how

'Catholic' equates to 71. Adding to the ritual, he died in 1943, at the age of 86, a number corresponding with the term "eighty-sixed" meaning to get rid of. In gematria terms, both 'blood sacrifice' and 'human sacrifice' equate to 86 as well. And since we're talking Nikola Tesla and numbers, it is important to remember his quote, "If you only knew the magnificence of 3, 6 and 9, then you could have a key to the universe." In light of his quote, it makes you wonder if it was an accident that the August 24, 2016 earthquake was reported to have happened at 3:36 local. That also happened to be the day of Los Angeles, California's first Kobe Bryant Day, the basketball star, who had played his last game in the NBA that prior April, and who would go on to die in the ritual of rituals to start the year, January 26, 2020, that we will uncover ahead. For now, just remember Kobe grew up in Italy, and his fatal crash came after attending Catholic mass. Also important, 3:36 is the 216th minute of the day, what is the product of 6x6x6, and as we learned, in Jewish Gematria, 'prophecy' sums to 666. That earthquake was said to be the worst in Italy since 1980, 36 years earlier, and as we have learned, 666 is the 36th triangular number.

Sticking with the Catholic theme, I have to encourage you to watch the film *V for Vendetta*, where the protagonist is against a government that is very much like the one described in George Orwell's *1984*. The film is made in tribute to Guy Fawkes, the Jesuit, who in the Gunpowder Plot of November 5, 1605, attempted to assassinate King James and destroy the English Parliament. You'll notice November 5, 1605 was 65 years and 39 days after the Jesuits were recognized by Rome, on September 27, 1540. This matters because 'Gunpowder' sums to 39, and 'United Kingdom' equates to 65. At the same time, 'Gunpowder Plot' equates to 165, not too far off from 1605. As for the title *'V for Vendetta'*, it sums to 172, corresponding with 'Ad maiorem Dei gloriam', the Jesuit motto. For another Catholic connection, the film released on March 17, 2006, a date with 46 numerology, corresponding with the gematria 'Catholic'. It could also be expressed as 17/3, and 'Roman Catholicism' equates to 173. More important than the numbers though, is what the film is about, and what time period it is set in, which is around the year 2020, having been released more than a decade earlier. The story involves details that the U.K. is still standing despite the United States of America having already fallen due to terrorism, war, disease and poor government planning. In this dystopian world, curfews are in effect,

203

and liberties are few, especially when it comes to the type of information and entertainment one is allowed to have access to. In terms of symbolism, the film begins with the destruction of British Parliament, on the date of November 5th, thus the phrase, "Remember, remember, the 5th of November." You have to keep in mind this eye grabbing scene came less than five years after the destruction of the World Trade Centers, in the United States, an image still fresh in everyone's mind who was alive at the time. And for a math note on November 5th, 11 is the 5th prime number, and September 11, had very much to do with the master number, number 11. To take it even further, Guy Fawkes was born April 13, 1570, meaning he was on his 207th day of being 35 years old on the day of the plot. This is interesting because 'terrorist attack' sums to 207 with Simple English, similar to 'The Magician' summing to 207 with Reverse Simple. If you are not aware, The Magician is the first card of the Tarot deck, and in light of 9/11 happening in 2001, emphasis on '01, something like the first card, please know that the word 'magic' sums to 33 with Simple English, and 102 with Reverse Simple English. As you'll recall, the 9/11 attacks came 33 years after 1968, the year of years, and lasted 102 minutes. For Judy Wood researchers, you'll appreciate that 'direct energy weapon' also equates to 207, what some contend turned the World Trade Center buildings to dust on September 11, 2001.

In addition to books, TV shows and movies, the world of video games is also ripe with predictive programming for coronavirus. Take the game *Resident Evil* for example. On January 26, 2020, five days after coronavirus was confirmed in the United States and hours before the death of Kobe Bryant, news had gone viral on the web that the company out of Shanghai, not far from Wuhan, Ruilan Bao Hu San Biotech, had nearly the exact same logo as Umbrella Corporation, the source of evil in the *Resident Evil* series that is responsible for unleashing a virus that mutates the world into zombies. In light of the symbol being shared being a Maltese Cross, the symbol of the oldest order of knights in the world, that serve the Catholic Church, the same as the Knights Templar, and the Knights Hospitaller, and the Knights of Columbus, it should come as no surprise that 'Shanghai Ruilan Bao Hu San Biotech' sums to 132 with Pythagorean, similar to how 'Catholic Church' sums to 132 with Simple English. At the same time, the viral news took place on a date with 47 numerology, and 'Malta' sums to 47, the same as 'Vatican'. For more familiar numbers,

'Resident Evil' sums to 61, 142 and 182, the same as 'Year of the Rat', and the number 142 reminds us of 'coronavirus'. The name of the game also sums to 61 and 74, reminding us of the Event 201 date, October 18th, leaving 74 days in the year, and 61, the 18th prime number, reminding us of *Inferno* on Bill Gates' 61st birthday, a man who seems to think of himself as a 'god', based on his behavior and worldview. At the same time, let us not forget the Event 201 simulation runs 18 months, or that 'IHS' and 'sun' equate to 18.

For another Zombie hit summing to 61 and 74, try '*The Walking Dead*', a series that began October 31, 2010, the day leaving 61 days left in the year, and a date with 71 numerology. Keep in mind the show begins in Atlanta, home of the 'CDC', summing to 71, and established on July 1st, or 7/1. On March 22, 2020, ComicBook.com published an article after interviewing the creator of the *Walking Dead*, who revealed for the first time, that the zombie apocalypse in his hit show began because of "space spore". He did not elaborate. But in gematria terms, 'space spore' sums to 54 and 153, the same as 'Jesuit Order'. Furthermore, the creator's name, 'Robert Kirkman' sums to 155 with Simple English, and 65 with Pythagorean. As you know, 'coronavirus' sums to 155 with Simple, and 'pandemic' equates to 65 in the same cipher. I should also note, 'zombie' equates to 70, the same as 'coronavirus'. As for why the article was published on the date it was, March 22nd, it might be because Kirkman was 41 years old at the time, corresponding with the Pythagorean Gematria, of 'Skull and Bones', and beyond that, his birthday is November 30, meaning George Herbert Walker Bush, the 41st President, and the Skull and Bones alumni, died on the creator's birthday in 2018, at the age of 94. That also means Paul Walker, who starred in '*Skulls*', a film title having gematria equating 41 and 94, and being about Skull and Bones, died on his birthday, November 30, 2013 (41 is the 13th prime) in a red Porsche, just like the Porsche he drove in *Skulls*. I'll also note that '*Skulls*' sums to 68, in light of the year 1968, and how from George W. Bush's birthday to September 11th is a span of 68 days. And because I hate to talk about too many numbers at once, we'll ignore the fact that Paul Walker died on a date with 54 and 74 numerology.

Back on the subject of *Resident Evil*, and March 22nd, the first game in the series released on the infamous date of March 22, 1996. The year '96 is relevant because 'corona' equates to 96, and so does

'William Henry Gates' as well as 'Gavi, the Vaccine Alliance'. Keep in mind Gates had just become the world's richest man nearly a year earlier. And in light of March 22nd, don't forget that 'novel coronavirus' sums to 223 with Simple English- a novel virus that was foretold in a novel, truly. In terms of the details of the game, it was set in 'Raccoon City', summing to 54 with Pythagorean Gematria, the same as 'Jesuit Order', and while not being a perfect anagram, having the letters making up the word 'corona'. And with the Jesuits in mind, the video game was called '*Biohazard*' in Japan, summing to 84 with Simple English, same as 'Jesuit'. Also relevant, March 22, 1996 had numerology of 121 and the second game in the series released on January 21, 1998, 22 years before 'Wuhan', summing to 22 in Pythagorean, was confirmed in the United States of America. What's funny is Chris Redfield is the hero of the first *Resident Evil,* and Robert Redfield is the director the CDC during the time of the pandemic. Not by chance, March 11, 2020, the date the pandemic was declared, was 121 days before Robert Redfield's 69th birthday (meaning he is 68 at the time of the coronavirus pandemic), on July 10, 2020, what is the 191st day of the Gregorian calendar year in non leap years, corresponding with 'Society of Jesus', and the fact that he attended Georgetown, the Jesuit university. Even better, the names 'Robert Redfield' and 'Chris Redfield' both equate to 78, the same as 'Jesuit' and 'Wuhan Coronavirus'. For another 78, the hero of the second game is named 'Leon Scott Kennedy', summing to 78 and 201.

What was a haunting headline to read, on April 17, 2020, was that the voice actor for the same character, 'Leon Scott Kennedy', had died at 56, the 'coronavirus' number. He died 6 days prior to the story being reported, in Toronto, on April 11th, the 102nd day of the year and the 82nd day of coronavirus being confirmed in North America, counting from January 21st. I wonder if the reporting of his death 6 days later was by accident, because he died prematurely in 'Toronto', summing to 36 in Pythagorean, the same as his name, 'Paul Haddad'. Keep in mind 36 has a square root of 6, and 666 is the 36th triangular number, because 'Capcom', who makes the *Resident Evil* series, sums to 666 with Reverse Sumerian. For another example of 6 and Toronto, you might recall how the Toronto Raptors won 'The NBA Finals', summing to 666 with Sumerian Gematria, in Game 6, in a city known as "The Six' because of the rapper Drake, the man from Toronto and who the 2019 NBA Finals were scripted in tribute to. Furthermore, for the sports buff, you should know 'Canada' sums to 24 with Simple English, and it won its first championship after 24 years of being in the NBA. Of course, the number 24 is 6 in numerology terms. You should also know it was won on June 13th, where 13 is the 6th prime, and the Raptors motto, 'We the North', sums to 136, not unlike the date, 13/6. And for more familiar numbers, the name Paul Haddad sums to 54 and 72, the same as 'Jesuit Order'. You should also know, Ontario is a Jesuit stronghold, and 'Toronto, Ontario' sums to 74, the same as 'Resident Evil', and 'killing'. It also sums to 79, the same as 'Society of Jesus' and 'murder'. Also relevant, the date of the news of Haddad's passing, April 17th, can be expressed as 17/4, not unlike 174, corresponding with the gematria of 'number of the beast'.

Making matters even more disturbing, on the same day as the news of Paul Haddad's death at 56, April 17th, it was reported that video game voice actor Filipe Duarte had died at age 46, a number connecting to 'sacrifice', 'virus' and 'Catholic', and reminding us that *Genesis 46* begins with a sacrifice. The actor would have turned 47 years old on June 5, 2020, a date that can be written 5/6, or 6/5. The game he was remembered for being a part of is a survival game called *Days Gone*, that released on April 26, 2019. The game is set in 'Oregon', in the near future, two years after a pandemic has changed the world as we know it. In other words, both games are about surviving disasters, the same reality many people of the world are facing today, because of the problems the coronavirus has brought about, most of which have nothing to do with a virus itself. Even further, linking the reasoning for why the two deaths were reported on the same day in the same news cycle, is the fact that April 17, 2020 had 61 date numerology. As we covered, 'Resident Evil' sums to 61, and in the case of Filipe Duarte, he voiced the character 'Deacon St. John', summing to 61 as well. At the same time, The Cabal is playing 'God', a word having Jewish Gematria of 61, in the 'Year of the Rat'.

For another video game parallel, Elon Musk made waves on May 2, 2020, with headlines referring to himself as the hero of *Deus Ex*, a character named J.C. Denton. If you're not familiar with the video game, it is set in 2052, at a time when America has been wrecked by terrorism and plague, thus explaining the May 2nd, or 5/2 news. Also, as you learned earlier, 'technology' has Pythagorean Gematria of 52, and Elon Musk is Mr. Technology. Thus it is fitting that he would refer to himself as J.C. Denton, a fictional man with superhuman abilities, because of the nanotechnology that is operating within his body. In the video game, 'J.C. Denton' is in battle with factions known as the Illuminati, Triads and Majestic 12, and what really brings this fact to light, is that the character name sums to 131, and on May 11th of 2020, what is the 131st day of the year, Elon Musk made national headlines for defying California's state orders, by saying he was reopening his California Tesla plant. In response, a number of mainstream outlets referred to Musk's move as creating a 'standoff', a word equating to 131 with Reverse Simple, the same as 'J.C. Denton'. Even more, May 11th was 48 days before Musk's 49th birthday, meaning he was still 48 years old at the time, and 'Illuminati' has Pythagorean Gematria of 48, the main enemy of J.C. Denton in the *Deus Ex* series. For some more familiar numbers, '*Deus Ex*' sums to 78 and 84, the same as 'Jesuit'. And for one more thought, the number 131 is the 32nd prime, and the year 2052, that the game is set in, will come 32 years after 2020, the year of the outbreak. In light of the subject matter of the game, and the way predictive programming is often used to accurately forecast the future, these are things all people should consider, because before long, the youth of today, will be the young adults of 2052, and we don't want the world to be for them what it is projected to be in games such as *Deus Ex*. To put it into perspective how fast time goes by, development began for *Deus Ex* in 1994, the year Bill and Melinda were married, a year that was just 26 years prior to 2020. Of course Bill's former company is now making the nanotechnology that was only part of science fiction such as *Deus Ex* in '94. But for many of us, 1994 wasn't all that long ago, and we were just children then, not knowing that our futures were being plotted against. So as adults now, seeing what is coming, it is our responsibility to act on behalf of not only ourselves, but for the sake of the future generations who don't have the opportunity to.

Because of the mention of the Majestic 12 in the *Deus Ex* series, I am reminded of *12 Monkeys*, a film that has since been made into a TV show. In the film, a deadly virus is unleashed on the world in 1996, killing most of the earth's population, emphasis on '96, corresponding with the gematria of 'corona', equating to 96. In that film, Bruce Willis stars, and on April 6, 2020, what is typically the 96th day of the year, Bruce Willis, Demi Moore, and their children, were uploaded to social media in a family photo, quarantining together, and wearing the same green striped, matching pajamas. Then the next day, April 7ᵗʰ, emphasis on 4/7, or 7/4, all mainstream media had a story about the photo, pointing out that Bruce Willis and Demi Moore haven't been seen together in such a photo since their divorce in 2000. What made this funny is where 'Demi Moore', 'pajamas' and 'stripes' sum to 47, 'Bruce Willis' sums to 74. Thus, it was clearly all a ritual. And in light of the title *12 'Monkeys'*, the name sums to 102, one of the more important numbers in the coronavirus ritual. Let us not forget that film is set in 'Philadelphia', equating to 223, the same as 'novel coronavirus'.

For another dystopian piece of entertainment that gave us a look into the future, look no further than Comedy Central's *The Daily Show*, starring Trevor Noah, who on November 1, 2016, one week before the rigged selection of Donald Trump as president, did a comedy bit on what the world would look like on Halloween, October 31, 2020, about four years into the Donald Trump presidency. What the bit projects is that the United States of America is in ruins, there has been a total economic collapse, the dollar is worthless, China owns America after Trump's trade deals, people are in masks rioting, and the police have been disbanded and replaced by technology. Trevor Noah even brings up Tom Hanks in the bit. Worse yet, he makes a joke about Steve Harvey and a hurricane, 9 months before TMZ made a big deal about Steve Harvey sitting ringside at the Floyd Mayweather boxing match, that was taking place as the flood rains from Hurricane Harvey poured down on Texas, that led to the submerging of the state on August 27ᵗʰ, the 27 year anniversary of the death of Stevie Ray Vaughan, whose best selling album was Texas flood. As of the time of finishing this book, a little more than a few months before Halloween 2020, all of this is exaggerated except for Hurricane Harvey, but at the same time, there's no doubt that the comedy bit shed light on what we're now experiencing, and what some might have thought was impossible just four years ago. Furthermore, it shed light on the direction we're being taken, that must be stopped.

On the subject of hurricanes, and weather warfare, if you have not read my first book, you really should. In it you will learn that weather warfare, and the ability to induce flooding was admitted by the Royal Air Force in 1952, emphasis on '52. They admitted it in that year because 'earth', 'flood' and 'hurricane' each equate to 52. And in

209

the case of the Texas flooding, August 27, 2017, that was a date with 52 numerology, plus it was the 239th day of the year, the 52nd prime number. And in very recent history, on July 25, 2020, the first hurricane of the season to make landfall, Hanna, did so on Texas, and once again on a date with 52 numerology. In light of it happening on the 25th, 'hurricane' also sums to 97, the 25th prime, and 'flood' equates to 25 as well. Furthermore, with the base ciphers, 'Hanna' sums to 97 and 25, as well as 20, the latter number making it the perfect trend setter for 2020. When you get a moment, look up the article from May 7, 2020, a date with 52 numerology, about how AccuWeather forecasted a very active hurricane season, predicting 11 hurricanes, and 4 major hurricanes for 2020. In light of the word 'hurricane' also having gematria of 56, and 2020 being a year of "56 related" stories, it is a safe bet to count on. And let us not forget the Houston Astros have won the World Series one time, and it was in their 56th season, after the flooding of Houston, Texas by Harvey. That was the same year Matt Harvey became the first pitcher to pitch in Houston, after the flooding, and his appearance was 52 days before the start of the World Series.

To conclude this chapter, something that is hard to do, because there are no less 500 other topics I would like to discuss in terms of predictive programing for both coronavirus and 9/11- such as Ozzy Osbourne biting the head off of a bat on January 20, 1982, a date that can be written 20/1, in the "Year of the Computer", in light of bats being blamed for coronavirus after Event 201- and Season 3 Episode 20 of *Are We There Yet?*, titled *The Quarantine Episode,* that debuted on October 12, 2012, where Ice Cube's character explains, while under government stay at home orders, that the "Monkey Flu" is a government drill, to test the emergency response systems, and to see how well the populace obeys their commands...- and the August 1997 U.S. Department of Justice document titled *Emergency Response to Terrorism Self Study,* that shows a picture of the New York skyline, with a bullseye on the World Trade Center- and '*The 10th Kingdom*' television miniseries, summing to 56, like 'Rockefeller', that debuted on February 27, 2000 and concluded March 26th of that year, the date written 26/3, like 263, the 56th prime and reminding us of the three planes that hit targets on September 11th, with their flight numbers equating to 263, and all of this mattering because the World Trade Center towers are shown crumbling to the ground in this fictional series- and Disney's *Gargoyles* series, that began October 24, 1994, the day leaving 68 days left in the year, in light of it beginning with an attack on the 'World Trade Center', having gematria of 94, and having opened on the 94th day of 1973, after construction began on the buildings in 1968- and the '*Last Man Standing*' series, summing to 68 and 94, that pays tribute to Elvis, and debuted its second season on September 27th, the date the Jesuits were recognized by Rome, and concluded on May 6, 2018, emphasis on 5/6- and the secret about Supertramp's 1979 album cover artwork for *Breakfast in America*- and the details of Bill Gates 1997 interview in George magazine, a must read, that focused on the future, and the year 2020 specifically. If you can find the issue, I suggest you read it. And for the record, I have much of the contents of that article posted on my website, GematriaEffect.news, where you can also find the source information and references for what is written in this book. Also, I have a chapter dedicated to the predictive programming for 9/11 in my first book, *Letters & Number*, if you are interested.

What is essential to takeaway from this chapter is simply put, we are being conned. And worst of all, we are being conned by people who we are allowing to be in charge of us because of our own behaviors and actions, or lack thereof. We are allowing this by paying taxes. We are allowing this by shrugging our soldiers and voting for the "lesser of two evils," what amounts to choosing between two puppets that are working for the same puppet masters. And we are allowing it by supporting their enterprises with mass consumerism, as well as by supporting Hollywood and cable television with our dollars, the same things that mock us with our planned dystopian destiny. It is our duty then to change this, because for us to be under their control much longer, will ensure the doom of not only ourselves, but future generations. This is the 666 clan after all that we're allowing to lead us around. And to illustrate this point, I want to leave you with one more example of predictive programming, from the old television show, '*Trackdown*'. The episode of focus debuted May 9, 1958, and was about a conman named Trump, who arrived in a small Texas town, telling the people who inhabited it that a great storm was coming and only he had the solution to save their lives. The name of the town was 'Talpa, Texas', equating to 119 with Simple English, like 'Donald' with Jewish Gematria, reminding us of Trump's Serta ad with sheep numbered 11 and 9, and that he was announced as President elect on November 9, 2016, winner of the 58th U.S. Presidential Election, 58 years after this television show aired, in 1958, complimenting how Trump announced he was running for president from the 58 story Trump Tower and before hiring the 58 year old Steve Ray for inauguration day. As for the date May 9th, or 9/5, or 5/9, the latter reminds he is now running for reelection in the 59th U.S. Presidential Election. Getting back to the show, what the conman Trump tells the people of Talpa is that if they don't buy the miracle solution he is selling, they will all die on November 14th, the day leaving 47 days left in the year, the number corresponding with the gematria of 'Trump', 'president', 'government', 'authority', 'Vatican', and 'The Cabal'. If somehow you still think this episode is a coincidence regarding the current president, Donald Trump, think again, because 'Trackdown' sums to 37 with Pythagorean Gematria, and it released 37 days before Trump's 12th birthday, June 14, 1958, where 37 is the 12th prime. Personally, it reminds me of the time we called American Pharoah, the misspelled Triple Crown winner, foaled on the 33rd day of the year, in 2012, to win the Triple Crown in 2015, before a single race was won by the horse, because it had been 37 years since the last Triple Crown winner, and American Pharoah was to become the 12th, Triple Crown winner as he did. Keep in mind 'American' sums to 37 in Pythagorean, explaining why Donald Trump was at 'Mount Rushmore' on July 3, 2020, or 3/7, the site of the great American monument, campaigning under the slogan, 'Keep America Great', the same one used in The Purge. And regarding the gematria of the slogan, equating to 138, the same as 'Donald Trump', it's not by chance that 'Mount Rushmore National Memorial' sums to 138 with Pythagorean. It's also not a coincidence that 'Rushmore' sums to 45 with both Pythagorean ciphers, the same as 'Mike Pence', the Vice President to number 45, Donald Trump. And it's also not a coincidence that 'Mount Rushmore' sums to 65 and 151, the same as 'pandemic', or to 70 in the same cipher as 'coronavirus'. This was made clear when the mainstream media immediately began to broadcast that the gathering could spark an outbreak in South Dakota, a state that had drastically less cases than many other members of the "lower 48". So think about it truth seeker, and ask yourself, do you want to stand up to this tyranny, or do you want to continue to be played for fools, up until the moment we get purged by this cabal, that literally mocks us, day, after day, year after year, decade after decade?

15 | Super Bowl 54, the Kansas City Chiefs & Coronavirus

2020, the year of Super Bowl 54, was 54 years after the Church of Satan was founded in San Francisco, having been established in 1966, the season of the first Super Bowl. I bring this up because San Francisco is the home of the 49ers, the team who lost to the Kansas City Chiefs in Super Bowl 54. And because I haven't checked on anyone's amnesia lately, as a reminder, 'Jesuit Order' equates to 54 in Pythagorean Gematria, and 'sun' equates to 54 with Simple English. If you want to get more technical, in alchemy, the sun represents gold and the San Francisco 49ers are named after the 1849 gold rush. For another 54, it is the name 'Joe Montana', equating with Reverse Pythagorean, who went to Notre Dame, a Catholic school, and I bring up his name because Super Bowl 54 had much to do with Joe Montana, considered one of the greatest NFL quarterbacks ever. The connection to Super Bowl 54 and Joe Montana was created by the fact the two teams he played for in his NFL career, the 49ers and the Chiefs, were facing each other. It was an easy riddle to solve, largely because Montana wore the number 16 for the 49ers, who he won Super Bowl 16 with, and he wore the number 19 for the Chiefs, who went on to win Super Bowl 54, concluding the 2019-20 season, emphasis on '19. Never mind 'Kansas City' equates to 67, the 19th prime number. It was only fitting then that the Super Bowl came 54 days after Joe Burrow's December 10, 2019 birthday, another Joe, who won the college football championship with the LSU Tigers, defeating the Clemson Tigers, on January 13, 2020, in the battle of the Tigers, in a year that would become even more about tigers, with hit shows like *Tiger King*, and a year where Joe Burrow would become the #1 overall pick, by the Cincinnati Bengals, who Joe Montana defeated twice in Super Bowls, 16 and 23, two numbers adding to 39, like the 39 gematria values of 'Montana', 'Bengals', 'Tigers' and 'Masonry'. Let us not forget, the 2020 NFL Draft was the first ever draft where all the players being selected stayed home, because of the coronavirus-, as opposed to meeting in a large building, and walking across a stage, and shaking someone's hand, while fans either cheered or booed the selection, what typically occurs at the event. And getting back to 54, I should note LSU won the championship in their own backyard, in 'New Orleans', equating to 54 with Reverse Pythagorean, on a 54 date numerology, January 13, 2020 (1/13/2020 = 1+13+20+20 = 54).

Adding to the list, Super Bowl 54 was played on February 2, 2020, a span of 54 days from Nancy Pelosi's March 26th birthday, the Speaker of the House in 2020, a Catholic, who calls San Francisco home, the city named after Saint Francis of Assisi, the same as Pope Francis. The symbolism in this distance in days was observed through the riddle of the Kansas City "Commander and Chiefs", defeating Pelosi's San Francisco 49ers, three days before Donald Trump defeated the impeachment brought on by Pelosi, on February 5, 2020, a date that can be expressed a 2/5, like 25, and having 47 numerology, both numbers corresponding with the gematria of 'Trump' and 'time'. And never mind that Patrick Mahomes, the quarterback of the Chiefs, went to White House High School in Texas, or that the Super Bowl was 138 days after his September 17, 2019 birthday, corresponding with the Simple English value of 'Donald Trump'. To make a long story short, it was all a ritual, and even synced with the 2019 World Series, where the Washington Nationals won the championship on October 30, 2019, precisely 138 days after Donald Trump's birthday, corresponding with the gematria of 'Nationals', 'Donald Trump', and 'Dave Martinez', the latter being the manager of the team, and each equating to 138. It was on that same day the impeachment process against Donald Trump was brought out from behind closed doors, by Nancy Pelosi, a ritual we discussed earlier. It was one of many that are a part of an ongoing circus of number games that bring together professionally rigged sports, and professionally rigged politics, things that should be so obvious, especially after rituals such as September 11, 2001, the PATRIOT Act, and the New England Patriots. Yet somehow, so few see the obvious. As for how the Nationals World Series and impeachment came together in numbers, 'impeachment' and 'Washington Nationals' both equate to 107 with our base ciphers. And for your list, 'baseball' sums to 54 in two of the four base ciphers, with Simple English, and Reverse Pythagorean. And if you don't already know, there are 54 outs in a complete baseball game, a game that is not as much about time, as it is about counting. Regarding counting, the Nationals threw 159 pitches in Game 7, winning the 115th World Series, 138 days after Donald Trump's birthday, who won the election and took office with the 115th U.S. Congress, and while 'Donald Trump' sums to 138 with Simple English, his name sums to 159 with Reverse Simple, the latter value being the same as 'Scottish Rite'. Adding insult to injury, on the same night the Washington D.C.

214

baseball team, the Nationals, beat the Houston Astros with 159 pitches to win the World Series, the Washington D.C. basketball team, the Wizards, lost in D.C. to the Houston Rockets, with a score of 159-158, in a thrilling comeback by the Rockets. If you're asking how these things can be so exact, the answer is technology, and counting, old tricks of the magician. Adding to the riddle of the basketball game was that Mike D'Antoni, the coach of the Houston Rockets, earned his 631st regular season win in that game, the 115th prime number, corresponding with the 115th World Series. Better yet, using Simple English, his name 'Mike D'Antoni' sums to 115, proving that his entire multi-decade career was scripted up to that moment, and reminding us how sports announcers always repeat, "You couldn't have scripted it any better." I repeat, they are not kidding! For years we've been calling games and championships correctly, as well as news stories, long in advance, and showing how these same types of riddles and patterns play out day after day, season after season, and year after year. Once you learn the code, you'll be amazed, but you'll also come to understand the patterns are the most broken record there ever was.

For one more on the 115th World Series, recall the number connecting the 32nd degree of the Scottish Rite and the Jesuits who established 'Georgetown' in D.C, is 115, through the motto, 'Ad majorem Dei gloriam', equating to 115 with Reverse Pythagorean. I bring this up because the 'Nationals' gave the Houston Astros their 57th postseason loss by winning Game 7, and in gematria, 'Nationals', 'World Series', 'Dave Martinez', 'Scottish Rite' and 'Georgetown' each equate to 57, a number that comes up with sports championships, college and pro, season after season. Case in point, Vanderbilt won the College World Series in June of 2019, just before the Nationals big win, and their manager, Tim Corbin, was 57 years old at the time. This should remind you that George Washington, in the land of the Jesuits and Scottish Rite, Washington D.C., became the first recognized President at age 57, and how 'Georgetown', equating to 57, was established in 1789, the year George Washington turned 57. For one last thought on the number, and with regards to all things being about time, 'Moon' sums to 57 with Simple English, and as you know, the moon has a 19 year pattern with the Gregorian calendar, and 57 is divisible by 19, three times. And last, I'd be amiss if I didn't let you know Game 7 of the World Series was won by the Nationals 6-2, on

215

October 30, the day leaving 62 days left, by defeating the team from 'Houston, Texas', summing to 62 with Reverse Pythagorean. Keep in mind, that same MLB season began with the other team from Washington winning the first game of the year, the 'Seattle Mariners' summing to 62 with Pythagorean, a game played in Japan, where 'Ichiro', summing to 62 with Simple English, the longtime Japanese star of the Mariners, would announce days later he was retiring. And for the record, we called it right then, that the World Series would go to Game 7, the day leaving 62 days in the year, because year after year, it is the same types of rituals, paying tribute to certain numbers that spell out what's to come. If you want to keep going, the Mariners won the season opening game 9-7, and both 'Mariners' and 'Athletics' sum to 97 with Simple English. If you want to go even further, 'Oakland Athletics' sums to 97 with Reverse Pythagorean. Even further, it was played on March 20, 2019, the 79th day of the year. And to bring us back to where we started, the first two games of the 2019 MLB season, were both played between the Mariners and the Athletics in Japan, and the Mariners won the second game with a score of 5-4, a lot like 54, starting off their season 2-0, before eventually improving to 12-2 by beating 'Kansas City', summing to 122 with Simple English, the same as 'San Francisco', and reminding us that both Seattle and San Francisco are on the 122nd Meridian West, and that the Kansas City Chiefs would go on to beat the San Francisco 49ers in Super Bowl 54, the 50th of the modern era, where the Chiefs would win the big game for the first time in 50 years, and where 'Chiefs' sums to 50 with Simple English, and 'San Francisco', who hosted Super Bowl 50, sums to 50 with Pythagorean. And of course, this came right after the other 'Washington' team, the Nationals, had won the World Series, where 'Washington' equates to 50 with Reverse Pythagorean, and 'America' sums to 50 with Simple English, the same as 'Donald', the man and president who was perfectly synced with both rituals. And for the person who fears I'm only going after Trump, it wasn't an accident the Chicago Blackhawks became the cream of the NHL after Barry O. accepted the presidency from Chicago.

On the subject of U.S. Presidents and rigged sports, I should also let you know how I called the outcome of the 115th World Series, Nationals over Astros in Game 7, over a month in advance, based off of what transpired on September 27, 2019, the anniversary of the Jesuits being recognized by the Roman Catholic Church, in a game between the Washington Nationals and the Cleveland Indians. The riddle had everything to do with Skull and Bones, and an old story about Prescott Bush, a Washington man, likes the Nationals, and the father of George H.W. Bush, who became a U.S. Senator, years after stealing the skull of Geronimo for Yale's fraternity when he was a member. For starters, from the anniversary of the death of Geronimo, who passed on February 17, 1909, to the September 27th game, the Nationals hosting the Cleveland Indians, was a span of 223 days, the 48th prime number, corresponding with the gematria of 'Cleveland', equating to 48, and making it easy to see that the Nationals would pick up their 48th home win in the September 27th game, on the 48 date numerology, similar to how they would pick up their 49th and 50th home wins over the course of the next two days, on 49 and 50 date numerology, also corresponding with the gematria of 'Washington'. Furthermore, the manager of the Nationals, Dave Martinez, was coaching his 322nd game on September 27th, and he came in with 149 losses, corresponding with the Simple English Gematria of 'Skull and Bones', equating to 149, which is the 35th prime, corresponding with 'Catholic'. When I identified this ritual, it too me back to April 20, 2019, and a game between the Texas Rangers and Houston Astros, where I predicted the Rangers, who were severe underdogs, would beat the Astros, and improve to 11-8 overall, and 9-4 at home, which they did, winning the game 9-4. I knew this was going to transpire, because 'George Herbert Walker Bush' equates to 118 with Pythagorean Gematria, and he had just died at 94, November 30th, 2018, before the start of that MLB season, plus he had history with the ownership of those two respective teams. Keep in mind the game was on the 110th day of the year, and 'President' sums to 110. Also, for your learning, when you write out 'Skull and Bones', it equates to 41, and when you write out 'forty one', it equates to 118, similar to how 'ossuary' equates to 118, and Skull and Bones gets their symbolism from an 'ossuary', what the Knights Templar of the Church would use to bury their dead, in the time of the crusades. And let us not forget that H.W. was the 41st President. Thus, because the Nationals won in a Skull and Bones ritual, and the Astros lost, the riddle was clear to see, and very lucrative. And please keep in mind, I did take the time to decode every single game in the 2019 MLB season, giving me the opportunity to unlock the riddle that I did, meaning the hard work eventually paid off, literally, and in a very big way.

I really could go on all day, about presidents, sports, news and more, but instead I'll transition to the most important thing you need to know about Super Bowl 54, and that is what Andy Reid accomplished, the coach of the Kansas City Chiefs, who earned his 222nd win in the NFL, on the date written 2/2/2020, and precisely 222 weeks after the Kansas City Royals defeated the New York Mets in the 111th World Series on November 1, 2015, a date written 11/1. Factoring in with the riddle linking the Kansas City Chiefs and Kansas City Royals, it was reported on July 28, 2020, that Patrick Mahomes became a part owner of the Kansas City Royals, exactly 45 weeks after his September 17, 2019 birthday, corresponding with the gematria of 'Major League', equating to 45 with Pythagorean. Keep in mind, 45 is the 9th triangular number, and baseball is a game of 9 innings. Furthermore, the date Mahomes became a part owner of the Royals, was also 177 days after Super Bowl 54, where 'The Jesuit Order' equates to 177, and 'Jesuit Order' alone equates to 54. And continuing with the patterns of twos, the Chiefs picked up their second Super Bowl win, and the 49ers earned their second Super Bowl loss, in what was the second ever Super Bowl played on the 33rd day of the year. Keep in mind, it was just days before Super Bowl 54 was played, that Donald Trump appeared at the 'World Economic Forum', equating to 222, on his 222nd day of his age, gloating about his trade deal with China, at the same time 'Wuhan Coronavirus', equating to 222 was being confirmed in the United States. And in light of the Kansas City Royals beating the New York Mets in the 111th World Series, 222 weeks before the Chiefs Super Bowl 54 win, let us not forget that from the attack on New York, on September 11, 2001, the day leaving 111 days in the year, to the coronavirus pandemic, declared March 11, 2020, was 222 months later. I should also note, 'February Second' sums to 222 with Reverse Simple English, the date of Super Bowl 54, and Andy Reid's 222nd win- and yes, it truly is all one interrelated ritual, and it's a form of spell casting. As we learned, two is a number that can be used to symbolize division, and taking apart, and that is what 2020 was much about, in terms of the controllers agenda, the same controllers who own the sports teams and leagues of the world, that are used symbolically, year after year, in rituals such as this. For one more point on Andy Reid, Super Bowl 54 was his 122nd game coached with the Kansas City Chiefs, and as we covered earlier, both 'Kansas City' and 'San Francisco' sum to 122 with Simple English, whereas 'satanic' sums to 122 with Reverse Simple English. Of the 122 games, Andy Reid had coached 112 in the regular season, and 10 in the playoffs, with the 10th being Super Bowl 54. Keep in mind, 'satan' sums to 10 with Pythagorean, and regarding the 112 regular season games, 'Chiefs' sums to 112 with Reverse Simple English, the same as 'Super Bowl'. Let us not forget the 112 countries the Jesuits operate in, or the 112 connection to 'Catholicism'.

Since we brought up the 111th World Series, we might as well revisit the ritual that all but ended the championship series on November 1st, or 11/1, because it further proves how scripted these games are. To take you back in time, Eric Hosmer stepped up to the plate in the top of the ninth inning, and the stat was displayed on the screen that Hosmer had a .111 batting average for the 111th World Series. Fittingly, on Matt Harvey's 111th pitch of the game, Hosmer nailed a line drive in the gap, driving in a run and giving the Royals their first score of the game. Matt Harvey was then pulled with 111 pitches, on 11/1, in the 111th World Series. From there, the Royals would go on to win the game 7-2, and fittingly 'Royals' sums to 72. As you will learn, it is the same type of obvious rituals that take place season after season, in all of professional sports, and before long, you'll be calling the outcomes of the games before they happen, just as I called the Mets to be in the 111th World Series in Spring Training of that season, reminding of Matt Damon's line from the film *The Informant,* where he explains the obvious math behind the World Series being rigged before Spring Training begins, which marks the start of the baseball season. Also important, Dave Henderson, a former star of the New York Mets, died at age 57, exactly 57 days after the World Series concluded, passing away on December 27, 2015. As we have just learned, 'World Series' sums to 57, and in this case, so do 'Mets' and 'New York Mets'.

Back on the subject of Super Bowl 54, another ritual worth recognizing, is how Patrick Mahomes, the quarterback of the Kansas City Chiefs, became the 33rd quarterback to win a Super Bowl, in only the second ever Super Bowl played on the 33rd day of the year. This is fitting because the name 'Patrick' sums to 33 with Pythagorean Gematria. Furthermore, his full name, 'Patrick Lavon Mahomes II' sums to 333 with Reverse Simple, and February 2, 2020, fell in a leap year, meaning there were 333 days left in the year on that date as well.

For another 3, he became the third black quarterback to win a Super Bowl. The first was Doug Williams with the Washington Redskins, who won Super Bowl 22, with a score of 42-10. The second was Russell Wilson, who won Super Bowl 48, 43-8, the only other Super Bowl ever played on the 33rd day of the year. What brings these rituals together is the number 42, where Doug Williams scored 42 points after throwing 4 touchdowns in the 2nd quarter, and then Russell Wilson, representing the 42nd state, Washington, brought the championship home for Seattle. Adding to the pattern, Patrick Mahomes won the big game after throwing exactly 42 passes, a number coded all over black history. As you might be aware, Jackie Robinson wore the number 42 and is credited with breaking the color barrier in MLB, in the year 1947. Not by chance, the name 'Jackie' sums to 42, and so do many words pertaining to black history, starting with 'February', the month that is referred to as black history month. Adding to that list is 'slavery', 'Tuskegee', 'nigger', 'brothers', 'bus', 'Martin', 'Malcolm X', 'Muhammad Ali', 'Huxtable', 'Cosby Show', 'LeBron James' and more. The next time you watch the sitcom *Martin*, you won't miss that he lives in apartment number 42. And if you want to rewind the clock, Jackie Robinson wasn't actually the first black baseball player in white major league. It was 'Moses Walker', summing to 42 with Pythagorean Gematria, who played in exactly 42 games. For another recent example, look no further than the Tyson Fury and Deontay Wilder fight of February 22, 2020, or 2/22/2020. In that fight, in black history month, the white fighter Tyson Fury defeated the black fighter Deontay Wilder in what looked like a fight where Deontay was told to lay down. Of course, the fight was easy to call in advance, because Wilder came in with 42 wins, and 'Tyson' sums to 42, the name of his opponent, reminding us of the 42-to-1 fight where Buster Douglas upset Mike Tyson on February 11, 1990, the 42nd day of the year, 30 years earlier. And the 30 years earlier mattered too, because all of these words sum to 30 and 42. They are 'slavery', 'Tuskegee', and 'nigger'. In this case, the name 'Deontay' sums to 30 with Pythagorean as well, and it was crystal clear that Tyson Fury would be picking up his 30th win, as a white man, beating the black man, in black history month, again, leaving Wilder on 42 career wins. Sure enough, he did. For one more 42, in February of 2021, the 56th and final themed "America the Beautiful Quarter" is being released, and it is in tribute to the 'Tuskegee' Airmen. It shows two planes, one with a 4, and another with a 2. The 'math' is simple on that one.

In addition to the number 42, the second parallel between the three black quarterbacks winning Super Bowls with the Redskins, Seahawks, and Chiefs, is that they are the only three teams in the NFL with clear Native American symbolism. The Redskins and Chiefs don't need explanation, but the Seahawks might. If you're not aware, Seattle is named after Chief Seattle, a Native American. And the Seattle Seahawks logo comes from the local Kwakwaka'wakw tribe. Thus, it appears the controllers of the NFL, are trying to tell us something about Native American history, and perhaps what they are attempting to say is, that long before African slaves arrived here, there were already Africans who had likely come to the continent in advance, and very possibly by their own ships that they had constructed and sailed with, since Africa was a very advanced continent, from a time in history that is nearly all but forgotten, outside of the pyramids. And let us not forget ancient Egypt and the 42 Laws of Ma'at. With this in mind, consider 'Native Americans' sums to 64 with Pythagorean Gematria, the same as 'Kansas City Chiefs', and the day they won Super Bowl 54, was precisely 64 weeks after Patrick Mahomes beat Len Dawson's 1964 Kansa City Chiefs' touchdown passing record. That accomplishment occurred November 11, 2018, and it should be noted that the same day Mahomes beat Dawson's record, Mahomes' girlfriend was watching in the stands, next to her father, who dropped dead, at the game. Of course the word 'kill' has gematria of 64, and on the subject of the number, Doug Williams had turned 64 years of age, August 9, 2019, 177 days before Super Bowl 54, the latter number connecting to 'The Jesuit Order'. For one more fact about 64, the Chiefs have now played in three Super Bowls, losing Super Bowl I by a score of 10-35, winning Super Bowl IV by a score of 23-7 and winning Super Bowl LIV 31-20. If you add it up, the Chiefs have scored 64 points in Super Bowls, and had 62 scored against them. Not by chance, if you write out 'Forty-Niners' the name of their last opponent, it has Pythagorean Gematria of 64, and Reverse Pythagorean of 62. For a bit more gematria fun, 'Forty-Niners' sums to 163 with Simple English, which is the 38th prime number, corresponding with the Simple value of 'gold', and reminding us that the 49ers hosted the "golden anniversary" of the Super Bowl, 50, on February 7, 2016, the 38th day of the year, only for it to be won by the

38th state, 'Colorado', equating to 38 with Pythagorean Gematria, who defeated the 'Panthers', summing to 38 in the same cipher. It also reminds us that it was the 38th President, Gerald Ford, who ended FDR's orders, effectively allowing Americans to buy 'gold' again, legally.

With regards to the Chiefs most recent score, in Super Bowl 54, winning 31-20, there must be something else said about this. Number 20 for the Chiefs, Morris Claiborne, was reported to be having Super Bowl 54 blues, because not long before it, his brother, had unexpectedly died, at age 31, on January 5, 2020. Thus, 31 and 20, a sum of 51, and his brother had died on a date that can be written 5/1. Keep in mind 'death' sums to 20 in Pythagorean Gematria, and that Morris Claiborne played his college football for the 'LSU Tigers', summing to 113 with Simple English, who won the college championship over the Clemson Tigers 8 days later, January 13th, or 1/13. The distance of 8 days matters as well, because 19 is the 8th prime, and the football championships at the start of 2020 for college and pro, were for the 2019 season, emphasis on '19.

Regarding the 2020 college football championship, if you watched the game, you might have caught the announcer's numerology lesson as he put it, while accusing the people of New Orleans of being into "those things", meaning numerology, in the fourth quarter, when LSU had all but won the game. The lesson was on the number 20, in regards to the death of 'Billy Cannon' on May 20, 2018. If you missed it, the announcer first pointed out that in 1959, 'Billy Cannon', summing to 59, the same as 'LSU Tigers', and even 'Tiger' alone, won the Heisman with LSU, and defeated Clemson, in the college championship, that was played in New Orleans- very similar to how in 2020, Joe Burrow of LSU became the second player from the school to win the Heisman, the highest honors in all of college football, and to defeat Clemson in the championship, in New Orleans. Beyond that, the announcer pointed out with "10:10 to play in 2020", how Billy Cannon wore the number 20, and how history was repeating itself, about 60 years later, which was divisible by 20, in 2020, when he had just died in recent history at age 80, another number divisible by 20, on May 20, 2018. Keep in mind, if you were watching and listening, the first down marker was set at the 20 yard line during the numerology lesson, and the camera crew went to an angle that captured Joe Burrow with an orange sign in the background next to his head with the number 20 on it. The only thing the announcer forgot to tell the audience, was that Joe Burrow had transferred from Ohio State to LSU on May 20, 2018, the same day Billy Cannon died, and that in gematria terms, 'LSU' equates to 20 with Reverse Pythagorean, whereas 'death' and 'time' equate to 20 with Pythagorean. Personally, I was so provoked by this incident, I traveled to LSU's campus in January of 2020, to educate the students of LSU about this. And as we'll get to, it was a beautiful thing, that I'll discuss more in the last chapter.

Coming back to the ritual of Super Bowl 54, on July 3, 2020, the last day before the United States 244th birthday, it was reported that the Washington Redskins and the Cleveland Indians were thinking about changing their names in the wake of the Black Lives Matter protests, and the extra attention brought to racism with them. Since the United States of America was technically still 243 years old on this date, it is worth nothing that 'Native American' sums to 243 with Reverse Simple English. This wasn't the first time the two teams from the NFL and MLB were used in such rituals either. For another recent example, on Christopher Columbus Day, October 8, 2018, a date with 56 numerology, the Saints wasted the Redskins on Monday Night Football, 43-19, and in the MLB, the Indians and the Braves, the two teams with native symbolism, were eliminated from the postseason the same day. In addition to these native teams all losing on the day to remember Columbus, the man who was paid for by the Catholic Church to voyage the world, and who is falsely credited with the discovery of America, a land where people lived long before he arrived, they were all shamed by the numbers as well. Consider the Braves lost to the Dodgers 6-2, going with the 62 points scored in the Monday Night Football game, corresponding with the Simple English Gematria of 'genocide', summing to 62, and the Indians were creamed by the Astros, 11-3, the team who had won the 113th World Series, over the Dodgers, a year earlier. That was the one given away by Matt Harvey being the first pitcher to pitch in Houston after the flooding of Hurricane and Tropical Storm Harvey, 52 days before the start of the World Series, where 'flood' and 'hurricane' both equate to 52. It is to say, it's all number games, and that is why A.J. Hinch, the manager of the Houston Astros, who won the 113th World Series, was fired on January 13th, or 1/13, and the following day, January 14th, or 1/14, Alex

Cora, who won the 114th World Series, met the same fate, because he was part of the "cheating" Houston Astros team, from the year prior. And please realize, there is no "cheating" when all of these games are 100% and undeniably fixed.

It should also be noted that the potential name change news for the Redskins and Indians came on July 3rd, a date that can be expressed as 7/3, like 73, and Doug Williams, the first black QB to win a Super Bowl, who accomplished this with the Redskins, has a full name, 'Douglas Lee Williams', equating to 73 with Pythagorean. Furthermore, the date July 3rd can be expressed as 3/7, like 37, and the announcement came 37 days before Doug Williams August 9th birthday, corresponding with the gematria of 'Native', equating to 37, the same as 'Zachary', the Louisiana town where he was raised, reminding us what state won the college championship to begin 2020. Adding insult to injury, July 3rd leaves 181 days left in the year, the 42nd prime number, bring us back to square one. And with that fact in mind, they are debating changing the name to the Washington Redtails, in tribute to the 'Tuskegee' Airmen. While it seems nice, it is truly sick. And if it eventually happens, expect another book about it, because I have a lot more to say on the subject matter. *For the time being, as of July 23, 2020, they have changed the name to Washington 'Football Team', where the new nickname equates to 122, the same as 'National Football League', as well as 'Kansas City' and 'San Francisco', who just faced each other in Super Bowl 54. Adding to the ritual, 'Redskins', the old name, equates to 54, and the temporary name change came 172 days after Super Bowl 54, where 172 corresponds with the Jesuit motto, 'Ad maiorem Dei gloriam', a motto also summing to 100 with Pythagorean, reminding us that Super Bowl 54 concluded the 100th NFL season.

For one last ritual, on July 6, 2020, a few days after the Redskins and Indians potential name change announcements, Patrick Mahomes signed a new contract worth reportedly over $400 million dollars, replacing Russell Wilson, the Seahawks quarterback, as the highest paid player in the National Football League. Not by chance, the date July 6th can be expressed as 7/6, reminding of *Acts 7:6* and the prophecy of people being mistreated as slaves for 400 years in a foreign land, tying in with the "$400 million" headlines. Of course, August 20, 2019, marked 400 years since slaves arrived in America, and the 100th NFL season that Mahomes won, began days later. It was for this reason 'ESPN' called the 100th NFL season that concluded with the Chiefs championship the "Year of the Black Quarterback". This prediction by the "54 network", ESPN, was made prior to the season beginning and prior to Kyler Murray, a rookie black quarterback, winning the NFL's Rookie Offensive Player of the Year award, and Lamar Jackson, a black quarterback, winning League MVP, and Patrick Mahomes, a black quarterback, winning Super Bowl MVP. Keep in mind 'African American' sums to 100 with Reverse Pythagorean, coinciding with the 100th NFL season. Furthermore, it sums to 71 with Pythagorean, the 20th prime, and all of these awards were given at the start of 2020, including the top honors to Lamar Jackson and Patrick Mahomes on the first and second day of 'Black History Month', respectively. For another riddle, this $400 million contract came 5 months and 4 days after Super Bowl 54, a game that was played on February 2nd. The signing of the contract also came 293 days after Patrick Mahomes September 17, 2019 birthday, which is the 62nd prime number, and with Pythagorean Gematria, 'Patrick Mahomes' sums to 62, same as 'four hundred', and similar to 'Forty Niners', also equating to 62, and reminding us that the Chiefs have allowed 62 points to be scored against them in Super Bowls, after holding the 49ers to 20 points in the 2020 Super Bowl, meaning that the Chiefs had allowed 42 points coming into the game. As you have learned, 'genocide' sums to 62, and there is symbolism with that to think about, in light of the "native team" having that many points scored against them in Super Bowls, to start 2020, the year of the deadly virus- but not as deadly as the smallpox that wiped out Native Americans. Back on the subject of the contract, it also came on a date that can be expressed as 6/7, like 67, and 'Kansas City' equates to 67 with Reverse Pythagorean. Furthermore, July 6th is the 187th day of the Gregorian year, and 'Society of Jesus' sums to 187, reminding us who is in charge of the rituals. With the Jesuits in mind, Super Bowl 54 was won by Patrick Mahomes 177 days after Doug Williams 64th birthday, and 'The Jesuit Order' equates to 177, reminding us that 'Jesuit Order' equates to 54, just like 'Joe Montana', the good Catholic, who Super Bowl 54 was in tribute to, coming a span of 131 days from his 64th birthday, on June 11, 2020, having been born in '56. For the record, both 'championship' and 'Super Bowl' equate to 131 with Simple English, which is the 32nd prime number, reminding us

225

that the NFL has 32 teams, and 'NFL', 'America' and 'Scottish' each equate to 32, matching the number of sun rays on the Jesuit logo. To add to your list, both 'Kansas City' and 'Chiefs' sum to 32 with Pythagorean. And never forget, 7/4/1776 = 7+4+1+7+7+6 = 32.

Of course, America began with a genocide of the Native Americans, that was purposefully done by spreading a virus. That virus was 'smallpox' equating to 104, the same as 'Roman Catholic Church', and reminding us that the date July 4, 1776 also has a numerology path of 104, as follows, 7+4+17+76 = 104. In light of the significance of 104 to 'smallpox', it was for this reason the Supreme Court revisited Jacobson v Massachusetts, a 1905 ruling on vaccinations in the time of smallpox, April 10, 2020, emphasis on 10/4, like 104. Thus the symbolism is clear. In the year of the purposefully spread virus, Covid-19, that changed the continent of North America, just as the genocide of the natives once did, it was only fitting to have the Kansas City Chiefs win the Super Bowl, in a massive 222 ritual, syncing with 'Wuhan Coronavirus', and the Jesuit motto, 'order out of chaos'. Furthermore, it was in 1798, 222 years prior to 2020, that Edward Jenner demonstrated the inoculation of humans with a live vaccinia virus, or cowpox, could protect against smallpox. And keep in mind 'Wuhan' alone equates to 67, the same as 'Kansas City', and the July 6th contract, or 6/7, was completed 155 days after Super Bowl 54, corresponding with the Simple English Gematria of 'coronavirus', 155. And for one last familiar number, it was signed on a 33 date numerology (7/6/20 = 7+6=20 = 33), only fitting for 'Patrick', equating to 33, the man who became the 33rd quarterback to win a Super Bowl, who did it on the 33rd day of the year, February 2, 2020, leaving 333 days left in the year, again, corresponding with the gematria of 'Patrick Lavon Mahomes II', summing to 333, who surpassed Russell Wilson as the highest paid player, a man who was born November 29, the 333rd day of the year. As a reminder, Russell Wilson is the only other player to win the Super Bowl on the 33rd day of the year to date, and what's funny about that is, 'Indian' sums to 33 with Pythagorean Gematria, the term often associated with Native Americans due to the false history we've been taught. For another joke, it was reported on July 24th, or 24/7, that Russell Wilson and Ciara had just given birth to a boy, 'Win'. As you know, 'Seattle, Washington' equates to 247 and 2020 marked the 247 year anniversary of the banning of the Jesuits. *Russell Wilson = 54

16 | Kobe Bryant's Burial & the NBA's March 11ᵗʰ Suspension

Coincidence. It's a word many use far too often to explain away things that are not. For example, many would claim it is a coincidence that LeBron James passed Kobe Bryant in points scored, in what was Kobe Bryant's hometown, in the Lakers' one game of the season in Philadelphia, thus a 1 out of 82 chance, because the Lakers play an 82 game schedule, and only 1 game at Philadelphia each year (*Game = 82, Reverse Simple English). Those same people would likely also call it a coincidence that LeBron James passed Kobe Bryant in points scored, while playing for the Los Angeles Lakers, and then the next day Kobe Bryant died in Los Angeles, exactly what was reported to have happened January 25ᵗʰ and January 26ᵗʰ, 2020 respectively. They would likely also call it a coincidence that Kobe Bryant was then buried in Corona del Mar in the time of a coronavirus outbreak. They might even call it a coincidence that LeBron James got his 24ᵗʰ tattoo on his body in tribute to Kobe Bryant, who wore number 24, with a picture of a black snake, and the words 'Mamba 4 Life', days after Kobe's death, and after passing Kobe Bryant in points scored on Philadelphia's court, that was decorated with a black snake, chopped into pieces, from the 'Join, or Die' flag. They'd likely even call it a coincidence that the Lakers became 24-8 at home, after defeating the Los Angeles Clippers, when the NBA returned from its coronavirus break, July 30, 2020, despite 24 and 8 being the jersey numbers of Kobe Bryant. And they might even call it a coincidence that Beyonce won her 24ᵗʰ Grammy at the Staples Center where the Lakers play on the same day Kobe died, being the same woman that opened up his memorial with a song on the 24ᵗʰ of February in the same building. But if you show them what is in the remaining pages of this chapter, you might very well cure their **coincidence theory** problem. Information is the key, and those same people might have never heard of a death pool, or gematria, or how it is used ritualistically- and in that regard, here is what is interesting about Kobe Bryant's death, in light of a death pool and gematria.

First, the way the odds for a death pool work are by taking the age of a person, and subtracting it from 100. So in the case of Kobe Bryant, who died at 41, you would subtract 41 from 100, meaning Kobe Bryant paid 59:1 in a death pool, huge odds. This becomes interesting because Kobe Bryant was known as the 'Black Mamba', and he crashed in his Black Mamba painted helicopter, in 'Calabasas', where both the names 'Black Mamba' and 'Calabasas' sum to 59, with Simple English, the same as 'blues', 'Rasta', 'negro' and 'slave'. This is why at first it was reported that 5 people were killed, including Kobe Bryant and his daughter in the crash, before the death toll jumped to 9 killed. This is also why it was later reported that Lisa Marie Presley's son died in Calabasas, July 12, 2020, a date with 59 numerology, the grandson of 'Elvis Presley', a name equating to 59 with Pythagorean Gematria, who was once accused of making "black music". As you'll recall, the number 59 is encoded into black history in a number of ways, from the establishment year of Motown, 1959, to the fact that Black History Month, February, ends on the 59th day of the year, except for in leap years. And while death pools and betting on them might not be common amongst ordinary people, we are talking about the games of those who are often referred to as elites. Again, I'll ask you to read and listen to the lyrics to the song *Murder by Numbers*, a song about how killing is the sport of the elite, and it is as simple as A, B, C is 1, 2, 3. And as you read and listen, consider how games, such as the knocking off of celebrities for the sake of winning a death pool, could fit into the schemes that are sung about.

Moving on. The man born 'Kobe Bean Bryant', summing to 54 with Pythagorean Gematria, and his daughter 'Gianna Bryant', also summing to 54 with Pythagorean, shocked the world when they were reported dead exactly one week before Super Bowl 54, to an unsuspecting public, even though the event had been foretold nearly a decade in advance in the 2011 film *The Black Mamba*, that we'll soon get to. Keep in mind, their respective ages, 41 and 13, add to be 54, and as you know, the number 54 connects the 'Jesuit Order', and their logo, the 'sun', both equating to 54 --- the latter being the object that is measured in a 24 hour cycle, similar to how Kobe Bryant finished his career with the jersey number 24, after beginning his career with the number 8, two numbers that when added together equate to 32, reminding us of the number of sun rays in the Jesuit logo, 32. With regards to the sun, and the Gregorian calendar that is based on the solar cycle, you will notice that the name 'Kobe Bryant' and the phrase 'solar cycle' are identical in all four base ciphers, equating to 41, 58, 113 and 157, numbers we will come to understand very well before the end of this chapter, especially in how they relate to the life of Kobe Bryant, and what really happened the day he was reported dead, his

157th day of being 41 years old. As we move through the chapter, keep in mind that 'Sun God' sums to 26, like 'Bryant', and he died on the 26th day of the Gregorian year, in the 74th NBA season, while having a first name, 'Kobe', equating to 33 in Simple English. As you have learned, the numbers 33 and 74 are often brought together, seemingly in tribute to 'Jesus', summing to 74, the same as 'cross', the former being the man who is believed to have been crucified at age 33, and whose existence is debated, and sometimes debated as being the sun of God, as opposed to the son of God. And in that breath, keep in mind Kobe Bryant died on a Sunday, the Catholic Day of worship, named in honor of the sun. With these parallels between Jesus and Kobe in mind, the latter being a man who is truly worshipped by many for his athleticism, professional success and celebrity, it is only fitting then that 'crucify' sums to 41 with Reverse Pythagorean, matching Kobe Bryant's age of demise.

As for the parallel to Super Bowl 54, it becomes all the more curious when you realize that 'Kobe Bryant' alone sums to 41 with Pythagorean, the same as 'Super Bowl', and that Patrick Mahomes, number 15, became 26 for 41 on passing attempts after connecting with Damien Williams, number 26 (15+26 = 41) on the Chiefs, for a touchdown, helping add 7 points to the scoreboard, and giving his team the lead for the first time in the 'game', a word equating to 26, in Super Bowl 54, 7 days after Kobe Bryant died on the 26th of January, at age 41. And again, 'Bryant', like 'Jordan', sums to 26 in Pythagorean- the 'God' number. Bringing Kobe Bryant's death even closer to the sport of football, January 26, 2020 happened to be the 37 year anniversary of the death of Bear Bryant, who passed January 26, 1983, a man who is considered the greatest college football coach of all time, and who coached for Alabama, *where Forrest Gump* played. It was only fitting he would die in '83 then, because 'football' sums to 83 with Simple English, similar to how 'basketball' sums to 22 with Pythagorean and Kobe died in 2020, the same year David Stern died, who became the commissioner of the National Basketball Association (NBA) in 1984, before dying on January 1, 2020, a date with 22 numerology, which stands out, because both 'David' and 'Stern' sum to 22 with Pythagorean, the same as 'basketball', connecting back to the key digits in 2020, 2 and 2. As for why I bring up the part about the 37 year anniversary, it is because the name 'Bryant' sums to 26 with Pythagorean Gematria, like dying on the 26th of the month, and 37 with Reverse Pythagorean, like dying on the 37 year anniversary of Bear Bryant, and similar to dying on the 157th day of his own age, because 157 is the 37th prime number.

To further illustrate the significance of 26, in light of both Bryants dying on January 26th, and not to be confused with Al Bryant of the Temptations who died on October 26th, we need to revisit the college football Championship won by Alabama on January 8, 2018. We will examine this game because it was from recent history, and it was when Nick Saban won his 6th college football championship, tying Bear Bryant for the most college football championships ever. Not by chance, he did it by scoring 26 points, beating Georgia 26-23, on the date of January 8, 2018. So I ask, is it a coincidence both 'Georgia' and 'Los Angeles' equate to 37, the latter being where Kobe Bryant and his daughter died? In light of of the tragic news from the 26th, that of Kobe Bryant dying at age 41, along with his daughter at age 13, in 'L.A.', equating to 41 and 13, that same Alabama championship game that was won by Nick Saban, to tie 'Bear', a name also summing to 26, concluded in overtime with a 41 yard touchdown pass from the quarterback wearing number 13 to the receiver wearing number 6, in a beautiful mathematically driven riddle, because 41 is the 13th prime, and 13 is the 6th prime. The winning quarterback's name, 'Tua', sums to 6 as well, and he brought home Nick Saban's 6th championship, despite being down 0-13 at halftime. Adding to the riddle of 26, the winning play and 26th points for Alabama happened on 2nd down and 26, that was set up by taking a purposeful big loss on the down prior. Keep in mind Nick Saban was coaching 'Alabama', Bear Bryant's old school, summing to 13 in Pythagorean Gematria, the 6th prime number. As for the greater meaning of 26 and 6, it goes back to *Genesis 1:26*, where mankind is made in the image of 'God' on the 'sixth' day, and where 'sixth' equates to 26 with Pythagorean, similar to how 'Adam' sums to 26 in Reverse Pythagorean, the name 'God' gave to the first man. The numbers 26 and 6 also reminds us of Pope Francis, the first Jesuit Pope, the 266th, and the fact that Kobe Bryant died while traveling from Catholic mass. Let us not forget the value of 'Iesus Hominum Salvator', equating to 266, because as we'll soon get to, Kobe Bryant died 266 days after his wife's May 5, 2019 birthday, the day she turned 37. He was also drafted into the NBA on June 26th, or 26/6, in 1996. And for the record, 'Iesus Hominum Salvator' means 'Jesus, savior of men', a phrase equating to 211, the same as 'Black

Mamba', and in Kobe Bryant's case, he died 211 days before the next Kobe Bryant Day, August 24, 2020, celebrated on 8/24 in Los Angeles annually. The celebration began in 2016, the year Kobe retired from the NBA, and on the date August 24th, because Kobe Bryant wore the numbers 8 and 24. The number 211 is also the 47th prime, and Kobe Bryant died on a date with 47 numerology, a number connecting to the 'Vatican', that was established in history on February 11th, or 2/11, in 1929. Sadly, on February 11, 2020, it was reported that Joseph Shabalala had died at age 78, and reminding us that Kobe was born in '78, and Shabalala was born in '41. What makes the parallel between the two men's deaths all the more clear, is that Joseph Shabalala was the singer for the band 'Ladysmith Black Mambazo', equating to 211 with Simple English, similar to 'Black Mamba', equating to 211 with Reverse Simple. Thus it was a very sick joke, on the 30th anniversary of Nelson Mandela being freed on the 42nd day of the year, and also on the Vatican's 91st birthday, the 13th triangular number.

On the subject of 13, and to get back to the Alabama championship game for a moment, it was January 3rd of that year, or 1/3, like 13, that Donald Trump, the "winner" of the 58th U.S. Presidential Election, announced he was going to be attending the 'Alabama' championship (58 is 5+8 = 13), one of many signs the game was all about 13, and in favor of 'Alabama', equating to 13, before it was even played. And as we had stated that day after hearing the news, it was a done deal, the game was Alabama's, and it would be all about the number 13- and it was, with the biggest storyline being number 13, Tua Tuanigamanuolepola Tagovailoa, replacing Jalen Hurts, number 2, at halftime, down 0-13, and coming back to win the championship under the highest pressure. And if you want to get cute, 'two' has a Pythagorean value of 13. And if you want to get cuter, there were 49 points scored in the game in total (49 is 4+9 = 13). And now this year, in 2020, Tua was drafted by the NFL's Miami Dolphins, a city that's name begins with the 13th letter, M, becoming the first quarterback to wear 13 for the Dolphins since Dan Marino, who was coached by Don Shula, who passed recently at age 90, on May 4th, 2020, a date with 13 numerology (5+4+2+0+2+0 = 13), and even more, being written 5/4, after Miami hosted Super Bowl 54. His date of passing also came 13 weeks and 1 day after Super Bowl 54, reminding us that 'Super Bowl' sums to 131. And in light of Don Shula dying at 90 on May 4th and being a Miami legend, never mind

231

that 'Miami' sums to 45 with Simple English and 90 with Reverse Simple, or that the date can also be written 4/5, like 45, corresponding with the Pythagorean and Reverse Pythagorean values of 'thirteen', equating to 45 with both. For your learning, 45 is the 9th triangular number, and 9 represents completion. In numerology terms, both 45 and 90 equate to 9 as well, thus making Don Shula's "completion" ritual all the more fitting, especially after Super Bowl 54, another number having 9 numerology.

And for more familiar numbers, you might have noticed I brought up Donald Trump being the winner of the 58th U.S. Presidential election in light of his January 3rd announcement about attending Alabama's championship. I did that because 'Alabama' sums to 158 with Reverse Simple English, similar to how 'Kobe Bryant' sums to 58 with Reverse Pythagorean, and similar to how 'Forrest Gump', set in Alabama, sums to 58 with Reverse Pythagorean, and also 158 with Simple English. And for another, 'Tuanigamanuolepola Tagovailoa' equates to 158 with Reverse Pythagorean, the star 'Alabama' product, who is now off to the Jesuit and Scottish Rite controlled NFL, where once again, the Jesuits were formed in France on 15/8, or August 15th, and 'Freemasonry' sums to 158 with Reverse Simple English and also 58 with Pythagorean.

For another synchronicity between the deaths of Kobe Bryant and Bear Bryant, as we have learned, the name 'Kobe Bryant' equates to 157, and having been born August 23, 1978, he died on his 157th day of his age, 41, which again, becomes all the more curious when you recognize that 'Kobe Bryant' equates to 41 and 157. Regarding the number 157, it is the 37th prime, and in light of dying on the 37 year anniversary of Bear Bryant's passing, 'Tuscaloosa, Alabama', where the University of Alabama is located, sums to 157 with Simple English. And with the number 157 in mind, let us add to the list, in light of the ritual of Kobe Bryant's very suspicious death, while traveling from Catholic mass in 'Los Angeles', a city equating to 37 with Pythagorean Gematria.

On the day of his demise, the Grammy Awards were being hosted at the 'Staples Center', in L.A., a building name summing to 157 with Simple English, where Kobe Bryant used to play his home games with the Lakers. During the Grammy's, 'Alicia Keys', summing to 41 with Pythagorean, the same as 'Kobe Bryant', paid tribute to his name. Also standing out, is the fact that Beyonce won her 24th Grammy award at the ceremony, on the date of the death of number 24, Kobe Bryant, and in the building that is often referred to as the one "Kobe built." If you think that's a coincidence, try again. When Beyonce was with Destiny's Child, they released the album *The Writing's On The Wall* on the date of July 27, 1999, the day leaving 157 days left in the year. This matters because Kobe Bryant appears in the music video for the song 'Bug-A-Boo' off the same album, and the song name sums to 126, the same as 'Gianna Bryant', and corresponding with his date of death, 1/26. Furthermore, that music video released after the album, on Kobe's 21st birthday, August 23, 1999, where 21 is the number corresponding with 'Jesuit' as well as 'Lakers', using Pythagorean Gematria for both, and corresponding with the fact that 1999 was 21 years before 2020. To take it further, 'Saturn' sums to 21 with Pythagorean Gematria, and Saturn is the 6th planet, corresponding with 21 being the 6th triangular number. Saturn is also connected to death and judgement, and in Tarot, the 20th card is the judgement card, bringing us to 2020, the year of Kobe's demise. Keep in mind 'Tarot' sums to 74, and so does 'Destiny's Child', because Kobe Bryant died during the 74th NBA season. And in light of this riddle running through Beyonce and her 24th Grammy on the day of Kobe Bryant's death, for her husband, Jay-Z, it was his 54th day of his age… and in case I'm giving you number shock, 'Kobe Bean Bryant' equates to 54. Furthermore, he died 144 days after Beyonce's 38th birthday, that fell on September 4, 2019, and as you know, 'Jesuit Order' equates to 54 and 144. Never mind that September 4th is also Los Angeles' birthday, and for good reason. It is because September 4th leaves 118 days in the year, and 'Los Angeles, California' is not only located on the 118th Meridian West, but it equates to 118, the same as the name of their current Mayor, 'Eric Garcetti'. It reminds us a little bit of how 'Los Angeles, California' and 'Paradise, California', both summing to 118, burned on November 8, 2018, emphasis on 11/8, in the deadliest California wildfires in history. It should also remind you that the word 'death' has Simple English Gematria of 38, and Jewish Gematria of 118, since Beyonce was 38 years old at the time of Kobe's tragic "accident." And if you caught the July 4, 2020 news of a political candidate going by the name K.W. Miller stating that Beyonce was really a member of the Italian 'Lastrassi' family, the name 'Lastrassi' sums to 118 with Simple English, and the prospect of her being Italian is very interesting, because Kobe Bryant grew up in Italy where his father also played professional basketball. Furthermore, the candidate said her real name was 'Ann Marie Lastrassi', equating to 193 in the same cipher as 'Roman Catholic Church', and 67 like 'Italy', and 122 and 266 in the same ciphers as 'Iesus Hominum Salvator'.

Back on the subject of the 'Staples Center', it is also the same building that Steph Curry's record streak of 157 games with a three-point shot made came to an end, November 4, 2016. At the time, it reminded me of the Warriors record home winning streak ending at 54 games, at 'Oracle', equating to 54 with Simple English, on April 1, 2016, April Fools Day, the same day the Cavaliers picked up their 54th win of the season, in back to back games that were broadcast on 'ESPN', a network equating to 54 in two of the four base ciphers, and reminding us that Steph Curry and LeBron James were both born in Akron, Ohio, in the same hospital, only to have the fate of playing each other four straight times in the NBA Finals. *The coincidences!* And don't even get me started on Nate Thurmond, also born in Akron, Ohio, who had his jersey number 42 retired with the Warriors and Cavs, the same teams that met in four straight NBA Finals led by Steph Curry and LeBron James, and who died at age 74, 27 days after LeBron scored 27 points in Game 7, defeating the Warriors on the real King James birthday, June 19, 2016, in what was his 103rd game of the season, the 27th prime, and where right before the game, the actor Anton Yelchin died, in a freak accident, at age 27, having 103 birth numerology, having been born March 11, 1989. As we'll get to, March 11th is a very important date to the NBA in terms of numbers, and it is the date the 74th NBA season would eventually be suspended on in 2020, due to "coronavirus". In the case of Yelchin, his birth year, '89, also mattered, because 'King James' sums to 89 with Simple English, the same as 'religion', and reminding us of the 89 chapters that make up the *Gospel*, the story of Jesus. Adding even more relevance to the number 89, hours after Yelchin's death, the Warriors would lose to LeBron, 'King James', in Game 7, with 89 points. And let us not forget that occurred during LeBron James' 13th season, similar to how the real King James became a king at 13 months of age, and reminding us that the son of King James, was King Charles, and the people who fought for him were called Cavaliers, just like the name of the team LeBron played for at the time, the Cleveland Cavaliers.

Moving on and continuing with the subject of 157, this number connects to many more important things regarding Kobe Bryant, including his father, who was once an NBA star himself, having been drafted by the Warriors before playing for the Philadelphia 76ers, the San Diego Clippers and the Houston Rockets. His NBA nickname was 'Jellybean', equating to 157, as in Joe Jellybean Bryant. For another 157, Kobe's death was blamed on an 'accident', equating to 157 with Reverse Simple, the same as 'Jellybean'. Furthermore, the day of his death, the WWE's 33rd Royal Rumble was taking place, corresponding with 'Kobe' equating to 33, and for the first time in the history of the WWE, a man from Scotland won the event. He was 'Drew McIntyre', having a name equating to 157 with Simple English, and reminding us that the top of the Scottish Rite of Freemasonry, created under the Jesuit umbrella, is the 33rd degree. Keep in mind, Vince McMahon, a Scottish Rite Freemason, born on August 24, 1945, "Kobe Bryant Day", owns and operates the WWE, and he was 74 years old at the time of Kobe's death, reminding us that Kobe died during the 74th NBA season, and Bear Bryant's full name, 'Paul William Bryant', sums to 74 with Pythagorean Gematria, the man who Kobe Bryant's death was coordinated with. For another 74, you can add 'Mahomes' to the list, a name summing to 74 by using Simple English, and the surname of the man who appears to have been a beneficiary of the greater Kobe Bryant death ritual, where you could say one star died, and another was truly born, by winning Super Bowl 54.

Continuing with the subject of 157, Kobe Bryant's father still is, and Kobe Bryant was a member of the Boule, as many black entertainers are. I bring this up because the date Joe Bryant was born, October 19, 1954, was 157 days after the Boule's 50th birthday, having been established May 15, 1904. And don't overlook that his father was born in '54, in light of the sacrifice ritual that Kobe Bryant became a part of before Super Bowl 54, where in that game, another young black superstar, in black history month, put his stamp on the NFL, winning his first Super Bowl, that couldn't have been scripted any better. If you are not familiar with the Boule, it is similar to Prince Hall Freemasonry, which is Freemasonry for black men. It is for this reason Kobe Bryant's autopsy was released on May 15, 2020, on the anniversary date of the establishment of the Boule, a fraternity also known as Sigma Pi Phi. With your gematria lens, you can verify that both 'Boule' and 'Sigma Pi Phi' equate to 55 with our base ciphers, similar to how the letters Sigma (18) Pi (16) and Phi (21) of the Greek alphabetic add up to 55 (18+16+21 = Sigma + Pi + Phi = 55), and it is for this reason Kobe Bryant's February 24th memorial was held at the 'Staples Center', on the 55th day of the year. That last stat becomes all the more interesting when you recognize that 'Los Angeles Lakers' sums to 257 with Reverse Simple, the 55th prime, and Kobe Bryant died on the 257th day of the Boule's age. At the same time, 'blood sacrifice' equates to 257, as well as 67, the latter number corresponding with the gematria of 'Black Mamba' and 'Calabasas', as well as the 67 date numerology that he died on. The significance of 55 also explains why he was in an arranged marriage with Vanessa Bryant, a woman born on May 5th, or 5/5. And on the subject of her birthday, I should remind us, Kobe Bryant died 266 days after her 37th birthday. As you have learned, 266 is a special number to the Jesuits, through the gematria of the motto 'Iesus Hominum Salvator', equating to 266, and the fact that the first Jesuit Pope is the 266th. This detail reminds us that modern Freemasonry, and its many wings, including the Boule, a fraternity just for black men, are under the Jesuit umbrella, the "divide and conquer" cartel.

For another 157 riddle, the NBA All Star Game was played on February 16, 2020, a date with 58 numerology, and it was dedicated to 'Kobe Bryant', equating to 58, the same as 'Los Angeles Lakers', and the same as 'star'. And for a reminder, all of these words sum to 58 with the base ciphers, and they all relate to time. They are 'calendar', 'Gregorian', 'Zodiac', 'solar cycle', 'star', and 'stars'. Let us not forger the sun is considered our nearest star, or how 'Kobe Bryant' relates to 'solar cycle'. And with the concept of all things being of God recognized, including time, the four letter name of God, the 'Tetragrammaton' sums to 58. As for the 157, instead of playing with a game clock for the 2020 All Star Game, a target score was set at 157, meaning the first team to score 157 points was the winner. Sure enough, Team LeBron James won, defeating Team Giannis, scoring 157, and what makes this all the more creepy, is that prior to the coronavirus suspension, the NBA Finals were originally set to begin on June 4, 2020, precisely 157 days after LeBron James' December 30th birthday, the star of the Los Angeles Lakers who joined the team after Kobe's retirement. Furthermore, heading into the 2020 NBA Playoffs, LeBron's postseason record is 156 and 83, meaning his next win is 157. Keep in mind, that measurement of 157 days was from LeBron's 35th birthday, and 'King James' sums to 35 with Pythagorean Gematria, the same as 'Catholic', and the real King James became a 'Freemason' when he was 35 years of age. Furthermore, the real King James died unexpectedly, at age 58, and he was a Freemason and a 'Rosicrucian', the latter equating to 58 the same as 'Freemasonry', both with Pythagorean. If you break 58 down in numerology terms, 5+8, it equates to 13, and then you can break 13 down to 1+3 is 4. Recall, LeBron, nicknamed King James, passed Kobe Bryant in points scored, in Philadelphia, Kobe's hometown, dropping Kobe to 4th in scoring in NBA history, and as we learned earlier, the number 4 is associated with not only the Tetragrammaton, but death, especially in the far east, because in both Mandarin and Japanese, you pronounce "four", the same way you pronounce "death". And with Japan in mind, and the 'New World Order', or better said, 'The Jesuit Order' pulling the strings, I must mention that Kobe Bryant died on 1/26 in the time of the 126th Emperor of Japan, Naruhito, and that Kobe, Japan was founded on April 1, 1889, emphasis on 4/1, similar to 'Kobe Bryant' equating to 41, dying at age 41. If you want to go even further, Naruhito took office May 1, 2019, meaning the day Kobe Bryant died, was his 271st day as emperor, and 271 is the 58th prime. I should also mention, in light of LeBron James passing Kobe Bryant in points scored, that the NBA All Star Game was captained by the stars of the Los Angeles Lakers and Milwaukee Bucks, the two teams that Kareem Abdul-Jabbar once played for, the same man who leads the NBA in scoring all time, as of 2020. And never mind that 'Abdul-Jabbar' sums to 74 with Simple English, coinciding with the death ritual in the 74th NBA season, and reminding us of 'Muhammad' Ali, another athlete who changed his name to an Islamic name, and who died at age 74. *In light of the Islamic parallel between Abdul-Jabbar and Ali, it should be noted that an infamous episode of *South Park* is titled "*201*", and it was banned because it outraged Muslims for the way it mocked the Prophet Muhammad. And let us not forget, Event 201 was held on the day leaving 74 days in the Gregorian year.

For yet another 157 pertaining to the premature death of the basketball star, Kobe Bryant and Kanye West, along with Bruce Willis, did a short film called *The Black Mamba*, that was made for Nike, and

237

that was released in February of 2011. The film concludes with Kobe Bryant throwing a basketball with a bomb inside of it at a helicopter, that houses an escaping villain, played by Kanye West, leading to the helicopter exploding in midair. This obviously reminds us of Kobe's fatal helicopter accident. If you look at the poster made for that film, that depicts an exploding helicopter behind Kobe Bryant, at the top it says, **'You lose this road game, you don't go home'**, equating to 157 with Pythagorean Gematria. Again, this number connects to the gematria of 'Kobe Bryant' and the fact that he died on the 157th day of his age, and the fact that the day before his death, the Lakers lost a road game, in Kobe's hometown, Philadelphia, where LeBron James surpassed Kobe Bryant in all time points scored, scoring an easy layup, for the 54th points of the game for the Lakers, corresponding with the Pythagorean Gematria of 'Kobe Bean Bryant', as well as 'Gianna Bryant'. I'll also add, regarding the logo of the black snake on the court, it is from the 'Join, or Die' flag, and 'Join, or Die' equates to 54 with both Pythagorean cyphers. Furthermore, LeBron's basket brought the score to 54 to 74, in the 74th NBA season, meaning that moments before, the score was 52 to 74, thus 126 points in total, similar to the date of his passing, 1/26, as well as *Genesis 1:26*, and the fact that 'Gianna Bryant' sums to 126 with Simple English, similar to 'Bug-A-Boo', also equating to 126. Keep in mind, LeBron James passed Kobe on January 25th, a date that can be written 25/1, like 251, the 54th prime number, and on a date that was 26 days after LeBrons' birthday. Furthermore, Kobe died a span of 54 days from Bruce Willis 65th birthday, March 19, 2020, who again, also starred in *The Black Mamba*. And regarding Willis turning 65, 'Philadelphia' equates to 65 with Pythagorean Gematria, reminding us that Kobe's father was 65 years old at the time of his death, and Philadelphia's date of establishment, October 27th, leaves 65 days in the year. As you know, that is the 'pandemic' number, and Kobe's death was woven into the web of coronavirus pandemic riddles when it was reported that he and his daughter were buried in 'Corona del Mar', equating to 56 and 70, in the same exact same ciphers as 'coronavirus'. Even further, it was reported they were buried February 7th, the 38th day of the year, corresponding with the gematria of 'pandemic' as well as 'death' and 'R.I.P.', making the span of days, from the accident to the burial, 13 in number. And further tying his death in with the pandemic riddle, it was reported that Kobe Bryant was in a legal battle with a

238

pharmaceutical company at the time of his demise, over the fact a company was attempting to capitalize on his Black Mamba branding without his permission. Of course, this was at the same time when pharmaceutical giants in the (201) area code of New Jersey and elsewhere were racing for the coronavirus cure.

Further bringing Kobe and Kanye West together, it was reported that the accident was very close to Kanye West's Calabasas home, and it came a span of 135 days before Kanye's 43rd birthday, June 8, 2020, connecting to the Simple English Gematria of 'Kobe Bean Bryant', summing to 135, and reminding us that the Boule's birthday, in non leap years, is May 15th, the 135th day of the year. And in light of Philadelphia being where the Boule was originally established, and where Kobe was born, there is something special about 135 and Philadelphia, that is biblical, and it is explained through Philadelphia's establishment date on October 27, 1682, a date with 135 numerology (10+27+16+82 = 135). This number matters because Philadelphia is a name used in *Revelation*, and in the letter written to the Church of Philadelphia in *Revelation 3:7*, 'The Key of David' is mentioned, equating to 135 with Simple English. And I promise you, from this day forward, when you pay attention to Philadelphia sports and history, you'll notice a lot of 135 riddles. Case in point, Carson Wentz, as a rookie with the Philadelphia Eagles, set an NFL record, not throwing an interception until his 135th pass.

Speaking of Carson Wentz, you might recall the time Kobe Bryant was in attendance at his game on December 10, 2017, when the Philadelphia Eagles were visiting the Los Angeles Rams, and Kobe Bryant received national attention for singing 'Fly Eagles Fly', the Philadelphia Eagles team song, equating to 135 and 54, in the exact same ciphers as 'Kobe Bean Bryant'. That was the game where the Eagles won, but Carson Wentz was badly injured, giving rise to Nick Foles, who lead the Eagles to a Super Bowl victory over the Patriots, in Minneapolis, the original home of the Los Angeles Lakers. I know my followers do, because they hit for six times their money when the Eagles won that game, as huge underdogs, who I predicted would be winning that symbolic game prior to facing the Patriots in the Super Bowl, after just Week 3 of the NFL season. And again, I was able to make this prediction because of what Donald Trump did on September 23, 2017, when he took on the NFL protesters of the National Anthem and U.S. Flag, reminding us that the date is written 23/9, similar to 239, the 52nd prime, and Super Bowl 52 was upcoming in 'Minnesota', equating to 52, and more importantly, the flag was sewn at 239 Arch Street, in Philadelphia- a city that gets its name from a book of prophecy, *Revelation*, and where 'prophecy' equates to 52 with Pythagorean and 'prophet' equates to 98 with Simple English. I bring up the part about 98 because Super Bowl 52 concluded the 98th NFL season, and it was hosted by the Minnesota Vikings, where again, 'Minnesota' sums to 52, and 'Vikings' sums to 98. So as we asked then, what could be more symbolic than the team with the flag on their helmet, the Patriots, playing against the city that gave birth to the flag, Philadelphia, the city named after the 'church' of prophecy? The answer came the next day, when the Eagles field goal kicker set a new team record, with a 61 yard make. This mattered in gematria terms, because both 'church' and 'Philadelphia' equate to 61, along with 'Christian', 'Christmas', 'Jesus' and 'cross'. And if you're asking the logical question that is to be asked, "How do you make sure a 61 yard kick goes in?", the answer is technology, in the balls, that you're not ever allowed to take home in the NFL, or the NBA, as a fan. Keep in mind, 61 is the 18th prime, and the Eagles would take the Vince Lombardi trophy, to start 2018.

Adding to the riddle with the flag, the Patriots and Eagles had played each other in Super Bowl 39, 13 years earlier, reminding us of the number of stripes on the U.S. flag, 13. And with 13 in mind, don't overlook the fact that the Eagles scored 41 points in 'Super Bowl' 52, the 13th prime number, or that a deck of cards is 52 in number, and divided into four sets of 13. And don't overlook that 'NFL' sums to 13 with Reverse Pythagorean, or that 'U.S.A.' sums to 41 with Simple English, the nation that began with 13 colonies. Also for the memory bank, the final score of 'Super Bowl' 52 was Eagles 41, Patriots 33, for 74 combined points, in tribute to the nation born on July 4th, or 7/4.

Having recognized the Super Bowl matchup months in advance, thanks to Donald Trump's September 23rd antics, and understanding how the number games unfold, year after year, season after season, as we have been proving since 2014, it allowed me to call in advance, that if the Eagles were to win, Zach Ertz, number 86 for the Eagles, would score the winning touchdown in Super Bowl 52, 86 days after his November 10th birthday, because the National Anthem had been adopted by the U.S. 86 years prior to the 98th NFL season, thus bringing the riddle full circle. And sure as the sun, Zach Ertz scored the winning touchdown, on a pass from Nick Foles, a man having N.F. initials, or 14.6., similar to the birthday of Donald Trump and the U.S. Flag, June 14th. Even more, the name 'Nick Foles' sums to 149 with Reverse Simple English, the 35th prime, and he defeated 'Tom Brady', also summing to 35, on February 4, 2018, the 35th day of the year, reminding us who wrote the script, the same entity that controls the nation, the 'Catholic' Church.

It should also be noted, that in light of Donald Trump having the same birthday as the U.S. Flag, that was born in Philadelphia, on June 14, 1777, and 'president' equating to 52, you can understand why the ritual would run through the presidency for Super Bowl 52, as it did. And keep in mind Super Bowl 52 was played prior to the start of the 99th NFL season, that was a continuation of the same ongoing storyline, where 'New England', summing to 99, would go on to win the Super Bowl, in the most symbolic of fashion. To understand the symbolism, you must keep in mind 'The United States of America' sums to 99, and it was named that on September 9th, or 9/9 of 1776. Furthermore, 'thirteen' written out as a word sums to 99, reminding us of the 13 stripes on the U.S. Flag and the 13 colonies, as well as the number of families that founded the Bavarian Illuminati, May 1, 1776, a date with 99 numerology. Of course, in the 99th NFL season, the New England Patriots, lead by 41 year old Tom Brady, would defeat the team from 'L.A.', equating to 13 and 41, with a score of 13-3, giving Tom Brady his 6th Super Bowl ring, and reminding us that 13 is the 6th prime. And adding on to that riddle, the state of California joined the United States of America on September 9, 1850, 74 years after the U.S. was named, the home state of the Los Angeles Rams, making them all the more a perfect opponent for 'New England' for the 99th NFL season. We won't even touch the fact that the Rams star, 'Aaron Donald', equating to 99 with Simple English, wears the number 99, or that his birthday is May 23rd, or 5/23, similar to 523, the 99th prime, and that he laid down in the Super Bowl against old man Brady, who lead the Patriots into the 99th NFL season, as a franchise with 523 wins before a single game was played, a major tell that the 99th season was theirs.

And to get back on the subject of 157 and Kobe Bryant, there is another very important story to tell. That is of Damian Lillard, the man born July 15, 1990, a date that can be written 15/7, like 157, stealing the show on *'Remembering Kobe'* night, leading the Portland Trail Blazers to a road win in Los Angeles, while being on the team from 'Oregon', the only state having Simple English Gematria of 74, and also being the 33rd state in order of statehood, perfect for the 'Kobe' ritual in the 74th NBA season. This matchup only occurred on *Remember Kobe* night because the Lakers and Clippers game was immediately rescheduled in the wake of his death, making the Lakers next game in the Staples Center against the Portland Trail Blazers. In terms of gematria, 'Remembering Kobe' sums to 263, the 56th prime number, and 'Damian Lillard' equates to 56 with Pythagorean. Another tell for the numerical ritual that was created by the rescheduling of the Lakers' next game after the death of Kobe, was that the date of the game against the Blazers, on January 31st, or 1/31, was something like 131, the 32nd prime, corresponding with the gematria of 'Lillard', equating to 32, as well as the sum of Kobe Bryant's jersey numbers, 8+24. Plus, as you know, the 'Society of Jesus' logo, a name equating to 56, has 32 sun rays. From that game, Lillard would take the league by storm, tying Kobe's 6 game scoring high of 293 combined points, the 62nd prime number. This was all in the days leading up to NBA being suspended, and the 'coronavirus pandemic' being declared, a phrase equating to 293. As for the star's full name, 'Damian Lamonte Ollie Lillard Sr.', it equates to 118 with Pythagorean Gematria, and as a reminder, Kobe Bryant died in 'Los Angeles, California', equating to 118, on the 118th Meridian West, 118 days after it was top news on October 1, 2019, that Lillard had a rap beef with Kobe's old teammate, Shaquille O'Neal, who was 47 years old at the time. Regarding the rap beef, on the same day as the Kobe Bryant remembrance game, where the Lakers lost at home, to Damian Lillard's Blazers, Lil Wayne's new rap album 'Funeral', equating to 32 with Pythagorean, the same as 'Lillard', released. Keep in mind Lil Wayne is a rapper having a birthday of September 27, 1982, the same day the Jesuits were recognized by Rome in 1540. As for the album *Funeral,* a curious title, releasing just five days after Kobe's death, the 8th track was titled *'Bing James'*, and it featured 24 seconds of silence at the end in tribute to Kobe. Also, that title, 'Bing James', equates to 35 and 55 in the same ciphers as 'King James', as in LeBron, who was 35 years old at the time, the most important person in the riddle of Kobe's demise, after Kobe, whose death, had much to do with 55. For another important point, the album was released 126 days after 'Lil Wayne's birthday, a rap name summing to 101, the 26th prime, and reminding us of Kobe Bryant's 1/26 'accident', reportedly along Highway 101. As for another significance to the number 126 and the Jesuits, from the death of Ignatius of Loyola, the first Superior General of the Jesuits, July 31, 1556, to the day he was replaced by Diego Laynez, July 2, 1558, was 701 days later, the 126th prime number. And for another point on the number 126, Nike claims that the first Air Jordan shoes sold $126 million units worth in their first year. This is an interesting stat, because in *Ephesians 2:2*, it is stated that satan is the prince of the 'air', a word equating to 26, the same as 'Jordan', the same as 'Bryant', and the latter being the man who died 1/26, after emulating Michael Jordan's career.

With this knowledge, you can really begin to appreciate just how scripted things are, from history (his story), to news, to sports, to entertainment, to politics- and better yet, you can escape the matrix of deception that they are a part of because of this knowledge. On the subject of entertainment, I want to revisit the man who directed the short film, *The Black Mamba*, the same film that gave aways Kobe Bryant's fate nearly 9 years in advance. That was Hollywood's 'Robert Rodriguez', a man having a name summing to 201 with Simple English, and a man born in 1968, two stats that aren't to be glossed over. As we have learned, 201 is a very important number to 'The Jesuit Order', and it is also a number that corresponds with the gematria of '*The Holy Bible*', as well as 'Seven Churches' and 'Seven Churches of Asia', each equating to 201. If you're not familiar with the 'Seven Churches' or the 'Seven Churches of Asia', they are the churches referenced in *Revelation*, where each of the seven receive a letter, including the Church of Philadelphia, that receives the letter warning of the false Jews, referred to as 'The Synagogue of Satan', equating to 223, the same as 'Philadelphia', and that also discusses the instrument of prophecy, 'The Key of David', equating to 135, the same as 'Kobe Bean Bryant'. If you are asking who the false Jews are, look no further than the head of the NBA right now, Adam Silver, or the man who came before him, David Stern. And with 'prophecy' in mind, that is where the detail of Kobe Bryant dying in a 'helicopter' accident comes into play. A 'helicopter' is a vehicle name summing to 666 with Sumerian Gematria, whereas 'prophecy' equates to 666 with Jewish Gematria. Keep in mind the musician Stevie Ray Vaughan died in a helicopter crash as well, a man with a best selling album of *Texas Flood,* only for Texas to suffer historic flooding on the 27 year anniversary of his fatal accident, August 27, 2017, a date with 52 numerology, and on the 239th day of the year, the 52nd prime, where the number 52 corresponds with the gematria of 'prophecy', as well as 'California', the latter being where Kobe Bryant died. Of course, the number 52 connects to 'flood' and 'hurricane' as well, and the latter word 'hurricane' also sums to 56, and again, the Houston Astros, in their 56th season, would win the World Series that began 52 days after Matt Harvey became the first pitcher to pitch in Houston after the flooding done by Harvey. I should mention, in that rigged 113th World Series, the Astros beat the Dodgers, from Los Angeles, 'California'. The number 666 also reminds us that Kobe Bryant had an official workout called the "666 Plan" and that his career high in points scored, came in his 666th game, January 22, **2006,** when he scored 81 points, corresponding with the gematria of 'Kobe Bean Bryant', equating to 81 and 54, the exact same as 'mark of the beast', equating to 81 and 54. Let us not forget the rest of his team scored 41 points, corresponding with 'Kobe Bryant', thus totaling 122 points, on January 22nd, or 1/22, corresponding with the gematria of 'satanic', summing to 122, the latter being the name of a values system that is about self worship, that coincides with the idea of putting the star of the team before the rest of the team, which is the NBA's marketing strategy. The 81 point 'ritual' reminds us of Kobe Bryant's last game as well, where he scored 60 points, and his team scored 101 total, thus the rest of his team scored 41 again, in a game, where Kobe Bryant would exit the court for the last time in his NBA career, with 4.1 second left on the game clock, after making his last shot while number 41 of the Utah Jazz was guarding him. As for the 101 total points, it is the 26th prime number, and his hometown 'Philadelphia' equates to 101 with Simple English.

Regarding the tributes to 666, the number of the beast, the number of a man, and Kobe's reported death on January 26th, or 1/26, let us not forget significance of *Genesis 1:26,* or that *'Genesis'* sums to 666 with Reverse Sumerian, or that God sums to 26 with Simple English, who regrets making 'mankind', summing to 66 with Simple English, in *Genesis 6:6.* It is also for this reason that Nick Saban won his 6th championship at age 66 with 26 points, and building onto that riddle, he used to coach with Bill Belichick, who went on to win his 6th

244

championship, at age 66, in Super Bowl 53, in the same stadium Nick Saban accomplished the feat in, one year earlier. For the record, that stadium was 'Mercedes Benz Stadium', equating to 307, the 63rd prime, where in that same game, Belichick and Tom Brady became 6-3 together in Super Bowls, in Tom Brady's 307th NFL game. Even more, Sony Michel scored the only touchdown of Super Bowl 53 for either team, scoring at exactly the 53rd minute of the game, in a sport that plays on a 53 yard wide field, and where the NFL allows 53 man rosters, and in a game between the 'Patriots' and 'Los Angeles', both being names equating to 53. What made Sony's touchdown special, is that he was wearing the number 26, and the Super Bowl was 351 days after his birthday, the 26th triangular number, and a year earlier, he had lost in the college football championship to Nick Saban, who scored 26, while Sony was playing for Georgia, his home state- thus the bitter taste of losing the rigged college football championship a year earlier was washed away by winning the rigged Super Bowl, that we called dead on, Patriots over Rams, before the season even began, just as we had called Alabama to win the championship before the prior college season had started. It is to say, it was all too predictable. And when Sony Michel put away Super Bowl 53 with two 26 yard runs in the closing moments of the fourth quarter, we laughed all the way to the bank. I imagine somewhere else some Jesuit was saying, 'For the greater glory of God', equating to 351 the 26th triangular, because that phrase in Latin, 'Ad maiorem Dei gloriam', equates to 172, and Sony Michel's birthday is February 17, or 17/2, the same as Michael Jordan's, another person having a surname summing to 26, and who was 56 years old when Kobe Bryant died, the latter number connecting to 'Society of Jesus'. As for the relationship between 351 and the Jesuits, let us not forget that the first Jesuit pope, Pope Francis, has a December 17th birthday, the 351st day of the year. And furthermore, if you search through the most iconic images of Michael Jordan dunking, you won't have to look long before you find the one of him soaring from the free throw line, with his legs back, with the game clock shown in the background at 3:51 (351, 26th tri. number *Jordan = 26).

For one more stat you should know about Super Bowl 53, when you write our 'six', it sums to 16 with Pythagorean, and there were 16 points scored in Super Bowl 53, reminding us that 53 is the 16th prime number, and Tom Brady and Bill Belichick picked up their 6th scripted Super Bowl win together. The 16 points were the result of the Patriots 13-3 win over 'L.A.', equating to 13, which is the 6th prime number. And further, in *Daniel 8,* there is the story of how the goat destroys the ram, and Tom Brady was referred to as the "G.O.A.T.", meaning greatest of all time, after beating the Los Angeles Rams at age 41, at the start of 2019, reminding us that 19 is the 8th prime. Not by chance, 'goat' sums to 16 with Pythagorean as well, topping off the ritual. It was at this same moment in history ESPN began the debate of who was the better G.O.A.T.- Jordan or Brady? When you have eyes to see, the riddles are laughable, and demented.

As for the biblical narratives and the subject of prophecy, keep in mind Kobe Bryant's death in a helicopter was also foreshadowed in a Comedy Central cartoon, *Legends of Chamberlain Heights,* where Kobe Bryant literally dies in an exploding helicopter, in an episode titled *End of Days,* that released on November 16, 2016, a date that can be written 16/11, similar to 1611, the year the *King James Bible* was published, and reminding us that King James, or LeBron, surpassed Kobe Bryant in points scored, one day before his demise. You'll notice November 16, 2016 was also a date with numerology of 36, and 666 is the 36th triangular number (11+16+(2+0+1+6) = 36).

If you can, please take a moment to search for the small group of graphics used to advertise the show *Legends of Chamberlain Heights,* you should discover what I have. For starters, there are multiple graphics with a group of young men wearing basketball jerseys, and they are three in numbers, and the jerseys they are wearing from left to right are 55, 54, and 100 in each ad, with 54 front and center. Now if you think about it, you will notice they're not in order of counting, because if they were, 54 would come before 55, and furthermore, we have discussed each of these numbers extensively in this chapter. Consider, Super Bowl 54 concluded the 100th NFL season one week after the deaths of 'Kobe Bean Bryant' and 'Gianna Bryant', both equating to 54, and as we stated, the number 55 is very important to the Boule or Sigma Pi Phi, and the fact that Kobe Bryant, a member, died on the 257th day of the Boule's age after their May 15, 2019 anniversary, when 'Los Angeles Lakers' and 'blood sacrifice' sum to 257, and 257 is the 55th prime number. Also, as we learned in the last chapter, the 100th NFL season was called the "Year of the Black Quarterback" by 'ESPN', prior to it beginning, only for three black men to take the top honors in the league, all of whom were quarterbacks, and in a season equating with the gematria of 'African American', summing to 100.

The greatest 54 ritual of all with *Legends of Chamberlain Heights* however, is how it relates to Kobe Bryant and the Lakers winning the NBA Finals on June 19, 2000, the real King James birthday, to conclude the 54th NBA season, 251 days after the death of Wilt Chamberlain, who passed on October 12, 1999, and was from Philadelphia, before dying in Los Angeles, the same as 'Kobe Bean Bryant', equating to 54. Of course, 251 is the 54th prime. And in light of what we uncovered about Kobe Bryant, the 'sun', and the solar cycle, take another gander at the *Legends of Chamberlain Heights* advertisements, and notice how some of them show the sun setting with the three boys in jerseys, 55, 54 and 100, left to right, with 54 front and center. As you know, 'sun' equates to 54.

Another point that should be made, is Wilt Chamberlain died in Bel Air, the wealthy and well known neighborhood in Los Angeles, largely due to the hit TV show starring Will Smith, the *'The Fresh Prince of Bel Air'*. As you'll recall, in the TV show, Will Smith, who plays himself, is sent from Philadelphia to Bel Air Los Angeles, because of the trouble he was getting into on the basketball courts around his hometown, a story with clear parallels to the life of Kobe Bryant. In gematria terms, 'Fresh Prince' equates to 59 and 67, the same as 'Black Mamba' and 'Calabasas', the latter being where the crash occurred, on a date with 67 numerology (1/26/2020 = 1+26+20+20 = 67). Further connecting the pieces of the puzzle, from Will Smith's 51st birthday, September 25, 2019, to the date Kobe Bryant died, was 123 days later, and *'The Fresh Prince of Bel Air'* equates to 123 with Pythagorean Gematria. Keep in mind 'helicopter' equates to 51, the same as 'conspiracy', a word that also sums to 123, and Will Smith was 51 years old at the time. You could also say 'Kobe Bryant', equating to 41, died 4 months and 1 day after Will Smith's birthday, a man who wore the jersey numbers 14 and 41 in varying seasons of *The Fresh Prince,* playing for the 'Bel Air Academy' basketball team, equating to 54 and 81 in the exact same ciphers as 'Kobe Bean Bryant'. Even more, the acronym on the jersey, 'IYT' sums to 54 with Simple English. And to add to our list of 41, here are a few more. It was reported that Kobe Bryant's helicopter departed at 9:06 and the crash was reported at 9:47, 41 minutes later.

Furthermore, it was reported the pilot's name was 'Ara Zobayan', summing to 41 and 58 with the Pythagorean methods, in the same ciphers as 'Kobe Bryant'. Even more, Kobe Bryant died 41 days after Lakers owner JoAnn Buss, who passed December 16, 2019. For another, he died a span of 41 days from his longtime teammate Shaquille O'Neal's March 6th birthday, causing Shaq to put up a billboard in tribute to Kobe at the LSU campus, his alma mater, who had just won the football championship 13 days before Bryant's demise. For another, Utah, who Kobe Bryant played his last game against in the NBA, was established January 4th, a date that can be written 4/1, similar to April 1st, the date Kobe, Japan was founded. For another 41, Kobe Bryant retired from the NBA in 2016, 41 years after his father was drafted by 'Golden State', equating to 41 and 58, just like 'Kobe Bryant'. And on the subject of Golden State, you might recall when Kobe played his last game there was a double header on ESPN taking place with two games being shown at the same time. One was Kobe Bryant hoisting up 50 shots to score 60 against Utah, and the other was the Warriors eclipsing the Chicago Bulls season record of 72 wins, by winning their 73rd game in their last game of the season, led by Steph Curry, born on the 73rd day of the year, March 14th, and whose father, Dell Curry, faced Jordan in his 73rd game of the respective season that the Bulls set the record with 72 wins. I bring this up because Kobe Bryant played his last game exactly 678 weeks after Michael Jordan, and at the same time, Steph Curry and Klay Thompson set an NBA record with 678 three pointers made by two teammates in a single season on the same day. What makes this "678 coincidence" meaningful, is that both 'Michael Jordan' and 'Kobe Bryant' equate to 678 with Sumerian Gematria. And for one last 41, if you take the time to watch the short film *The Black Mamba,* before Kobe hoists the basketball bomb at the helicopter, you see the timer on the bomb count down to 4.1, and not a tick lower, before the camera cuts to the next shot. It is reminiscent of how Kobe came off the court, in his last game against Utah, with 4.1 on the game clock, after scoring 60 points, compared to his team's 41 points scored, no different than his career high, when he scored 81, and his team scored 41, bringing the team's total score to 122, on January 22nd. Once again, that number 122 has a 'satanic' connection, as does 67, the latter number, again, connecting to 'Black Mamba', 'Calabasas' and 'Fresh Prince'.

With regards to Will Smith, the *Fresh Prince*, he is a man who has had some very dark rituals taking place around him, as is so often the case in the world of celebrity. If you have not read my first book, I cover the story of the death of Will Smith, the NFL star, on the same day Will Smith, the actor, received a lifetime achievement award from MTV, on a stage with a gold and black color theme, the same color theme of the New Orleans Saints, who the NFL player Will Smith played for. Let us not forget 'New Orleans' equates to 54, the same as 'Kobe Bean Bryant' and 'Jesuit Order'. Also relevant, at the time, Will Smith the actor had just finished the movie *Focus*, set in New Orleans, a film about football, gambling, and numbers. If you have seen that film, you might recall the numerology lesson Will Smith gives on the number 55. Not by chance, both 'numerology' and 'Will Smith' equate to 55, and this is in part why you read about the death of his co-star from *Fresh Prince, Galyn Görg*, at age 55, on July 14, 2020, one day before her July 15th birthday, a date that can be written 15/7, like 157. As we'll get to, Smith's song *Just the Two Of Us*, also has to do with the drowning of Naya Rivera on July 8, 2020, a date with 55 numerology. I should note, Naya Rivera is remembered as the love interest in the Kobe Bryant jersey filled B2K music video, *Why I Love You*. And on the subject of Will Smith, Kobe Bryant, Bel Air, and helicopters, keep in mind the same actor, Will Smith, starred in the film '*I Am Legend*', where his family is killed in a helicopter accident. That film title has gematria of 47, the same as 'Bel Air', reminding us that Kobe Bryant died on a date with 47 numerology (1/26/20 = 1+26+20 = 47), and that the emergency phone call for the crash was made at 9:47 AM local time, further reminding us that the first 9-1-1 called was made on the 47th day of 1968. Let us not forget 'Black Mamba' equates to 211, the 47th prime number. At the same time, 'beast' equates to 47, corresponding with how 'helicopter' sums to 666. For another 47 word, it is 'legend', with Simple English, and it reminds us of the cartoon *Legends of Chamberlain Heights* and how it also foretold the fateful end of Kobe Bryant in a helicopter. On the subject of legends, you should seek out the interview Tracy McGrady did with ESPN, immediately after Kobe Bryant's death, where he told the reporter that when he and Kobe Bryant were young men in the NBA, Kobe confided in him that he wanted to die early, so he could be immortalized as a legend. If that is true, he got his wish, but perhaps not in the way he would have hoped, with his daughter dying as well, and reportedly 7 other people.

Coming back to the jerseys shown in the graphic for *Legends of Chamberlain Heights*, 55, 54, and 100- to go even further on 55, I will tell you something that I have not told you thus far. There is a complimentary rule to the Pythagorean ciphers, and it is for the 19th letters in each respective cipher. When you use these rules, words such as 'Los Angeles' equate to 55, and 'YHWH', the four letter name of God, sums to 26, the same as it does in the Hebrew language, thus being the reason why 26 is the **God** number. With Pythagorean Gematria it is 's', and with Reverse Pythagorean, it is 'h'. The rule is created because the 19th letter is the only letter you must reduce two times using numerology, to get to a single digit number, in the 26 letter alphabet. For example, S=19=1+9=10. Then, S=10=1+0=1. It is the same with H in Reverse Pythagorean, breaking down from 19 to 10 to 1. So the rule becomes, that S can be 1 or 10 with Pythagorean Gematria, and H can be 1 or 10 with Reverse Pythagorean Gematria. And for the record, up to this point in the book, we have not used this rule for any calculations, outside of the 'Trump Heights' ritual on his 74th birthday that we briefly mentioned earlier, the one that happened the same day the 74th Charles Schwab Challenge concluded, won by the 'Jewish' golfer with the 7/4 birthday, and where 'Trump Heights', being established in the Jewish nation of Israel, equates to 74 using the rule with Pythagorean Gematria. That said, I want to emphasize that all you really need are the four base ciphers (not including the rule with the 19th letter) that you learned in the first chapter to decode adequately, and that is why up to this point in the book, at least 98% of the calculations made, have been with the base ciphers exclusively. The advantage of being aware of more ciphers, is that as you become more experienced with gematria, it can be insightful to start picking up on rituals that are hidden beyond the first layer of decoding, such as how 'Los Angeles' equates to 55, in a very 'Los Angeles' related death that brought together the people of L.A. on February 24th, the 55th day of the year, for Kobe Bryant's Staples Center memorial, or as mentioned, how the four letter name of God, 'YHWH', equates to 26, corresponding with the Hebrew language --- and if you want to learn more about this, I highly suggest reading the first chapter of my first book, that begins with why there are 26 letters in the English alphabet, something you will find is a major compliment to learning about Kobe

Bryant's death on the 26th day of the Gregorian year. Also, keep in mind that the four letter name of God is the 'Tetragrammaton', summing to 58, the same as 'Kobe Bryant', who again fell to fourth in scoring after being passed by LeBron "King" James the day before Kobe's death, and reminding us that the real King James, who had the Bible printed in his name in 1611, died at 58, and like Kobe Bryant, he died unexpectedly. To be fair, you could call it a hazard of being in secret societies, and as we know, 'secret society' equates to 58.

On the subject of secret societies, death, and Kobe Bryant, who died on the 26th of January in 2020, 1,383 days after scoring 60 points in his last NBA game on April 13, 2016- that last game came 213 days after the death of Moses Malone, at age 60, on September 13, 2015. This was a curious distance in dates because Los Angeles, where Kobe played, is the (213) area code, and in Satanic Gematria, that you learned about earlier, 'death' sums to 213. If you're not aware, Moses Malone was a Philadelphia basketball star, the same as Kobe Bryant. What else brought the two men together was the fact that they were both drafted into professional basketball from out of high school, and in the case of Moses Malone, he was drafted by the Utah Stars, similar to how Kobe Bryant finished his career against the Utah Jazz. And since we brought up the number 213 and the date September 13th, I'd be amiss if I did not tell you that 'Tupac Shakur' sums to 139 with Simple English, and he died on 13/9, or September 13, 1996, 213 days after releasing his last album while he was alive, *All Eyez On Me*. That album was released on February 13, 1996, or 2/13, corresponding with how 'Black Panther' equates to 213, and his mother was a Black Panther, who was announced dead in headlines on the real Machiavelli's birthday, May 3, 2016, one day after her passing, a fact that matters because her son's rap alias was Makaveli, named after Machiavelli, a man who faked his death. Furthermore, like Kobe Bryant, Tupac called the (213) area code his home at the time of his demise, even though he was originally from New York. And for one more parallel, Tupac's last album, '*Makaveli*' equating to 74 with Simple English, the same as 'Jesus', 'cross', and 'rapper', had album artwork depicting 'Tupac' nailed to the cross, reminiscent of the crucifixion of Jesus. Let us not forget, 'Tupac' sums to 74 with Reverse Simple English. And for the icing on the cake, the *Makaveli* album released on November 5, 1996, Guy Fawkes Day, a Jesuit day of remembrance, and the day leaving 56 days left in the year, taking us back to the 'Society of Jesus'. And for one more 213, 'The Black Mamba' equates with Jewish Gematria, the name of the film that foretold Kobe Bryant's fate.

Adding to the darker side of the ritual of Kobe Bryant's last game, where he scored 60 points, was the death of 'Darryl Dawkins', summing to 60 with Pythagorean Gematria, another Philadelphia basketball star, who died just before Moses Malone, on August 27, 2015, the day leaving 126 days left in the year, not far off from the date Kobe Bryant would eventually die, written 1/26, and also corresponding with the Simple English value of 'Gianna Bryant', summing to 126, the daughter of Kobe who died with him. Furthermore, Darryl Dawkins died at age 58, connecting to the gematria of 'Kobe Bryant' and 'Moses Malone' both equating to 58 with Reverse Pythagorean Gematria, as well as 41 with Pythagorean. And as a reminder, 'Los Angeles Lakers', the team Kobe played for, also sums to 58 with Pythagorean. And notice, if you add the ages of death, 60 and 58, they equate to 118, corresponding with the gematria of 'Los Angeles, California', and 'Philadelphia, Pennsylvania', as well as 'death'. Even more, Dawkins died a span of 33 weeks from Kobe's last game, and 'Kobe' sums to 33 with Simple English, a man who died during the 74th NBA season. As you learned about in the first chapter, the ritual of 74 and 33 is common.

And speaking of 74, for the 74th NBA season, the biggest story outside of Kobe's demise, was 'Zion Williamson', equating to 74 with Pythagorean. His NBA story began with the "Zion" Williamson sweepstakes, on the 71st birthday of Zionist Israel, May 14, 2019, where 'Catholic' equates to 71 and 145, the latter being like the date of establishment, 14/5. You should also know that 'Zion Williamson' sums to 74 with Pythagorean, and has overlap with 'Society of Jesus' in three out of four ciphers, 79, 187 and 191, where one of those three values corresponds with the fact that his birthday is July 6, 2000, the 187th day of the year in non leap years. And just so you know, we have not bounced from Darryl Dawkins dying at age 58, to Zion Williamson by accident. That's because, on January 26, 2020, after Zion Williamson finished his third career NBA game, the same day Kobe Bryant reportedly passed, he had totaled 58 points, scoring 22 in his debut on the 22nd of January, a span of 22 days from the death of 'David' 'Stern', then 15 on the 24th, and then 21 on the 26th. Keep in mind, 'Pelicans' and 'New Orleans Pelicans' equate to 79, like 'Zion Williamson', and 79 is the 22nd prime, corresponding with his 22 point NBA 'basketball' debut on the 22nd day of the year. And with regards to the 21 he scored the day Bryant died, 'Lakers' as well as 'Jesuit' sum to 21 in Pythagorean, and from the date Darryl Dawkins died, to Kobe's last game, was a span of 231 days, the 21st triangular number. As we know, the number 21 also connects to '*Bible*', and in that breath I will remind you that Kobe Bryant's death was foreshadowed on November 16, or 16/11, on Comedy Central, in a King James tribute, who has a *Bible* named after him, that was published in 1611, right after English was standardized with a 26 letter alphabet, and the Gregorian calendar had been introduced. And with King James in mind, let us not forget that 'biblical' equates to 58. At the same time, '*King James Version*' equates to 74 with Pythagorean, and Kobe's very King James related death ritual came in what NBA season? Of course, when the Lakers returned from the coronavirus break on July 30, 2020, and played the Clippers, in the battle of Los Angeles, they gave the Clippers their 21st loss of the season, while improving to 24-8 at home, corresponding with the jerseys Kobe Bryant wore, 24 and 8. In that same game, the score was tied at 74-74 late, and then 101-101, before LeBron scored the winning 103rd points, reminding us of the ritual of the Cavs winning with LeBron on the real King James birthday, June 19, 2016, in their 103rd game of the season. And never mind July 30th was the day leaving 154 days left in the year, and 'King James' sums to 154 with Reverse Simple English.

To transition to what Kobe Bryant's death had to do with the league being suspended on March 11, 2020, or 11/3, after a member of the Utah Jazz tested positive for coronavirus, the team Kobe finished his career against, we'll begin with the number 113 and how it relates to Kobe Bryant. Using Simple English, 'Kobe Bryant' equates to 113, the same as 'Michael Jordan', a man whose career he emulated, and who he passed in points scored on December 14, 2014, 113 days after his August 23rd birthday. And keep in mind, Kobe did that in a win against the team from Minneapolis, the original home of the Lakers, and he helped his team become 8-16 for the season, meaning it was their 24th game, like how Kobe wore 8 and 24. At the same time, only one team in the league equates to 113 using their full name, and that is the 'Utah Jazz', who Kobe finished his career against, and who Jordan once beat in the NBA Finals. For the record, the only other team with

253

a connection to 113 is 'Dallas', the city name equating to 113 with Reverse Simple, and sure enough, they beat the Denver Nuggets 113 to 97, on March 11, 2020, the day the league was suspended. Speaking of Colorado, 'Eagle, Colorado' sums to 113 with Simple English, where 'Kobe Bryant' was accused of rape, and a town reminding us of Kobe's hometown football team, the Philadelphia 'Eagles', where the nickname sums to 113 with Reverse Simple English. Keep in mind 'Eagle, Colorado' also sums to 59 and 67, the same as 'Black Mamba'. As for 113, it matters to the NBA because 'The National Basketball Association' sums to 113 with Pythagorean Gematria, the 30th prime number, explaining why the NBA has been capped at 30 teams since 2004. Furthermore, when Kobe Bryant retired, he wrote a basketball poem titled *'Dear Basketball'*, equating to 113 with Simple English and 41 with Pythagorean, identical to 'Kobe Bryant'. He was even nominated for an Oscar award for *'Dear Basketball'* on January 23, 2018, Georgetown's anniversary, 41 days prior to the ceremony, March 4, 2018. If you have not seen the *'Dear Basketball'* short film, it begins with 13 seconds on the clock, and of course, 41 is the 13th prime number. Building on the 13 connection, from the day Kobe Bryant received the Oscar, to his death, was 99 weeks later, and as you have learned, when you write out 'thirteen', it equates to 99. And keep in mind, LeBron James passed Kobe Bryant in points scored in his 99th game with 'L.A.' The date of the nomination was also 153 days after Kobe's birthday, connecting to 'Jesuit Order'. Furthermore, 153 is the 17th triangular number, and 'NBA' sums to 17 with Simple English. It should also be noted that in *'Dear Basketball'*, Kobe talks about giving his soul for basketball, and the word 'soul' has gematria of 67, matching 'Calabasas', 'Black Mamba', 'Fresh Prince' and the numerology of the date of his demise, January 26, 2020.

Back on the subject of 113 and Kobe Bryant in relation to the league being suspended on March 11th, or 11/3, Kobe Bryant was drafted in Round 1, with the 13th overall pick, by the North Carolina team, in tribute to Michael Jordan, in 1996, thus on the draft sheet he was taken 1:13. Furthermore, after being traded from Charlotte, he made his debut for the Lakers, on November 3, 1996, a date that can be written 11/3. Keep in mind, that game was against Minneapolis, the original home of the Lakers, and the Lakers won with 91 points, the 13th triangular number, scoring 26 in the fourth quarter. More recently, on December 13, 2019, Kobe Bryant had 'mainstream' headlines written about him for being a good samaritan for assisting with a car accident in L.A. that he supposedly witnessed. Not by chance, that was his 113th day of his age, and 'mainstream' equates to 157, 113 and 41 with the same ciphers a 'Kobe Bryant'. As we learned earlier, 'accident' sums to 157, it also sums to 59, the latter like 'Calabasas' and 'Black Mamba'. As you can verify, the date of the car accident, December 13, 2019, was a date with 44 and 64 numerology, corresponding with the gematria of 'kill'. Adding to the riddle with his own fatal accident, after helping with the car accident, Kobe Bryant would die 44 days later, at least reportedly, in the 'mainstream'.

Thus, in light of how well planned and coordinated it all was, it is no accident that the league was suspended on March 11th, 45 days from the death of Mr. 113, 'Kobe Bryant', when 'Jazz' equates to 45, and so does 'ritual'. It was also a span of 46 days, and as you know, 'virus' sums to 46, corresponding with how 'coronavirus pandemic' equates to 113, along with 'The National Basketball Association' and 'Utah Jazz', the latter tying in perfectly with the date March 11th, or 11/3. And in light of Kobe Bryant traveling from 'Catholic' mass at the time of his accident, let us not forget that 'Catholic' equates to 46 as well as 71, because the league was suspended on the 71st day of 2020, after supposedly 7'1" Rudy Gobert of the 'Utah Jazz' tested positive for the virus. That was also the day 'March Madness', equating to 71 was put on hold, before being cancelled the next day, March 12, the 72nd day of the year, corresponding with 'Jesuit Order'. Keep in mind, Rudy is from France, like the Jesuits, and he was born on June 26th, or 26/6, the same day of the year that Kobe Bryant was drafted into the NBA, and of course reminding us that Kobe Bryant's death came 266 days after his wife's birthday, something that can't be repeated enough, in light of who is truly responsible for these evil acts. Case in point, the name 'Rudy Gobert' sums to 135 and 54 in the same ciphers as 'Kobe Bean Bryant', meaning 54 in the same cipher as 'Jesuit Order'. And I should point out, March 11th was 37 weeks after Gobert's birthday, corresponding with 'virus', as well as 'Bryant', two words that have gematria of 26 and 37 in identical ciphers, similar to 'Covid', equating to 26 with Pythagorean.

For another important point about Rudy Gobert, he had been criticized on March 9, 2020 for making fun of coronavirus after purposefully dragging his hand over every microphone on the podium as a way of showing he was not scared of the virus- a virus that was just beginning to take hold in the media. The date of his stunt, two days before the pandemic was declared, part of the ongoing and well planned storyline and agenda we're now living out, could be written 9/3, much like 93, corresponding with 'Wuhan Coronavirus'. For another familiar number, the March 9th incident took place 257 days after his 27th birthday, the 55th prime.

On the subject of 93 and 55, these are numbers that bring together the killing of George Floyd in 'Minneapolis', the original home of the Lakers, and the death of Kobe Bryant, two men who were reported to have daughters named Gianna, as odd as that is, especially since the All Star Game paid tribute to Kobe, and it was between Team LeBron and Team Giannis. Giannis? Gianna? Before we get to the 93 and 55 part, I must point out that Kobe and George Floyd died a span of 121 days apart, and L.A. is 12.1. At the same time, the phrase 'blood sacrifice' equates to 121, and where Kobe Bryant and Gianna are reportedly buried is 'Pacific View Memorial Park', equating to 121 with Pythagorean. Keep in mind, the number 121 relates to the gematria of 'Revelation', and an alternative word for *Revelation* is 'apocalypse', equating to 113 with Simple English, the same as 'Kobe Bryant'. In light of the *End of Days* cartoon being released by Comedy Central on 16/11, foretelling the death of Kobe Bryant, you cannot deny the 'biblical' riddles. And to build on your gematria learning, Kobe's hometown, 'Philadelphia, Pennsylvania', equates to 1611 with Jewish Gematria, a fitting sum for being biblically named, in the post 16th century world, and the post *KJV* world.

As for the numbers 93 and 55 they relate to 'Minneapolis', in several ways. Starting with 93, the city is located on the 93rd Meridian West, and better yet, 'Minneapolis, Minnesota' sums to 93 with Pythagorean. It reminds us how Tom Brady ran 93 offensive plays in Super Bowl 51, a record, including 62 passes, and as I had pointed out then he was definitely going to be back in Super Bowl 52, in Minneapolis, because of the gematria connections, including the fact that 'Minneapolis' sums to 62 with Reverse Pythagorean, similar to how 'Floyd' and 'riot' equate to 62. On the subject of 55, 'Minneapolis' sums to 55 with Pythagorean, reminding us it is where the Patriots fell to 5-5 in Super Bowls after losing to the Eagles in Super Bowl 52, after a sack fumble caused by number 55 of the Eagles put the game away in their favor. Beyond the numbers, the connection with Kobe Bryant and George Floyd, is that in the wake of the deaths of both men, in 2020, 'I can't breathe' became a popular motto, just as it had been in 2014, in the wake of the killing of Eric Garner. And in 2014, Kobe Bryant led the charge in the NBA with his 'I can't breathe' protest t-shirt after the death of Eric, a slogan equating to 74, reminding us that Kobe Bryant would die during the 74th NBA season. For the record, 'protest' also sums to 113 with Simple English, making Kobe a fitting leader. And also for the record, Eric Garner's killing was on July 17, 2014, a date that can be written 17/7, and with 58 numerology as well as 38, reminding us that George Floyd was killed in 'Minnesota', equating to 38 with Pythagorean, on 38th Street, before the murder trial date was set to begin on March 8, 2021, emphasis on 3/8, and that his killing officer's name, 'Derek Chauvin' equates to 58, the same as 'Benjamin Crump', the latter being the attorney for the family of George Floyd, who is a member of the 'Boule', as well as 'Prince Hall', both equating to 55, and being 'fraternal' organizations that in the case of the Boule, 'Kobe Bryant', equating to 58, and his father were and are members of, as well as Martin Luther King Jr., a man I must speak on briefly, in relation to the deaths in his family, and the repetition of the number 38, so as the emphasize the repetition of the evil that is taking place, and who is responsible.

For starters, 'The Boule' equates to 38 with Reverse Pythagorean. Now to build, Martin Luther King Jr. was killed in 'Memphis', equating to 38 in Pythagorean, the same as 'killing' and 'gematria'- let us not forget about the song *Gematria the Killing Name*, by the band Slipknot, where the first member of the band to die, Paul Gray, passed at age 38, on May 24, 2010, the 144th day of the year, the number corresponding with 'Jesuit Order', reminding us that the Boule as well as the rest of the world of modern Freemasonry fall under the umbrella of the Jesuits. One of many examples making it clear this is the case, Martin Luther King Jr.'s brother, Alfred A.D. King was found drowned in a pool on July 21, 1969, at the age of 38, the date in history the Jesuit Order was banned by the Pope. And on the subject of 38, 163 is the 38th prime number, and July 21st leaves 163 days in the year, plus 'drowned' has a Pythagorean value of 38. Also noteworthy, the date he died had numerology of 116, and he was most commonly called 'A.D. King', equating to 116 with Reverse Simple, similar to how 'Ad maiorem Dei gloriam', the Jesuit motto, sums to 116 with Reverse Pythagorean. In other words, "his number was up," and we know who was counting. For another 38, MLK's father died November 11, 1984, a standout year and date, 38 days before his 85th birthday, meaning he died at age 84 in '84. As you know, the number 84 connects to 'Jesuit', 'savior' and 'The Catholic Church', and his son, Martin Luther King Jr., was killed on the 95th day of 1968, on a date with 95 numerology as well, a number reminding us that Martin Luther, who died in February of 1546, six years after the Jesuits were formed, led the Protest Reformation against the Catholic Church with the *95 Theses*. I should also note that MLK's father was killed on the 316th day of the year, corresponding with the Hebrew Gematria of 'Jesus Christ', a number reminding us of *John 3:16*, about God sacrificing his son, similar to how MLK Jr., the son of Sr., had been sacrificed in 68, corresponding with the gematria of 'crucifixion', equating to 68.

Out of all the deaths in MLK's family however, the one that screams Boule the most, is the death of Yolanda King, who died on the 103rd anniversary of the Boule's establishment, May 15, 2007. Recall, in 2020, they released Kobe's autopsy on May 15th, and I should note, the film that predicted his helicopter related demise, '*The Black Mamba*', the gematria equates to 38 with Pythagorean. As for Yolanda King, she was fitting for the ritual, because 103 is the 27th prime, and like 'ritual', the name 'Yolanda' sums to 27 with Pythagorean, thus explaining the reasoning behind the infamous "27 Club." Adding to the list of 38, she died in 'Santa Monica' equating to 38 with Pythagorean, and being located on the 34th Parallel North, similar to how 'murder' equates to 34 and 38, and reminding us that 'The Boule' equates to 34 and 38 as well. On the subject of 34, A.D. King's son would be killed at age 34, after he died at 38, and where MLK died, 'Memphis', equates to 34 and 38 as well. Keep in mind 'Santa Monica' also sums to 187 in the same cipher as 'Society of Jesus', and 'Yolanda King' equates to 58, like secret society. For one more on Yolanda, she died 179 days after her November 17, 2006 birthday, and 179 is the 41st prime number, and that matters because the name 'King' sums to 41 with Simple English. It's similar to how Nick Cordero was reported dead at age 41, on July 5th, the 187th day of 2020, and on the day leaving 179 days left in the year, and also being a man having a September 17th birthday, emphasis on 17/9, similar to 179. You'll recall we covered his death earlier, having happened 201 days after

Pope Francis' birthday, the first Jesuit Pope, who lives in Suite 201, where no other Catholic Pope has lived before.

For more familiar numbers, MLK Jr.'s mother was assassinated in church, June 30, 1974, emphasis on the year '74, and reminding us of the gematria values of 74 for 'Jesus', 'killing', and 'gematria'. Even more, the assassin was said to be 'Marcus Wayne Chenault', equating to 74 with Pythagorean, and once again putting the 'Jesus' stamp on the matter, something only the Society of Jesus would do. The date she was killed had 110 numerology as well, and I bring this up because 'Santa Monica' also equates to 110, a number connected to 'prophecy', and it is something that is being fulfilled, by a code. In the eighteenth chapter, we'll discuss how this factors into George Floyd being killed in 'Minnesota' equating to 110, and Ahmaud Arbery and Rayshard Brooks being killed 110 days apart, with the second killing being in Atlanta, Georgia, the home of the King family, and also the current headquarters of The Boule.

Adding to riddle of the assassination of MLK's mother is the fact that she was killed on the 181st day of the year, the 42nd prime number, and 'Martin' equates to 42, same as 'February', the same as 'Jesuit', whereas 'Black History' equates to 181, reminding us that from Barack Obama's August 4th birthday to the start of the next Black History Month is 181 days each year and that 'Barack Obama' sums to 181 with Jewish Gematria, and also that George Floyd was killed on 'Memorial Day', equating to 181 --- not to mention the media's detail about how Amy Klobuchar could have put away Derek Chauvin in 2006 for wrongfully killing a 42 year old person, but she didn't --- and also not to mention the detail that George Floyd died on her birthday, the same day it was reported a white woman, Amy Cooper, a similar name to Amy Klobuchar, in Central Park in New York, choked her dog, while calling the police on a black man who was bird watching, only for it to be reported 42 days later by the New York District Attorney, July 6, 2020, there would be charges against 'Amy Cooper', a name equating to 42, the same as 'Amy' alone. And never mind that in February of 2020, while Trump was campaigning for reelection, he said Amy Klobuchar was a choker while putting his hands around his neck, and mimicking being strangled, and playing it up with his own improvised choking sound effects. It should serve as a reminder, it is called "political theater" for a reason.

Back on the subject of MLK's mother's assassination, she was killed in the 'Ebenezer Baptist Church', equating to 228 with Simple English, the same as 'Martin Luther King Jr.' and 'United States of America'. At the same time, 'St. Joseph's Hospital' equates to 228 and 93, the same as 'Martin Luther King Jr.', the location where MLK was pronounced dead. Keep in mind 'death' equates to 228 with Sumerian Gematria, and with that thought in mind, please realize that Martin Luther King Jr. is the only person born in the history of the United States who has a holiday named after them to date, and his assassination is largely the reason for this. And on that matter, the last state to recognize the MLK holiday, because of political opposition, was 'Arizona', equating to 42 and 84, the same as 'Jesuit', reminding us of the 'divide and conquer' tactics that are utilized in government and media with every major event that happens in the history of "this great nation", a nation also having a name equating to 84. And in light of 'death' being encoded in the country's name, let us not forget the U.S. is a nation that was founded on genocide, war and slavery, despite the rosy pictures so often painted in our government controlled schools, where topics such as genocide are justified because of 'Manifest Destiny', a term I could write a book about. For now, I'll let you know that in Jewish Gematria, it sums to 929, the same as 'United States of America', and reminding us that the Old Testament has 929 chapters in it.

And for one last point on MLK's mother's death, she died 193 days after her husband birthday, reminding us of how Bill Gates mother died on the 193rd day of the father's age, a number that is the 44th prime, connecting to 'kill' and 'execution', and reminding us of the date MLK was assassinated, 4/4, or that 'Seattle', where the Gates family is from, equates to 44. In this case, 193 also corresponds with 'Roman Catholic Church', equating to 193 and 94 as well, and reminding us that MLK's death is remembered each year on April 4th, the 94th day of the year except for in leap years, where it is the 95th, and also corresponding with how Bill Gates' mother died in 1994, the year Bill was married, and before he announced his "Decade of Vaccines" on the 94th day of his age. Again, the parallels are no accident. It is because they are parts of scripts, from the same Jesuit Order, working on behalf of the same Roman Catholic Church, working by the same repetitive code, year after year, cycle after. And on that topic, Martin Luther King Jr.'s birthday is January 15th, a date that can be written

1/15, the same day coronavirus supposedly showed up in the United States. You'll recall from our learning earlier, the significance of 115 to the Jesuits, and the nation of 'France', equating to 115, where they were formed, the same nation the Scottish Rite of Freemasonry came to power in, the secret society that the Jesuits share a motto with --- the same two entities that now have headquarters in Washington D.C., the "Masonic City", where 'masonic' equates to 115 as well.

On the subject of 'Scottish', let us not forget that it equates to 113 with Simple English, the same as 'Kobe Bryant', bringing us back to the date of March 11th, the date the NBA was suspended due to coronavirus. For the record, that was the 142nd day of the 74th NBA season, a season that began on October 22, 2019, the day leaving 70 days left in the year. And as we know, 'coronavirus' equates to 142 and 70 with the base ciphers, and proving it was no accident, the NBA would announce that the season was set to return on July 31, 2020, 142 days after it was suspended, despite later adding a double header for one day earlier, July 30th, where LeBron won on "King James Day." Better yet, July 31st is the date Ignatius of Loyola, the founder of the Jesuits, died in the year 1556, emphasis on '56. It was a fitting date because July 31st leaves 153 days in the year, and 'Jesuit Order' equates to 153. It was also for this reason the Rockets played the last game of the day on the July 31st return, scoring 153 points, and giving the Mavericks their 28th loss of the season, where 'Rockets' equals 28 in Pythagorean. Furthermore, 'ESPN', equating to 54, had a double header for the return, and the Bucks picked up their 54th win of the season, in the 'Jesuit Order' salute, both of which were easy games to call in advance, knowing the code. And in that same Bucks game, you had to laugh when Giannis gave his team an early 17-2 lead, much like 172, the Jesuit tribute number. As for the year 2020, July 31st was a date with 78 numerology, corresponding with both 'Jesuit' and 'Scottish Rite', as well as 'Wuhan, Coronavirus', and the year Kobe Bryant was born, 1978.

Adding to the riddle of the NBA's planned return date, July 31st was the 213th day of the leap year, similar to the LA area code, (213), and similar to how LeBron ended up playing July 30th, 213 days after his 35th birthday. And in the case of the 74th NBA season, the NBA's advertising campaign was 'The codes we live by', equating to 74, and being about the area codes NBA teams call home. Furthermore, that same phrase equates to 79, the same as 'Society of Jesus', and 'helicopter crash' and '*The Black Mamba*', the latter being the film that foreshadowed Kobe Bryant's death in Los Angeles, a title that also sums to 213 with Jewish Gematria. Adding to the area code riddle, the NBA's July 31st planned return date was on LeBron James' 215th day of his age, and that is the Philadelphia area code, (215), where he passed Kobe Bryant, in Kobe's hometown, the day before Kobe died, and shortly before the season was put on pause. Also not by chance, the NBA announced its July 31st return date on May 29th, 2020, 79 days after the league was suspended, on a date with 54 and 74 numerology. In that announcement, it was stated all remaining games would be played in the brand new 'ESPN Wide World of Sports Complex', equating to 373 with Reverse Simple, the 74th prime number, a perfect concluding spot for the 74th NBA season. Plus, the complex is in 'Orlando', equating to 79, or otherwise said 'Orlando, Florida', equating to 72 and 144, the same as 'Jesuit Order'. If you need one more proof of who is behind the rituals, July 31st will be 187 days after Kobe Bryant's reported death, reminding us of the California homicide code, as well as the fact that 'Society of Jesus' sums to 187. And if you still need another, July 31, 2020 will have 42 and 78 date numerology, equating with the gematria of 'Jesuit'.

On the subject of the NBA returning on July 31st, a date that can be written 31/7, something like 317, I must bring up another important point that connects back to the memorial for Kobe Bryant on February 24, 2020, the 55th day of the year, as well as the ceremony where he won his Oscar for *Dear Basketball*. It is that Jimmy Kimmel, who broadcasts his late night TV show out of the Masonic Temple of Hollywood, who has a November 13th birthday, the 317th day of the year, was the host for both, and in the case of the February 24th memorial, it was titled '*A Celebration of Life Kobe & Gianna Bryant*', equating to 317 with Simple English Gematria. The greater significance of the number 317 is that it is the 66th prime number, and fittingly, February 24, 2020 had 66 date numerology (2/24/2020 = 2+24+20+20 = 66). In addition to 'number of the beast' equating to 66, a phrase that had much to do with Kobe Bryant's "666" ending in the 'helicopter', the number 66 connects to the gematria of 'Lakers', 'LeBron' and 'LeBron James' --- the latter being the man who in recent history was reported to have gone to 6 straight finals for the first time since Bill Russell did it in 1966, and who also tattooed 'Mamba 4

Life' on his body, equating to 66. And never mind that both 'Bill Russell' and 'LeBron James' both equate to 42 with Pythagorean, reminding us that the beast rules for 42 months in *Revelation*, and that 'basketball game' has Sumerian Gematria of 666, the number of the beast. It was also for this reason that at the same ceremony it was discussed how Kobe Bryant learned to play 'Moonlight Sonata' on the piano, equating to 66 with Pythagorean Gematria, in record time, as a way of showing how talented and determined he was. And with regards to 'piano', it equates to 26 and 80, the same as 'Bryant', and 26, 55 and 80, in the same way as 'Boule'. *Satan = 55 / 80

In light of the significance of 317 in the ritual, and Beyonce's parallels to Kobe through *Bug-A-Boo* and winning her 24th Grammy, the same day Kobe, number 24, died, as well as opening his ceremony on February 24th with singing, I should bring up the release of her '*Black is King*' musical on Disney+, July 31, 2020, a date that can be written 31/7, much like 317, the 66th prime, corresponding with the fact that 'king' equates to 66 in Jewish Gematria, and Kobe Bryant, of the 'Lakers', had a tattoo on his arm, of a crown. And let us not forget, 66 is the 11th triangular number and 'black' equates to 11 with Pythagorean Gematria, corresponding with the title, '*Black Is King*'. Speaking of which, the title sums to 201 in the Jewish cipher, the number of the Jesuit Order. And for one more connection to 11, 31 is the 11th prime, and it released on the 31st of July, corresponding with the NBA's planned return date for the NBA, the day leaving 153 days in the year. As a reminder, 'Jesuit Order' equates to 153, as well as 144 and 54, and Kobe died 144 days after Beyonce's 38th birthday and on the 54th day of Jay-Z's age, 50, who also stars with his wife in the musical, along with Jessie Reyez, who we'll learn about later, in the death of Naya Rivera, in light of her name sounding like Nile River, and the Nile River being shown in Beyonce's film. To take it a step further, Beyonce's film is 85 minutes in length, corresponding with the gematria of 'basketball', equating to 85 with Simple English, and the year of the first *March Madness* tournament, '85- the one where a Catholic school, Villanova, outside of Philadelphia, beat a Jesuit school, Georgetown, to win the first tournament championship. In this case, May 8th, or 8/5, or 5/8, was also the date NBA teams were allowed to resume practicing after the coronavirus quarantine. And let us not forget that it was 'Utah' who was blamed, because like 'Kobe Bryant', 'Utah' equates to 58, syncing with the May 8th return. And keep in mind, the rumor has recently circulated that Beyonce is from Italy, and wouldn't it make too much sense, with Kobe growing up in Italy as well, and the concept of the Church picking their pawns to do their bidding, in terms of people like Beyonce and Kobe Bryant? If you take the time to watch the film, you'll understand the biblical and occult symbolism within it having read this book, especially when they get to the part about 'knowing good and evil', that is shown with imagery of a chessboard, and a heavy white and black focus. If you watch, you'll also notice it is full of card symbolism, something that should remind you of Tarot. And let us not forget, the oldest Tarot deck traces back to Italy, the nation that was hit the hardest by the virus after the "outbreak." *'Italy' = 'Wuhan' in 3 out of 4 base ciphers

As for the satanic numbers being assigned to the ritual, there is a reason, and it begins with the fact that 'Italy', the home of the Catholic Church, and 'satanic' equate. Beyond that, basketball is a game of 5 versus 5, and as we know, 'satan' sums to 55 with Simple English. Regarding the number 55, it is one we have covered in great detail regarding Kobe Bryant's death, as well as the 'Boule', and how the number 55 factors into the ritual of the death of George Floyd in 'Minneapolis', the original home of the Lakers. And please know, that these numbers don't mean it is evil to play basketball. What they mean are that the insane psychopaths who are effectively running the world, as well as the NBA, and who enjoy number games and riddles, are using the things they control, that have the right number relationships, to lay down the tracks of their contrived 'prophecy', a word, again, equating to 666 with Jewish Gematria.

The evidence of this is in things such as the Comedy Central cartoon, about Kobe Bryant dying in the helicopter, that released on November 16, 2016, the 16/11 date, in relation to the *KJV Bible*, not too many years before Kobe's planned demise, and how it was titled *End of Days*, a biblical concept, and it became part of a story that involved LeBron "King" James passing Kobe in points scored, in Kobe's biblical hometown, the day before Kobe's death in a "666copter." Then consider how at that same time, and in the time shortly after, there were countless headlines written comparing the coronavirus outbreak to the "end times", with the word "apocalypse" scattered here and there. Then consider further, at the same time this was going on, the U.S. Government was busy working on H.R. 6666, and a pandemic was landing exactly 666 days after the Clade X simulation that laid out something very similar to what we're currently living out, just not as drastic, at least not yet, as of July 2020, when I am putting the final ink on these thoughtfully written pages.

And speaking of 'LeBron James' and 66, the man with the biblical nickname, in connection to a text that is 66 books in length, the *Holy Bible,* let us build on the prophecy riddle by revisiting his last game as a member of the Cleveland Cavaliers while playing against the Los Angeles Lakers. If you search for it, you'll find that game was played March 11, 2018, a span of 113 days from LeBron James signing with the Lakers on July 1, 2018, and the March 11th game between the two teams was the 66th for both, and the Cavaliers lost 113 to 127. Regarding that score, as you learned earlier, 'Scottish' sums to 113, and 'Scottish Rite of Freemasonry' equates to 127 as well. And for the record, that July 1st deal was reported to be worth $154 million, a funny payout, when you recognize 'King James' equates to 154 with Reverse Simple English. And please don't overlook that July 1st can be written 7/1, like 71, as in 'Catholic' and similar to 71, the 20th prime, reminding us of 2020, the year all these riddles are aligning for something that is as horrific as it is fascinating. Of course, July 1st can also be written 1/7, and 'NBA' equates to 17 with Simple English, reminding us of the Celtics who lead the NBA with 17 titles, and who are trailed by the Lakers with 16. Let us not forget 'Los Angeles' sums to 53, the 16th prime, or that 'Black Mamba' sums to 59, the 17th prime, or how Boston and Los Angeles came together in Super Bowl 53, where the spoils went to the New England 'Patriots', 13-3, in what was considered a dud of a game, contrived for the 'G.O.A.T.' As for why 'Boston' is the leader in the NBA, gematria tells the tail. 'Boston' and 'basketball' are identical in Simple English and Pythagorean, equating to 85 and 22, similar to how 'Brady' and 'National Football League' equate to 85 with Simple English, and Boston (New England) is currently tied for the lead in most Super Bowls as well. The 85 connection is the reason the NBA allowed teams to resume practice on May 8th, or 8/5, or 5/8. It's also the reason the first March Madness was in 1985. And while we're off on the championship leading cities tangent, let us not forget that the'New York Yankees', identical to 'Society of Jesus' in half the base ciphers, lead the 'MLB', equating to 27 with Simple English, with 27 championships.

To fill in a few more dots about Kobe Bryant's death and the larger ritual, including the coronavirus agenda and the rioting in the wake of George Floyd, consider that at the beginning of the outbreak, 'Italy', the home of the Vatican, where Kobe Bryant grew up, was the hardest hit country in terms of cases and deaths, with the virus taking a toll on the elderly and impoverished. In gematria, 'Wuhan' and 'Italy' are identical in three out of the four ciphers, summing to 22, 67 and 68, and where they don't match, 'Wuhan' sums to 23, and 'Italy' equates to 32. As for the numbers 22 and 68 in both 'Wuhan' and 'Italy', those coordinate with the gematria of 'basketball', also summing to 22 and 68, thus how Kobe fits in. Of course, the term coronavirus was coined in 1968, explaining why these elements fit together in the ritual, that is all about numbers, and time, reminding us of the title of the fourth book of the *Holy Bible, Numbers* --- and again, Kobe fell to fourth in scoring, one day before his death.

In terms of time, as a reminder, 1968, the infamous year, was 52 years before 2020, and Kobe Bryant was part of the Super Bowl 52 ritual, won by Philadelphia, the biblically named city, in a Super Bowl played in 'Minnesota', equating to 52, like 'prophecy'. And furthermore, after the George Floyd killing in Minnesota, on the 93rd Meridian West, a number central to 'Martin Luther King Jr.', the phrase 'I can't breathe' became very popular, that Kobe championed in 2014, a phrase having gematria of both 52 and 74, and all of this shortly after the prophecy of *Acts 7:6* was fulfilled in terms of U.S. history, and just before Patrick Mahomes, who made the 49ers 5-2 in Super Bowls by beating them, signed what was reported to be a $400 plus million contract on July 6, 2020, emphasis on 7/6. Again, it was the first Chiefs Super Bowl victory since they had beat the 'Minnesota Vikings', 50 years earlier, a team name equating to 201, like 'George Perry Floyd', going with the rest of the 201 list.

In the eighteenth chapter we'll discuss why the killing of George Floyd took place 75 days after the NBA was suspended, when both 'Kobe' and 'Martin' sum to 75, the latter being the name of Martin Luther King Jr., who was in the Boule, and was pronounced dead at 7:05 PM local time. Keep in mind 'Catholic Church' also equates to 75, the same as 'New World Order'. And as a reminder, please seek out the New York Times story from October 6, 1940, with a top headline that day reading, 'New World Order' Pledged to Jews.

Not by chance, that date had 75 numerology, a number that also corresponds with the gematria of 'order out of chaos' and 'order' itself. And adding to your 75 list, it was not by chance that Martin Luther King Jr.'s mother was assassinated June 30, 1974, 75 days before her September 13th birthday. And on the subject of the 'Catholic Church' and 'New World Order', she was 69 years old, and both entities equates to 69 and 75, whereas 'The Jesuit Order' equates to 69 alone.

For another parallel between the Boule, Kobe Bryant, and Martin Luther King Jr., it is the number 80. With Reverse Simple English, Boule sums to 80, and Martin Luther King Jr. died April 4, 1968, 80 days after his January 15th birthday. At the same time, 'Bryant' sums to 80 with Simple English and 26 with Pythagorean, whereas 'Boule' equates to 26 with Reverse Pythagorean and 80 with Reverse Simple, bringing us back to Kobe's demise on the 26th day of the year. For another recent example of the number 80 in terms of "black history", 'Kofi Atta Annan', summing to 80 with Reverse Pythagorean, who received the 'Nobel Peace Prize', equating to 80 with Pythagorean, on October 12, 2001, the day leaving 80 days left in the year, died at age 80, on August 18, 2018. He was the first black leader of the United Nations in Switzerland, a nation that has very much to do with world affairs, from the World Health Organization, to the World Economic Forum. Keep in mind, Kofi Annan died on a date with 44 and 64 numerology as well, corresponding with the gematria of 'kill', equating to 44 and 64, just after Obama's birthday, the man known as Number 44, who became the 44th U.S. President, 44 years after the 1964 U.S. Civil Rights Act, running on 'hope', a word equating to 44 and 64, similar to how 'Barack Hussein Obama' and 'Civil Rights' both sum to 64 with Pythagorean. Let us not forget, 1964 was 56 years before 2020, the year of all these running agendas coming together.

And to further illustrate the point of how all these agendas are truly coming together in 2020, we'll examine the death of Lisa Marie Presley's son on July 12, 2020, in greater detail and in relation to the death of Kobe Bryant. As we connect the dots, keep in mind Elvis's daughter was born in 1968, the infamous year, 52 years prior to 2020, before reportedly losing her son at age 27 to suicide, the 'ritual' number, in Calabasas, the same city Kobe Bryant and eight others fatally crashed in, to begin the year. As you know, Elvis Presley has much to do with the coronavirus riddle, and so does Kobe Bryant. So to prove these two celebrity related deaths in Calabasas in close proximity to one another were no coincidence, and that they were carried out by the same Jesuit-Masonic network, we'll examine a few telling signs. For starters, July 12, 2020 had 59 date numerology, connecting the gematria of 'Calabasas', 'Black Mamba' and 'Elvis Presley', each equating to 59 and 67. And keep in mind 'kill' sums to 59 with Jewish Gematria and 'killer' sums to 67 with Simple English. For another parallel between the two deaths, her son's name 'Benjamin Keough' equates to 135 and 243, in the exact same ciphers as 'Kobe Bean Bryant'. Let us not forget the U.S. was 243 years old when Kobe died, or that there is now a movement to make the NBA's logo the likeness of Kobe Bryant, replacing Jerry West, who happened to be 81 years old and 243 days past his birthday when Kobe died, having been born May 28, 1938, corresponding with the fact that 'Kobe Bean Bryant' equates to 81 and 243. And regarding the example of Kofi Annan, he died on the day leaving 135 days in the year, connecting to the fact that the Boule's birthday is the 135th day of the year. At the same time, 'Boule' sums to 277 in Jewish Gematria, the 59th prime. And I should note, some researchers contend the Boule are very fixated on Lucifer. With that in mind, let us not forget that 'Lucifer' sums to 74 with Simple English, or that Kobe Bryant's demise came during the 74th NBA season, or that Kobe Bryant was born the day the Boule turned 74 years and 101 days old, the latter number, 101, corresponding with 'Philadelphia', the original home of the Boule. For another parallel between the deaths of Benjamin Keough and Kobe Bryant, they came a span of 169 days apart, the number having a square root of 13, corresponding with 'L.A.', equating to 13. At the same time, 'L.A' equates to 41, the 13th prime number, the same as 'King', equating to 41 and 67, and that links to 'Kobe Bryant' dying at 41, a man who had a tattoo of a crown on his arm, whereas Elvis Presley was called "The King" of Rock and Roll. And then consider, these riddles in the time of coronavirus, where corona is the Spanish word for crown. And let us not forget, all of this came not long after the death of Aretha Franklin, The Queen of Soul, who died on the 41 year anniversary of Elvis, sometime before the first case of coronavirus was confirmed in the U.S. in King County. Brandon Keough also died on his 163rd day of his mother's age, the 38th prime number, corresponding with 'death', 'murder', 'killing', 'R.I.P',

'Memphis', 'Graceland', and *'The Black Mamba'*…. As well as George Floyd, on the 38th Street, before the murder trial was set for March 8, or 3/8…

As for the Jesuit fingerprints on the ritual, the name "Lisa Marie Presley' sums to 79 and 187, the same as 'Society of Jesus', and reminding us that both 'helicopter crash' and *'The Black Mamba'*, equate to 79, the same as 'murder'. Let us not forget Elvis died at age 42, corresponding with the gematria of 'Jesuit', and the fact that every mainstream media outlet reported Kobe Bryant's helicopter crashed on the "4200 Block" even though it crashed in the middle of a field. Beyond that, her son, Benjamin Keough died on his 266th day of his age, a number that should go without saying at this point, and that points straight at the Society of Jesus, a.k.a, the Jesuit Order.

To further the case on the relevance of 266 in relation to the Jesuits and the agendas we're exposing, in case somehow the evidence is lacking thus far, we'll examine what happened with 'Eminem', the 'Elvis Presley' of his time, in the sense both white men, were and are accused of making "black music," and both men's names equate to 59. On July 9, 2020, it was Eminem's 266th day of being 47 years old, having been born October 17, 1972. That also happened to be a date having 56 numerology and being written 7/9, while also being the 191st day of the year, corresponding with the gematria of 'Society of Jesus', equating to 56, 79 and 191. On that day Eminem released the song, *'The Adventures of Moon Man and Slim'* equating to 135, the same as 'Central Intelligence Agency' and its current director, 'Gina Cheri Haspel'. The lyrics of the song received mainstream attention because they criticized people not wearing masks in the time of coronavirus, and police brutality in the time of Ahmaud Arbery and George Floyd. In other words, it was the culture creators, the Jesuits, using their musician puppet, to create more divisive content for the currently forming "mask culture", that is part of the 'new normal', a term equating to 47. And keep in mind, when this song came out, major cities were introducing hotlines to text images of people not wearing masks to, thus a tattle-tell line, for the purpose of governments being given the opportunity to test the capabilities of their facial recognition technology systems, that coronavirus created the excuse for.

On the subject of 135, I should note that Eminem released a music video on January 16, 2020 titled *'Darkness'*. It paid tribute to the Route 91 Harvest Festival shooting, and it showed the recreated hotel room of the October 1, 2017 shooter, with the room number chosen for the video being 135. Proving that this was no accident is the fact that 'Darkness' sums to 91 with Simple English Gematria, and the Route 91 Harvest Festival shooting was on October 1st, the day leaving 91 days left in the year, and to top it off, the music video released 91 days after Eminem's 47th birthday. And never mind that 91 is the 13th triangular number, and CIA equates to 13, or that images shown in the media of the Route 91 Harvest Festival shooter featured a 13 tattooed on his neck. And since Eminem was 47 at the time of release, also never mind that it was reported the October 1st shooter owned "at least 47 guns" in light of the shooting happening in 'Nevada', one of two states with a Simple English Gematria of 47, the other being 'Ohio', where 'Kid Cudi' is from, a rap artist having 47 name gematria, and who shares the track *The Adventures of Moon Man and Slim* with Eminem. And for the person asking, yes, 'Capital Steez' sums to 47 with Pythagorean… as well as 187… and for people who don't know, he was a rapper who died young, who often expressed his fascination with the number 47. Also noteworthy, Eminem's Darkness song was part of an album that was released one day after the music video, on January 17, 2020, a date with 58 numerology, reminding us that 58 were reportedly killed at the Route 91 Harvest Festival shooting, on the 58th day of then Nevada Governor Sandobal's age, a man born on August 5th, or 5/8, and who was 54 years old when it happened. Adding to the riddle, Eminem's album with the song 'Darkness', titled *Music to be Murdered By,* was in tribute to monologues done by Alfred Hitchcock, in the year 1958.

It is fair to say then that there is no doubt Eminem was chosen as a 'government' pawn at the age of 47 in his career, intentionally, in light of how important the number 47 is to 'government', a word equating to 47, and a number being especially important to Washington D.C., the nation's federal headquarters, as you learned about earlier, the city that is a Jesuit and 'Vatican' stronghold. If you have not seen the *Darkness* music video, it ends with an advertisement for the U.S. Federal Government, instructing people how they can turn in their weapons, making it all the easier from the government's perspective to have dominion over the masses. And let us not forget, the C.I.A. was created in 1947, and is interested in mind control, and when it comes to mind control, the power of celebrity is very, very, persuasive.

To make another point about celebrity, and the Jesuits, and the repetition of ritual, and in another story taking place on July 9, 2020, and also related to Eminem, it was the assumed drowning of the 3rd member of the TV show *Glee*, and that was Naya Rivera, at age 33. She was the same actress who sang the song *"If I Die Young"* in an October 10, 2013 episode of the hit show. In that song there are lyrics about being laid down in the river at dawn, a body of water that is spelled very similar to Rivera. Furthermore, the title of the song sums to 56, matching the date numerology of the news of her disappearance. And further, her full name, 'Naya Marie Rivera' equates to 79 with Pythagorean Gematria, and the show '*Glee*' equates to 79 with Reverse Simple, similar to how 'murder' sums to 79 with Simple English, connecting with the date 7/9. Keep in mind, 'Society of Jesus' equates to both 56 and 79, as well as 187 and 191, and in the case of Rivera, the news came on the 191st day of 2020, and 187 days before her upcoming birthday, January 12, 2021. Adding to the riddle, her body was recovered on July 13, 2020, a date that can be written 13/7, like 137, the 33rd prime. Worse yet, it was the seven year anniversary, in the seventh month, of the death of Cory Monteith, the first member of *Glee* to die. Not by chance, when you write out 'thirty-three' it sums to 66, and that is also true with 'Cory Monteith' and 'Naya Rivera'.

As for how Eminem fits in, it is through his hit song '97 *Bonnie & Clyde*, where there are lyrics about drowning the mother of his child, as well as the use of the words "just the two of us", from the Bill Withers hit song by the same name, a song that was sung by the same man who died by the code to start 2020- and again, it was also sung by Will Smith. This matters because Naya Rivera's last Instagram post was on July 8th, with the words "just the two of us." Of course, the date of the news, July 9th, can be written 9/7, similar to 97, corresponding with the gematria of 'death' and Eminem's hit song, '97 *Bonnie & Clyde*. What makes this riddle undeniable however, is that on April 2, 2020, it was reported Maeve Kennedy and her son disappeared in a 'canoe' accident, a word equating to 20, 25, 38 and 97 in all the exact same ciphers as 'death', and a date that was precisely 97 days before the disappearance of Naya Rivera, July 8, 2020. Furthermore, when their bodies were found, April 6, 2020, it was the

97th day of the leap year, and they were said to be recovered in 25 feet of water (97 is the 25th prime), in the town of 'Shady Side, Maryland', equating to 97 with Reverse Pythagorean. The clincher is that Eminem's rap alias is Slim Shady. Never mind that the family surname 'Kennedy' equates to 33 and Naya Rivera was 33, or that Eminem lost his close friend and rap associate Proof when Eminem was 33 years old. That killing happened April 11, 2006, a date with 51 numerology, corresponding with the gematria of 'conspiracy'. I bring it up because the words "Just the two of us" equate to 51 and 156, the same as 'Naya Rivera'. And while we're at it, 'thirty-three' also sums to 156 with Simple English. For another, 'Lake Piru' equates to 51, and that is where Naya Rivera reportedly drowned. If you're not aware, the word 'Piru' means devil in Finnish, and Eminem has an album called *Devil's Night* as well. Even further, Naya Rivera starred in the film *At the Devil's Door,* that premiered March 9, 2014, 56 days after Rivera's 27th birthday, and a date that can be written 9/3, like 93, corresponding with the fact that 'Lake Piru' sums to 93 with Simple English, the number of 'Saturn', who to the occult is also recognized as satan. In that film, she is often shown wearing a red sweater with the number 33 on it, the age of her planned demise. And because the number 33 also resonates with the 'Kennedy' family, I'll note that Rivera disappeared 93 days after Maeve Kennedy and her son were found, on April 6th, or 4/6, reminding us of JFK's death at age 46, and the greater parallels to the number, such as 'Catholic' and 'sacrifice'. In this case, Rivera's character in the film, *At the Devil's Door,* is named 'Vera', a name equating to 46 with Simple English. Keep in mind the name of the film sums to 84 and 177, the same as 'The Jesuit Order', corresponding with how it premiered 56 days after her birthday, the number matching 'Society of Jesus' and the date numerology of the news of her disappearance, as well as the gematria of 'If I Die Young', the song she sang in 2013. And as if the case wasn't already closed, Naya Rivera also played the part of 'Blanca Alvarez', equating to 46 with Pythagorean, a character that dies in the 33rd episode of *Devious Maids,* that released July 13, 2015, five years to the day of her body being recovered. I'll add, the title '*Devious Maids'* sums to 51, connecting to both 'Lake Piru', 'Naya Rivera' and 'Rome'. Furthermore, the title sums to 75, like 'Catholic Church'.

I should also point out that the riddles connecting news, sports and entertainment, are international, and that I am only focusing on a small group of examples in the U.S. because this happens to be the nation I live in, as the author. But to make the point about these same things happening over seas, in European football, Real Madrid, with their crown for a logo, reportedly lost their former owner Lorenzo Sans, to coronavirus, or the "crown" virus, at age 76- an age corresponding with the gematria of 'Spain', where Madrid is. What made this riddle all the more interesting is the fact that his death came while Real Madrid's league was paused due to the "coronavirus outbreak", and they were stuck on 56 points in league play, corresponding with the gematria of 'coronavirus'. They were only trailing Barcelona who had 58 points, whereas 'Barcelona Spain' sums to 58 with Pythagorean. And for more familiar numbers, 'Real Madrid' equates to 68, the same as 'basketball' and 'Wuhan', and reminding us of 1968, the year 'coronavirus' was coined. And if you want to practice your gematria skills, go back and revisit the first ten or so NBA players to come down with coronavirus in the headlines, and you won't be surprised to see that nearly all of their names equate to 68, including 'Kevin Durant', who was drafted by the Supersonics out of 'Seattle, Washington', also equating to 68, where the outbreak in the United States began. At the time of the diagnosis, he was playing for the Brooklyn Nets, owned by Jay-Z, reminding us of how Kobe Bean Bryant died on Jay-Z's 54th day of his age, and that the Nets used to be in New Jersey, home of the (201) area code, what is the pharmaceutical giant mecca. It it to say, it reminds us of how it all comes full circle, kind of like *The Lion King*, that released July 19, 2019, 54 weeks before Jay-Z's wife's '*Black Is King*', a related film.

For one more point on the number 68, I must mention the film '*Space Jam*', equating to 68 with Simple English. It involves a plot with details of the NBA season being suspended due to a virus caused by aliens, and it released November 15, 1996, a span of 13 days from Kobe's November 3rd debut in the NBA, while Michael Jordan, the star of the film, was 33 years old. The film also released 94 days before Jordan's February 17, 1997 birthday, and as we know, 68 and 94 have quite the relationship, connecting to things we have covered ranging from MLK's assassination, to the World Trade Centers, to 'Seattle, Washington', to 'Davos, Switzerland' to the word 'terror' itself. In this case, 'coronavirus pandemic' also equates to 94, and the word 'corona' alone sums to 96, corresponding with the year the film came out- and let us not forget that the name "coronavirus" was coined in 1968.

Furthermore, the movie released on the day leaving 46 days in the year, and 'virus' sums to 46, same as 'Chicago', where Michael Jordan was the big star at the time. And please also keep in mind, Chicago is where Tom Hanks moved from in *Sleepless in Seattle,* and that Seattle and Chicago were the first two cities in the U.S. to confirm cases of coronavirus. Let us also not overlook that Michael Jordan was 56 years old at the time of Kobe Bryant's burial in 'Corona del Mar', and let us also hope that a celebrity, such as Michael Jordan, will pick up this book, and be inspired to spill the beans, because Jordan's tears at the Kobe Bryant memorial, February 24, 2020, told me he knew something, that he did not speak on, that was truly tearing him apart inside. In my opinion, if he were a real legend, he would have let it out, because the world needs to know the truth.

To close with a few more familiar numbers, I want to bring attention to the two books that Kobe Bryant released shortly before his death. The first was released March 19, 2019, 157 days before his 41st birthday, titled *The Wizenard Series: Training Camp.* You know the drill with 157 and 41 in terms of 'Kobe Bryant', and to add to the list, the protagonist of the story is 'Rolabi Wizenard' equating to 157 with Simple English. The other thing to see in the book is that '*The Wizenard Series*' sums to 251, the 54th prime, again, corresponding with 'Kobe Bean Bryant'. With this title and numerical relationship of 54 and 251 in mind, recall what we learned earlier about the cartoon *Legends of Chamberlain Heights* and the deaths of both Wilt Chamberlain and Kobe Bryant. What I did not mention about that cartoon before, is that it released on Kobe Bryant's 86th day of his age, a number connecting to the gematria of 'blood sacrifice' as well as 'human sacrifice', plus the term 86'd. Even further, 'John Wayne Airport' equates to 86, where Kobe Bryant reportedly was traveling from when he died. I bring it up now because the name 'Rolabi Wizenard' sums to 86 as well. And while we're at it, it also sums to 76, like 'negro', and like how Kobe Bryant grew up a Philadelphia 76ers fan, and reportedly crashed in a helicopter called a Sikorsky S-76, named after 'Igor Ivanovich Sikorsky', summing to 126, and who died on the 26th of October. Further connecting dots, the fictional character Mr. Wizenard teaches a group of boys to play basketball at the fictional 'Fairwood Community Center', equating to 118 and 125 in the same ciphers as 'Philadelphia, Pennsylvania'. At the same time, 'Fairwood' alone sums to 125, just like 'Training Camp', the second part of the title, *The Wizenard Series: Training Camp*. The number 125 also connects to 'numerology', same with 55. This detail reminds me of Darren Daulton, who played for the Philadelphia Phillies, and who wrote the book *If They Only Knew*, about numerology and sports, and who died 215 days after his 55th birthday, similar to the Philadelphia area code, equating to (215). His death came just before the Philadelphia Eagles won the Super Bowl in 'Minneapolis', equating to 55, and making the Patriots 5-5 in Super Bowls. Furthermore, he died on August 6, 2017, emphasis on 8/6, reminding us that the Eagles won the Super Bowl on the touchdown catch from number 86, Zach Ertz, 86 days after his birthday, in a season played 86 years after the National Anthem was adopted. His death was also a span of 183 days before the Eagles won the Super Bowl over the Patriots, from 'Massachusetts', a state equating to 183. And in Darren Daulton's case, August 6th also leaves 147 days left in the year, and 'Darren Daulton' sums to 147 with Simple English, same as 'World Series'. Again, it speaks to how repetitive the rituals are.

As for the second book Kobe Bryant released, it was '*Epoca the Tree of Ecrof: The Island of the Gods*'. It's about a fictional world filled with magic and basketball, having a title equating to 178 with Reverse Pythagorean, similar to how 'Kabbalah' equates to 178 with Reverse Simple. On the cover of the book, it shows a bright and colorful tree above ground, and a dark and withered tree below ground. Of course, this is paying tribute to Kabbalah's Tree of Life and also the dark half, known as the 'Qliphoth', a word having gematria of 51 and 666, the same as 'helicopter'. I'll finish by saying it was no accident this book released on November 12, 2019, 81 days after Kobe's birthday, and 75 days before his death. As you know, 'Kobe Bean Bryant' equates to 81 (*Wizard = 81 with both Simple and Reverse Simple), and he was the man who had a career high of 81 points in his 666th NBA game, scoring 66% of the points. And at the same time, the name 'Kobe' alone equates to 75, the same as 'New World Order', and 'Catholic Church', reminding us that the term The Cabal comes from Kabbalah, a secret society that grew out of the Church, and the language of gematria comes from within Kabbalah. If you take the time to seek out the cover of this book, *Epoca the Tree of Ecrof: The Island of the Gods*, you'll be reminded of the phrase, a picture is worth a thousand words. And for the record, 'Epoca' equates to 95, reminding us once again, who is in charge, the Jesuit Order.

17 | The Qasem Soleimani Assassination & WWIII Rumors

Had Qasem Soleimani not been assassinated on January 3, 2020, he would have celebrated his birthday 68 days later on March 11, 2020, the date the coronavirus pandemic was declared and the NBA was suspended, having been born March 11, 1957. As you'll recall, he was reportedly killed on January 3, 2020, a date with 44 numerology, a number corresponding with the 44 gematria values of 'military', 'execution' and 'kill'- and in the wake of his death, rumors of World War III began. As you're likely aware, "rumors of war" is a biblical concept from *Matthew 24:6*. Keep in mind Soleimani was a military general in 'Iran', a nation equating to 42 with Simple English, the same as 'Japan', the nation blamed for attacking 'Pearl Harbor', the event that gave the U.S. a reason to become involved in World War II. And let us not forget 'war' also sums to 42 with Simple English, reminding us that 'world war' equates to 42 with Pythagorean, and this is similar to how 'Jesuit' and 'Freemason' equate to 42 as well, something that we the people of the U.S. should remember, because our nation's capital is a Jesuit cesspool, named after a freemason war general, and our nation has been at war for nearly all of its existence- with either some foreign enemy, or some domestic threat, and the reasoning for war has always been based upon some lie, or set of lies- and often lumped together with the word 'freedom', a word that apparently doesn't end with the *dumb* sound arbitrarily. Also keep in mind, all of U.S. history has happened in the time of this post 16th century New World Order operating system if you will, that involves working by the code of letters and numbers and Gregorian dates, as well as other occult staples, such as astrology, astronomy, alchemy, Tarot and hermeticism. And for the record, in World War II 'history', 1942 was the year the 'Holocaust' began, a word equating to 33 with Pythagorean, and 42 when you utilize the rule you learned about regarding the 19th letter, similar to how 'Zionism' equates to 42 with Pythagorean, and it was the Holocaust that provided the reasoning for the establishment of a permanent home for the Zionist people of Europe and elsewhere. For yet another connection to 42, on November 29, 1947, the United Nations recognized the boundaries of Israel with Resolution 181, and as you know, 181 is the 42nd prime. And in terms of all rituals being done in relation to time, keep in mind the name Soleimani relates to the sun and the moon, and he died on January 3rd, a date that can be expressed as 1/3, similar to 13, reminding us of the 13 cycles of the moon in the time of a Gregorian year, a solar based year. In that same breath, 'clock' has Simple English Gematria of 44, bringing us back to the date numerology of his death. And on the subject of 44, it was the 44th person to be President of the United States, Donald Trump, taking credit for the 'kill'. As you'll recall, Donald Trump is number 45, but he is only the 44th person to be the U.S. President thanks to Grover Cleveland's split terms, making him the 22nd and 24th U.S. President.

On the subject of the Holocaust, I should mention that in the time of Nazi interment camps, Freemasons were made to wear armbands with red triangles drawn on them. As you are likely aware, the viral image of the coronavirus is illustrated with red triangles, and both 'coronavirus' and 'Freemasons' equate to 56 and 155. And let us not forger that the people who illustrated the coronavirus have names equating to 56 and 201, as we learned earlier. At the same time, 'red triangle' equates to 113, reminding us that the pandemic was declared on March 11th, or 11/3, and 'red triangle' also equates to 67, the same as 'Wuhan'. Keep in mind, 67 is the 19th prime number, corresponding with the viral outbreak beginning at the end of 2019, and the virus being named Covid-19, where the number 19 is associated with 'chaos', as well as the agenda of order out of chaos.

For another 56, recall that at Soleimani's funeral it was reported by nearly every major news network in mainstream media, "at least 56 people" were stampeded and trampled to death. It was a very specific count, used by all major mainstream media outlets, similar to how all of the same channels quoted Gavin Newsom on March 18, 2020, saying "56% of Californians" would have coronavirus in "eight weeks", or otherwise said, 56 days. And in the same way it is no coincidence 'Gavin Newsom, 'coronavirus', 'Washington D.C.', 'Anthony Fauci', 'Society of Jesus'., 'unemployment', and 'toilet paper' each sum to 56, or that Donald Trump began his Jesuit education 56 years prior to 2020, at Fordham in 1964, or that the 56th Governor of New York, Cuomo, also went to Fordham- it is no coincidence 'Soleimani' sums to 56 with Reverse Pythagorean. And if you want to read a headline that'll make you smile, look up the April 23, 2020 story of the nurse who won $56,000 on Wheel of Fortune. She was reported as being on the front lines of the 'coronavirus' fight. And for a few more 56 connections, they include the gematria of 'mind control', 'all seeing eye', and 'magic spell', along with 'Eye of Horus', the latter being a well known occult symbol, where the word 'cult' itself sums to 56 with Simple English. It's also for this same reason, 'Black Lives Matter', equating to 56, is coming to power in 2020, 56 years after the U.S. Civil Rights Act of 1964, and it is also for this reason that 16th Street of 'Washington D.C.' was painted with 'BLACK LIVES MATTER' on June 5th, a date that can be expressed as 5/6. To be short, the paint job was an example of DIVIDE AND CONQUER by the numbers. And on the subject of these matters, I assure you that for the rest of your days you will understand why numbers are inserted in headlines and stories that are far too specific, given that they are for estimates, such as "at least 56 dead", or "56% will have coronavirus", or similar to another story we covered earlier, where the first believed death from 'coronavirus', in 'Mumbai, India', equating to 201, a city having a population greater than 18 million, was said to be that of a "56 year old".

Further adding to the 56 ritual with the reported killing of Soleimani, was what took place on March 11, 2020, and 56 days later, May 6, 2020, emphasis on 5/6, the latter being the 127th day of the leap year, reminding us of Pearl Harbor, on December 7th, or 12/7, and Buildings 1, 2 and 7 on September 11th, in the "New Pearl Harbor", and where the site of the 9/11 tragedy is now known as 'Ground Zero', equating to 127 with Reverse Simple, the number that is the 31st prime number, and where 31 is the 11th prime number, coming back to the master number, 11. In addition to March 11th being the day the 'coronavirus' pandemic was declared, 68 days after the January 3rd assassination, it was the day the U.S. Congress passed the Iran War Powers resolution, on what would have been Soleimani's birthday, attempting to limit Donald Trump's power for starting a war with Iran. Then precisely 56 days later, May 6, 2020, again, emphasis on 5/6, Donald Trump vetoed the Iran War Powers resolution, saying it was an insult to his character. What made this all the more interesting is May 6th was 201 days after the Event 201 coronavirus outbreak simulation. And what made this even more interesting, is that May 6, 2020, was the 194 year anniversary of the establishment of the National Congress of Brazil, founded May 6, 1826, and further still, the National Congress of Brazil was in its 56th Legislature at the time of the Covid-19 outbreak. Of course, the outbreak begins in Brazil in the Event 201 simulation, a nation that is sometimes treated as a boogieman threat to the United States, the same as North Korea, who supposedly confirmed their first case of coronavirus on July 19, 2020, the 201st day of the leap year. And speaking of 56 and Event 201, it was first reported that the first confirmed case of coronavirus was on the date December 12, 2019, 56 days after the Event 201 simulation, that when written out as 'Event Two O One', equates to 56 with Pythagorean Gematria. Since the December 12th date was cited, it has changed to December 8th, then December 1st, and has since gone all the way back to November 17, 2019, the day leaving 44 days left in the year, where 44 stands for 'military' operation- and on top of that, November 17, 2019 was a date with 67 and 47 numerology as well, connecting to the 67 gematria value of 'Wuhan', and the 47 date numerology of Event 201.

On the subject of the number 201, and to further prove that it is a number the Jesuits use ritualistically, and in dark ways, I want to discuss a national news story from Sunday, July 19, 2020, the 201st day of the leap year, relating to a surprise attack on the husband and son of 'Judge Esther Salas', a title equating to 95. It was reported that in the attack, her 20 year old son, 'Daniel Anderl' was killed, having a name equating to 54 and 72, in the same ciphers as 'Jesuit Order', and also matching the gematria of the town where it happened, 'New Brunswick', equating to 54 and 72 in the same ciphers as well. Keep in mind, this was in New Jersey, not far from the (201) area code, and the 20th card of the Tarot deck is the judgement card. As for the judge's son being 20 years old, the number corresponding with the gematria of 'death', 'time' and 'judge', it is important to note that her name 'Esther Salas' equates to 71, the same as 'Catholic', and again, 71 is the 20th prime number. For one last point on the matter, the 20 year old who was killed, 'Daniel Anderl', had a name equating to 54, 72, and 225 in the same ciphers as 'Adolfo Nicolas', the Jesuit Superior General who died on the day leaving 225 days in the year, who we learned about earlier. And in the next chapter, we will learn more about the meaning of the number 225, and how it has been ritualistically used by the Catholic Church, and for what purpose.

To go off on another important tangent about how sinister and contrived things in the mainstream are, and regarding the other dates mentioned for the "first confirmed case of coronavirus", we'll begin with December 8th. *Imagine* the odds of it, because it is the day John

Lennon died by the numbers in history, and in more recent history, Juice WRLD as well, who died on that date in 2019, and who used the lyrics of Lennon in his own work, and who tweeted on April 25, 2017, "My goal is to get overly famous, shine for a couple years, then fake my death." What's funny, is his twitter handle was titled 'JuiceWorlddd', spelled exactly as shown, and equating to 128 with Simple English, similar to the date he supposedly died, December 8th, or 12/8. Even more, in the same ciphers as 'coronavirus', the handle 'JuiceWorlddd' equates to 56 and 70. And with regards to the other date, December 1st, it can be written 12/1, like 121, reminding us of the date coronavirus was confirmed in the U.S., January 21st, or 1/21, as well as the gematria of 'coronavirus outbreak' and '*Revelation*'.

What makes the Juice WRLD death ritual more relevant to the topic at hand, in terms of who is controlling the flow of information and how, is what happened 201 days after his death, on June 25, 2020, George Orwell's birthday. On that date there were international news headlines about a 16 year old TikTok star dying. If you're not familiar with TikTok, it is a company that allows people to upload videos that are 15 seconds to 1 minute in length, and it is very popular amongst teenagers, especially young women who like to dance on camera-exactly what 'Siya Kakkar' was known for, the name of the deceased 16 year old. In gematria terms, her name equates to 35 in Pythagorean, the same as 'Catholic', and she died on a date having 35 numerology. As a reminder, the head of the Catholic Church right now is Pope Francis, the first Jesuit Pope, who lives in Suite 201, a fact that begins a long list of number 201 connections that are related to 'The Jesuit Order' and the man born 'Jorge Mario Bergoglio'. This is also the same Church that is known for sexually abusing children and covering up crimes, and again, her death was reported 201 days after Juice WRLD's. Why it matters that this was 201 days after Juice WRLD's death, is because when Juice WRLD died, there was a strange "coincidence" brought up in the mainstream about his reported death being from a seizure, at the same time a viral challenge had just begun on TikTok called the 'Lucid Dreams Challenge'. To understand the "coincidence," the challenge was to upload a video of yourself listening to or dancing to the song Lucid Dreams, by Juice WRLD, and then fake having a seizure on camera. What makes this beyond chance is the gematria. 'Lucid Dreams Challenge', 'blood sacrifice', and 'human sacrifice' all equate to 86, the same as 'TikTok' and 'seizure'.

And then adding insult to injury, Eminem released the song 'Godzilla' featuring Juice WRLD on his social media on March 3, 2020, 86 days after Juice WRLD's reported death, where 'Godzilla' sums to 86 with Simple English. And knowing this, we can understand why mainstream outlets emphasized the phrase in headlines, 'you will always be the best', equating to 86 with Pythagorean, regarding the mysterious June 25, 2020 death of the 16 year old, Siya Kakkar. *On the subject of TikTok, I should note that on July 31, 2020, it was reported Donald Trump was considering banning TikTok. Not by chance, that story came 47 days after his 74th birthday, on June 14th. And what made it all the more interesting is that 'ByteDance' owns TikTok, a company name equating to 47, like 'time' and 'Trump', and of course, the hands of a clock make the tick tock sound. Furthermore, ByteDance is Chinese, and this story was symbolic of the growing tension between the United States and China, in the 'time' of 'Trump'.

Back on the subject of the May 6th ritual involving the Iran War Powers resolution, mainstream publications brought attention to the fact that Wikipedia and Google had promoted the date of May 6, 2020 as the start date of World War III in their search engines at the beginning of 2020, in the aftermath of the U.S. assassination of Soleimani for seemingly unknown reasons. Of course, World War III did not start this day, but the vetoing of the resolution on the same day by Trump, vetoing something meant to prevent war, was no doubt symbolic. And in light of the date May 6, 2020 being 201 days after Event 201, it also means that it was 201 days after the Military World Games began in Wuhan, China. And on the subject of Wuhan and 201, let us not forget Dean Koontz, who wrote about the 'Wuhan 400' virus in 1981, and who was on his 201st day of being 74 years old when the Chinese New Year began, the 'Year of the Rat', a detail not to be confused with Event 201 taking place on the day leaving 74 days left in the year.

Where the number 201 connects with war is through the planet 'Mars', equating to 201 with Jewish Gematria. In that same cipher, 'Roman' also sums to 201, and Mars is the Roman God of War. Let us not forget that both 'Roman' and 'Roman Catholicism' equate to 74, and since the times of ancient Rome, the church has been waging war in God's name. As we'll get to in the next chapter on George Floyd's killing, 'Confederate' sums to 201, and that was the name of the southern army in the U.S. Civil War, an army that was financed by the Jesuits and Catholic Church, for the purpose of breaking and bankrupting the U.S. nation, that the Church then effectively bought in 1871, emphasis on '71, shortly after the conclusion of the U.S. Civil War, as we covered in the first chapter, when we learned about the District of Columbia Organic Act of 1871. And for another related thought, the day of the week named after Mars is 'Tuesday', having Simple English Gematria of 95, bringing us back to the Jesuits, as well as the year the Military World Games began, in 1995, in Rome. And for a strong 201 war ritual on a Tuesday, think of September 11, 2001. For an even more recent and more subtle ritual, think of Tuesday, July 7, 2020, when the President of Brazil, Jair Bolsonaro, was diagnosed with coronavirus. As you'll recall, in the Event 201 coronavirus war games simulation, the outbreak begins in 'Brazil', and in this case, the news came 263 days after the Event 201 simulation, the 56th prime number. Not to be outdone, 23 days later, July 30th, corresponding with 'Wuhan', his wife, with the March 22nd birthday, tested positive. It was a story that reminded of Canada's Sophie Trudeau coming down with the virus March 11th, 2020, 322 days after her April 24th birthday.

Thus, there are no two ways about it, the rituals that are shaping our world are numerical and purposeful, and in 2020, 56 has been the most repetitive number used in the spell casting, from the killing of Soleimani, to the death of Kobe Bryant, who is now buried in 'Corona del Mar', equating to 56 and 70, in the same ciphers as 'coronavirus', and who died a span of 23 days before Michael Jordan's birthday, 'MJ', number 23, who was at the tail end of being 56 years old when Kobe's accident happened, having a February 17, 1963 birthday- reminding us of Michael Jordan's father's death at age 56. And let us not forget Kobe was traveling from Catholic mass, and Soleimani was killed in the holy lands, where the crusades once took place- wars waged by the Catholic Church, that is now clearly under the leadership of the Jesuit Order, or the 'Society of Jesus', the 56 'cult'. In addition to 'Soleimani', Kobe Bryant, 'coronavirus', 'unemployment' and 'Black Lives Matter', each equating to 56, the year has been full of other stories relating to the number 56 as well, including the deaths of Naya Rivera and Pop Smoke. In total, this barrage of encoded information has captured the mind's eye of the masses, and let us not forget that 'all seeing eye' equates to 56 in Pythagorean, the same as 'mind control' and 'magic spell'. And again, these stories, collectively, are a form of magic and spell casting, thus the word *spelling.*

So do the spells work? I cannot confirm, but I do lean towards thinking the answer is yes. That is because I have noticed many people seem to be under some sort of hypnosis when it comes to falling in line and not asking questions anytime it comes to the government's very obvious, and very big lies and agendas- including September 11, 2001, and the 'Wuhan Coronavirus' pandemic 222 months later. And in light of the discussion of magic, let us not forget the first card of the Tarot is The Magician, and in '01, when 9/11 happened, the attack supposedly lasted 102 minutes and came 33 years after 1968, corresponding with the gematria of 'magic', equating to 102 and 33. As for spell casting, and good and evil, and light and dark, I should also mention that 'as above so below' sums to 222 and 78, the same as 'Wuhan Coronavirus' and 'order out of chaos'. If you're not aware, "as above, so below" is a common phrase used by magicians, and the occult, and it is a concept illustrated within the symbol that is the Star of David, the flag of Israel. And on the subject of Israel, if you have not seen *World War Z*, you should. I recommend it only because the movie is about a deadly 'virus' that is part of a conspiracy, that traces back to Israel, a nation that exists because of the ongoing agendas of the Catholic Church. And regarding the title of the film, keep in mind Z is the 26th letter, and 'virus' equates to 26 with Pythagorean, same with 'Covid'. Furthermore, regarding the words "world war" in the title *World War Z*- from the U.K. to the U.S. to Israel and beyond, headlines have been written during the time of the "coronavirus pandemic" comparing the outbreak and the consequences of it to World War I, and World War II. There have even been stories calling the pandemic World War III, from The Hill to the Washington Post, so the riddles are definitely there, especially in light of the fact that the idea of Israel's creation was one of the key contributing factors to both World Wars.

In regards to war, there is another point that needs to be made about the number 56. That point is the word 'Abrahamic' sums to 56 with Simple English, and the major world shaping events of the 21st century, that got off to a bang with September 11, 2001, have been about dividing the people of the world, and this is especially true regarding religion, such as blaming 9/11 and other related attacks on "radical Islam", something our U.S. government has admitted to funding through the CIA, including the funding of Osama bin Laden himself, who had the CIA codename 'Tim Osmond', equating to 41 with Pythagorean, the same as 'Saudi Arabia' and similar to how 'al-Qaeda' sums to 41 with Simple English, the number also corresponding with the numerology of September 11, 2001, equating to 41- and even more, being the 13th prime, connecting back to the gematria of 'CIA', an acronym that also equates to 68, and reminding us that Soleimani was killed on January 3rd, or 1/3, like 13, 68 days before his birthday. As for the Abrahamic religions, you'll recall they are Judaism, Christianity and Islam, and I write them in that order, going from oldest to newest. All 'three' of the religions are based out of the *Torah*, that is 187 chapters in length. And as you know, 'three' sums to 56, and 'Society of Jesus' sums to 56, as well as 187. Furthermore, the words 'Jesuit', 'math' and '*Bible*' each equate to 21, connecting with the 21st century of the Gregorian Calendar, a Catholic system, and reminding us that the date September 11, 2001 had 21 date numerology as well. The number 21 also reminds us of when Agenda 21 is supposed to be in effect, by the start of the year 2021, a goal that was reaffirmed at the Agenda 2030 launch, concluding on September 27, 2015, the anniversary date of the Jesuits being recognized by Rome. As you'll recall, President Obama, the winner of the 56th and 57th U.S. Presidential Elections, was on his 54th day of being 54 years old, when he attended and spoke at the same Agenda 2030 event.

It is to say that these numbers are being used in rituals and spells that are in their favor, but not so much everyone else's. Case in point, on September 11, 2001, the 'three' planes that hit structures, were flight numbers 11, 77 and 175, adding up to 263, the 56th prime. And do you remember how that day benefited you? Me neither. But I know how it benefited the 'Rockefeller' Foundation, who helped mastermind it, as well as the warmongers and corporate beneficiaries in 'Washington D.C.' And in case you have forgotten, 'Rockefeller' sums to 56 with Pythagorean, the same as 'Washington D.C.', and the same as 'Society of Jesus'. For another thought, in light of the one world order that the satanic cabal is building, consider that Abraham, is the person who is credited with changing the world's thoughts about God, in the sense that prior to him, people believed in many different Gods, such as Mars, the God of War, or Zeus, the God of all Gods. But it was Abraham who said no, it wasn't so, and there was one God, and he is a God that demands being worshipped, and worshipped alone. And for his services, Abraham was given Canaan by God, as is told in *Genesis 13*. And keep in mind, today Canaan is situated in the territory of the southern Levant, encompassing Israel, the West Bank, Gaza, Jordan, and the southern portions of Syria and Lebanon. In other words, it is the land that is suffering from some of the greatest religious divisions in the world, that over the centuries, have been brought about predominantly by the Roman Catholic Church.

In light of 9/11, and so many other divisive deceptions in the mainstream media, recall that a Jesuit tactic is 'divide and conquer', equating to 84 in Pythagorean, the same as 'United States of America' and 'Jesuit'. With divide and conquer in mind, think of the Church's occupied territory, 'Washington D.C', and their two party federal system that is all about choosing the "lesser of two evils." Think about it. Really, think about it. Because most people never do. They just shrug their shoulders, and walk through life doing what they see everyone else doing, from voting in elections that they know are scams, to marching along and agreeing with obvious lies that are no good for society, whether it be 'Santa Claus', equating to 666 with Sumerian Gematria, or 9/11 in 'New York', the state summing to 666 also with Sumerian Gematria. Sadly, as they march, it appears they do not realize they're being herded, like cattle, or sheep, or like characters in George Orwell's *Animal Farm*, a classic, and being herded by a code- as they're driven to a cliff, and as I say they're, I mean we're, because we're all part of this society, and that is why it is all of our jobs to do something to inform the herd, and change the direction of things. While so many are too busy fighting between the choices of A and B that are given to them, such as to wear a mask or to not wear a mask, they're forgetting to ask more important questions, such as, should I be overthrowing this tyranny, or standing down, and hoping someone else comes along and does it for me?

On the subject of war games and rumors of war, let us once again discuss Sun Tzu's famous text, *Art of War,* translated by the Jesuit in France, Jean Joseph Marie Amiot, in 1772, reminding us that 'Jesuit Order' equates to 72. As you'll recall, *'Art of War'* itself equates to 102 and 114, the same as 'World War', and it connects to the fact that 'Pearl Harbor' equates to 114, and the U.S. Civil War began April 12, 1861, the 102nd day of the year, as well as the 9/11 attacks lasting 102 minutes, and 'al-Qaeda' equating to 102 with Jewish Gematria. And on the subject of 'magic' equating to 102, let us not forget 'The Magician', the name of the first card in the Tarot, equates to 207, the same as the name 'Jean Joseph Marie Amiot', the man who translated *Art of War*. Let us also not forget that the oldest Tarot deck in the world traces back to Italy. And in light of coronavirus being compared to war, it is important to keep in mind that it has been compared to Spanish Flu, an outbreak that began after World War I, in 1918, 102 years before the "coronavirus outbreak" of 2020. And furthermore, one of the main consequences of coronavirus for us as a people is what we now refer to as 'social distancing', causing a world of inconvenience and also having gematria of 102 using Reverse Pythagorean.

On the subject of social distancing, if you missed it, on March 25, 2020, Deborah Birx, born April 4th, in '56, part of team 'Anthony Fauci', told the story of how her ancestors didn't social distance way back in 1918 and it caused the Spanish Flu to rapidly spread in her family. What made her story funny, is that her full name, 'Deborah Leah Birx' equates to 'social distancing', showing why it was her job to tell such a tall tale. At the same time, her full name also sums to 78 and 84, the same as 'Jesuit', as well as 132, like 'United States of America' and 'Catholic Church'. Even more, 'Deborah Birx' equates to 191, the same as 'Society of Jesus', and also 65, like 'pandemic'. Further still, 'Birx' alone equates to 26 with Pythagorean, the same as 'virus', 'Covid' and 'China', making her the perfectly named puppet for the task at hand. And because we are practicing the tactic of "*know your enemy*", a concept from Sun Tzu's *Art of War*, it is easy to see who she operates on behalf of.

For one last detail about Deborah Birx, her official title, 'Coronavirus Response Coordinator' equates to 155 with Pythagorean, similar to how 'coronavirus' equates to 155 with Simple English, and something that is also true of 'Michael Richard Pence', equating to 155 with Simple, the name of the Vice President, who was given the title "Coronavirus Czar" during the time of the "pandemic." His big decision as Czar came on June 26th, or 26/6, to allow the airlines to begin contact tracing people, following the tradition of H.R. 6666. It was only fitting his decision came on that date, because as we learned earlier, when President Trump made him Coronavirus Czar, on

February 27, 2020, the 58th day of the year, it was Mike Pence's 266th day of his age, having a June 7, 1959 birthday. For another fun stat on Mike Pence, he turned 58 years old 138 days after the inauguration of Donald Trump, in the 58th U.S. Presidential Election, where the ceremony was led by the 58 year old Steve Ray of the Washington Nationals, and where 'Donald Trump', 'Nationals' and 'federal' each equate to 138, and reminding us that the Washington Nationals won the World Series October 30, 2019, 138 days after Donald Trump's June 14, 2019 birthday. Keep in mind 'Major League' sums to 45, the same as 'Mike Pence', which is the 9th triangular number, tying in perfectly with the 9 innings of a baseball game, and the 45th POTUS.

Speaking of the Jesuit puppet that is Donald Trump, let us examine the significance of his remarks that made international headlines on September 15, 2019, when he said he was "locked and loaded" in regards to being ready to go to war with Iran after an attack on a Saudi oil field that was blamed on Iran by U.S. intelligence. Because the date could be written 15/9, it made sense for 'Donald Trump' equating to 159, the same as 'Scottish Rite', to make big news with a bold statement on this date. Furthermore, 'locked and loaded' equates to 110 with Simple English, the same as 'president', and 'airstrike', the latter being what reportedly killed Qasem Soleimani on January 3, 2020, exactly 110 days after Trump's remarks. Continuing with the pattern, it was reported that after the retaliatory attack of January 8, 2020 by Iran on the U.S.'s 'Ayn al-Asad Airbase', equating to 110 with Reverse Pythagorean, that 110 soldiers were treated for traumatic brain injuries. As you have learned, 110 is a very significant number to the events of September 11th, connecting to the name 'Osama bin Laden' and the height of the WTCs, each 110 stories tall, where the first plane hit at 8:46 AM, a similar detail to the one in the story of the killing of George Floyd, where it was reported the officer was on George Floyd's neck for 8 minutes and 46 seconds in 'Minnesota', a state equating to 110 with Simple English, and reminding us that the same officer's pretrial for the murder of 'George Floyd', a name equating to 119 with Simple English, will begin September 11, 2020. As you have also learned, the word 'prophecy' equates to 110, and that is what it is all about, pushing us closer and closer to a planned apocalypse, and our planned demise, as foretold in the *Holy Bible*, one story at a time, by the same old numbers. And speaking of which, I should mention, in light of 9/11, let us not forget

Building 7, the 'Salomon Brothers Building', that collapsed for no good reason, and had a name equating to 110 with Pythagorean, and a name also paying tribute to objects in the sky that measure time, the sun and the moon, no different than the name Soleimani. At the same time, 'Salomon Brothers' alone sums to 68 with Pythagorean, reminding us of not only of 1968, but that Soleimani died 68 days before his birthday, and just how repetitive the code of the 'age' is, another word equating to 68. And for one last 68 riddle, at least for now, in the days after the assassination of Soleimani, and Iran's response attack on January 8th, Iran's lone female 'Olympic Medalist', a title summing to 68 with Pythagorean, 21 year old Kimia Alizadeh Zonouzi, announced she was leaving Iran for Europe on January 12, 2020, due to Iran's oppression of women, 187 days after her July 10, 2019 birthday. As you know, 21 and 187 connect to the Jesuits, and the number 187 also connects to the 'Abrahamic' religions, as in the religions that are purposefully being divided, by headlines such as these.

For the clincher, in terms of exposing just how much of a show it all is, and who is responsible, the supposed attack on 'Ayn al-Asad Airbase', January 8, 2020, in response to the killing of Soleimani, came exactly 54 weeks after Donald Trump visited the same base, in a surprise visit, December 26, 2018, a date having 56 numerology as well. Regarding the number 54, as you know, the 'Jesuit Order' equates to 54, and so does their logo, the 'sun'. At the same time, the Jesuit acronym, 'IHS' equates to 18, and so does the word 'sun', similar to the January 8th date of attack, emphasis on 1/8. And with the sun being the topic at hand, think about what you learned regarding Sun Tzu, and the *Art of War*, translated by the Jesuits. And in light of Iran and the U.S. both operating by the code, let us not forget that 'The Jesuit Order' equates with the 'New World Order', and 'New World Order' also equates with 'Catholic Church'. And with *Art of War* still in mind, I will say, because most people do not know their enemy, it is the same reason they do not recognize the enemy's operations, as repetitive as they are. Case in point, you might recall it was reported that Iran accidentally shot down a Ukrainian commercial jet in their attack on the U.S. on the date of January 8, 2020, a plane that was reported to be a Boeing 737. Not by chance, this element of the contrived story, was a subliminal cue to trigger memories of 9/11, and true to the code, both 'Boeing' and 'Ukraine' equate to 110. And yes,

288

110 is the reason 'Ukraine' was chosen for the impeachment theater of Donald Trump, the 'president'. It is also why the 'War Powers Resolution' was named as such, because it equates to 110 as well.

And for the person reading and still doubting, I'll leave you with a challenge, because it is important. It is important in the sense that either I am right, or I am wrong about what I am writing, and you are reading- and if I am right, that means the 1,000 people from the U.S. 82nd Airborne Division who were deployed to Iran after the January 3rd airstrike, were deployed as part of a ritual that put them in harms way- and was completely needless- not to mention all the time and energy and taxpayer money wasted. It also means the same thing happened after September 11, 2001. So think about that. That's the challenge. And then think about this too. The name 'Qasem Soleimani' sums to 62 and 82 in the base ciphers, and he was reportedly killed at age 62, and 1,000 members of the 82nd Airborne Division were deployed to the region after his killing.

For your gematria learning, the word 'soldier' sums to 82 with Simple English, and in addition to the numbers, notice the word begins with sol, the Spanish word for sun and the beginning of the word solar. Now pair that thought with Sun Tzu, *Art of War,* the Jesuits, the sun, the calendar, and the language, and how it all comes together. While you're doing that, don't overlook that the word die is also in soldier. And ask yourself, in the time of the Church and the Jesuits, and under many cycles of the sun, what have so many young people really been dying for in wars? Has it been about people and freedom, or has it been more about The Cabal's agenda? If you take a look around, and you see as I see, it definitely appears to be a lot more about the latter.

In light of it being the Jesuits behind all of this, for some historical perspective, I offer the well put and entertaining quote from *V for Vendetta,* in regards to the November 5, 1605, the date of the Jesuit attack on the United Kingdom, known as the Gunpowder Plot. The dialogue from the film puts it, *"Remember, remember! The fifth of November, the Gunpowder treason and plot; I know of no reason, why the Gunpowder treason, should ever be forgot! Guy Fawkes and his companions did the scheme contrive, to blow the King and Parliament all up alive. Threescore barrels, laid below, to prove old England's overthrow. But, by God's providence, him they catch, with a dark lantern, lighting a match! A stick and a stake for King James's sake! If* *you won't give me one, I'll take two, the better for me, and the worse for you. A rope, a rope, to hang the Pope, a penn'orth of cheese to choke him, a pint of beer to wash it down, and a jolly good fire to burn him.*" As a reminder, the gematria of *V for Vendetta* is 172, the same as the Jesuit motto, 'Ad maiorem Dei gloriam', equating to 172, something that is only fitting, because the film is in tribute to the Jesuits. And never mind the detail that the main character of the same film is masked, for the entire film, in light of living with the "new normal", with required masks in public places, especially since the film's plot involves the storyline of the U.S. having fallen to terrorism, wars and a virus. And for one last gematria proof, *V for Vendetta* released March 17, 2006 in the U.S., on a date with 26 and 46 numerology, corresponding with the gematria of 'virus' as well as 'chaos', both equating to 26 and 46, as well as 89. If you take the time to watch the film, you'll be astonished for multiple reasons, mostly because of how the storyline relates to the present conditions we're living with, but also because of the discussion of tactics such as order out of chaos. *And for another joke being had at our expense, you'll understand just how deep the mocking of our times are when you realize that in history the film *V for Vendetta* was made by the Wachowski Brothers, who now years later want to be called the 'Wachowski Sisters', because they consider themselves transgenders, a concept that relates to Kabbalah, the same as gematria. This is because in Kabbalah, it is believed God is male and female.

With regards to transgenderism and the Jesuits, I'll say this much- it's not an accident that NBA star Dwayne Wade, who attended Marquette University, the Jesuit school in Wisconsin, is parading around his little boy Zion, as a young transgender. It's also not an accident that his child changed his name from Zion to 'Zaya', where the latter equates to 53, the same as 'transgender', and reminding us of Bruce Jenner's transgender 'Vanity Fair' cover, a magazine name equating to 53, in the exact same way as 'transgender'. Of course, Bruce Jenner is now known as 'Caitlyn Jenner', a name equating to 201, the same as 'The Jesuit Order'. At the same time, 'Caitlyn' equates to 84 and 42 in the exact same ciphers as 'Jesuit'. And as for why all this likely is the case, goes back to the Knights Templar, who served the Catholic Church, and who were accused of worshiping baphomet before they were burned at the stake, October 13, 1307. Of course, baphomet is male and female.

18 | I Can't Breathe & George Floyd's Killing On 38ᵗʰ St.

On May 26, 2020, mainstream media captured the mind's eye of the masses in record time with the disturbing story and video footage, reportedly from one day earlier, of the killing of 46 year old George Floyd by 44 year police officer Derek Chauvin, on the 44ᵗʰ Parallel North, in Minneapolis, Minnesota. As you'll recall, the word 'execution' has gematria of 44 and 46, pairing with how 'kill' and 'officer' equate to 44, and similar to how 'sacrifice' sums to 46, as well as 'chaos' and 'ordo ab chao', the latter being the Latin motto for order out of chaos. In the case of 46 year old George Floyd, he had the double headed eagle of the Scottish Rite of Freemasonry tattooed on his chest, that is often adorned with the words *ORDO AB CHAO*, with the AB around the 'neck' of the two headed bird, the part of George Floyd's body that was kneeled on by Officer Chauvin, and the part having a Simple English value of 33, reminding us that the rioting in response to the killing of George Floyd began on East 33ʳᵈ Street in Minneapolis, similar to how the beating of Rodney King by the 'LAPD', an acronym equating to 33, just like the words 'police' and 'race war', happened on March 3, 1991, emphasis on 3/3, the same day in history Trayvon Martin was buried, March 3, 2012, 21 years later. As you have learned, the number 33 relates to 'Kundalini' energy, rising up the 33 bones of the human vertebrae, and where 'Kundalini' equates to 58, so does 'Derek Chauvin', 'Benjamin Crump', the Floyd family's lawyer, 'Freemasonry', 'fraternal', and 'secret society'. In light of the number 58, let us not forget its relationship with 33, reminding us that 'masonry', 'federal', 'order' and 'secrecy' equate to 33, and all in the same cipher as 'police', Pythagorean. And to get back to the point of how the story captured the mind's eye of the masses quickly, recall that 'pineal' equates to 33, and at the same time, 'Fraternal Order of Police' equates to 119, the same as 'George Floyd', along with the phrase 'all seeing eye', something that is clearly part of the design of the logo for the Fraternal Order of Police, or F.O.P., if you care to look it up. Speaking of which, it was April 29ᵗʰ, the 119ᵗʰ day of the year in non leap years, in 1992, when the police were acquitted for the vicious beating of Rodney King, also captured on camera, something that was unprecedented at the time, triggering rioting, especially in 'Compton', equating to 33 with Pythagorean, and being located on the 33ʳᵈ Parallel North. And in light of the number 119 list we've compiled, please don't overlook that it is 9-1-1 in reverse, the number we dial for police in the U.S., as well as emergency services.

In the case of George Floyd's tattoo, if you want to see it for yourself, search for the image of the porn star named 'Floyd the Landlord'. I kid you not, because that is the stage name of George Floyd in his scene with adult actress 'Kimberly Brinks'. And regarding her name, part of me wonders if it is an accident that he was chosen to film this scene with this specific actress whose name has gematria of 93, the same as 'Minneapolis, Minnesota', the city on the 93rd Meridian West, where Floyd was killed, and reminding us of the rituals with 'Martin Luther King Jr.' and 'Malcolm X', who both went by names other than their birth names, and who both were assigned names equating to 93, something that becomes more interesting when you realize they met only one time in history, March 26, 1964, a date with 93 numerology, and where 93 is the reflection of 39, the age both Martin and Malcolm died at. Keep in mind, the number 39 also corresponds with the Pythagorean Gematria of 'George' and 'Gemini', since this killing came in the "Twin Cites" in the time of Gemini, the "Twins". And in light of George Floyd reportedly being killed by a 44 year old officer on the 44th Parallel North, let us not forget that both MLK and Malcolm X were killed on dates with clear 44 connections, and in Malcolm X's case, his assassin's name, 'Thomas Hagan', equated to 44, and he received 44 years in prison. And for even more familiar numbers, the porn name 'Floyd the Landlord' has gematria of 76, the same as 'slave', 'negro' and 'blues', reminding us that the Million Man March was October 16, 1995, the day leaving 76 days in the year, and at the same time, the phrase 'order from chaos', which is sometimes used instead of "order out of chaos", equates to 76- and let us not forget *Acts 7:6* either. Furthermore, both 'Floyd the Landlord' and 'order from chaos' equate to 77, reminding us of the ritual of Flight 77 on September 11, 2001, as well as the gematria of both 'police officer' and 'police department', equating to 77, the same as 'September Eleventh' and 'World Trade Center'. Tying this together further is what we have already covered, and that is, 'George Floyd', equating to 119 with Simple English, is similar to the date of September 11th when written as 11/9, plus the most crucial reported fact of all, and that is Officer Chauvin was on George Floyd's neck for 8 minutes and 46 seconds, not unlike how it was reported that at 8:46 AM, Flight AA-11 became the first plane to hit the World Trade Center on September 11, 2001. And then as if the riddle wasn't already made clear enough by The Cabal, they set the pretrial date for Derek Chauvin's accused murder of George Floyd for September 11, 2020, on the 19 year anniversary of the infamous attack. Of course, 'Floyd' equates to 19 and 26, the same as 'chaos', the same as 'knee', and it is for this reason the footage of the killing of George Floyd was saved for the 26th of May, to spark the chaos that it did on the same day (keep in mind 8:46 AM is the 526th minute of the day, like date 5/26). Adding to the riddle, both 'Floyd' and 'riot' equate to 26, and as we know, 26 is the 'God' number- and what we have observed through the worldwide response to the video of George Floyd needlessly having his life taken away from him by the "authority figure," through the protesting and rioting, is that The Cabal can move the people of the world in ways that only God, or even Gods, should be able to. Then again, we've been witnessing this for some length of time, including the incident of April 29th, the 119th day of the year, when the police were acquitted for the beating of Rodney King, setting off severe rioting in one of the world's largest cities, Los Angeles, California.

As a reminder, 'Rodney King' equates to 59 with Pythagorean, the number corresponding with the Simple English values of 'slave', 'negro' and 'blues'. Furthermore, his birthday is April 2nd, or 4/2, and his father was born in 1942 and died at age 42 in the infamous year of 1984- and if you have read my first book, you know about the repetitive nature of bringing the numbers 42 and 59 together in national headlines involving black people, numbers that represent the gematria of 'slavery' and 'slave' respectively, and reminding us further, that Black History Month, 'February', sums to 42, and in non-leap years it ends on the 59th day of the year- and further still, Motown was established on the 42nd Parallel North in Detroit, in the year 1959, emphasis on '59, and that in 2020, the 42nd pick of the NFL Draft was 'Laviska Shenault Jr.', equating to 59 with Pythagorean, in the most recent of many related draft rituals, where mostly wealthy white men bid for and trade men that are often of darker complexions, if you catch my drift. It was for this same reason that on May 9th, or 5/9, you likely read the stories about the deaths of Little Richard, as well as the CEO of Motown, who died at 59, Andre Harrell, and who were both black entertainers. In the case of Harrell it was reported the news of his death was broken at 'Club Quarantine' equating to 59 in Pythagorean, and by 'Derrick Jones', the DJ, a man having a name equating to 59 and 76 with both Pythagorean ciphers. Also curious about Harrell's death, is that it was reported he had helped Sean Combs establish 'Bad Boy Records', equating to 59 and 76, and the May 9th news of his death came 187 days after Sean Combs' 50th birthday, celebrated on November 4, 2019. Then right after that news, it was reported the next day, 'Betty Wright', equating to 59, was dead 44 years after winning her Grammy in '76.

In the case of George Floyd, his death was on 'Memorial Day', equating to 181, the 42nd prime, and in the month of 'May', the only month in addition to 'February', Black History Month, that equates to 42. And don't let it slip away that 'Black History' equates to 181 as well, the 42nd prime number, or that the killing of Floyd was on Minnesota Senator 'Amy' Klobuchar's 60th birthday, and the story emerged days after Floyd's killing that she could have put Derek Chauvin away in 2006 for the wrongful killing of a 42 year old man (*Police = 60; *Nigger = 42 & 60). Also, don't forget that on the same day as the supposed killing of George Floyd, a woman named 'Amy Cooper', equating to 42, made national headlines for choking her dog in 'Central Park', something that was captured on video, like George Floyd's fatal ending, while at the same time she was calling the police to report a black man who was bird watching, only because she felt threatened after he asked her to leash her dog. And never mind that on July 6th, 7/6, 42 days later, the New York DA said Amy Cooper would face charges, or that the word 'twin' equates to 42, and both stories happened in the time of Gemini, the "Twins", and George Floyd was killed in the 'Twin' Cites, whereas Amy Cooper was close to where the 'Twin' Towers once stood. Even better, Stephen Jackson of the NBA, who was 42 years old at the time, and who grew up in Houston, like Floyd, said he was George Floyd's twin, and then seemingly in the same motion, he uploaded to his Instagram profile an image of his relative's Freemason apparel, reminding us of the killing of Philando Castille on June 7, 2015, a date that can be written 7/6, by Minnesota Police, and how in the aftermath of his death, Philando Castille's uncle went on primetime television to talk about the death of his nephew while wearing his Freemason pin. And for the record, 'Central Park', where Amy Cooper choked the dog, the day George Floyd was choked to death, equates to 119 with Simple English, the same as 'George Floyd', and the same as 'all seeing eye'- the latter being masonic terminology. As for the 59 part, George Floyd's killing came 59 days before the Minneapolis Mayor's 39th birthday on July 23, 2020, meaning he was 38 years old at the time, having been born as Jacob Lawrence Frey, July 23, 1981, a name we'll get to.

Speaking of the number 38, for me personally, when the news of what happened to George Floyd broke, the detail that struck me first was the reported killing on the corner of 38th Street and Chicago Avenue. As you know, 'Chicago' equates to 46, going with what we discussed prior. And as for 38, as you have learned, it connects to the gematria of 'death', 'murder', 'killing' and 'R.I.P.', each equating to 38. For a good visual, and as another reminder, seek out the movie poster for *Murder by Numbers,* where the letters for 'b' are changed to 8 and the letters for 'e' are changed to 3, and no other letters are tampered with- and this matters because 'murder' has gematria of 38 and 83, and the song *Murder by Numbers* was released in 1983 by the band The Police, not to mention George Floyd was arrested next to a police cruiser with the number **83**0 on it after being taken from his Mercedes ML 320, and prior to being kneeled on in front of police cruiser 320, when 'Roman Catholic Church' equates to 320 and 'Mercedes Benz' equates to 119 and 56 --- numbers that should remind you of the Jesuits and 'Vatican', and I'll say no more on the matter, except that you should look into the July 17, 1944 Port Chicago Disaster that reportedly killed 320 people, most of whom were black. As we'll soon get to, Eric Garner's choking related death that was also caused by a police officer, an incident having clear parallels to George Floyd's murder, occurred on July 17, 2014, 70 years after the Port Chicago incident. Now to get back on the subject at hand, the number 38- 'asphyxiation' equates to 163, the 38th prime number, and in this case, that is what George Floyd's death was blamed on, an asphyxiation in 'Minnesota', one of five states having a Pythagorean Gematria of 38. Those five are Oregon, Colorado (the 38th state), Minnesota, Louisiana and Florida. And for some examples of their relevance, consider, 'Trayvon', as in Trayvon Martin, a first name equating to 38, was killed in 'Florida', and buried March 3, 2012, a date with 38 numerology. And more recently, in the wake of George Floyd, the story has emerged of the chokehold killing of Elijah McClain by police, in 'Denver, Colorado', a city equating to 74, the same as the phrase 'I can't breathe'. Furthermore, this case was reportedly reopened because of George Floyd's killing, due to the fact that Elijah was killed on Kobe Bryant Day by police, using a chokehold, August 24, 2019, the day named after the man who would go on to die in the NBA's 74th season, after championing the phrase 'I can't breathe'. And as you might recall, Kobe Bryant had a rough time in Colorado as well, being accused of sexual assault and infidelity. To keep this riddle short, the name 'Elijah McClain' sums to 55 and 251, the latter being the 54th prime, big numbers in Kobe's death, and when Kobe Bryant was accused of rape in Colorado, it was on July 1, 2003, a span of 54 days from his upcoming birthday, meaning he was 24 at the time, and the name of the building he supposedly raped the young woman in was called the 'Spa at Cordillera', summing to 251, the 54th prime. And getting back on the subject of the 38 states specifically, if you have a good memory, you might recall July 6, 2015, emphasis on 7/6, when there were two viral stories in the news, at the same time, about the killing of black men by police officers, both captured on video, and they were Alton Sterling in 'Louisiana' and Philando Castille in 'Minnesota', thus two states from our list of 38. And if you do the math, there is a 5 in 50 (or 1 in 10) chance of a state having gematria of 38, meaning that the odds of two similar stories being in the news on the same day, both with states having 38 gematria, is one in ten, times one in ten, meaning 1 in 100, meaning 1%, meaning not likely. Keep in mind July 6th, 2015, the day those stories were reported, was the 187th day of the year, corresponding with the police homicide code, as well as the phrase 'Society of Jesus'- and in the case of George Floyd, 'Minneapolis Police' also equates to 187. And then as if the pattern of 38 wasn't established enough, the murder trial for George Floyd has been set for March 8, 2021, a date that can be expressed as 8/3 or 3/8, corresponding with the 38 and 83 gematria of 'murder'. Furthermore, on August 3, 2020, or 3/8, or 8/3, new body cam footage was released of George Floyd resisting arrest, and it was the same day John Hume was reported dead at 83, having joined British Parliament in 1983. And let us not forget it is the band **THE POLICE**, that sing the song *Murder by Numbers*, that released in 1983, and is on the album *Synchronicity.*

In addition to the obvious 'murder' connection, the March 8, 2021 trial start date will be a date with 52 numerology (3/8/2021 = 3+8+20+21 = 52). And as you have learned, 'Minnesota' equates to 52 with Reverse Pythagorean, the state that hosted Super Bowl 52. The greater significance of the number 52 in this case is through the phrase that became popular after the killing of Eric Garner in 2014, and again after the killing of George Floyd. That phrase is, 'I can't breathe', equating to 52 with Pythagorean. Proving that the use of these numbers in this way was a ritual was demonstrated through multiple stories. One was the story from May 29, 2020, a date with 74 numerology, telling of how the rapper 'Trae the Truth', equating to 52 and 74 in the exact same ciphers as 'I can't breathe', had traveled from Houston, George Floyd's hometown, to Minneapolis, to pay his respects to his fallen friend George Floyd. Beyond that, the day of the news, May 29, 2020, was 331 days after Trae the Truth's July 3, 2019 birthday, having been born July 3, 1980 with the name 'Frazier Othel Thompson III', equating to 331 with Reverse Simple. Furthermore, 331 is the 67th prime number, a number connecting to 'blood sacrifice' as well as 'human sacrifice', and reminding us of the demise of Nipsey Hussle, on March 31, 2019, another story for another time.

Further proving that the number 52 was being used for ritual in the matter I am asserting, is what happened on July 15, 2020, a span of 52 days from the reported May 25th killing of George Floyd. On July 15, 2020, Benjamin Crump filed a civil lawsuit against the city of Minneapolis and its police on behalf of George Floyd's family. The number 52 was also the reason that on the same day, Minneapolis police released new body cam footage of the death of George Floyd, where you could more clearly hear him utter the words, "I can't breathe", as his last words, a quote that was emphasized through all of mainstream media in the July 15th headlines. Another thing to consider is that the date of July 15th can be expressed as 15/7, similar to 157, the number that much of Kobe Bryant's death was centered around, along with his daughter Gianna, where again, it was reported that like Kobe Bryant, George Floyd had a daughter named Gianna, a name that isn't all that common. And in terms of parallels, 52 is divisible by 26, and both 'Bryant' and 'Floyd' equate to 26 with Pythagorean, reminding that Kobe died on the 26th day of the year, and then on the 26th of May, the world saw the video of George Floyd's demise, leading to 'chaos', for the sake of order out of chaos. Remember, these are the number games of 'The Cabal', and when most of us play games, we do it with 52 cards, but when they do it, they play with people.

For yet another example of how the number 52 was being used ritualistically in relation to George Floyd's killing, it was reported that on July 18, 2020, on the 52nd straight day of protests in Portland, Oregon (one of the 38 states) in tribute to George Floyd, a stretch of days that was emphasized in headlines, that federal police were capturing protesters by pulling them into unmarked vans. Keep in mind, Oregon is the 33rd state, and both 'federal' and 'police' equate to 33 with Pythagorean, and the George Floyd protests began on East 33rd Street. Furthermore, the date of July 18th can be expressed as 18/7, similar to 187, corresponding with the gematria of 'Washington D.C.' and 'Society of Jesus'. At the same time, the 52nd day factors in with the gematria of 'government' and 'authority', also equating to 52. And better yet, days later, it would be reported that federal police had quietly been in Oregon, monitoring protesters, since July 4th, emphasis on 7/4, because as you learned in the first chapter, 'Oregon' is the only state having Simple English Gematria of 74. At the same time, it was reported that Donald Trump had named this federal police mission 'Operation Legend', equating to 74 with Reverse Pythagorean.

Now to transition between numbers, let's discuss 62, the reflection of 26, because it connects everything from the location of the incident, to what the video of the killing provoked, to it happening in the time of Gemini, under the watch of the Minneapolis Mayor, in the time of the "coronavirus pandemic", where many people reportedly couldn't breathe, because of a deadly virus, that made many require 'ventilators', a word having gematria overlap with 'coronavirus' in three out of the four ciphers. To begin on the subject of 62, both 'Floyd' and 'riot' equate to 26 and 62. Beyond that, 'sacrifice' and 'Minneapolis' equate to 62 with Reverse Pythagorean, the latter being the city where Floyd's killing happened, and in light of Minneapolis being considered one of the Twin Cities, in astrology terms, the twins are 'Castor and Polydeuces', equating to 293 with Reverse Simple, the same as 'coronavirus pandemic', and as you'll recall, 293 is the 62nd prime number. For more insight on the number pairing, if you followed my YouTube channel on March 29th, or 29/3, it was a day of nonstop headlines involving 293 and 62, with several reported deaths and hospitalizations in the world of celebrity, connected to coronavirus, including names such as Alan Merrill. March 29th was also the day 'Queen' Elizabeth's 'Royal Footman' tested positive for coronavirus, and where 'Queen' sums to 62, 'Royal Footman' equates to 'coronavirus' in the same ciphers, summing to 56 and 155, similar to how 'Royal Family' equates to 56. Building onto our 293 list, 'Jacob Lawrence Frey' equates to 293, the full name of the 38 year old Minneapolis' Mayor at the time of Floyd's death- and I'll add that he is

Catholic educated, having attended Villanova, just outside of Philadelphia. Furthermore, George Floyd was reported to be from 'Houston, Texas', equating to 62, and reminding us that the Houston Astros lost in Game 7 of the 115th World Series, and were defeated by the Nationals 6-2, on the day leaving 62 days in the year. At the same time, 'Houston, Texas' sums to 46, matching Floyd's age of demise. For another 62, it is the state 'Georgia', similar to the name George, and where just 20 days before the reported killing of George Floyd, on May 5th, the video released of the Ahmaud Arbery killing in Georgia.

Another important word having gematria of 62 is 'Mason', equating with Simple English. And in the case of George Floyd's death, the knee on his neck was symbolic to the Freemasons, who have a kneeling ritual of their own. It is in tribute to 'Hiram Abiff', a name equating to 62 with Reverse Pythagorean, the Master Mason, who according to the Freemasons, built Solomon's Temple, and who died keeping the 'three' secrets of the first three degrees of Freemasonry. In the Hiram Abiff related ritual, a candidate who is going through the masonic initiation process, lays on the ground, on his back, blindfolded, while his brethren take a knee, surrounding the initiate in close proximity. To cut to the point, the ritual involves the story of Hiram Abiff, who ends up being murdered by the West Gate of Solomon's Temple. Consider the sun sets in the west, and on the date of George Floyd's death, it was reported that the sun set at 8:46 PM local time, corresponding once again, with the detail of 8 minutes and 46 seconds on the neck. In short, this is how it all comes together.

At the same time, the name 'Hiram Abiff' equates to 55 and 62 in the exact same ciphers as Minneapolis. With regards to 55, that is the number we discussed earlier, having a great deal of significance to 'Sigma Pi Phi', also known as the 'Boule', as well as 'Prince Hall' Freemasonry, each equating to 55. In the case of George Floyd, the lawyer his family hired, Benjamin Crump, is a member of both the Boule and Prince Hall. And in that breath, let us recall that 'Boule' equates to 26, because the surname 'Crump' sums to 26 just as well, and Benjamin Crump was named as the attorney of George Floyd's family on May 26th, the day the video of Floyd's demise went viral. Further adding to the list of coincidences is the fact that the Prince Hall Lodge for Minneapolis is located a stone's throw from the crime scene, at the address of 310 E. 38th St #224, Minneapolis, Minnesota (Prince = 38). And as a reminder, Prince Hall is a sect of Freemasonry for black men, who are often entertainers, as was the case with George Floyd, who was a rapper, pornography actor, and semi-pro basketball player, as well as being a bouncer at a nightclub where Derek Chauvin, the officer who reportedly killed him, also worked. And if you saw it yourself, and your eyes were open then, you had to appreciate when the media released the image of George Floyd posing next to a Corona Light poster, in the time of coronavirus, at supposedly the same nightclub where he and Chauvin worked. Personally, I wonder if it is a coincidence that 'Corona Light' equates to 59, because it does remind me that Eric Garner's family was paid $5.9 million for his wrongful death after being choked by the police, and that George Floyd died 59 days before the Minneapolis Mayor's birthday. Making the chance of a coincidence all the more unlikely, is the fact that the name of the nightclub the two men worked at was'El Nuevo Rodeo', equating to 56, the same as 'coronavirus'. And never mind that it was a club with a Spanish name, similar to corona being a Spanish word.

Regarding the familiar number 59, the June 4, 2020 news story about the choking of 27 year old 'Patrick Carroll' contributed further to the use of it. In his case, it was reported a police officer knelt on his black neck on May 18, 2020, 7 days prior to George Floyd, and the story came out of 'Sarasota' equating to 59, the reflection of 95, the latter being the number equating with the gematria of the name of the victim, 'Patrick Carroll'. And not losing track of the fact the word 'slave' sums to 59, 'Sarasota, Florida' sums to 102, the same as 'slavery' and 'police'. A little further ahead, we'll discuss how the full name 'George Perry Floyd' also equates to 102, and what the clear symbolism is behind it. For now, I'll point out that the Patrick Carroll incident took place on May 18, 2020, a date with 43 numerology, connecting to the gematria of 'Florida', 'George Floyd', 'policeman', 'masonic', 'killing', and 'civil war'.

I should also note that May 18, 2020 was a date with 63 numerology, connecting to the gematria of 'racism'. And on the subject of 63 and racism, I want to briefly discuss the fraternity Alpha Phi Alpha, that claims to be the nation's oldest black fraternity, something also claimed by the Boule. They were established on December 4, 1906, and on their 63rd birthday, Fred Hampton, the Black Panther, was murdered in Chicago, supposedly in cold blood, in his bed, while sleeping, by the FBI. Keep in mind 'Fred Hampton' sums to 177, like 'The Jesuit Order', and his full name, 'Fredrick Allen

Hampton', equates to 110, the same as 'prophecy'. As you know, that number connects from the height of the WTCs that fell on 9/11, each 110 stories, to the gematria of 'Minnesota', to the gematria of 'Dave Chappelle', the latter being the once funny comedian who told the story of being born at 8:46 in the morning in a skit made in tribute to George Floyd- and for another 110 ahead, when we talk about the killings of Ahmaud Arbery and Rayshard Brooks in Georgia, be sure to note that their killings were 110 days apart, from February 23, 2020 to June 12, 2020, respectively. As for the date of Hampton's murder, it was the same day the rapper Jay-Z was born, who did the series *'Rest In Power'*, in tribute to Trayvon Martin and other slain black Americans, a film inspiring the Black Lives Matter movement and the push to end racism. Not by chance, the title of that film *'Rest in Power'*, equates to 63 with both Pythagorean ciphers. The symbolism behind this number is also why it was reported after the killing of George Floyd, in national headlines, that Sambo's, in Santa Barbara, would be changing their name after 63 years, a name that is based in an Indian racial slur.

As for what got my attention about Alpha Phi Alpha, it was an NBC news broadcast with an interview of 'Brady Bobb', reported to be a childhood friend of George Floyd, and a member of the fraternity, who attended Floyd's funeral. For the sake of moving onto more important things, I'll ignore that the name 'Brady Bobb' equates to 55, the same as 'Minneapolis', and 'Boule', and 'Sigma Pi Phi', and 'Prince Hall'. The more important point that needs to be made about Alpha Phi Alpha, is that from their establishment date, to the death of George Floyd, was 173 days later, and 'Black Lives Matter' as well as 'Roman Catholicism' equates to 173 with Simple English. The number 173 is also the 40th prime, and Shaun King, the leader of Black Lives Matter, was 40 years old at the time of George Floyd's death, having been born September 17, 1979. Keep in mind this means he was approaching his 41st birthday, on 17/9, something like 179 the 41st prime, which becomes all the more interesting when you recognize that 'King' equates to 41 with Simple English, and 'Shaun King' equates to 41 with Pythagorean. Also, don't overlook that Shaun King attended Morehouse College in Atlanta, the home of MLK's family. With regards to 'Moorehouse', it equates to 119 and 43, the same as 'George Floyd', and 'Moorehouse College' equates to 178 with Simple English, the same as 'George Floyd' with Reverse Simple English.

For a couple more familiar numbers, 'Moorehouse College' also sums to 74, and 'Moorehouse' alone equates to 47. I should also note that Alpha Phi Alpha was originally established at 'Cornell', equating to 38 and 110, the same as 'Minnesota', essentially showing that the universities that gave birth to these fraternities, have their stamp on the George Floyd killing ritual, on 38th Street, in Minnesota.

Back on the subject of the killing of George Floyd, if you watched the video of his death that was initially released by the media, it was just over 10 minutes in length, and within the first 40 seconds of the recording, there is something very crucial that happens. At the very beginning of the video, the person filming backs up from where George Floyd is being assaulted, and makes sure to capture the artwork on the concrete structure built to hold the garbage can that is nearby. The artwork is a colorfully painted number 6. After keeping the number in the shot for a considerable period of time, around the 40 second mark, the person filming then moves closer to where George Floyd is being kneeled on. This detail matters because in the wake of the news of his killing, it was immediately compared to Eric Garner's murder in New York by police on the date of July 17, 2014, nearly 6 years earlier. Furthermore, once the rioting began on East 33rd Street in Minneapolis, the incident was compared to the rioting in Ferguson, Missouri, after the reported death of Michael Brown, that also occurred in 2014, on August 9th. And for the record, both 'Michael Brown' and 'George Perry Floyd' equate to 201, the number of the Jesuits. And let us not forget, where 'The Jesuit Order' sums to 201 with Reverse Simple, the same phrase equates to 177 with Simple English, much like the date July 17th, or 17/7, when Eric Garner was killed. At the same time, as you know, the number 56 is very important to the 'Society of Jesus', and it also connects to 'Black Lives Matter', equating to 56, an organization reaching peak power in the wake of George Floyd's televised death, in the year 2020, 56 years after the 1964 Civil Rights Act.

With the year '64 in mind, let us not forget that 'Civil Rights' equates to 64, and in this case, so does the name 'Eric Garner', and the word 'asphyxiation'. At the same time, 'Eric Garner' and 'asphyxiation' both equate to 62, a number we have made our point about. And to build on the 62 and 64 list, 'Alpha Phi Alpha' equates to both, the fraternity that had a presence at George Floyd's funeral, through Brady Bobb. For another 64, 'cigarettes' equates to 64, and the story in 2014 was that Eric Garner was illegally selling cigarettes, whereas with Michael Brown, he had allegedly stolen cigarettes, and then more recently in 2020, regarding George Floyd, he had tried to purchase cigarettes with a counterfeit $20 bill. Keep in mind 'tobacco' sums to 59, and goes without saying, and please also know 'cigarettes' sums to 163, the same as 'asphyxiation', and again, 163 is the 38th prime, bringing us back to George Floyd on 38th Street, as well as history's past, because both 'Africa' and 'Jamaica' equate to 38 with Simple English. Please keep in mind, these are important locations in the history of U.S. slave trading, and that is much of what this 2020 narrative is about, the prophecy of *Acts 7:6*, and the punishing of the nation that comes after the period of 400 years of slavery, that is stated in *Acts 7:7*. As another reminder, 'United States' sums to 77, and in this case, so does 'police officer'. And to further comprehend how calculated it all is, keep in mind that 2020 is the year of the 59th U.S. Presidential Election, and on August 4, 2020, shortly before that election, 'Barack Obama', a name equating to 76, will turn 59 years old, the two numbers related to the gematria of 'negro', 'blues', 'Rasta' and 'slave', and reminding us further that Obama became the 44th President, 44 years after the Civil Rights Act of 1964, running on 'hope', a word equating to 44 and 64, and having the full name, 'Barack Hussein Obama', equating to 64, the same as 'Civil Rights'. And for one more 44, 'cigarettes' equates to 44 with Pythagorean, reminding us of the coordinates of Minneapolis, and the age of Officer Chauvin- 44 and 44, as well as the fact that it was reported Obama smoked. You should also know that there is another important cipher that I have not yet taught you, called Septenary, and in that cipher, 'African American' sums to 44, shedding light on why the number has been so persistent throughout black history. If you would like to learn the cipher, it is located for free on my website GematriaEffect.news, along with all the other ciphers you have learned about in this book. You can also read my first book, where I educate about the relevance of the Septenary cipher, one worth knowing, but not necessary.

Moving on and further connecting the dots between George Floyd's killing and Eric Garner's, was the ritualistic use of the number 99, a number that when written out, is not all that different than 44, and strangely enough, when you write out 'forty four', it has gematria of 99. More importantly, you'll recall, the officer who is said to have killed Eric Garner with a chokehold in 2014 was wearing a t-shirt with a giant number 99 on the back. If you have forgotten this fact, the image is easily searched for in the information age, and it is also documented in my first book. As for the symbolism of 99, let us begin with the word 'racism', equating to 99 with Reverse Simple, the same as the surname 'Garner'. Let us also recall that 'The United States of America', a nation where we've been reminded about racism for all of our lives, was named as such on September 9th, emphasis on 9/9, and also has a gematria value of 99. And in the case of Eric Garner, he was killed in 'Tompkinsville, Staten Island', equating to 99 with Pythagorean Gematria, whereas George Floyd was choked to death in front of a 'Cup Foods', equating to 99 with Simple English. Furthermore, through much of the video showing Floyd's demise, you can see the gas station across the street, and on the fuel price board, you can clearly see that they are selling coffee for $0.99, something I would otherwise say was a coincidence.

Building on the riddle of number 99, two days after the video of George Floyd's death was shown on the nightly news, there was an updated story, showing the 'AutoZone' in Minneapolis burning. Not by chance, 'AutoZone' equates to 99, and if you go back and look carefully at the footage and images presented in the mainstream, the words "Autonomous Zone" were spray painted on the outside of the AutoZone structure that burned, days before the "Autonomous Zone" was launched in Seattle, Washington, in response to the George Floyd killing. That area was created reportedly after the police abandoned their precinct on June 8, 2020, in 'Capitol Hill', right next to one of the nation's limited Jesuit universities, Seattle University. That's something we'll touch on more ahead. And equally as important, in the wake of Michael Brown's death, the first thing to burn in the Ferguson riot was an auto parts store as well. It speaks to symbolism, and history repeating itself, by the numbers.

Back on the subject of number 99, it was no accident that boxing superstar, Floyd Mayweather, on his 99th day of his age, June 1, 2020, paid for the funeral of George Floyd, having been born February 24, 1977. And don't overlook the fact that his birthday is the 55th day of the year, the same day the Kobe Bryant memorial took place, reminding us of the Boule and 55. Furthermore, 'Mayweather' equates to 52, the same as 'Minnesota' and 'I can't breathe'. Beyond that, he was 43 years old at the time, and the name 'George Floyd' sums to 43, same as 'pandemic', and 'civil war', the latter being a topic just ahead, when we get to the new number 43 car in NASCAR, the 'Black Lives Matter' car, that debuted on June 10th, a very specific date to the ritual at hand. And for another number 99 in the world of sports and pertaining to the ritual, 'Drew Brees', equating to 99 with Simple English, received ample criticism in the wake of George Floyd's death, for offering a counter perspective to the Black Lives Matter movement's. Keep in mind he plays for the New Orleans Saints, the most Catholic team in the NFL in terms of symbolism, and also reminding us that his coach Sean Payton caught the coronavirus, by the numbers, as we covered. Let us not forget 'football' equates to 43, tying in with 'pandemic', also equating to 43. At the same time, Drew Brees ended up apologizing for his remarks on June 3rd, 99 days before the scheduled start of the NFL season, September 10th. In light of the date of apology, keep in mind 'racism' equates to 63 and 99, and 'New Orleans Saints' sums to 63 with Pythagorean, similar to June 3rd, or 6/3. For another 99, on May 31st and June 1st of 2020, curfews were being installed across the United States because of the protesting, looting, and rioting that was taking place, and those dates fell on the 99 year anniversary of the Tulsa Race Riots, that lasted from May 31st through June 1st, 1921. What made the ritual impressive, is that Tulsa is in 'Oklahoma', a state having gematria of 76 and 31 in the exact same ciphers as 'curfew', and May 31, 2020, when the curfews were beginning nationwide, was a date with 76 numerology, plus being the 31st day of the month. Furthermore, 'Tulsa, Oklahoma' alone equates to 76. And even further, 'Tulsa Race Riots' equates to 181, the same as 'Memorial Day', which again, is the 42nd prime number, and the date George Floyd was reportedly killed. And if you recall the recent killing of Terrence Crutcher by police, September 16, 2016, in Tulsa, Oklahoma, you learned the story of the 'Crutcher Twins', equating to 181, the 42nd prime number. At the same time, the surname 'Crutcher' alone sums to 42 with Pythagorean, the number stamped on black history, and equating with 'twin'.

Thus, there can be no doubt the Crutcher Twins story, part of the same contrived mainstream news cycle that gave us the killing of George Floyd in the Twin Cities, in the time of Gemini, the Twins, on 'Memorial Day', was part of the ongoing script, leading up to the moment where we now are. This is proven further with the following facts. September 16th, the date of the Crutcher killing, is the 259th day of the year, corresponding with the gematria of 'Black Lives Matter', as well as 'Roman Catholicism', the latter being who is behind this purposeful divide and conquer agenda. At the same time, September 16th leaves 106 days left in the year, a number that matters for many reasons, including the gematria of 'prophecy', equating to 106 with Simple English- once again reminding us of *Acts 7:6*. For another connection to 106, 'Greenwood' sums to 106, and that is the neighborhood that was attacked during the Tulsa Race Riots of 1921, that began May 31, 1921, a date with 76 numerology. Then beyond that, 'I can't breathe', 'Black Lives Matter' and 'black' itself each sum to 106 with the base ciphers. Beyond that, 'NASCAR' sums to 56 and 106, the same as 'Black Lives Matter', and on June 10, 2020, or 10/6, like 106, a date with 56 numerology as well, NASCAR debuted the number 43 car, the 'Black Lives Matter' car, while also announcing that the Confederate Flag was no longer allowed at the races, something we'll touch on more ahead when we discuss the significance of 'Confederate' and 'George Perry Floyd' both equating to 201. For now, don't forget that both 'George Floyd' and 'Civil War' equate to 43, what is the 14th prime number, taking us back to 2014, the year Eric Garner and 'Michael Brown', the latter being another name equating to 201, were both killed in incidents related to race and authority. And of course, 'slave' equates to 14 with Pythagorean.

On the subject of 106, contrived prophecy, and the Jesuits pulling the strings, I should mention the July 17, 2020 death of C.T. Vivian, at age 95, the civil rights leader who served with Martin Luther King Jr., the man who was assassinated on the 95th day of 1968, and a man easily confused with Martin Luther, who wrote the 95 *Theses*, against the Catholic Church, leading the Protestant Reformation, and causing the creation of the Jesuit Order. And it is interesting to note that Vivian was just 43 years old on the date of April 4, 1968, the date of King's end. As for Vivian's connection to the number 106, he was born 'Cordy Tindell Vivian', equating to 106, the same 'as 'Black Lives Matter' and 'black'. And for another 106, it was around this same time, Joe Biden, on July 20, 2020, what is the 201st day of the year in most years, announced he would be naming "one of four black women" for his Vice President running mate, a date that was 106 days prior to the November 3rd election. And since Vivian died on July 17th, or 17/7, corresponding with 'The Jesuit Order', it is important to note that he is remembered for being one of the Freedom Riders in the U.S. civil rights movement, a movement that began on May 4th, emphasis on 5/4, like 54, the 'Jesuit Order' number, and in the year 1961, the 100 year anniversary of the Civil War. For his efforts, he was offed on the same date Catherine the Great's husband was in history, and what happened to be a date with numerology of 28, 44 and 64, as well as being the 17th of the month, where the gematria of 'kill' equates to 17, 28, 44 and 64. At the same time, it is said that Vivian began his civil rights campaign in 1947, 17 years before 1964. Furthermore, 'civil rights' equates to 64, and he died in Atlanta, Georgia, the current home of the Boule, on the 64th day of the Boule's age, having originally been established May 15, 1904, meaning they turned 116 years old. Not by chance, 'C.T. Vivian' sums to both 116 and 100, the same as 'African American'. For another, 'Barack Hussein Obama' equates to 64 and 116, and of course, Obama was elected as number 44, 44 years after the Civil Rights Act, while running on 'hope', equating to 44 and 64 as well. Better yet, Obama nominated C.T. Vivian for the Presidential Medal of Freedom in 2013, and Vivian died 13 days before his 96th birthday, July 30, 2020. I doubt it is an accident, because he received the medal November 20, 2013, a date with 44 and 64 numerology, and the day leaving 41 days left in the year, the 13th prime number.

Then on the back of C.T. Vivian's death, on the very same day, July 17th, the one with the 'kill' numerology as well as 'civil rights' numerology, it was reported that civil rights leader and U.S. Congressional Rep. John Lewis of 'Georgia', the same state the Boule is now headquartered in, a state equating to 44, had died at age 80. As we know, 'Boule' sum to 80, and Martin Luther King Jr., from Georgia and a member of the Boule, died 80 days after his birthday, on April 4th, or 4/4. Adding insult to injury, Lewis died 147 days after his February 21, 2020 birthday, and both 'conspiracy' and 'Freemason' equate to 147. At the same time, the White House has 147 windows on it, and both 'U.S. President' and 'President of the United States' equate to 147, and July 17th, the date of John Lewis' death, was 33 days after Trump's 74th birthday on June 14th, and for one more 33, John Lewis had become a congressional representative in 1987, 33 years earlier. Just ahead, we'll get to how these numbers come together in another important pattern with the killing of Rayshard Brooks on June 12, 2020 in Atlanta, the date that was the 147th day of Atlanta Mayor Bottoms' age, having been born January 18, 1970. This stat is very important because 'police' sums to 147 with Jewish Gematria and 612 with Reverse Sumerian, the latter being similar to the date of the shooting, June 12th, or 6/12, as well as the Minneapolis area code, (612), and also having happened in the city known as 'ATL', equating to 33 (1+20+12), on the 33rd Parallel North, and where 'police' sums to 33 with Pythagorean. Then right on script, on June 14th, Trump's 74th birthday, Mayor Bottoms', from the 33rd Parallel, called on 'police' reform, echoing the 'I can't breathe' marchers, but then at the same time, days later, made it mandatory for people in her city to wear masks outside, a city known for heat and humidity. That order from Bottoms came on July 8th, or 7/8, reminding us that 'Jesuit' sums to 78, and so does 'Wuhan Coronavirus'- plus, George Floyd was born October 14th, the day leaving 78 days left in the year, a number also corresponding with the gematria of 'order out of chaos', exactly what was taking place, with the puppet politicians doing their part. It's also important to note that her order came two days after she tested positive for coronavirus, on July 6, 2020, a date reminding us of *Acts 7:6*, and a date that can be written 6/7, like 67, corresponding with the gematria of 'Mayor Bottoms' as well as 'Wuhan'. And please don't overlook that her birthday can be written 18/1, like 181, or that 'Houston, Texas', Floyd's hometown equates to 181. And to think, they're all new storylines for 'black history', also equating to 181.

For another 106 parallel, we have discussed the death of Naya Rivera in light of the riddles connecting Maeve Kennedy and Eminem, the latter being a Detroit rapper, the same as Big Sean, who used to be in a relationship with 'Naya Rivera'. I bring these points up because Naya Rivera died on Big Sean's 106th day of his age, a man born March 25, 1988. When you consider that she drowned, and 'drowned' equates to 106, the same as the phrase 'I can't breathe', you see how the ritual comes together, especially since on the day of the news of her disappearance, Eminem put out the new song criticizing those who weren't wearing masks in the time of coronavirus- *and wearing a mask makes it harder to breathe, especially in the summer. To further remind of the parallels between the rituals over the years, both the names 'Naya Marie Rivera' and 'Rodney Glen King' equate to 79, the 22nd prime, and both people drowned, Naya at age 33, Rodney at age 47. Furthermore, 'Naya', 'Rodney' and 'water' each equate to 22 and 67, showing in part, why they were chosen for these water rituals. And where the news of 33 year old Naya's disappearance was July 9th, or 7/9, Rodney King, the man beaten on March 3rd, or 3/3, had his death announced on June 17, 2012, a date that three years later, June 17,

2015, would become the date of the Charleston Church shooting, blamed on Dylan Storm Roof, and where in the televised aftermath, a big red firetruck pulled up and parked in front of the church with the number 106 on it, and I pointed out that day, the ongoing pattern with 106 and contrived prophecy, and that there could be no doubt it was a tribute to the 16th Street Baptist Church Bombing, that happened September 15, 1963, a date with 106 numerology. Thus, what seems arbitrary, and separate, is not, but instead, is holistic, which is what the Jesuits promote to market their educational offerings, holistic learning. Little do most of their students know however, how this "holistic" worldview is being utilized by some of their teachers, in a very demented way. *On June 24, 2020, the 106th day of the pandemic, Covid-19 vaccine testing began on 'black' Africans.

For one more point on Naya Rivera's drowning, which will help us understand how history repeats itself, and also transitions us into the topic at hand, George Floyd, it was compared to the drowning of Natalie Wood on November 29, 1981, a little more than 38 years earlier, the number connected to 'death'. To add to the list, 'drowned' equates to 38 with Pythagorean and Natalie Wood was born July 20th, in the year 1938. And as we covered earlier, Naya Rivera's death connected very heavily with the code of the Jesuit Order, being presumed dead on July 9th, the 191st day of 2020, and a date with 56 numerology, as well as being 187 days before her 34th birthday, January 12, 2021, because 'Society of Jesus' equates to 56, 79, 187 and 191. And with regards to 191, from Rivera's birthday, January 12th, to Wood's birthday, July 20th, is a span of 191 days in 2020. At the same time 'The Jesuit Order' sums to 177 and 201, and from Natalie Wood's birthday on July 20th, to what would be Rivera's next birthday, is 177 days, plus as we know, July 20th, the anniversary of the moon landing, is the 201st day of the year. And let us not forget that July 20th is in the time of cancer, and cancer is ruled by the moon, and cancer is a water symbol, adding to the relevance of Naya Rivera drowning July 8th, 2020, in the time of cancer, and also a cancer like Natalie Wood, drowning. Furthermore, the father of Naya Rivera's child, Ryan Dorsey, celebrated his birthday on July 19, 2020, the 201st day of the leap year. And further connecting the ritual to the Jesuits, his name, 'Ryan Dorsey', equates to 144 and 54 in the same ciphers as 'Jesuit Order', similar to how Naya Rivera played the part of 'Santana Lopez' in *Glee*, equating to 144 as well. Also, let us not forget what we learned earlier, about the parallels between the "Glee curse" and the

"Kennedy curse", and the deaths of Maeve Kennedy and Naya Rivera, where 'Kennedy curse' equates to 144 and 54 as well.

With regards to 177 and 201, and further connecting the dots between George Floyd in 2020, and Eric Garner and Michael Brown in 2014, was the story released by the mainstream media in the wake of George Floyd's killing, about the assault of 'Lamar Ferguson' in 2014, by Minneapolis Police Officer, Tou Thao. Keep in mind, Ferguson, Missouri is where Michael Brown was reportedly killed in 2014. As for this more recent story, it emerged in the international news almost as fast as the George Floyd killing video went viral. If you forget who Tou Thao was, he was the asian officer, standing between the person filming the George Floyd scene, and the officers on top of George Floyd. In regards to the Lamar Ferguson story, where he retells his tale from 2014, the DailyMail had 'punched and kicked him until his teeth broke' emphasized in headlines, equating to 177 and 201. The phrase was in regards to what Officer Thao allegedly did to 'Lamar Ferguson', a name also equating to 201, back in 2014. The reason we can be certain the encoding of these numbers is no accident, is because once again, in 2014, Eric Garner was killed on July 17th, or 17/7, and 'Michael Brown' equates to 201, and those two events sparked the movement that is 'Black Lives Matter', equating to 56, the same as 'Society of Jesus'- and once again, it is coming to power 56 years after the 1964 Civil Rights Act, in 2020. And for the record, as most people know, the 1964 Act was nothing but symbolism, unlike the war on drugs, which is part of the 19 year cycles, that has devastated black communities, by design. The same is also true of Black Lives Matter, a movement that has black people targeting their own communities, only helping further the same stereotypes that the mainstream media has assigned to black people for all of their lives- that is they're criminal, violent, immoral, etc., all of which are false.

To build on our list of 201 connections, the mother of George Floyd's child, Gianna, was reported to be 'Roxie Washington', equating to 201 in Simple English, and also 78 and 84 with the Pythagorean ciphers, all of which are numbers pointing back to the Jesuits. Furthermore, George Floyd's international traveling basketball team paid tribute to his passing on their website. They were the 'TGBTG Quest Team' out of Houston, equating to 177 and 201. If you take the time to look up the team's page, you will notice their logo is a basketball with a cross on it, with the letters 'TGBTG' beneath the ball, letters equating to 56 and 79, the same as 'Society of Jesus'. It reminds me that Manly P. Hall wrote the United States of America was truly founded by a secret society called the 'Order of the Quest', equating to both 79 and 74, the latter reminding us that the George Floyd story came during the time of the 74th NBA season. It also of reminds us of 'The Black Mamba', equating to 79, and Robert Rodriguez, equating to 201, the director of the short film that foretold Kobe Bryant's death. And in that breath, while remembering the Lakers are originally from Minneapolis, I encourage you to look up the image used by mainstream media of the unnamed Minneapolis protester shown across all major networks, sporting a purple and gold Lakers jacket, while holding a sign, 'Justice for George Floyd' in front of Cup Foods, equating to not only 322, but also 106 and 110, the latter two numbers connecting to 'prophecy', and the last connecting to 'Minnesota'. Also, with regards to 106, it was for this reason that on June 10th, or 10/6, headlines were run in Houston saying that there could soon be the 'George Floyd Sports Complex' named in his honor. Personally, that reminds me of how they opened up the musician Prince's home in Chanhassen, Minnesota, as a museum, on the date of October 6, 2016, emphasis on 10/6. If you look back, you'll see the announcement about the October 6th opening came on August 24, 2016, the first ever Kobe Bryant Day, and it was noted the museum would be maintained by the same organization that takes care of Graceland, Elvis Presley's estate. And on the subject of the 106 like date, October 6th, if you listened to Prince in his last interview with Tavis Smiley, he said, "all we can go by now is prophecy." Keep in mind Prince had a June 7th birthday, a date that can be written 7/6, similar to *Acts 7:6*, and he was speaking on how sour the times were when he made the remark, noting that people didn't even recognize what was right before their eyes, the chemical trails in the skies above. If you're not familiar with Prince's remarks on Tavis Smiley's show, it is an audio clip you should seek out.

For another important thought, regarding the encoding of 322 in the sign paying tribute to George Floyd, a man killed in 'Minnesota', the land of 'prophecy', Prince's home state, and in light of the significance of 76, 'Skull and Bones' equates to 76, the secret society that identifies by the number 322. And with Prince in mind, please recall that he died at age 57, corresponding with the gematria of 'George' and 'Gemini', and further, from the anniversary of his death,

April 21st, to Floyd's death, May 25th, is 34 days later. This matters because 'Prince' equates to 34, the same as 'murder'. Beyond that, 'Prince' equates to 65, the same as 'George Floyd', and the musician's name also sums to 38, the same as 'Minnesota' and reminding us of 38th Street. The name Prince also equates to 97, the 25th prime number, corresponding with how George Floyd was killed on the 25th of May and 'death' equates to 97 and 25. That's also the reason why when Maeve Kennedy and her son were found dead on the 97th day of the year, April 6, 2020, it was reported they were found beneath 25 feet of water, in 'Shady Side, Maryland', a town equating to 97. Let us not forget their death was blamed on a 'canoe' accident, a word equating to 97 and 25, or how the riddle relates to Eminem, a.k.a. Slim Shady.

Back on the subject of 201, days after the killing of George Floyd, on May 30, 2020, it was reported that a "white bar owner" killed a "black George Floyd protester" named 'James Scurlock', a name equating to 42, 84, 150 and 201 with the base ciphers. As you know, 42, 84 and 201 connect to the Jesuits, and in the case of 150, it connects to May 30th being the 150th day of the year in non leap years, and it also connects to the gematria of 'Illuminati', reminding us that the Illuminati was established by the Jesuit, Adam Weishaupt, May 1, 1776, a date with 99 numerology, one of the more important numbers in the George Floyd ritual, and being the number connecting the ritual of Eric Garner and George Floyd directly. As for the Scurlock killing, it happened in 'Omaha', equating to 38, connecting to 'death', and where George Floyd died, 38th Street. Even further, 'Omaha, Nebraska' equates to 46, and 'Nebraska' alone sums to 26, numbers connecting to George Floyd, as well as the words 'riot' and 'chaos', words that defined the moment of Saturday, May 30th, 2020, in the wake of the May 26th George Floyd video.

As for arguably the most important 201 riddle in the George Floyd killing, was the killing of Adama Traore in Paris, France, also by police, the original home of the Jesuits, on July 19, 2016, the 201st day of the leap year. After the news of George Floyd's death, a death that came exactly a span of 201 weeks from the killing of Adama Traore, a protest was scheduled for Paris, France, for the date of June 1, 2020, to honor the names of both men. Of course in 'France', they chose a date with 47 numerology, and notice that same date, June 1st, can be written 1/6, not unlike 16, reminding us that Washington D.C., the "Land of 47" and the city laid out by the French Freemason L'Enfant, made 16th

312

Street, Black Lives Matter Plaza, four days later, on June 5th. At the same time, the 106 gematria of 'Black Lives Matter', reminds us of the 16th Street Church Bombing, September 15, 1963, a date with 106 numerology, and the fact that 16th Street in D.C. is known as 'Church Row', equating to 54, like 'Jesuit Order', in the Jesuit city. Even further, the official name given to the road on June 5th, was 'Black Lives Matter Plaza', equating to 76, the same as 'Floyd the Land Lord' and the list of related words equating to 76, including 'slave' and 'negro'. And let us not forget the Million Man March, October 16th, 1995, the day leaving 76 days in the year. And for another riddle, from 1963 to 2020, is 57 years later, corresponding with the gematria of 'George' and 'Georgetown', the latter being the Jesuit University established in 1789, the year George Washington, the slave owner, turned 57 years old- the same man the city is named after.

The other 201 ritual that was a real smack in the face, was when Steve Mnuchin announced in the days before the George Floyd killing, that the Federal Reserve would not be debuting the new Harriet Tubman $20 bill as planned, and instead, were pushing the date back 8 years, to 2028. For starters, this mattered because George Floyd was arrested for using a counterfeit $20 bill, a fitting detail for 2020. And for some gematria, 'Harriet Tubman' sums to 201 and 84 in the same ciphers as 'The Jesuit Order'. Beyond that, she was a member of the 'Underground Railroad', equating to 102 in Pythagorean, the same as 'George Perry Floyd', and 102 is a number that reminds us the U.S. Civil War began April 12, 1861, the 102nd day of the year. Speaking of which, from the painting of Black Lives Matter on 16th Street in Washington D.C. on June 5, 2020, to September 15, 2020, the upcoming 57th anniversary of the 16th Street Church bombing, is precisely 102 days later. And let us not forget of *'Art of War'*, the Jesuit translated text, summing to 102, and reminding us of the 102 minute long 9/11 attack, an incident having clear parallels with George Floyd, as we covered. In that breath, let us not overlook that 'civil war' and 'George Floyd' both equate to 119 with Simple English. And in case you're not familiar with the Underground Railroad, it was a system for slaves to escape their bondage, connecting to the fact that both the words 'slavery' and 'nigger' equate to 102. It was for this same reason, on June 4, 2020, 102 days after the killing of Ahmaud Arbery on February 23rd, a story released that he had been called a 'nigger' in the video captured just before his execution.

If you go back and check, you'll see the news of the $20 Harriet Tubman bill delay was published in the New York Times and the rest of mainstream media on May 22, 2020, even though Mnuchin had made the announcement days before that. This date can be expressed as 22/5, and this matters because it was reported George Floyd was born October 14, 1973, meaning he was killed on his 225th day of his age. Adding to the riddle, on May 27th, national headlines emerged that a Minnesota Catholic diocese was to pay $22.5-million to sexual assault victims. For another familiar number, it was 'The Diocese of Saint Cloud' paying the settlement, equating to 119. In light of 'George Perry Floyd' equating to 201, let us not forget that Event 201 was advertised as being 3 hours and 45 minutes long, which is what it ended up running, and that is precisely 225 minutes. Let us also not forget that the related simulations, Event 201 and Clade X, the latter coming 666 days before the pandemic was declared, involved scenarios of civil unrest, protesting, rioting and "violent police crackdowns." As for the number 225, it gains its significance through a couple of related things. First, it is the 'Trinitarian Formula', equating to 93 with Pythagorean, the same as 'Minneapolis, Minnesota'. The Trinitarian Formula is something you have likely heard spoken before, "In the name of the Father, and the Son, and the Holy Spirit", a saying equating to 225 with Pythagorean. The other 225 connection, and the one that should make you really take notice, is the phrase 'The Great Tribulation', equating to 225 with Simple English. This is what Jesus said would be the name for the period of time before the end, where the world would befall many consequences. The Great Tribulation also involves the period of time described in *Revelation*, where people are being forced to take the mark of the beast if they want to buy or sell, and by the way, 'mark of the beast' equates to 144 and 54 in the same ciphers as 'Jesuit Order'. At the same time, I should note Kobe Bryant died January 26, 2020, a span of 121 days from the death of George Floyd, May 25, 2020, and in addition to L.A. being 12.1., *'Revelation'* equates to 121- and let us not forget the Kobe Bryant centered cartoon that foreshadowed his death in a 'helicopter', equating to 666, wast titled *End of Days*. I should also remind us, in light of Kobe Bryant scoring 81 points in his 666th game, not only does 'Kobe Bean Bryant' equate to 54 and 81, so does 'Mark of the Beast' in the same ciphers. Think about it, and don't forget both men had a daughter named Gianna. Parallels. And I haven't even mentioned that

'Gianna' sums to 35 and 46, the same as 'Catholic', or 116, like 'African American' and the Jesuit motto, 'Ad maiorem Dei gloriam'.

Speaking of basketball, the Jesuits and 225, on May 22, 2020, or 22/5, it was reported that Patrick Ewing, the Georgetown basketball legend, tested positive for coronavirus. And let us not forget the death of 'Adolfo Nicolas', equating to 225, the former Superior General of the Jesuits, who died May 20th, 2020, the day leaving 225 days in the year. As for Patrick Ewing, it wasn't by chance that he was 57 years old at the time of the news, because as you'll recall, 'Georgetown' equates to 57, the same as 'Scottish Rite', and it was established 1789, the same year George Washington turned 57 years old- plus 'George' sums to 57 with Simple English. To go even further, 'Patrick Ewing' sums to 71, the same as 'Catholic', the 20th prime number, tying in with 2020, and the fact that the "coronavirus pandemic" was declared March 11, 2020, the 71st day of the leap year, essentially cancelling 'March Madness', another 71, and suspending the NBA season. It also reminds us the Church bought Washington D.C. in 1871. And adding to the ritual even further, the news came 75 days before Patrick Ewing's 58th birthday on August 5th, and 'Catholic Church' sums to 75.

With Georgetown on your mind, think about this as well. If I say "Georgia and George" in relation to this story, what pops into your mind? For me it is the release of the Ahmaud Arbery killing video on May 5th, or 5/5, in Georgia, and then the killing of George Floyd in 'Minneapolis', equating to 55, and then the June 12th killing of Rayshard Brooks in Atlanta, Georgia, emphasis on the date 6/12, after the killing of George Floyd in Minneapolis, home of the (612) area code, and then the burning of the Wendy's on June 13th in Atlanta where Rayshard Brooks was reportedly killed, which was the day leaving 201 days left in the year.

If you look at the details of these three stories more carefully, you'll notice the fingerprints of the Jesuits all over them. For example, it was reported that 'Ahmaud Arbery', equating to 54 and 72 in the same ciphers as 'Jesuit Order', was killed on February 23, 2020, 72 days before the release of the video on May 5th, a fitting date because 'video' sums to 55 with Simple English. Then on May 7th, 74 days after the 'killing', where 'killing' equates to 74, the father and son responsible for the murder of Arbery were arrested. If you think about the riddle, it involves the "father and the son", and the man who is now

315

just a "spirit"… and I am assuming you recall the connection to 'Jesus' and the number 74. *Forgive me father if you don't!*

Now for a bit more on the number 72, in the wake of the killing of 27 year old Rayshard Brooks in Atlanta, it was the 'Wendy's' that burned, and the name of the restaurant equates to 72 as well as 27. In light of 27 being the reflection of 72, keep in mind both the words 'race' and 'racism' equate to 27, and that is what these stories were centered on. Furthermore, the 27th book of the New Testament is *Revelation,* and when the Wendy's burned on June 13th 2020, a date with 59 numerology, corresponding with the gematria of both 'Atlanta, Georgia' and *'Revelation',* both equating to 59, that was Georgia Governor Brian Kemp's 225th day of his age, having been born November 2, 1963. As you have learned, this has to do with 'The Great Tribulation', part of prophecy, connecting to *Acts 7:6,* and it was for this reason that on July 6th, or 7/6, the same day Mahomes signed for $400 plus million, Brian Kemp deployed the 'National Guard', equating to 56 like 'Black Lives Matter', to Atlanta, Georgia, to deal with the ongoing protests and the protesters. Keep in mind Brian Kemp's announcement was 247 days after his birthday, and out of all the major cities in the U.S. nation, the only two equating to 247 are 'Atlanta, Georgia', the home of the CDC, that turned 74 on July 1, 2020, and 'Seattle, Washington', where the virus arrived in January, and where big tech companies have taken over the city in recent years and benefited from the pandemic, tremendously, especially Amazon, led by Jeff Beezos, the Vatican stooge. And on the subject of 247, July 21, 2020 marked 247 years since the Jesuits were suppressed by Pope Clement XIV, on July 21, 1773.

As for June 13th, the day leaving 201 days left in the year, it was also the date Stacey Abrams, who lost the rigged election to Kemp, spoke out about the shooting of Rayshard Brooks and against police brutality, and not by chance, her media moment came precisely 187 days after her 46th birthday, on December 9, 2019. *If you have read my first book, where I reveal a few additional ciphers, you know how 'Fraternal Order of Police' equates to 187. To be quick about it, if you use the master numerology of the letters in Reverse Pythagorean, that is where the name equates to 187. To be clear, the only difference is you don't reduce the master letters with the Pythagorean Methods, so in the case of Fraternal Order of Police, the letter 'p' would be worth 11 and the letter 'e' would be worth 22, as opposed to 2 and 4 respectively. The same is also true with Pythagorean, where 'k' becomes worth 11 and 'v' becomes worth 22, as opposed to 2 and 4 respectively. And as a reminder, these rules are not necessary, but they do provide additional understanding, and with that said, they can also be abused, so please, stick to the four base ciphers, until you feel you have really gained a strong grasp of those, because they are more than enough to prove the points that need to be proven.

Another important detail to keep in mind about Governor Kemp's ordering of the National Guard to Atlanta on July 6th, is that he is the 83rd Governor, and on the same day of his order, 83 year old musician Charlie Daniels died, of course an age connecting to the gematria of 'murder'. Furthermore, it was reported Charlie Daniels died from a 'hemorrhagic stroke', equating 193 and 94 in the same way as 'Roman Catholic Church', and 266 in the same way as 'Iesus Hominum Salvator'. The reason Daniels death appears to be connected to the governor's orders, is because Daniels had the song *The Devil Went Down to Georgia*, which released in history on May 21, 1979, a standout year, and the anniversary of its release was 46 days before the National Guard was deployed to quell the 'chaos' in Atlanta, Georgia, in the wake of the killing of 46 year old George Floyd, from 'Houston, Texas', and the ongoing protests fueled by the deaths of Ahmaud Arbery and Rayshard Brooks. In regards to the latter death, if you research, you'll find that it was the 43rd minute of being interviewed by the Atlanta police, per the body camera footage, that the deadly confrontation began, and in addition to 'George Floyd' equating to 43, again, so does 'masonic', 'killing', 'police man' and 'civil war'. Even further, Abraham Lincoln, the U.S. Civil War president, was born on the 43rd day of the year, and Obama, who carried his legacy, became the 43rd person to be President of the United States of America. As for the civil war pattern with Ahmaud Arbery, he was killed in 'Brunswick, Georgia', equating to 97, the same as 'civil war' with Simple English. And on the subject of 'civil war', you should know that with the base ciphers it equates to 43, 56, 97 and 119, and at this point you should know how to connect each number to the greater George Floyd ritual. If you a need another reminder, 'George Floyd' equates to 43 and 119, 'Black Lives Matter' equates to 56, and 97 is the 25th prime number, where George Floyd died on the 25th of May, and 'death' equates to 25 and 97, similar to 'Omaha', where James Scurlock died, while protesting George Floyd's name, a town equating to 20, 25, 38 and 97- identical to 'death'. And whatever you do, especially if you're trying to explain this to people, don't forget the 'NASCAR' example with the Black Lives Matter car, the number 43 car, on the date June 10th, or 10/6, with the 56 date numerology, where on the same day, they banned the Confederate Flag, the symbol of the U.S. Civil War for the South, and how this happened one day before the stock market fell 1861 points, proving just how contrived every last detail in the mainstream is. Again, the Civil War began in 1861 and Lincoln was shot at the end of war in a Jesuit plot, by John Surratt, in a theater. And for the record, the date of that symbolic fall in DowJones points was June 11th, or 11/6, like how 'country' sums 116, the same as 'autonomous', a word meaning to be self governing, as the Confederate states once fought to be in the Civil War. Of course, it was June 11th that the national coverage of the Autonomous Zone in Seattle began, which was three days after it was started. In other words, The Cabal was once again communicating their intentions, through ritual, to divide we the people.

It is for this reason, I have a dream, that the knowledge within the pages of this book will reach the world, and this nonsense will be brought to an end. And as I echo the words of Martin Luther King Jr., who asked for the end of The Cabal on April 4, 1967, a year to the day of his assassination, I should point out that national headlines on June 23, 2020 brought attention to the fact that 'Rayshard Brooks', having gematria overlap with 'Number of the Beast' in three out of four ciphers, had his funeral at the same church 'MLK' spoke at, a man remembered by an acronym that equates to 36 with Simple English, connecting to the fact that 666 is the 36th triangular number. Keep in mind 'Charlie Daniels' is also identical to 'number of the beast' in three out of four ciphers, and he died exactly 36 weeks after his 83rd day birthday, October 28, 2019, the same birthday as Bill Gates, who has a full name, 'William Henry Gates', also equating to 'number of the beast'. Of course, Daniels became part of the riddle thanks to dying at age 83 on the same day the 83rd Governor of Georgia deployed the National Guard to Atlanta, to extinguish the protests.

As for another part of the country protesting George Floyd's death, as well as the deaths of Breonna Taylor and David McAtee, that was 'Louisville', equating to 62 and 46, the latter like 'chaos' and 'ordo ab chao'. Of course, it is the hometown of 'Muhammad' Ali who died at age 74, and where 'Muhammad' equates to 74,

'Muhammad Ali' equates to 201, reminding us that the TV show *South Park* deleted the episode called "201" from their archives, because it was found to be too offensive to Muslims for how it portrayed the Prophet Muhammad, who Muhammad Ali was killed in tribute to, on June 3, 2016, as we discussed earlier. On the subject of Louisville and 'George Perry Floyd', from the killing of Breonna Taylor by Louisville Police, March 13, 2020, to the killing of George Floyd, May 25, 2020, was a span of 74 days. Not by chance, the name 'Breonna Taylor' also sums to 74, in the same cipher as 'I can't breathe'. In addition to that, her name sums to 191, the same as 'Society of Jesus'. At the same time, her killing was on a date with 56 numerology, corresponding with 'Black Lives Matter' and 'Society of Jesus', the latter being the organization name also equating to 187, and this is why on July 18th, or 18/7, the headline emerged via CNN that Breonna Taylor had lived for '5 to 6 minutes', as CNN emphasized it, after being shot. It made me wish I had Lawrence Taylor's number, so I could tell him to be safe, because you never know. Of course he is the NFL great who wore the number 56 for the New York Giants. And back on the subject of Breonna Taylor's death, March 13th can be written 3/13 as well, similar to 313, the 65th prime number, connecting back to the gematria of 'George Floyd'. Furthermore, the date can be written 13/3, like 133, equating with the gematria of 'Minnesota'. And in light of 'Muhammad Ali' being part of the riddle, keep in mind he changed his name in 1964, the year of the Civl Rights Act, 56 years prior to 2020. Furthermore, keep in mind that 'Muhammad Ali' sums to 42 with Pythagorean, and on June 1, 2020, it was reported that police killed 'David McAtee' during the protests, a Louisville restaurant owner, and a man also having a name equating to 42 with Pythagorean, the number that syncs with George Floyd being killed on 'Memorial Day', equating to 181, the 42nd prime. Also noteworthy, 'McAtee' sums to 47, the same as 'news', and he made the headlines the date of his reported killing, a date with 47 numerology. Keep in mind the number 47 also connects with 'government', as well as 'policeman' and 'cop', and the date after his death, June 2nd, or 6/2, the police chief of 'Louisville', equating to 62, was fired over the combined outcomes of the Breonna Taylor and David McAtee incidents. This was largely due to the fact the chief's officers let the body of David McAtee lay in the street for reportedly 12 hours before it was taken away, even more extreme than what happened with Michael Brown's body, the latter being a man who was loaded into the back of a police SUV, as opposed to an ambulance, after laying in the street for 4 hours, the number associated with death. Then on June 27th, the day leaving 187 days in the year, Louisville had another nationally reported incident at a protest, where 27 year old Tyler Gerth was shot to death, precisely 106 days after Breonna Taylor's death, brining us back to 'black', 'prophecy' and 'Black Lives Matter'. The shooter was reported to be 'Steven Nelson Lopez', equating to 76, and reminding us yet again of *Acts 7:6*. Furthermore, the shooting was at 'Jefferson Square Park', equating to 225, another recurring number in the related rituals, that connects directly to prophecy, as we have covered.

I should note, the name of the victim from the June 27th shooting, 'Tyler Gerth', equates to 57, the same as 'George'. In the same way his fateful headline was connected to the larger George Floyd ritual, so was the reported death of 57 year old Rev. Vickey Gibbs, on July 18, 2020, in 'Houston, Texas', equating to 181, the 42nd prime, George Floyd's hometown. On that date it was reported she had fallen victim to coronavirus and died days earlier, July 10, 2020, a date with 57 numerology, matching her age of death, 57. Even further, it was reported that she had tested positive for coronavirus just 5 days before her death, July 5th, or 5/7. Recall, 'Georgetown', equating to 57, the nation's first Jesuit university, was established the year George Washington turned 57 years old, on January 23, 1789, and keep in mind 'Rome' sums to 57. At the same time, don't forget that date can be written 23/1, like 231, the 21st triangular number, corresponding with the gematria of 'Jesuit'. In this case, the number 21 corresponds with the surname, 'Gibbs', equating to 21 with Pythagorean, the same as 'Jesuit'. Also relevant and further connecting the dots, 'George Perry Floyd' equates to 231, the 21st triangular number. In articles written about her, she was referred to as 'Rev. Vickey Gibbs', equating to 84, connecting to both 'Jesuit', as well as 'United States of America'- reminding us that this is propaganda for a nation, and part of a storyline, attempting to guide us to our self destruction. If you research the articles on her passing, you'll see all mainstream media made sure to point out that she had been a supporter of Black Lives Matter, and was an outspoken critic in the recent killings of Ahmaud Arbery and George Floyd. And to make one last point on the matter of her death, July 10th was 46 days after the killing of 46 year old George Floyd on May 25th, and as we have covered, 46 is very symbolic,

320

especially in this case, because 'Houston, Texas' equates to 46 with Pythagorean, the same as 'sacrifice'. And let us not forget *Genesis 46.*

On the subject of them tying the stories of Black Lives Matter and its 'I can't breathe' movement together with coronavirus through the story of the death of Rev. Vickey Gibbs from coronavirus, it is important to note that it was reported she was born December 1, 1962, emphasis on '62, as well as 12/1… meaning she died 222 days after her birthday, the number connecting back to 'Wuhan Coronavirus'. And with the number 222 in mind, please recall how it connects 9/11 and the coronavirus pandemic declaration 222 months later, of March 11, 2020, as well as how George Floyd fits in, in addition to the Black History Month tribute, with Patrick Mahomes of the Kansas City Chiefs helping Andy Reid win his 222nd career game in Super Bowl 54, on 'February Second', equating to 222, a date also written 2/2/2020, and coming precisely 222 weeks after the Kansas City Royals won the World Series. And let us also not forget 'baseball' equals 54, or that 'Jesuit Order' does as well. It is a number connecting details such as 'Tyler Perry', equating to 54, reportedly helping pay for the funeral of Rayshard Brooks.

As for the topic of 'coronavirus' connecting to the George Floyd story, let us not forget that on June 3, 2020, while the Global Vaccine Summit was taking place in London, there were national news headlines that George Floyd had tested positive for coronavirus. This was comical, because it was the 155th day of 2020, and 'coronavirus' sums to 155 with Simple English. It is a detail that should remind us of Clade X as well, hosted May 15th, or 15/5, that simulated massive protests and rioting, and "violent police crackdowns." Furthermore, from Floyd's May 25th death, to what would have been his upcoming birthday, October 14th, was 142 days, and 'coronavirus' also sums to 142. As we have covered, there are parallels with the George Floyd story, to the NBA, including the details of Kobe Bryant and Stephen Jackson, and as we know, the NBA season was suspended on the 142nd day of the year, before being declared to start again July 31st, 142 days later (prior to them adding a double header to the schedule for July 30th, a span of 142 days from the league suspension). Proving that the patterns are no fluke, is the fact that NASCAR returned from its coronavirus break on May 21, 2020, the 142nd day of the year, as well as the PGA charity tournament for coronavirus, the special between Tigers Woods and Phil Mickelson, where 'Tiger', equating to 201 with

Jewish Gematria, in a year of Tiger symbolism, took the winning honors, in an event called, 'The Match: Champions for Charity', equating to 142, and pairing nicely with the surname 'Mickelson', summing to 142 as well. It should be noted, that the tournament was played May 24th, 2020, what is normally the 144th day of the year, but in 2020, was the 145th, corresponding with the gematria of 'Catholic'. On the subject, Tom Brady was also a participant in the event, losing to Payton Manning, 71 days before Brady's 43rd birthday, August 3, 2020, and as we know, 'Catholic' sums to 71.

On the subject of 71, I should note that the George Floyd killing video released May 26, 2020, a date with 71 numerology. It is important to pay mind that in addition to 'Catholic', the number connects to the Pythagorean Gematria of 'African American', as well as the title of the recent film '*Birth of a Nation*', both equating to 71, and the latter supposedly being a film that made only $7.1 million at the box office in a disappointing opening weekend. Once again, that film is about Nat Turner and his life leading up to his execution, November 11, 1831, a date with 71 numerology. At the same time, the name 'Crump' equates to 71 with Simple English, the 'Boule' lawyer that was announced as George Floyd's family attorney on May 26, 2020. Then it was on May 28th, the AutoZone burned, as well as the 'Target' in Minneapolis, the latter store name equating to 71 with Simple English. Then in the aftermath of those events, footage was shown all over the news of mostly 'African American' looters, rummaging through the store, a trend that setoff a nationwide pattern of people looting Target stores, causing Target to close many of its nationwide locations temporarily. For everyone, this should have been an eye opener, because Target is headquartered in Minneapolis, and they are the sponsors for the stadiums that both the Minnesota Twins and Minnesota Timberwolves play in. With the subject of gematria aside, everyone should have asked- why attack Target if the societal response is based in being outraged by injustice caused by governments through their violent and oppressive measures? That said, I do understand big corporations have a lot to do with government wrongdoing and corruption, and in that breath, let us not forget the nation is a corporation itself, thanks to the Act of 1871.

In light of who is responsible for systemic oppression, conversations of shutting down authoritarian mechanisms did transpire in the wake of George Floyd's death, including the outright disbanding of police by cutting off all funding. This exact conversation is what reportedly lead to the "Autonomous Zone" being formed in Seattle, again, an event that was foreshadowed in Minneapolis, when images that were presented on May 28th, showed the words "Autonomous Zone" spray painted on the Minneapolis AutoZone, the same one that burned. And if you have investigated the burning of that store, you're likely aware of the man referred to in the mainstream media as "Umbrella Man", who while holding a black umbrella, and dressed in all black, including a black gas mask, carefully broke all the windows of the AutoZone, that was then set on fire soon after. Later, this same man was accused of being a police officer who worked at the nearby police precinct, just blocks from the store, an allegation the department denied. Regardless of the truth of the allegations, the ritual is clear, and it is one that reminds us of the "Umbrella Man" in the *Zapruder Film*, who is shown during the assassination of JFK in Dealey Plaza. In that parallel, let us not forget 'Dealey Plaza' equates to 54, because soon after the Minneapolis incident with Umbrella Man at the AutoZone was captured on film, Seattle's Autonomous Zone was born-on a date with 54 numerology, June 8, 2020. This happened because the Capitol Hill Police of Seattle abandoned their precinct on this date, in response to the many protesters who were demanding for police to be defunded and disbanded. In addition to the 54 date numerology, matching the Pythagorean Gematria of 54 for both 'Jesuit Order' and 'Capitol Hill', the site was formed next to Seattle University, one of the nation's 27 Jesuit universities. Also, in light of the date of formation for the Autonomous Zone, June 8, 2020, let us not overlook that it can be written 6/8, in 'Seattle, Washington', the 68 city, that is home of the construction firm that began building the World Trade Centers in 1968, in New York, New York, Amy Cooper's hometown. And because I haven't said it in some time, all of this ritual is based in 'Kabbalah', equating to 178 with Reverse Simple, the same as 'George Floyd', and 'Central Park', the latter being where Amy Cooper choked her dog on the same day George Floyd was choked to death. At the same time, I would like to remind us that 'Ancient Mystery Religions' equates to 119, the same as 'George Floyd' and 'Central Park', where Amy doesn't like to use a leash. And as if the jokes weren't already terrible enough, on June 11th, the same day the market fell 1861 points, the Autonomous Zone had risen to the top story in the nation, and it was stated on numerous cable outlets that the leader of Seattle's

Autonomous Zone, was a man named Solomon Samuel Simone, a local rapper, and the CEO of **Black Umbrella**, a company that produces music videos and other related content. Even better, his birthday was said to be January 15, 1990, meaning he turned 30 years old the same day the virus arrived in Seattle, per the official narrative. At the same time, the name 'Capitol Hill Autonomous Zone' equates to 115 with Pythagorean, what he was the "leader" of. In addition to that key detail, the entire area was spray painted with symbols ranging from umbrellas, to all seeing eyes, and where the gematria of 'all seeing eye' equates to 'Vatican', the gematria of 'Umbrella,' equates to 84 and 132, connecting the 'Catholic Church', its 'Jesuit' army, and the 'United States of America'. As for the importance of the symbolism of the 'umbrella', it is an object that can only be taken down from within, and that is a Jesuit tactic, to infiltrate other organizations, and either take them down from within, or use them to their advantage. Consider what we discussed earlier, with the "coincidences" of the *Umbrella Corp.* from the *Resident Evil* video game. And don't forget what JFK said about secrecy and infiltration either, in light of the fact that he was assassinated not long after.

With the idea of the Jesuits infiltrating other organizations, consider that at the site of Seattle's Capitol Hill Autonomous Zone, was the Odd Fellows Temple, overlooking the area, part of an organization established April 26, 1819, 201 years earlier, the number of 'The Jesuit Order', as well as the 'Order of the Illuminati'. What brings even more intrigue to this organization, is that their structure is referred to as 'Odd Fellows Hall', equating to 68, the same as 'Seattle, Washington', and reminding us of the June 8th date of establishment for the 'CHAZ', as it was called for short, having a lot to do with the gematria of 'anarchy', as well as 'pandemic', and the fact that George Floyd was killed on 38th Street. I'll let you practice and verify for yourself. At the same time, 'Odd Fellows' sums to 115 with Simple English, similar to how how 'Capitol Hill Autonomous Zone' equates to 115. With the base ciphers, 'Odd Fellows' also sums to 43, like 'George Floyd' and 'pandemic', and June 8th was precisely 43 days after their establishment date, April 26th. The name 'Odd Fellows' also sums to 47, matching Seattle's coordinate, on the 47th Parallel North, and last but not least, it also sums to 155, corresponding with 'coronavirus' and the fact that George Floyd was said to have had it on the 155th day of 2020, in the June 3rd news, courtesy of AP.

Sadly, as I predicted, the CHAZ, equating to 38 and 70, the same as 'anarchy', and having that connection to 'death' through 38, would end with a tragic death, which came on June 20th, the same date I predicted it would, because the date can be written 20/6, similar to how 'sacrifice' equates to 206 with Jewish Gematria, and Seattle is home of the (206) area code. Beyond that, it's the home of Mark Hubbard, a Freemason and a skateboarding legend in the area, who was found dead at age 47, on June 8, 2018, the day leaving 206 days in the year, a date that came two years before the establishment of the 'CHAZ'. It is a reminder rituals come annually, and when you know the numbers that pertain to your city, you can really see through local news. Case in point, the person killed on June 20th, was reported as being a "19 year old", and 'Seattle' sums to 19 with Pythagorean. Furthermore, the date of the shooting had 46 numerology, and where 'chaos' sums to 19 and 46, 'ordo ab chao' equates to 46. And for one more point on the matter, you might be asking what about the other name it was called by, the 'CHOP', standing for 'Capital Hill Occupied Protest'? I'll have you know that 'CHOP' sums to 42, the same as 'Jesuit', and the full name sums to 144, the same as 'Jesuit Order', reminding us that 'Capitol Hill' also equates to 'Jesuit Order' through 54, and the entire area was established June 8, 2020, the date with 54 numerology. Let us not forget that Washington state is the 42nd state in order of statehood, jiving with 'Georgetown', equating to 42, the first Jesuit University established in the U.S., in Washington D.C.

With regards to the significance of the number 68 to Seattle, this is why the Seattle police announced on June 22, 2020, a date with 68 numerology, they were returning to the abandoned precinct. Predictable. Also predictable, the 56th Seattle Mayor, Jenny Durkan, said on June 30, 2020, a date with 56 numerology, that everyone was to evacuate the CHAZ / CHOP, or they would be arrested on July 1, 2020, a date coming 23 days after June 8th when it began, connecting to the fact that 'end' sums to 23 with Simple English, and 'Jenny' sums to 23 with Pythagorean. I should also note that 23 is the 9th prime number, and the number 9 represents completion.

On the subject of the 56th Mayor of Seattle, Jenny Durkan, there is something important that must be said. It is proof she is part of the 'cult' that is responsible for so much of the wrongdoing we're undressing in this book. And as we look at the evidence of her attachment to the cult, keep in mind that The Cabal she serves, has much to do with the existence of the big tech companies in Seattle, Washington, that are also some of the biggest beneficiaries of the "pandemic," and could be described as the leaders of the technocratic take over. Again, Amazon is led by 56 year old Jeff Beezos (at the time of the pandemic), and Google is led by Mr. 201, 'Sundar Pichai', and Microsoft is the brainchild of 'William Henry Gates', another Mr. 201. As for the proof of her being in the 'cult', a word equating to 56, it came on June 11, 2020, when she made a remark about the 'Summer of Love' while referencing what was taking place in her city's Autonomous Zone, a phrase equating to 56, in a CNN interview with 'Chris Cuomo', a name equating to 56 and not to mention a person who was a main part of the daily CNN news cycle after he caught the flu, or I mean 'coronavirus', equating to 56- and who so just happens to be the brother of the 56th Governor of New York, Andrew Cuomo, the most covered governor in the nation in the time of the "pandemic." What made her 'Summer of Love' remark all the more bizarre, was the national reporting on July 4, 2020, the nation's birthday, that in Seattle, Washington, women with the names Summer Taylor and Diaz Love, had been fatally injured in a car crash at a Black Lives Matter related protest. There ages were reported as 24 and 32 respectively, thus adding up to 56, and reminding us that not only does 'Society of Jesus', equate to 56, but their symbol is 'the sun', equating to 24, and in their illustration of the sun with the 'three' nails, the sun has 32 rays comings off of it. For another miraculous catch, and more 'Jesuit Order' fingerprints, where their name sums to 72, 144 and 153, 'Summer Taylor' equates to 72, 144 and 153, the woman who died soon after the news broke. Furthermore, the mention of a severely wounded 32 year old on July 4th reminds us that July 4, 1776, was a date with 32 numerology, and both 'America' and 'Scottish' equate to 32 in Pythagorean- and America is wounded. And please, use your skills, and decode the name Diaz Love. You should find many familiar numbers, including 68 and 94, corresponding with 'Seattle, Washington', and 122, corresponding with 'satanic', and Seattle being on the 122nd Meridian West. You should also find that the name 'Love' equates to 54, the same as 'Jesuit Order' and 'Capitol Hill'.

In addition to those points, further exposing the Seattle Mayor's puppet strings connecting back to The Cabal, is that from Durkan's remarks on June 11th, to the accident in her city on July 4th, was a span of 24 days. And even further, from her 62nd birthday on

May 19, 2020, to the interview on June 11th, was also a span of 24 days. And then for the cherry on top, that means from her birthday to the July 4th ritual was her 47th day of her age, factoring into being on the 47th Parallel North, and on a date that can be expressed 4/7, not to mention the name 'Jenny Durkan' sums to 47 with Pythagorean Gematria and the name 'Durkan' alone equate to 24 with the same cipher. As we know, 47 is the number of 'government' and 'authority', as well as 'time'. And let us not forget the tropics of this earth, that measure the solstices, thus measuring 'the sun', are separated by 47 degrees. So for anyone out there doubting she is an agent of the 'Vatican', think twice. And oh by the way, until the Space Needle in Seattle was recently remodeled, it had a rotating restaurant that did a full rotation every 47 minutes. And on the subject, I suggest you look up the June 14, 1974 movie, *The Parallax View*, only because it came out on Trump's 28th birthday, and is about a presidential assassination, at Seattle's Space Needle, located on the 74 acre Seattle Center campus, reminding us that Donald Trump turned 74 years old this year, the 46 year anniversary of the release of the '74 film. Also noteworthy, the title of the film equates with 'The Jesuit Order' in three out of four ciphers, summing to 69, 84 and 177. It's a number 'Tamara Braxton', equating to 177, can tell you about, because on July 17, 2020, or 17/7, she was a national news headline for being in the hospital after attempting to commit suicide.

Getting back on the subject of 56th mayors, Lori Lightfoot, the 56th Mayor of Chicago, on May 26, 2020 (yes the day of the George Floyd video showed him being killed on the corner of Chicago Avenue), asked for $56 million for contact tracing the people of Chicago, 70 days from her August 4th birthday, reminding us that 'coronavirus' sums to 56 and 70, and at the same time, 'martial law' equates to 70- what has been hinted at by Donald Trump, in the wake of the George Floyd related protesting. Case in point, Donald Trump threatened to use federal force to shutdown the Autonomous Zone, that was formed on June 8th, Andrew Jackson's death date anniversary, who passed in 1845, emphasis on '45, the first U.S. President to declare martial law. It's a reminder that the riddles are deep. At the same time, let us not forget that 'Bobby L. Rush', equating to 56, also serving the federal government in Illinois, is who introduced H.R. 6666, the contact tracing bill. At the same time, let us appreciate that Barack Obama, another man with big ties to Illinois, is who won the

56th U.S. Presidential Election, and like Lightfoot, has an August 4th birthday, the 216th day of the year, the product of 6 times 6 times 6. This should remind you, the mainstream media called it a "coincidence" when the Illinois' Pick 3 Lottery was 6-6-6 on November 5, 2008, the day after Obama accepted the presidential nomination in Grant Park, Chicago, Illinois. Keep in mind, that is Guy Fawkes Day, the day leaving 56 days in the year, and to bring it all together, 'Illinois' sums to 54, the same as 'mark of the beast', and 'Jesuit Order'. And do me a favor, go back and revisit the headline from August 1, 2018, emphasis on 8/1, where Obama endorsed 81 candidates for the upcoming November election. As we learned earlier, 'mark of the beast' also equates to 81, as does 'ritual', and that is who The Cabal performs for, the 'beast', or the '47', reminding us that Obama took office at age 47, alongside the 47th Vice President, Biden, who now runs against the orange over grown Oompa Loompa, 'Trump', also equating to 47, who sat in the 47 story Midtown Hilton Hotel the night he was named 'president' elect. Personally, as I think about it all, I am reminded of Kurt Vonnegut, who wrote that only terrible people become President of the United States. He wasn't wrong. But in the same breath, all of this can change if we act as a people, and stand up to the deception and tyranny, as well as the unwarranted oppression.

On the subject of 'beast', let us not forget the film series *The Purge*, where the New Founding Fathers encourage people to unleash the beast, participating in crime and murder, on the dates of March 21st and 22nd every year, where it is legal to do so. Let us also not forget from the same series, the film titled *Election Year*, uses the exact same campaign slogan as Donald Trump in 2020, "Keep America Great." And in 2020, for a period of time after the killing of George Floyd, we witnessed mainstream networks cheerlead the uprising in America, that mostly resulted in the vandalism and looting of property, and authoritarian measures such as curfews put in place and national guard deployments, including to Atlanta, Georgia, a predominately black city, and reminding us that in *The Purge* the federal government targets black communities for extermination through policy, while covering up the truth of the matter. Furthermore, it reminds us that the TV show *Containment* concluded on July 19, 2016, the 201st day of the leap year, and again, it is about a virus being unleashed in Atlanta, by the CDC, for experimentation purposes, events that lead to protesting and rioting. Altogether, it reminds us that the same people responsible for our entertainment, are the same people responsible for the agendas we are living out, where entertainment is essentially a form of public relations for The Cabal, slowly preparing us for the world they are building around us, day by day, riddle after riddle.

To further the point on the connection between entertainment and what we perceive as reality, I should mention the popular video game series *Mortal Kombat* added a new character to their franchise on May 26, 2020, the same day as the George Floyd killing video. That character was *RoboCop,* based on the 1987 film, from 33 years earlier, and the joke with this was hidden in the conversation that was sparked in mainstream media about replacing police with technology, and possibly even robots, the same kind that have been demonstrated in recent years to be the future soldiers of tomorrow. And if you're like me, robotic soldiers makes you think of *Terminator,* and fittingly, the *RoboCop* character was introduced on May 26th, alongside a *Terminator* character as well. And that's not even counting the fact that Detroit is busy erecting a *RoboCop* statue at the exact same time. In other words, The Cabal is gloating at what they've accomplished with technology, and the matrix of surveillance built around us, and how they duped us into paying for it, from our money taken in taxes, to the money we give to them at the box office and with their other consumerism gimmicks.

Speaking of consumerism gimmicks, did you catch when Ford announced they were releasing the Bronco for the first time in a long time on July 9, 2020, what was O.J. Simpson's 73rd birthday, having been born in '47, the man remembered in part for the white 'Ford Bronco' chase? If not, it was a big story leading up to the date of release, when Ford disappointed many people, announcing they were going to have to postpone the Broncos's release until 2021, the year O.J. will turn 74, meaning they got the hype out a year in advance. Keep in mind, the O.J. Simpson murder trial was very divisive, especially in terms of race, and this Ford Bronco news came while 'Black Lives Matter' was pounding pavement across the world, and equating to 56 with Pythagorean Gematria, the exact same as 'Ford Bronco'. At the same time, 'Bronco' alone equates to 95 and the O.J. Simpson trial was decided October 2, 1995, in '95. And don't overlook the 10/2 date either, because you know what 102 means. I'll add, O.J.'s first name sums to 42, reminding us that 'slavery' and 'nigger' both sum to 42 and 102, and of the story about Ahmaud Arbery being called a nigger 102 days after his killing, and how the U.S. Civl War began on the 102nd day of the year, and so on. You'll see, now that you've opened this can of worms, this infinite knowledge, the patterns are extremely redundant, throughout history, and you'll go back and look at things like the man who gave the black power salute at the O.J. Simpson verdict, 'Lionel Cryer', a name that goes beyond gematria, and you'll see his name sums to 64 and 62, and you'll go, "him too!?" Get used to it. You'll do it with O.J. Simpson as well, catching the 113 in his name, and that his full name sums to 84 in Pythagorean, a favorite number of the Jesuit Order, the same as 95 and 56, all pertaining to O.J.'s "trial of the century"- an event made for TV audiences for the sake of the distraction and division that it would cause in its viewers, that took place while the New World Order moved slowly against us, as it always is, amounting to where we now are, because most of us missed the major warnings, including September 11, 2001, or 9-11 as most people call it.

Back on the subject of corporate gimmicks, and getting back to the subject of the George Floyd killing, let us discuss how Nike and Colin Kaepernick fit in, the latter being the man blackballed from the NFL for kneeling during the National Anthem, beginning in 2016, a little more than a year before the Philadelphia Eagles won the Super Bowl. Before we connect the dots, I want to give you a few historical and geographic points to consider first. In case you have never noticed this before, San Francisco and the larger Bay Area are the home of the NBA's Golden State Warriors, and the MLB's Oakland Athletics, teams that are from Philadelphia originally, and for a period of time, 'San Francisco', equating to 122 with Simple English, the same as 'Liberty Bell', was the home of Philadelphia's Liberty Bell, on the 122nd Meridian West- the same city that's name originates with St. Francis of Assisi, who 'Pope Francis' is named after, and whose name equates to 122 with Simple English as well.

On the subject of rituals connecting the two cities, take a look at the date of August 11, 2019, when the San Francisco Giants hosted the Philadelphia Phillies, and in that game they remembered the Giants 1989 World Series Earthquake team, where the World Series and its live broadcast was interrupted because of an earthquake. If you don't recall the incident, it was a game between the Oakland Athletics and San Francisco Giants, that was interrupted on the date of October 17,

1989, at 5:04 PM local, when the earthquake struck (Baseball = 54; Jesuit Order = 54). If you go back and watch the footage, you'll see the last thing shown on the screen before it cuts to fuzz, as it did in those days when the signal was interrupted, was Jose Canseco crossing home plate, the man who wore number 33 for the Oakland Athletics, and who went on to win the World Series, but not on that day. It matters that he was the last person shown because the date of the incident was exactly 107 days after his July 2nd, birthday, having been born on this date in 1964, and the number 107 connects to the Simple English Gematria of both 'military' and 'earthquake', and it also connects to his full name, 'José Canseco Capas Jr.' equating to 107 and 55, the same as 'earthquake'. And for a teaching moment, when it comes to Spanish letters, if they have an accent on them, they are null values, meaning they are worth zero, thus é = 0. With this in mind, I should mention that the name 'José Joaquín de Ferrer' equates to 201 and 84, the same as 'The Jesuit Order', and he is the Spanish sailor and astronomer who coined the term "corona" in relation to an eclipse, and he did it in Kinderhook, New York, in 1806, not too far from the site of Event 201, where the coronavirus outbreak simulation took place. And if you search for his Wikipedia, you'll see it is currently showing an illustration of the man doing the hidden hand pose, popular amongst Jesuits and Masons, and it explains in part, why Derek Chauvin had his hand in his pocket while he was on George Floyd's neck. To verify this is the case, about the "hidden hand", do a search, and start with the names Pope Francis and Anthony Fauci. I should also mention, just as 'Fauci' equates to 95, a man born on a date with 95 numerology, December 24, 1940, the location of 'Kinderhook, New York' equates to 95 with Pythagorean, reminding that Event 201 took place the same day the Military World Games began in Wuhan, China, games that have origins in Rome, and that began in the year 1995.

Also, I'd be amiss if I did not tell you how 'Oakland Athletics', equates to 56 with Pythagorean, the same as 'Society of Jesus', and 'Athletics' alone equates to 56 with Reverse Pythagorean. At the same time, 'natural disaster' sums to 56 with Pythagorean, and 223 with Reverse Simple English. Regarding the latter value, that championship team and series was remembered at the Giants and Phillies game of August 11, 2019, the 223rd day of the year. Better yet, August 11th was the anniversary of the patent date for HAARP, the military technology that has the power to create earthquakes, which was filed August 11, 1987. The number for the patent is 4686605. And because of gematria, we can understand the date was purposeful, because HAARP stands for 'High Frequency Active Auroral Research Program', equating to 223 with Pythagorean. Let us not forget the Giants were hosting Philadelphia, and the biblical land of Philadelphia was known for earthquakes, and further, 'Philadelphia' equates to 223, the same as 'The Synagogue of Satan'- and as we learned earlier, in *Revelation,* a letter is written to the Church of Philadelphia, about the Synagogue of Satan, the false Jews, who are liars, as they are described in the *Bible.* Furthermore, 'High Frequency Active Auroral Research Program' sums to 457, the 88th prime number, and with Satanic Gematria, 'earthquake' equates to 457, whereas 'California' sums to 88 with Simple English. At the same time, 'HAARP' sums to 44 with Simple English, and 'earthquake' sums to 44 with Pythagorean, and August 11, 1987, was a date with 44 numerology. Keep in mind the number 44 has connections to 'military' and time, as well as the word 'prophet', as we covered earlier with the Dean Koontz joke, on the 44th day of February 2020, when it was announced that his book had foretold of the deadly coronavirus, through the story of the *Wuhan 400* virus, in a novel he wrote in 1981. In light of prophecy, I should also point out that August 11, 2019 was the second day of Tisha B'Av in 2019, associated with the coming prophecy of the Third Temple and the Jewish messiah, and it also happened to be Eid al-Adha, the Muslim day to give praise to 'Abraham', Mr. 56, who was willing to sacrifice his son for God. On that same day, August 11th, written 11/8, the Israeli Police fired 'tear gas', equating to 118, on the peaceful worshipers at Temple Mount, and as I said then, it was a sign things were getting hot and heavy, and we were nearing the end of 2019, and the 19 year cycle of 9/11 was upon us. Of course, I had told people all year to circle August 11, 2019 and the site of Temple Mount, because it was foretold in the news, and popular media, harm was coming to the site, including through the show *'Dig'*, where you must call 8-1-1 before you do dig deep, at least in the United States.

Now to get to the point about how 'Colin Kaeperick' fits in with George Floyd, it is that his name equates to 146, the same as 'Jesus Christ', which should make you think of *John 14:6,* and how the Society of Jesus runs the show. Furthermore, Kaepernick is known for kneeling in protest, and George Floyd was killed on May 25, 2020, the 146th day of the leap year, after being kneeled on. And since all of this relates to the flag, it's birthday is June 14th, a date written 14/6, and in the wake of the George Floyd killing video, the 'Confederate' Flag, a name equating to 201, was banned across the nation, no doubt a sibling of the U.S. Flag, and technically, a flag that you could say represented half the country's history.

As for Kaepernick, when he began protesting, in his own words (*but not really, think of him as an actor repeating scripted lines, and doing things like wearing a Fred Hampton t-shirt on December 4, 2016, in Chicago, after a road game with the 49ers, what was the 47th anniversary of Hampton's assassination), he said he was championing the cause of the 1968 Olympic protesters in Mexico City, emphasis on '68, that year again. On the subject of '68, I need to point out that 'afro' has gematria of 68, and Colin Kaepernick grew out his afro for the 2016 season, to play the part to a tee. And for a related story, please look up the death of Oscar Gamble, the MLB star known for one of the greatest afros in MLB history, who died at age 68, 42 days after his own birthday, on Jackie Robinson's birthday, number 42, a man having the nickname 'Jackie', equating to 42. On that same day, January 31, 2018, Rasual Butler, a former NBA star died in a car crash, like Jackie's son, and Don Lemon of CNN had his sister drowned in a frozen pond while walking on ice. Keep in mind all three of the deceased from that day, 'Oscar Gamble', 'Rasual Butler' and 'L'Tanya Lemon', had names equating to 42 with Pythagorean Gematria- of course, they were all black, and they were all news on the first day of Black History Month. And for the record, the man credited with Black History Month, is largely 'Carter G. Woodson', a name equating to 69, 177 and 201 in all the same ciphers as 'The Jesuit Order'.

Getting back to Colin Kaepernick, he once said he was taking a knee for the many people of darker complexions who were reportedly murdered by police brutality in his lifetime, and who were not truly represented by the supposed symbolism of the U.S. flag (not that I would say most people are, of any complexion, unless they're *American dreaming...*), especially in the post Eric Garner and Michael Brown killings era. As you'll recall, in the NFL seasons following their deaths, teams such as the St. Louis Rams and others often paid tribute to the motto, 'hands up, don't shoot', and the small protests eventually lead to Colin Kaepernick being seen as the leader of the movement due to his symbolic kneeling in the pregame. To be more specific about the timeframe, he was recognized as the leader shortly after the team he played for, the 49ers, hosted Super Bowl 50, what I called the *Race War Bowl*. To jog your memory, it was the one where the "White Broncos" defeated the "Black Panthers", a week after a new TV show debuted about the O.J. Simpson murder story, that began with a white Ford Bronco chase. That detail reminds me Henry Ford himself died on April 7th in the year '47, emphasis on 4/7 in '47, and reminding us that the first NFL Super Bowl season was the 47th. At the same time, Colin Kaepernick gave the 49ers their first Super Bowl loss, in Super Bowl 47, the 33 minute blackout bowl as some headlines put it, where it was the first time two brothers coached against each other in the NFL's big game, and the one with the name John Harbaugh defeated the one with the name Jim Harbaugh. Of course 'John' sums to 47 with Simple English, making him the fitting recipient of the Super Bowl 47 win. In addition to that, he coached the team from 'Maryland', equating to 47 as well.

To be more specific about when Colin Kaepernick became the face of the NFL's National Anthem protest movement, that is tied in with Black Lives Matter, it was on the 239th day of 2016, August 26, 2016, coinciding with what we learned about 239 Arch St., where the flag was sewn in Philadelphia, and 239 being the 52nd prime number, and the Eagles winning the rigged Super Bowl in 'Minnesota' equating to 52, after Donald Trump took on the NFL protesters on September 23, 2017 over the protests of the flag, the date that could be written 23/9, and reminding us that 'president' and 'White House' and 'government' and 'authority' all equate to 52, and so does 'Pope', and Pope Francis had been in D.C. years before, where he spoke on the White House lawn on September 23rd, beginning at 9:23 AM local. And then further, it also reminds us there are 52 weeks in the year, and there are 52 cards in the deck, and there is the terminology in cards, "Trump card." Thus, the number clearly has relevance, and let us not forget that 'Kabbalah' equates to 52 either, the source of the code being used daily by The Cabal, all 52 weeks of the year. It is to say, they're busy "spelling" for the sake of maintaining control and contriving 'prophecy', also equating to 52, and reminding us that the 49ers fell to 5-2 in Super Bowl 54, thanks to the mega "222 ritual" that was part of the year, 2020, defined by 'Wuhan Coronavirus', or 222 in gematria terms, and where the virus has been compared in the mainstream media to biblical prophecy concerning the "end times."

I should also note, in light of what we documented regarding 'Colin Kaepernick' equating to 146, and 'Jesus Christ' equating to 146, and *John 14:6*, and George Floyd being killed on the 146th day of 2020, in a kneeling ritual, there is something that needs to be said about Sleepy Floyd, the basketball star who played for the Houston Rockets, in George Floyd's hometown, after playing at Georgetown for his college years, the nation's first Jesuit university. This point needs to be made because it was emphasized that George Floyd said, "I can't breathe", "I want mommy", and "I am sleepy" in the disturbing recording of his death. Again, as silly as the riddle might seem, it is there, and to make the point, Sleepy Floyd's real name is 'Eric Floyd', equating to 146, the same as 'Colin Kaepernick'. In addition, 'Eric Floyd' also sums to 52, the same as 'Minnesota' and 'I can't breathe'. Beyond that, his 60th birthday was March 6, 2020, exactly 80 days before George Floyd was killed, and 'Sleepy' as well as 'Bryant' and 'Boule' each equate to 80, reminding us that MLK died 80 days after his 39th birthday, and 'George' equals 39, like 'Gemini', and reminding us that Malcolm X was 39 as well, and that George's twin incident was with 'Amy', a name equating to 39, in 'New York', equating to 39, that are the number of books from the Old Testament, 39 in number, that *Revelation* is based up on.

The subject of the number 39 brings me to 'Nike', a larger than life, international company, having a name equating to 39 with Simple English, and one that championed Colin Kaepernick's cause, when the NFL wouldn't. Their big statement was made September 3, 2018, a date that can be written 3/9, or 9/3, when they paid the NFL star big money for a new advertising campaign, as a way of endorsing his protest while capitalizing and selling merchandise to match. Keep in mind Colin Kaepernick's birthday is November 3rd, or 11/3, similar to 113, corresponding with the Simple English Gematria of 'protest'. In light of the date of endorsement, September 3rd, consider 'Colin Rand Kaepernick', the full name of the athlete, equates to 93 with Pythagorean, and 'Kaepernick' sums to 93 with Simple English, the reflection of 'Nike's 39. This action by Nike, by the numbers, reminds us of how the elite siphon the wealth of the public through their own psychological operations that are meant to exploit people's emotions and human nature, for the sake of getting them to buy into something, whether it is another Nike t-shirt with some slogan, or wearing masks in public, in the time of a virus that isn't deadly at all.

Continuing with the subject of 39 and 93, in regards to Nike and Colin Kaepernick, Nike is a company that is very much a part of The Cabal, and for their logo, they use a ring of 'Saturn', the planet equating to 93 with Simple English, making 'Kaepernick' a perfect match for one of their advertising campaigns. Furthermore, Saturn is a sacred symbol and astrological body to the occult, and of extreme importance to the 'cult' we are exposing- the planet that is said to be the keeper of time, and the 6th from the sun, reminding us that both 'Nike' and 'Saturn' equate to 21 with Pythagorean Gematria, the 6th triangular number. I should also note, Nike is headquartered in Oregon, a state that was established as the 33rd, on Valentine's Day, February 14, 1859, a date with 93 numerology. Of course, 33 in numerology terms, is 6, and in light of mankind being made on the 6th day, let us not forget that 'people' and 'person' equate to 33 with Pythagorean, or the 33 bones that make up the human vertebrae.

To help you understand the greater relevance of these numbers and their relationships even further, consider that the *Holy Bible is* 1189 chapters long, broken down to 929 chapters in the *Old Testament,* and 260 chapters in the *New Testament,* meaning the 930th chapter of the text, is where the Christian section begins. This becomes all the more interesting when you recognize that 'Christianity' sums to 930 with Sumerian Gematria (Where you multiply the alphabetic order by 6), the same as 'coronavirus', the virus outbreak that has 666 encoded all over it, and reminding us that '*Genesis*' equates to 666, and mankind is made on the 6th day, and the first man is Adam, who lives to be 930 years old in the *Bible.* And of course, in numerology terms, 930 is equivalent to 93.

And in light of one story building onto the next, as time passes on, let us not forget how central the number 93 is to the George Floyd killing ritual, in 'Minneapolis, Minnesota', equating to 93, and located on the 93rd Meridian West. Let us also keep in mind that 'crucifix', 'God's Son' and 'Nazareth' equate to 93, and Jesus was crucified between 9 AM and 3 PM in the *Bible,* and in recent years, modern science traced Jesus' crucifixion to April 3rd, the 93rd day of the Gregorian year, and a date written 4/3, like 'Jesus Christ', and like 'George Floyd'. While we're at it, 'Colin Kaepernick' sums to 74 and 146, also like 'Jesus Christ'. And I should note, in light of Jesus largely being remembered for his death and what his death meant for mankind, and Saturn being connected to death and judgement, there is a famous symbol you have seen that is connected to death, but you might not be aware of its relationship to Saturn. It is the scythe of the Grim Reaper, the same scythe that is part of Saturn's astrological symbol. Look it up when you get a moment.

Beyond the numbers, Jesus struggle was on behalf of the meek and the needy, and that is what is supposed to be the case with Colin Kaepernick's "struggle" as well, that is now directly connected to the George Floyd story- and for further proof the Kaepernick and Floyd stories are part of the same script, consider that September 3rd, when Nike endorsed Kaepernick's stand against authoritarianism, that was also the day leaving 119 days left in the year, connecting the gematria of both 'George Floyd' and 'civil war'. I should mention, NASCAR driver 'Ray Ciccarelli', having a name equating to 119, said he was quitting the sport when the 'Confederate' Flag ban was announced on June 10th, also part of the script. And because 'Confederate' sums to 201, and sports factor into the riddles in the news, keep an eye on the Minnesota Vikings if there is to be a Super Bowl 55, knowing that 'Minneapolis' equates to 55, and 'Minnesota Vikings' equates to 201.

In light of the discussion of 93, and the killing of George Floyd in what is perhaps the most 93 city in the world, 'Minneapolis, Minnesota', and to further connect the dots, let us not forget 'Wuhan Coronavirus' equates to 93. Of course, it is the same virus making it hard for people to breathe, causing the need for 'ventilators', a word overlapping with 'coronavirus' in three out of four base ciphers, plus being a word that equates to 930 in Sumerian. More importantly, because the 'recording' of George Floyd being killed on the 93rd Meridian West was shown across the world, it sparked protests worldwide, that are now being partially blamed for the "second wave" of coronavirus outbreaks. Of course the "coronavirus outbreak" is very much a ritual in time, corresponding with the year 2020, a year syncing with the gematria of 'time', equating to 20, and being a year having a relationship with Tarot, because the 20th card of Tarot is the Judgement card- and again, 'Saturn', equating to 93, is the keeper of time, and connected to judgement. I should also note, the word 'recording' sums to 93 with Simple English, the same as 'Saturn', and a recording is something that allows us to capture a moment in time.

If you would like to learn more about the occult, Saturn, and the number 93, I suggest you look into Aleister Crowley's work. I will point out he died in 1947, emphasis on '47, the number symbolizing 'time', because Saturn is the keeper of time and Crowley not only worshiped the number 93, but he also worshiped the planet. In your research of Crowley, you should discover that he founded the religion that worships the number 93, named Thelema. To them, 93 represents the word 'love', equating to 54 with both Simple English, and Reverse Simple English, like how 'sun' equates to 54 with Simple English, the object in the sky, that makes life on earth possible, and is also reported to be 93 million miles away from earth on average.

If you do research Crowley, you'll find that he is very influential in the world of entertainment, especially with regards to music, a trend that began in the 60's with emerging British rock and roll bands, including 'Led Zeppelin', equating to 47 and 61, the same as 'rock'. Other bands touched by his magical teachings included Black Sabbath, Pink Floyd, the Rolling Stones, the Beatles and many more, creating a tradition that has never left the music industry. If you've read my first book, you know just how many musicians and entertainers have been taken by the "93 code," if you will. And on the subject, when you have a moment, look up the song by Ozzy Osbourne of Black Sabbath, titled *Mr. Crowley*, about Aleister Crowley unleashing something evil in the world that cannot be undone, and that was beyond Crowley's comprehension. You'll find Ozzy Osbourne began recording that song on March 22, 1980, the 17 year anniversary of The Beatles releasing their first album, *Please, Please Me*, March 22, 1963, and I'm putting the emphasis on 3/22, as in 322, for 'Ancient Mystery Religions', and also 22/3, like 223, for 'The Synagogue of Satan', because as Osbourne points out in his song, Crowley waited on satan's call. At the same time, with Jewish Gematria, 'Beatles' sums to 223, and so does 'Masonic'. More importantly, the song '*Mr. Crowley*', equates to 666 with Reverse Sumerian, the same as 'rockstar', and tying in with the fact that 'Ozzy Osbourne', 'rock and roll' and 'number of the beast' each equate to 66. Again, if you research the man, you'll find that he was very much a gematria and isopsephy enthusiast. And with regards to his cult classic, *Mr. Crowley*, it released on September 20, 1980, the 263rd day of the year, the 56th prime, and also the day leaving 102 days left in the year, the latter connecting to the gematria of 'magic', what Crowley was into educating about, and practicing. On the subject of September 20th, that is also the date the Tavistock Institute was established in 1947, an entity controlled by the Jesuits, that is interested in steering the minds

338

of the masses for the purpose of government and military operations. It also has a major history in steering famous British entertainment acts, for the purpose of how they ultimately steer populaces.

To further emphasize the dark side of the number 93, and since we brought up the worshiping of 93 by Crowley, who is studied by those in the recording industry, and in light of what we have learned about this number, in terms of how it connects to tragic events ranging from the '93 WTC Bombing, to the 9/11 attacks, to the outbreak of 'Wuhan Coronavirus', I want to again visit the death of Naya Rivera an actress and a singer, in 'Lake Piru', equating to 93 with Simple English, where her body was found in the area of the lake known as "Devil's Canyon." I come back to her death again, because this example will really help you understand just how demonic, and evil things are, as well as connected, in the world of entertainment, that is controlled by the Jesuits and The Cabal, who have all the knowledge of Crowley, and ten thousand times more, at least. As a reminder, Naya Rivera passed at age 33, and prior to her passing, she had starred in the film *At the Devil's Door*, that premiered March 9, 2014, emphasis on 9/3, at South by Southwest. Further adding to the riddle is the fact that her last Instagram post was, "just the two of us", the lyrics to Bill Withers hit song, a man who died earlier in the year, March 30, 2020, but the news was not reported of his passing until April 3rd, what is typically the 93rd day of the year, and the date believed by science to be the date of Jesus' crucifixion, where 'crucifix' equates to 93. In addition to that, her death brought up the "Glee curse" in mainstream headlines, similar to the "Kennedy curse", and Maeve Kennedy and her son had been found dead in a boating accident, April 6, 2020, 93 days before Naya Rivera's death on July 8, 2020. As you'll recall, they were found in 'Shady Side, Maryland', equating to 97, on the 97th day of 2020, after a 'canoe' accident, where 'canoe' and 'death' equate in all four base ciphers, including 97 with Reverse Simple- and beyond that, their disappearance on April 2nd, was 97 days before Naya Rivera disappeared and drowned on July 8th. Please also recall that the day Naya Rivera was assumed dead, July 9th, or 9/7, like 97, was the day Eminem, who is known as Slim Shady (Shady Side, Maryland?), who had the hit song '97 Bonnie & Clyde, about drowning his significant other, a song that also sampled the words from Bill Withers' *Just the Two of Us*, put out a new song criticizing those who weren't wearing masks- a song also having lyrics discussing the dirty police killing of George Floyd, meaning two incidents that have to do with breathing in their own separate ways, the same as drowning.

At the same time, Eminem had another song from March 27, 2020, called '*Coffin*', on the debut album of the singer Jessie Reyez, who got her mainstream music start at a relatively old age, at the tail end of 28, before turning 29 on June 12, 2020, something that reminds us of Bill Withers, who began his music career around the age of 30 as well, relatively late for show business. And don't overlook that her album came out three days before Withers' death, or that Naya Rivera was the third member of *Glee* to die, dying at age 33, and having her death confirmed July 13th, or 13/7, like 137, the 33rd prime, the anniversary of the death of the first member of *Glee*, Cory Monteith, and also the 5 year anniversary of her starring in the 33rd episode of *Devious Maids*, that released July 13, 2015, and where she dies by hanging in the episode, thus having her air supply cut off. Even further, the name of that episode is *The Turning Point*, equating to 78 and 84, the same as 'Jesuit', and where 78 corresponds with the date she drowned, July 8th, or 7/8. As for the song '*Coffin*', Eminem once again raps about drowning his significant other, and what makes this all the more condemning, is that the name of the album the song is on, '*Before Love Came to Kill Us*', equates to 93 and 123, the same as 'Lake Piru', where the latter number, 123, connects to 'conspiracy', and reminds us of the riddle with Will Smith's 51st birthday, and Kobe Bryant's helicopter demise 123 days later, corresponding with the gematria of '*The Fresh Prince of Bel Air*'. In case you forgot, 'conspiracy' also sums to 51, same with 'helicopter', and in this case, so does 'Naya Rivera' and 'Lake Piru'. With regards to Will Smith, he also did a rap song using the words to Bill Withers' *Just the Two Of Us*', and even further, his name, 'Will Smith', equates to 55, reminding us that Naya Rivera died on a date with 55 numerology, July 8, 2020, connecting to the gematria of 'satan', an entity symbolized in occult astrology by 'Saturn', and an alias for the devil, connecting back to the fact that Piru is a Finnish word for Devil, and she was found in the Devil's Canyon section of Lake Piru, at age 33, only after wearing a red sweater with the number 33 on it in the film *At the Devil's Door*. Keep in mind that film title has gematria overlap with 'The Jesuit Order' in three out of four ciphers, equating to 69, 84 and 177, and reminding us that the news of Naya's disappearance came on July 9th, a date that connected to 'Society of Jesus' in all four ciphers (56, 79, 187, 191), coming on 7/9, like 79, and on the 191st day of the year, and on a date with 56 numerology, precisely 187 days before Rivera's 34th birthday. Furthermore, let us not forget that 'Naya Marie Rivera' and '*Glee*' both equate to 79, the same as 'murder'. At the same time, her character from *Glee*, 'Santana Lopez', has identical gematria to 'Jesuit Order' and 'Kennedy curse', summing to 144, the number we learned much about in chapter two. And we haven't even mentioned Eminem's album *Devil's Night*, or that July 8th, the day Rivera died, was Eminem's 266th day of being 47 years old, where the number 266 corresponds with the Jesuit motto, 'Iesus Hominum Salvator'.

I should also remind us, since we brought up the fact that 'Will Smith' equates 55, on July 14, 2020, it was reported that Will Smith's co-star on *The Fresh Prince of Bel Air*, Galyn Görg, was dead at 55, one day shy of her 56th birthday, that would have fell on July 15th, or 15/7, reminding of the ritual with the numbers 157 and 55, in the death of Kobe Bryant, a death very much connected to Will Smith through his once hit TV show, *The Fresh Prince of Bel Air*. And in light of her dying on July 14th, keep in mind that date can be written 14/7, like 147, corresponding with the Reverse Simple English value of 'conspiracy'. She also died on a date with 41 numerology, bringing us back to the death of 'Kobe Bryant', equating to 41, at age 41. Even further, she died 170 days after Kobe Bryant, and 'sacrifice' equates to 170. At the same time, she died 293 days after Will Smith's 51st birthday on September 25, 2019, and 293 is the 62nd prime number, connecting to the gematria of 'sacrifice', as well as 'Faustian bargain', the latter meaning a deal with the devil. She also died a span of 74 days from his 52nd birthday, or 73 days before his 52nd birthday, where 'sacrifice' equates to 73 with Simple English, and 'ritual sacrifice' equates to 73 with Pythagorean. Also noteworthy, between Galyn Görg's death and Kobe Bryant's, Will Smith, covered all the 'conspiracy' numbers from the base ciphers, a word equating to 51, 57, 123 and 147. Once again, 'helicopter' equates to 51 and 57, '*The Fresh Prince of Bel Air*' equates to 123, and Kobe Bryant died 123 days after Will Smith's 51st birthday in a helicopter, an event coming prior to the death of Galyn Görg, on July 14th, or 14/7, what is 'Bastille Day' in 'Paris, France', both equating to 187, the original home of the 'Society of Jesus'.

I should also note, on the subject of 55, if you listen to the recording of the song *Coffin*, you'll hear Jessie Reyez sing about jumping past the 5th floor, and the word 5th floor is echoed immediately behind it, thus you hear the number five repeated twice in close proximity to each other, something that becomes all the more interesting when you consider this song's release is synced with the death of Naya Rivera, who died on the date having 55 numerology. Furthermore, 'Jessica Reyez' sums to 55, as well as 71 and 145, like 'Catholic', and 179, like how Naya Rivera died 179 days after her own birthday. Keep in mind 179 is the 41st prime, and *'Glee curse'* equates to 41, as does the name 'Naya'. To further the point about satan, the album released March 27, 2020, the 87th day of the leap year. Beyond that, Naya Rivera was born in '87, and her date of death, July 8th, can be written as 8/7. Furthermore, Eminem put out the album *'Music to be Murdered By'*, equating to 87 with Pythagorean, on January 17, 2020, and of course, 'number of the beast' equates to 87 and 66 with the Pythagorean ciphers, where 87 has numerology of 6. More importantly, both 'Naya Rivera' and 'Lake Piru' equate to 66 as well, brining us back to her body being found in "Devil's Canyon." And to think, the people who used her beauty to sell shows, and movies, and ads and merchandise, they had her planned demise date written down all along, by the code. Sadly, this is true for many stars. And for one more proof of that, Eminem's album, *'Music to Be Murdered By'*, released a span of 174 days from her death, and 'number of the beast' sums to 174 with Simple English as well.

On the subject of 266 and the Jesuits, since we just brought it up with Eminem, and for yet another proof of who is behind this circus we're pulling the curtain back on, I should bring up what happened to the statue of Frank Rizzo in Philadelphia, shortly after the George Floyd protests began. On June 3, 2020, his statue that had been up since 1998, came down, being retired by Jesuit agents posing as protesters who said he was a racist cop. Not by chance, 'Frank Rizzo' equates to 63 with Pythagorean, similar to how 'racism' sums to 63 with Simple English, and being a number corresponding perfectly with the date June 3rd, or 6/3- thus making it the perfect target for the ritual in what became a national news story. If you go back in history, you'll find that Frank Rizzo died on July 16, 1991, having been born October 23, 1920, meaning he died on his 266th day of his age. And for one more Jesuit connection, 'Frank Rizzo' sums to 144 with Simple English, the same as 'Jesuit Order'. He also died on a date with 43 numerology, corresponding with the gematria of 'policeman', 'civil war' and 'George Floyd'. And in the case of his statue, it came down on the 155th day of 2020, corresponding with the gematria of 'policeman', also equating to 155, the same as 'coronavirus', further showing how the rituals intertwine, from George Floyd and "I can't breathe", to Covid-19. Let us not forget this was the day mainstream media let us know George Floyd had coronavirus, even though in those same reports they said he first tested positive on April 3rd, what is typically the 93rd day of the year, but in 2020, the leap year, it was the 94th, corresponding with the gematria of 'coronavirus pandemic'.

Because I brought up 155 again, and we're talking about the falling of statues connected to racism in the "post 400 years of American slavery", with prophecy and *Acts 7:6* in mind, the word 'statue' equates to 76, the name for the objects that came tumbling down across the U.S. and even other parts of the world after the televised death of 'Floyd the Landlord'. Furthermore, 'Christianity' sums to 155, and *Acts* is the 5th book of the *New Testament*, the Christian section of the *Bible,* corresponding with George Floyd being killed in the 5th month, May, on the 25th, having a square root of 5. Keep in mind, *Acts* is also the 44th book overall in the *Holy Bible*, a number corresponding very much with black history, as well as 'officer', and the word 'prophet' as in prophetic. Let us not forget George Floyd was killed by 44 year old Derek Chauvin on the 44th Parallel North, corresponding with Floyd's rap alias, 'Big Floyd', equating to 44 with Pythagorean. And recall, in *Acts 7:7*, the nation that is responsible for 400 years of slavery, is punished, and not only does 'United States' equal 77, but so does 'police officer' and 'police department', as well as the phrase 'order from chaos'. The point I am again making, is that The Cabal takes things, having the right numbers if you will, and forces them into their planned narratives, that treat the *Holy Bible's* scripture, as the script. With that said, 'christ' also sums to 77, and we have covered the numerous angles in the George Floyd story paying tribute to Jesus Christ, including The Great Tribulation. And that is the part of the biblical story that must be understood, we are to expect great suffering, destruction and war, before the return of Jesus, in the story handed down down to us, from the Church.

With regards to the number 77, connecting to the gematria of 'secret society', and with the title 'police officer' in mind, also equating to 77, many are members of the secretive Fraternal Order of Police. I bring this up in light of the story of the killing of David Dorn in St. Louis after the George Floyd protests broke out, a 77 year old retired officer, shot dead in the street, June 2, 2020, emphasis on 6/2 and 2/6. In regards to his killing, Fox News ran the headline, 'Murdered by a looter', equating to 84 and 201, numbers that remind us 'Michael Brown' equates to 201, and he was killed in 'Ferguson, Missouri', equating to 84, just outside of St. Louis. Even more, 'looter' equates to 77, corresponding with David Dorn's age of death. And for more familiar numbers, the name 'David Dorn' equates to 46, and it was reported he was a police officer in St. Louis for 38 years, comparing to how 46 year old George Floyd was killed on the corner of 38th Street and Chicago Avenue, where 'Chicago' equates to 46. To peel the onion back a bit more, 'St. Louis' sums to 25, the same as death, and reminding us that George Floyd was killed on the 25th of May. 'St. Louis' also sums to 74 and 115, the same as killing, and reminding ourselves of what we learned earlier about the killing of the rapper 'Huey' in St. Louis, on June 25, 2020. If I never mentioned it before, he had a hit song called, 'Pop, Lock & Drop It', equating to 71, the same as 'African American', and he died on a date with 71 numerology, a number we covered in connection to the release of the George Floyd killing video on May 26, 2020, reminding us of the repetitive nature of the code. And let us not forget that 71 is the 20th prime, and 'death' equates to 20. As for Huey's hit song, it also equates to 64 and 181, and those numbers were used in the killing ritual of the rapper George Floyd as well, a man of many talents.

This brings us to our last point, and that is what Shaun King, the leader of Black Lives Matter, said about white Jesus late June 22, 2020, on social media, a date with 68 numerology, that became top news the day after, June 23rd, where his message was condensed in headlines with phrases about white Jesus being a symbol of white supremacy, and the need to bring down all depictions of white Jesus, from artwork to statues. Not by accident, the news came on the day leaving 191 days in the year, corresponding with the gematria of 'Society of Jesus', the divide and conquer gang, and being the 43rd prime number, corresponding with the gematria of 'Jesus Christ', as well as 'George Floyd', and again, 'civil war', a target of The Cabal. In analyzing this ritual, it should summarize the point trying to be made in this chapter, and truly, this book. That is, we the people, are being played for fools, by the numbers, by the Jesuits, or the Society of Jesus (as well as other fraternities under their masonic umbrella), with biblical riddles, and historical riddles, and with divisive lies and stories told in the news, and by our governments and authority figures, and even churches. And understand, these lies are told for the purpose of keeping us fighting amongst ourselves, so that The Cabal can more easily rule over all of us. Again, The Cabal is at the very least, a three headed monster, that operates in the realm of spirituality through the Vatican, militarism through Washington D.C., and the financial world through the City of London, which controls things such as the Federal Reserve, and together, these entities have immense influence on the world and collectively, our lives.

Coming back to Shaun King's big statements about ending white Jesus, that were mainstream headlines on June 23, 2020, it is because of gematria that we can see why he was the perfect puppet for the ritual, and it was mostly because of his name. This is because 'Shaun King' sums to 139, the same as 'white Jesus'. More importantly, the artwork for white Jesus traces back to Cesare Borgia, born September 13, 1475, in Rome, emphasis on 13/9. You'll recall that is the day in 1996 that 'Tupac Shakur' died, having a name equating to 139, and then he had his album *Makaveli* release shortly after, with album artwork showing him crucified on a cross, the same as Jesus. As a reminder, that album released November 5, 1996, Guy Fawkes Day, a Jesuit remembrance day, and the day leaving 56 days in the year. As another reminder, 'Tupac' and 'Makaveli' equate to 74, like 'Jesus' and 'cross', and even 'Colin Kaepernick'. At the same time, let us not forget what happened to 'Kobe' either, in the 74th NBA season, or that 'Roman Catholicism' equates to 74.

And to add to our 139 list, I must thank my friend Rambo, who pointed out that in the film *The Matrix*, not only does Neo's passport expire on September 11, 2001, but his birthday is shown as September 13th, in the year 1971, emphasis on '71. Hopefully you get the joke from those crazy Catholics! And in the music video for '*Hate Me Now*', the rapper Nas, also black, is shown on the cross, portraying Jesus. Of course, the song name '*Hate Me Now*' equates to 139. As for Nas himself, his birthday is one day off, September 14th, but still in the time of Virgo, an astrological sign ruled by 'Mercury', equating to 103, the same as 'Cesare Borgia', reminding us that the Virgin Mary's birthday is celebrated in the time of Virgo, on September 8th, the 251st day of the year, the 54th prime. Let us not forget, some Coptic Christians contend Jesus' birthday is September 11th, what is their New

Years Day, and of course, also in the time of Virgo. And in light of Neo being born in '71, you should know that both 'Virgo' and 'Catholic' equates to 71 and 35 in the same ciphers.

For a bit more on 139, let us not forget that it connects to the name 'America', as well as the word 'Freemasonry'. And as we learned in the beginning, 139 is the 34th prime, and where 'Freemasonry' sums to 139 with Simple English, the word 'free' sums to 34 with the same cipher. Of course, in America, pictures of 'white Jesus' are very common, especially in churches, and with regards to 139 being the 34th prime number, let us recall that both 'Jesus' and 'church' also equate to 34 with the base ciphers. And that's the concern truth seeker. Can you imagine if The Cabal is allowed to continue to push the ball forward, as they are? How long until they're setting fires to churches with headlines blaming it on extremists who are erasing 'white Jesus'? And understand, my point in asking this question, is to get you to see that this is the direction we're being pushed, and just how divisive it can become.

In 2020 and going forward, we the people shouldn't be fighting over race, or anything else. We should be coming together and finding commonality in truth, and knowledge, and taking steps to take care of one another, and our world. All lives really do matter, and so does having a safe world to live in. So this is the only place our energy should be invested right now, and we can make it happen. We will do it for ourselves, our friends, our family, the children of the world, and the unborn generations. It is necessary, it is righteous, it is just, and it will happen! And as you likely know at this point, the knowledge you have learned within this book, truly is undeniable, and it has the power to awaken many, even the most closed minded, so don't be afraid to share it! And here's to it, truth seeker. Let's do it! Let's pull back the curtain on these monsters and bring an end to their games, based in numbers. Let's make it so we don't have to read headlines of needless tragedy anymore, from everything we've already covered, to the death of the 22 month old daughter of PGA Golfer Camilo Villegas, who was reported to have died on Sunday, July 26th, 201 days after Villegas 38th birthday, on January 7, 2020, or the death of Randall Cunningham's two year old in a 'hot tub' accident on June 30, 2020, 95 days after Cunningham's birthday, corresponding with the fact his name 'Randall Cunningham' sums to 95 and 76, and his child died on a 76 date numerology, corresponding with the gematria of 'hot tub'.

19 | What Happened to Me in Room 201 in New Orleans

At the beginning of 2020, great supporters of my work helped raise funds to pay for me to travel to the state of Louisiana for the purpose of educating the students of LSU and the people of the region about the very terrible rituals that took place just before LSU won the college football championship in New Orleans, January 13, 2020, defeating Clemson. Of course, the purpose of educating about such matters is so that people have an opportunity to become aware of the evil that is close to home, something that is true for most of us, so that we can do something to correct the problem. If you're curious about the topics I educated on, they involved the deaths of numerous people, connected to the January 13th championship game, including Billy Cannon, who passed the same day Joe Burrow transferred to LSU, and Nancy Parker, a New Orleans news anchor, who died on August 16, 2019, in a curious plane accident. As I taught people, her demise came precisely 150 days before LSU won the 150th college football season in Nancy's hometown, New Orleans. Further adding to the ritual, was that her name, 'Nancy Parker', equated to 54, the same as 'New Orleans', and the date LSU won the championship in the same city, was a date with 54 numerology (1/13/2020 = 1+13+20+20 = 54). In addition to that, I pointed out to them Parker's death came two days before the death of the 54th Governor of Louisiana, Kathleen Blanco, who died August 18, 2019, 119 days after her 77th birthday, on a date with 38 numerology. I also informed people about the rapper known as 5th Ward Weebie, who died at age 42, 42 days before his upcoming birthday, just days before LSU won the championship with 42 points, in the city known as 'NOLA', a predominantly black city, equating to 42 with Simple English, the same as 'five'. He died January 9, 2020, and was born February 19, 1977. Furthermore, I taught the New Orleans locals how his name 'Weebie' equated to 113, the same as 'LSU Tigers', who won the championship on January 13th, or 1/13. Even further, I taught them his birth name was 'Jerome Cosey' summing to 133, the same as 'football'. Beyond that, I reminded them that his hit song was titled *'Let Me Find Out'*, equating to 54 and 144, the same as 'New Orleans' and 'Jesuit Order'. And please keep in mind, New Orleans is home to the Jesuit university, Loyola.

On top of that, I did my best to help people see through the suspicious death of Carley McCord, the daughter-in-law of LSU's offensive coordinator, Steve Ensminger, who died in a plane crash on

347

the same day LSU advanced to the college championship. I also helped them connect the riddles relating to the two plane crashes, Nancy Parker's and Carley McCord's, telling the people who listened to keep in mind 'plane crash' equates to 97, the same as 'death', and in the case of the deaths being sacrifices for LSU's championship outcome, the names 'Burrow' and 'Orgeron' equate to 97 as well, the surnames of LSU's quarterback and coach. And on the subject of 97, I also let them know that 'Capricorn' sums to 97, and the game was in the time of 'Capricorn', as was McCord's fatal plane crash. And looking back, something that didn't seem as important then, as it does now, is the name 'McCord' sums to 56, same as 'Ed Orgeron', and he finished the 2019-20 season with 56 wins as a college football coach, in a year that would become much about 56, as you well know, from 'coronavirus' to 'Black Lives Matter'. And in light of 56 being a number of the 'Society of Jesus', let us not forget that the state of Louisiana became part of the U.S. with the Louisiana Purchase, involving France, the home of the Jesuits, who were formed in Paris.

In addition to those tragic stories, I educated about the death of Tyshon Dye, a former running back for Clemson, who reportedly drowned, July 5, 2019, exactly 192 days before the championship date was scheduled for, January 13, 2020. As I pointed out when the news of his death broke on July 6, 2019, Clemson would be in the championship, again, because 'Clemson Tigers' equates to 75 and 192, matching the 7/5 death, 192 days before the game. There was likely a historical joke in there that went over my head as well, because 'Louisiana Purchase' also equates to 75 and 192. At the same time, keep in mind Weebie's birthday was 19/2, like 192. And you have to understand, Clemson had a similar ritual with the death of C.J. Fuller the year prior, who died October 3, 2018, 97 days before the January 7, 2019 college football championship, that Clemson won over Alabama. They said he died from a 'seizure', equating to 103, matching his date of death 10/3, and the fact that 103 is the 27th prime, and 'Clemson' equates to 27, and he wore the number 27, and they went on to win the championship on a date with 27 numerology, in 'Santa Clara', equating to 27. And sadly, you must realize, these things take place every single sports season, college and pro, as I have been educating about for 7 years straight. They are not uncommon, and this was the same point I was attempting to make to the people of Louisiana, and this is the same point I am attempting to make to you.

What I want to transition to now, is what I refer to as the organic side of the code, meaning the synchronicity with numbers we have in our own lives, because that is what this chapter is really about. And as we move ahead, keep in mind, Hermeticism teaches that synchronicity is confirmation from the Creator, that we are on the right path. Furthermore, by understanding this subject, which you will soon be able to test with examples in your own life, you will gain understanding as to why The Cabal uses numbers ritualistically, in the way they do, because as you will come to understand, numbers are for purposes greater than just counting- and in my estimation, they are here to provide meaning to our lives, and to answer questions surrounding the mysterious qualities of our existence. It is to say, they are spiritual, and it should remind us that the fourth book of the *Holy Bible* is titled *Numbers*.

   To make the case, I will talk about a few things that happened to me while I was educating about these same subjects in Louisiana. For example, after landing in New Orleans at about 2:30 AM local time, January 31st, after several flight delays, I then had to pick up a rental car and drive to Baton Rouge, a little more than an hour away, where the LSU campus is located. When I arrived in Baton Rouge, it was nearly 4:00 AM and as I pulled off the freeway for the campus exit, I saw there was a Red Roof Inn, so I parked in their lot and asked the man at the front desk for a room. The rate was reasonable so I paid and he handed me a room key, it was for room number 131. I had to laugh! When I did, the man asked me what was so funny? I imagine he was half worried some late night psychotic had come through the door. I went on to explain to him what gematria was, and how the word 'championship' sums to 131 with Simple English, and how LSU had just won the championship on January 13th, a date that can be written 13/1, like 131, and I was down there to educate about the darker rituals connected to LSU's championship season. To make a long story short, by the time we finished talking, it was 6:30 in the morning, and another person had been awoken to the code. And for the record, 131 is a number that comes up ALL THE TIME in rigged sports championships, as I've also been educating about for years. Case in point, in addition to the word 'championship', 'Super Bowl' also sums to 131 with Simple English, and that is true of the word 'fifty seven' as well, which matters, because both 'World Series' and 'NBA Finals' equate to 57, another number to watch for in the world of rigged sports, reminding us of what we learned with the Nationals giving the Astros their 57th postseason loss, in the same game the Nationals won the 115th World Series.

Back on the subject of Room 131, I stayed in it for three days, during the time I was busy walking the LSU campus and talking to hundreds, if not thousands of students, including members of the LSU football team, as well as some staff, about the topics at hand. From the experience, I will always remember the eyes of the athletes I looked into, who I could tell were grasping what I was warning them about- that they could be the next Tyshon Dye. Sadly, he is one of many names in a long list of ritual sacrifices over the years, pertaining to major sporting events. I will also remember the compliment I received from a professor at the university, who after talking to him and his colleague for at least 30 minutes, said, "I normally don't care for conspiracy, but you're research and documentation is very compelling and I will look into it. Thank you very much." Sadly, he was not willing to be recorded on video with his thoughts, but I can't blame him, because in this world we live in now, there are consequences for pursuing truth. I will also remember Cade, the first gentleman to show up spontaneously and let me know he was a follower of mine on YouTube, and he was there to help educate- and he did. I will also always remember Jeremy, who drove all the way from West Texas, to help me get the word out, and he was tremendous in doing so, traveling with me from Baton Rouge to New Orleans for the same mission. It was especially nice to see his face, because I had known his voice for years from my radio show, a slow spoken gentleman who had become a regular caller after winning big on Super Bowl 50, having taken my advice in October of that season. What was cool, is in the season of Super Bowl 54, Jeremy and I had the opportunity to put our heads together, and be right about the outcome of the game before it happened, and then watch it happen in the company of each other, while at the same time educating those around us about how the rigging of the game was encoded and achieved in real time. This was made easier when the first interception of Super Bowl 54 was made by number 21, because I happened to be wearing my custom made Super Bowl 49 t-shirt, educating about how on the date of Super Bowl 49, February 1, 2015, emphasis on 2/1, on the down 2nd and 1 to go, Russell Wilson's 21st pass was intercepted by number 21 on the Patriots, with 21 seconds left, sealing the game in favor of New

England. On that same t-shirt it also shows how 'pick' equates to 21 with Pythagorean Gematria, the terminology for an interception. You might recall, that was the game Russell Wilson could have handed off to Marshawn Lynch on the 1 yard line, but didn't, throwing the interception instead, ensuring the scripted win for the Patriots.

As for the Louisiana trip, I will also remember all the others who showed up and helped out and did their part to bring this information into people's lives so we can change the course we're on, and of course, I will remember many of the faces and conversations I had with people, young and old, about the topics I went to Louisiana to discuss, including the gentlemen who said he felt this knowledge was going to change the world for the better. And I won't forget Billy either, a real life Forrest Gump, who was the groundskeeper at LSU, who got in a spirited debate with me, before coming around, and realizing he had some homework to do, because something certainly was eerie and seemingly beyond coincidence with the things I had to share regarding the rituals that pertained to the 2020 college football championship, especially the part about Billy Cannon, dying the day Joe Burrow signed with LSU, and Joe Burrow going on to join Billy Cannon, as the only LSU player to ever win the Heisman, or beat Clemson, in a championship, in New Orleans. And yes, if you're wondering, Billy was the very last person I talked to at LSU, a detail that couldn't have been anymore fitting, and tying in perfectly with the synchronicity of things. If you're familiar with Squire D. Rushnell, he'd say this detail about Billy, in terms of what happened during my trip to Louisiana, is *When God Winks At You.* That is also the title of Rushenell's best selling book, having a subtitle, *How God Speaks Directly to You Through the Power of Coincidence.* And to think, little did I know then that after being given room key number 131 on January 31st, or 1/31, and finishing my time at LSU with Billy, that the most meaningful "coincidence" was still yet to come.

As soon as I concluded with three days of educating in Baton Rouge, I traveled back to New Orleans to spend the next three days with the good people of that city, to educate about the same matters. And let me say, just as it went well in Baton Rouge, it went well in New Orleans, and as someone from the Pacific Northwest, visiting the South for the first time, I got to see that southern hospitality was a very real thing, and so were grits, something my mother told me I needed to try. Anyhow, when I arrived in town, I wanted to be in the 5th Ward, for the sake of Weebie, so I found a hotel there, which happened to be The Treme, at 1933 Ursulines Ave. When I asked for a room, they put me in number 201, at the top of the stairs, and my initial thought was, "Well, that's not as exciting as room 131." But that thought was soon to change in the most significant of ways. That's because within an hour of checking into the room, an unknown phone number began texting my personal cellphone, telling me to "research Event 201." I have to admit, I was a bit creeped out, because I felt that someone was playing a game with me, and they knew I was staying in room number 201. Eventually, the text messages turned to phone calls, but I didn't pick up or respond. Like I said, I was a little on edge, and it was late at night, and I was in strange city, and I was spilling the beans, in a neighborhood, about the killing of a man, in that very neighborhood, in a ritual for the college football championship, that had just been played weeks earlier, in that same city.

Soon after however, I started to see messages from the followers of my work, telling me that there was a man on YouTube, by the name of Dr. Paul Cottrell, uploading videos to his own channel, asking people in his community to please contact me for the purpose of having me research Event 201 in relation to the coronavirus outbreak. It turned out he was the same person who had come about my phone number and had been texting and calling me shortly after I checked into room number 201. When I asked him how he came about my number, he said a friend of his had it. And since I had been doxxed so many times, I assumed a lot of people had my phone number, and I didn't make a big deal about it.

What made the matter all the more strange however, is that his title, 'Dr. Paul Cottrell' equated to 201, and even further, his name was identical to 'The Jesuit Order' in three out of four ciphers. At the same time, 'Paul Cottrell' alone was identical to 'coronavirus' in two out of the four ciphers, and of course, he was asking me to research Event 201, the coronavirus outbreak simulation, in relation to the supposed actual coronavirus outbreak, and he was the first person in the world to ask me to do so. When I asked him about the gematria of his own name, he said it was just a coincidence. And as much as I don't like the word, anything is possible. That said, my take on the matter, is that it was synchronicity. And in case you have not read it, let me recommend the book to you titled the *Celestine Prophecy*, a book that echoes the teachings of Hermeticism, in the sense that it teaches what some people call coincidence, is really confirmation from the Creator that you are on the right path, and you are pursuing the right things. And let me also note, long before I knew anything about gematria, or even the existence of the book the *Celestine Prophecy*, I felt this to be the truth, and that is why I now recommend the book as good reading to you, along with the teachings of Hermeticism.

As for my own book, as I conclude writing it, about six months since being encountered by Paul Cottrell, what I can now confirm is that I am so grateful for his recommendation and the synchronicity of staying in room number 201 at the time of his contact, because it truly helped me advance this research, and identify the tip of the spear in terms of who is in control of the New World Order. To think, had I not been in room number 201, stirring up a personal curiosity for myself regarding the number, it might have made me less likely to follow through with the suggestion of researching Event 201. And it is possible that without his tip, this book would have never happened, because prior to his request, I did not recognize the significance of the number 201. And on the subject of synchronicity, it has been very peculiar for me to find out in the time of my research, that the Jesuits were suppressed in history, by their own Pope, July 21, 1773, a date that 210 years later, would become my birthday. And on the subject of 210 years, 'Wuhan Coronavirus' does have Gematria of 210, and again, it was through this Wuhan Coronavirus outbreak, that was simulated at Event 201, that made all of this possible. At the same time, let us not overlook that 210, 201 and 21 all have the same key digits, 2 and 1 for 21, the number syncing with the gematria values of '*Bible*', 'Jesuit' and 'math', as well as the 21st day of July. And in light of the number 21 being the 6th triangular number, and synchronicity, I should tell you one more thing about 6, because it is important, and it reveals to me, that perhaps there is such a thing as destiny.

After moving to Seattle at the end of 2006, I got the deal of a lifetime on a great apartment, because I was in the right place, at the right time. It was right across the street from a good friend, and at half the cost of comparable units in the area, and it was close to a park. Sadly, however, the park was just temporary, because soon after I had moved to the neighborhood, the Bill and Melinda Gates Foundation began construction on their headquarters that was built over the park, something that seems highly symbolic now. As for the number 6, the magical apartment was located at the address 211 Valley St., #6, and little did I know how relevant those numbers were then, with the key focus not being 211, the 47th prime, in Seattle on the 47th Parallel North, but #6. Adding to the riddle, I stayed in that apartment until the day I bought my first home, which was a process that closed on a Friday, January 13, 2012, where 13 is the 6th prime number. I felt that once again I had been blessed, receiving the keys to the address, 6 232nd Pl. SW, in 'Bothell'. And yes, the house number was just 6. And as was the case with my apartment, I got a very nice place to live in, in a great location, at a very great value. And making matters even more interesting, it was in that same home where I discovered gematria, in August of 2013, shortly after observing how the town of 'Bothell' seemed to be under some sort of trance at the annual July 4th celebration in the only two years I had ever attended it, something I pointed out to my sweet lady in both occasions. As for the interesting part about discovering gematria in Bothell, in addition to making the observation about the town's people on 7/4, it is that 'Bothell' equates to 74 with Simple English, the same as 'Simple', 'English', and 'Gematria'. And yes, if you're wondering, that is the same house that had a car crash through the side of it on Christmas Eve, December 24, 2016, what was possibly the strangest day of my life, while I was 33 years old, after more than three straight years of educating about gematria and the pattern of 33 and 74 in relation to 'Jesus'.

With regards to gematria itself, I still remember when it was new to me, and how I felt as though I had finally found what was hidden under my nose. I still do feel that way, and looking back, I wish in 2006, emphasis on '06, someone would have tipped me off to Mr. Bill Gates, Mr. 666, Mr. Number of the Beast, and what devious attentions he had for us, along with The Cabal he is a member of, or perhaps better said, puppet of. I wish they would have also tipped me off to gematria as well. Had I known either, I would have been out on the corner every day making noise, raising awareness, and been 14 years ahead of where I am now. But as they say, "better late than never," and- "the time is now." And the time is now truth seeker, and we need to make up for lost time, and stop overlooking our duty and what responsibility lies before us- that is ending this cabal, and ending tyranny with it, while restoring decency, and humanity and moral behavior. And we can do it with the pages of this book, if we will it. And with regards to overlooking, I should have seen it back in 2007, because when the Bill and Melinda Gates Foundation came into

Seattle, they came with a destructive act, destroying a public park, a beautiful place, to build another building, in a city full of buildings. Truly, in that single move, it showed what the Bill and Melinda Gates Foundation was, something that was not positive, and as we understand now, something sinister. That's why it seems so strange, that all these years later, I'm writing this book, with all these seemingly unrelated parts, becoming part of one full circle.

For another meaningful synchronicity, adding to the "full circle" if you will, I must share with you what happened on July 29, 2020, the first day of Tisha B'Av. It was a date I had to wait and see what would transpire on before I could hand this book over to the publisher, and I'm glad I did, because it was eventful. As you'll recall, Tisha B'Av, also known as the Ninth of Av, is to remember the destruction of the Two Temples, and every year, without fail, there is an act of destruction and tragedy reported on Tisha B'Av, in the form of a riddle. For example, in 2019, it was the attack of Muslim worshipers on Temple Mount with 'tear gas' by Israeli Police, and in 2018 it was the mass shooting in Toronto's Greektown. In the case of 2020, it was a terrible train wreck in Tempe, Arizona, a town that sounds much like 'temple'. As for how this most recent Tisha B'Av event synchronizes with me, I was attending Arizona State University, in Tempe, the day of September 11, 2001, when this journey I'm now on began. And it was sometime after that where I recognized the significance of Tisha B'Av, in regards to the events of September 11, 2001, a subject I have taught about continuously ever since, including how 'Tisha B'Av' equates to 911 with Jewish Gematria.

Regarding the July 29, 2020 train wreck in Tempe, it should be noted it occurred on a date with 76 numerology, corresponding with the gematria of 'Tempe', equating to 76. And in light of the accusation that the Catholic Church is pulling the strings, this train wreck was further confirmation that this is the case. Consider, 'Arizona State University' equates to 104, the same as 'Roman Catholic Church', and both 'Sun Devils' and 'Catholic' equate to 35, reminding us of number 35, JFK's assassination, on a sunny day in Dallas, and even further, ASU was established March 12, 1885, the 71st day of the year, also corresponding with 'Catholic'. Furthermore, the train crashed into 'Tempe Town Lake', equating to 191, the same as 'Society of Jesus', reminding us of the deceased Adolfo Nicolas on Arturo Sosa's 191st day of his age, as well as many other things. And with regards to the name Sun Devils, let us not forget the logo of the Jesuits, the sun, or that it is the Catholic Church that is solely responsible for making the Christian day of worship, 'Sunday', the lone day of the week having gematria of 33, similar to how Tempe is on the 33rd Parallel North. Adding insult to injury, CNN marketed the story of the crash with the headline, 'a scene from hell', equating to 71, the same as the word 'hell' itself, and the word 'Catholic'. At the same time, let us not forget that CNN operates from the 33rd Parallel North, and the 84th Meridian West, the latter coordinate corresponding with the gematria of 'Jesuit', as well as 'Arizona', both equating to 84 and 42.

Regarding CNN's Jesuit parallels, and to contrast the contrived side of the code, with the organic side, I highly doubt it was by the grace of God that CNN's co-founder Reese Schonfeld died on July 28, 2020, 266 days after his November 5, 2019 birthday. Let us not forget November 5th, Guy Fawkes Day, leaves 56 days left in the year, and where 'Society of Jesus' sums to 56, 'Iesus Hominum Salvator', their motto, sums to 266. Let us also not forget Pope Francis, the first Jesuit Pope, the 266th Pope, and the man born December 17, 1936, a date with 84 numerology, who happens to be in his 84th year of his life at the time of this death. Speaking of which, the death of Schonfeld was 224 days after Pope Francis' birthday, where the divisors of 84 sum to 224. At the same time, 224 days is 32 weeks on the nose, reminding of the number of sun rays on the Jesuit logo. And might I suggest that in the same way the Washington Redskins are changing their name, perhaps the true title of the pope should become the sun devil? In case you haven't noticed yet, 'pope' and 'devil' are identical with Simple English and Pythagorean Gematria.

With all things being good and bad, I must say that I feel more fulfilled than I ever have in my life in these times of uncertainty, only because I know that the things I have been working towards, since the time of September 11, 2001, and really even before that, have been justified, and necessary, as difficult as they have been. As I've been saying this entire time, if we don't stop The Cabal, it is going to be very bad news for us in the end, and as bad as things are at this very crucial moment, I am as hopeful as ever, because their *Art of War* if you will, is exposed, and I know that once enough people know about the shenanigans they're up to, things are going to change, and fast.

Altogether, it makes me feel that I found my life's purpose, and I achieved it by being true to myself, and not being afraid of my many critics, or the obstacles that have come at me, including the lost support of friends, family, and colleagues. It's why sometimes when I look at *Revelation 21:7*, something like my 21/7 birthday, a tear forms in my eye. It reads, "He that overcometh shall inherit all things; and I will be his God, and he shall be my son." Thus it speaks to perseverance, and that is the word that defines what it takes to go after the truth in this world. Perseverance is also the word that has defined my life, one that has been full of challenges, especially in the time of getting this research out to the world, where I have been harassed, followed, burglarized, jailed, censored, and even had a car crash through the walls of my home on Christmas Eve, something that happened December 24, 2016, while I was 33 years old, that magical age. And don't even get me started on the FBI agent coming to my house on August 21, 2018, the anniversary of the release of the film *Hitman*, about Agent 47, only to falsely accuse me of things I never did. I know now it was an intimidation tactic to try and get me to quit this work, but thanks to you truth seeker, I didn't quit, and I kept pushing forward for the purpose of getting this work to where it now is- truly undeniable, and to be taken notice of.

For the person out there who is interested in finding the numbers that relate to their own life, this is what I suggest you do. Using the Pythagorean cipher, decode your own name, as well as the names of the people in your family, from your parents, to your significant other, to your siblings, to your children, to your friends. Be consistent in how you decode, and decode the full names of the people you look at. In addition to that, examine the birthdays of these same people, and extract the birth numerology as well. You should be amazed by what you find. Using myself as an example, I was born July 21, 1983, what happens to be the date of the coldest recorded temperature in the history of such recordings, where the temperature was measured at 89 degrees below Celsius. This is interesting because my full name, 'Zachary Keefe Hubbard', as well as my father's full name 'Timothy Steven Hubbard', equates to 89 with Pythagorean. At the same time, my mother's birthday is September 8th, a date written 8/9 in the majority of the world. Making this even more interesting, my father's full name sums to 251 with Simple English, and my mother's birthday is the 251st day of the year. At the same time, from his birthday, April 18th, to her birthday, September 8th, is a span of 144 days, the 12th Fibonacci number, following 89, the 11th Fibonacci number. To get even more specific about it, 251 is the 54th prime, and 'baseball' equates to 54, the sport that brought my mother and father together. It only figures then that my dad's birthday is the 108th day of the year, matching the count of double stitches on a baseball. And in the same way my dad taught me to love baseball, he taught me to love numbers. Perhaps then it is not a coincidence both of our names sum to 89, and the word 'number' equates to 89 as well.

So yes, you can use the base ciphers in addition to Pythagorean, but it is best you start with that one. And if you do move to another, the next most logical is Simple English. For myself personally, I have been called 'Zach Hubbard' by most people for all of my life, a name that sums to 94 with Simple English, and 49 with Pythagorean, the latter number corresponding with my birth numerology. Making these numbers all the more interesting, my dad was born April 18, 1953, a date with 94 numerology, and my birthday comes 94 days after his, and 49 days before my mother's. And I haven't even mentioned my sister yet. Her and I have the same mother, but different fathers, and we have grown up to be total opposites, perhaps something that was foretold through our dates of birth. Her birthday is Pearl Harbor Day, December 7th, and mine is July 21st, thus 7/12, and 21/7, dates that are reflections of each other, or opposites. And please realize, not a single thing I have told you is false, and none of it was planned, it just is what it is, and it's organic.

The reason I have decided to close the book with this information is for multiple reasons. For starters, I want people to understand that the belief within Kabbalah, that God created the world through numbers, letters and words, as strange as it sounds, is entirely possible, and I would argue I am living proof, and you likely are as well. Furthermore, I want you the reader, to take greater interest in the work, and join me in terms of becoming part of the decoding community, connecting the dots that are not yet connected, from the organic side of the code, to the contrived side, where The Cabal specializes. And rest assured, despite working seven years straight at the task of understanding and comprehending this knowledge, I know I have only just begun. It is to say this research is in its infancy, and I need your help.

Another reason I am concluding the book this way, is because it is healthy to always challenge yourself and your beliefs. A question I have often been asked over the years, is if there is an organic side to the code, how can we be certain that everything we are witnessing, isn't organic, from 9/11 to coronavirus? It is a fair question, and my response is often along the lines of, "You have to use discernment." For example, when the Sandy Hook School Shooting happened, the image shown of Adam Lanza made many people lift an eyebrow, because his image looked like a contrived face, made by an amateur with Photoshop. Then began the needless reporting that he was 112 pounds, again a number connecting to the gematria of 'Sandy Hook', and the date numerology of the Dunblane Massacre, March 13, 1996, that resulted in gun rights being taken away in the U.K., after first graders were targeted, the same as at Sandy Hook. Plus, the number connected to Lanza's birthday being April 22nd, the 112th day of the year, and his initials A.L., equating to 1.12. Then on top of that, 1-1-2 is the alt dialing code for 9-1-1, and that incident set in motion a type of buzz in the U.S. that hadn't been felt since 9/11, the date of the big national emergency in 2001, where it was a clear numerical riddle, and a clear lie, that definitely wasn't the work of God, but was the work of psychopaths who want to be like God. At least that is how I see it, and I think that is how any sane person should.

To close, I want to say a few more things. First, please don't let numbers make you paranoid. If you see a number in your own name that was discussed in this book, do not fret. It is a fact of life, that all things are dualistic, meaning good and bad, and that includes numbers. Second, when you do start decoding news stories for yourself, don't overdo it. What I mean is, look first for the numbers that are that being reported in the story, and then see how the key details are encoded, such as the key names, locations and dates. As a rule, I have always started my decodes by looking at what numbers The Cabal is putting out through their propaganda, and leading from there, such as the clue with 112 pound Adam Lanza, or 'Gavin Newsom' saying 56% of Californians will contract 'coronavirus', etc. I'm telling you, with your eyes now open to this means of operating, you're not going to miss how it is done going forward, and it should reveal to you what it has revealed to me, and that is- it is being done purposefully, for the sake of agenda, and seemingly, mass rituals, that contribute to a massive spell over the populace, that must be broken, because if not, we will truly be enslaved to tyranny, with no recourse.

And for one last thought, I really do hope you'll eventually read my first book, *Letters & Numbers*, because there is so much information within it that will help you comprehend and appreciate the subject of gematria and how it relates to the English language all the more. For example, in this book, we haven't even uncovered one of English's greatest secrets, paying tribute to Pi, the number of numbers. If you're not aware, the mathematical shorthand to calculate Pi is to divide 22 by 7, and if you write out the phrase, 'twenty two divided by seven', with Simple English it sums to 314, similar to Pi, written 3.14. Furthermore, if you write out 'three hundred sixty', for the number of degrees in a circle, that Pi relates to, it sums to 227 with Simple English, similar to 22 divided by 7. Keep in mind, on a PC, if you type Alt+227, it gives you the output of the symbol Pi, or π. And in light of circles, and cycles and time, 360 months in 30 years, the age Jesus began his ministry at, and for many of us, a special year in terms of our own lives. As for my mother and my father, they were both 30 years old when I was born, and for me personally, I was 30 years old when I learned of gematria, a subject that has changed my life, and answered many questions. So cheers truth seeker. To gematria, and a better future.

Last, let me say thank you for taking the time to read this book, it means everything to me. And I hope you do share it with others, because that would mean even more. As they say, each one teach one. And thank you to my family, friends, and fellow truth seekers. I love you and stay strong. And let's win this fight too, because we need to. Case in point, as I hand this book over to the publisher on August 4, 2020, a date with 52 numerology, the eastern seaboard of the United States is being flooded by Hurricane and Tropical Storm Isaias, where again, as I wrote about in my first book, weather warfare was first admitted to by the Royal Air Force in 1952, and not by accident, but because 'hurricane', 'flood' and 'earth' equate to 52, as does 'prophecy', which they're contriving. And in this case, the name Isaias comes from Isaiah in the *Bible*, the prophet, and where 'prophecy' equates to 106, so does 'Hurricane Isaias'. At the same time, the storm is reportedly transitioning back and forth between a hurricane and a tropical storm as it travels north on August 4th, or 8/4, up the east coast, and not organically, but because of technology. For further evidence of the plotting, and who is responsible yet again, 'Tropical Storm Isaias' equates to 84, corresponding with what you learned in the first chapter, and that is- 'Jesuit', 'The Jesuit Order', 'The Catholic Church' and 'United States of America' equate to 84.

Outro | August 4, 2020 Beirut Explosion and Jesuit Terrorism

On August 4, 2020, Beirut was rocked with twin blasts that left a sizable crater in the city's floor. The explosion was treated as somewhat of a mystery, but blamed on fireworks that had been stored in a warehouse. The truth is, this incident was a ritual, carried out by the Jesuit Order, and paying tribute to the October 23, 1983 Beirut barracks bombing, and it wasn't an accident that the more recent explosion came on Barack's birthday, as in Barack Obama, a man having a first name sounding much like barracks. In addition to Barack and barracks sounding similar, 'President Obama' equates to 83, like the year of the attack on the American and French barracks, 1983, reminding us that the Jesuits were formed in France, and now have their greatest stronghold outside of the Vatican, in Washington D.C., where Obama was once the President of the United States. At the same time, let us not overlook that this occurred while Pope Francis, the Jesuit Pope, was 83 years old, and in his 84th year of life, being the man born on a date with 84 numerology, December 17, 1936. With regards to 'Obama', a name also summing to 84 in Jewish Gematria, it should be noted that the blast came on his wife Michelle's 201st day of her age, 56, having been born January 17, 1964. And as you know, 'The Jesuit Order' equates to 201, and 'Society of Jesus' equates to 56, and Obama won the 56th U.S. Presidential Election in 2008. And with regards to the number 201, as we learned earlier, 'Mars' and 'Roman' both equate to 201 with Jewish Gematria, and Mars is the Roman God of War, and Tuesday, the day of the blast, is named after the planet Mars.

Understanding that those points are the foundation of the ritual, let us now examine how the four base values of 'Jesuit' factor in, equating to 84, 78, 42 and 21. Of course, the attack took place on August 4th, or 8/4, like 84. At the same time that date can be expressed as 4/8, and 'explosion' equates to 48 and 42, the latter value corresponding with 'Jesuit', 'Beirut' and 'birthday', as in Barack Obama's 59th birthday, August 4, 2020, an age that matches the 59 gematria value of 'Pope Francis'. And with regards to 78, 'Beirut, Lebanon' equates to 78, and on August 4th, it was reported that "at least 78 people" had perished in the explosion, no doubt a severe understatement. In addition to that, it came 78 days before Netanyahu's 71st birthday, October 21, 2020, the Prime Minister of

Israel, the not so friendly neighbor of Lebanon, that is under the control of the Vatican. Furthermore, most headlines referred to the event as the 'Beirut explosion', a phrase equating to 78, 84 and 201. As for the number 21, the attack came 231 days after Pope Francis 83rd birthday, December 17, 2019, the 21st triangular number, reminding us that 'Georgetown', equating to 42, was established January 23rd, or 23/1, like 231. And with this most recent event having clear parallels to the October 23rd attack in 1983, the '83 incident fell on a 'Sunday', the day of the week equating to 21, 78 and 84 in the exact same ciphers as 'Jesuit'.

With regards to Georgetown, keep in mind that Saad Hariri, the Prime Minister of Beirut, who left office on January 21, 2020, a date with 42 numerology, is an alumni of 'Georgetown'. Making this detail all the more interesting is that his full name is 'Saad El-Din Rafik Al-Hariri', equating to 109 with Pythagorean, and in 2020, his April 18th birthday fell on the 109th day of the year, and the explosion came on his 109th day of his age. This number pattern stands out because the word 'military' equates to 109, and if you've seen the explosions with your own eyes, it looks as if the second blast was the result of a military grade weapon. As for his abbreviated name, which he went by as Prime Minister, 'Saad Hariri', it equates to 52, the same as 'pope', and the attack, which it is fair to call, fell on August 4, 2020, a date with 52 numerology.

On the subject of 52, the incident came on Donald Trump's 52nd day of his age, and he said the incident looked like an attack as well, plus 'president' equates to 52, and as we learned earlier, him and Pope Francis are attached at the hip, having birthdays a span of 187 days apart, corresponding with 'Society of Jesus', equating to 187, and the fact that Donald Trump became President elect in 2016, 52 years after attending the Jesuit school Fordham. Furthermore, 'fireworks' equates to 52, and that is what was blamed for the explosion, as ridiculous as it sounds. Even further, the structure that was the source of the blast was reported as being a 'fireworks warehouse', equating to 239, the 52nd prime number, and 95. As you know, the number 95 is highly symbolic to the Jesuits, as are the numbers 56 and 119, the latter two also corresponding with the gematria of 'fireworks'. It reminds us that 'Vatican' and 'Francis' equate to 119, and both Notre Dame and al-Aqsa Mosque burned on April 15, 2019, 119 days after Pope Francis birthday, corresponding with the gematria of 'fire ritual' as well, equating to 119 and 56, the latter number like 'pope' as well as 'Society of Jesus'. Of course, the April 15, 2019 ritual was in tribute to the Knights Templar, who are responsible for the construction of Notre Dame, and who used al-Aqsa Mosque as their base when they took over Jerusalem during the crusades, referring to it as Solomon's Temple. It is for this same reason the site is called 'Temple Mount' today, where the false ones intend to build their Third Temple, at the time of the Jewish Messiah. And please don't overlook that 'Temple Mount' equates to 46, the same as 'Catholic', the Church responsible for the establishment of modern Israel, and for forming the belief that Temple Mount is the destined location for the coming Jewish temple that is part of biblical prophecy. Once again, 'The Cabal', equating to 52, is contriving 'prophecy', also equating to 52, and as we know, they're doing it by the code, one act of terrorism at a time. In that breath, let us not forget that 'terrorist' equates to 52, or that Osama bin Laden was reportedly killed May 2, 2011, emphasis on 5/2, like 52, a span of 119 weeks from Obama becoming the U.S. President. And regarding Osama and 19 year cycles, he once said his inspiration to attack the U.S. in 2001 was the 1982 invasion of Lebanon by Israel, that ended September 29th, the day leaving 93 days in the year.

As for contriving prophecy, the August 4th explosion fell on the day leaving 149 days in the year, corresponding with the gematria of '*Revelation*', the book of prophecy, as well as 'antichrist', the entity the Catholic Church serves. And let us recall 149 is the 35th prime, and 'Catholic' equates to 35, plus Beirut is on the 35th Meridian East. And with regards to the explosion coming on Obama's 59th birthday, recall that '*Revelation*' also equates to 59. Furthermore, let us not forget that Obama took office as President in 2009 at age 47, with the 47th Vice President, Joe Biden, and their birthdays, measuring from Biden's on November 20th, to Obama's on August 4th, are 258 days apart, where 'beast' equates to 47, and 'number of the beast' equates to 258. In addition to that, in all years except leap years, August 4th is the 216th day of the year, the product of 6 times 6 times 6, where 666 is the number of the beast. That said, in a leap year, August 4th is the 217th day of the year, corresponding with the gematria of 'Whore of Babylon', what is the source of evil that is named in *Revelation 17*, where 59 is the 17th prime number. In addition to 'Whore of Babylon' equating to 217, it also sums to 71, the latter being the same as

'Catholic'. It reminds us that days before the Beirut blast, the good Catholic, Regis Philbin, died July 24, 2020, a date with 71 numerology, before being buried at 'Notre Dame', his Catholic alma mater, equating to 95, on July 31, 2020, a date with 78 numerology, the latter two numbers corresponding with the Jesuits.

In light of the Catholic and Jesuit trail we're following, it is worth pointing out that in the October 23, 1983 attack on the barracks, it was reported 75 people were injured. Not by chance, 'Catholic Church' and 'New World Order' equate to 75, and so does 'Beirut', explaining why the city is a target for Catholic and Jesuit rituals, having the right name, and the right coordinates- not to mention it is predominantly Muslim. At the same time, the October 23rd attack was on the day leaving 69 days in the year, and 'Catholic Church', 'New World Order', and 'The Jesuit Order' each equate to 69. Beyond that, 'Beirut' also equates to 87, like 'The Catholic Church' and 'number of the beast', shedding more light on why Obama, with the beast connections, became part of the riddle with the explosive tragedy in Lebanon's capital city. And in light of what we learned earlier about Naya Rivera's very Jesuit related death, that involved the numbers 33 and 87, I should note Beirut is on 33rd Parallel North, and the August 4th explosion came precisely 33 weeks after Pope Francis' birthday. Of course, the Catholic Church is abbreviated C.C., or 3.3. Furthermore, 'October' is the lone month having gematria of 33, and when you add 10+23 you get 33. And for one last point on the October 23rd attack, it fell on a date with numerology of 54, 116 and 135, corresponding with the gematria of 'Jesuit Order', equating to 54, the Jesuit motto, 'Ad maiorem Dei gloriam', equating to 116 and the fact that the August 4, 2020 attack came 135 days before Pope Francis 84th birthday.

Coming back to the August 4th attack, the bomb went off right next to Saint George Bay, and this is fascinating for a couple of key reasons. First of all, 'Saint George Bay' equates to 67 with Pythagorean Gematria, the 19th prime number, connecting to the gematria of 'chaos', equating to 19, and reminding us that the phrase 'order out of chaos' equates to 78, the same as 'Beirut, Lebanon'. At the same time, it was reported the explosions began at 6:07 PM local time, which is the 1,807th minute of the day, not far off from 'Society of Jesus', equating to 187. In addition to the gematria, as we learned earlier, Saint George's Cross is what is shown on the 20th Tarot card, the judgement card, and this explosion occurred in 2020. With regards to judgement, the planet 'Saturn' equates to 69 and 93, and as we have learned, it symbolizes judgement, as well as 'death'. Furthermore, the explosion was blamed on the firework ingredient, 'ammonium nitrate', equating to 69 and 93 as well. For the record, that is also what the bomb was reportedly made out of in the '93 World Trade Center bombing, that was blamed on the 'Blind Sheik', a title equating to 93. And since this entire ritual is coordinated with Pope Francis, let us not forget that his birthday is on December 17th, the day that Saturnalia is celebrated on, the festival for the planet Saturn. At the same time, let us not forget that both 'Saturn' and 'Jesuit' equate to 21 with Pythagorean Gematria, and this explosion came 231 days after Pope Francis' birthday, the 21st triangular number.

For another 67 connection, it is 'Peter Kolvenbach', equating to 67, who was the 29th Superior General of the Jesuits, and who died in Beirut on November 26, 2016, the day leaving 35 days in the year, and on the 35th Meridian East, just four days before his birthday, having been born November 30, 1928. That means he died at age 87, corresponding with 'Beirut' and 'The Catholic Church', as well as 'number of the beast'. Keep in mind, Arturo Sosa had just become Superior General on October 14, 2016, the day leaving 78 days in the year, corresponding with the gematria of 'Beirut, Lebanon' and 'Jesuit'. Furthermore, Kolvenbach died 43 days after Sosa assumed the position, corresponding with the gematria of 'Jesus Christ', or on the 44th day of Sosa being the Superior General, where 'kill' and 'execution' equate to 44. Also, in light of what we learned earlier about the 109 ritual with Georgetown grad and former Lebanese Prime Minister Saad Hariri, 109 is the 29th prime number, corresponding with the fact that the 29th Superior General died in Beirut.

For the clincher, and ensuring that there can be no doubt the Jesuits are responsible for everything exposed in this outro, as well as everything else exposed in this entire book, the August 4th explosion came 266 days after Arturo Sosa's 71st birthday on November 12, 2019, the current Superior General of the Jesuits, corresponding with the Jesuit motto, 'Iesus Hominum Salvator', equating to 266, and the fact that Pope Francis is the first Jesuit Pope, and the 266th Pope in the history of the Catholic Church. So please, for the sake of humanity, help me end The Cabal, that is the Whore of Babylon. It is righteous.